Inside *Paradise Lost*

Inside *Paradise Lost*

Reading the Designs of Milton's Epic

David Quint

PRINCETON UNIVERSITY PRESS
Princeton and Oxford

Copyright © 2014 by Princeton University Press
Published by Princeton University Press, 41 William Street,
Princeton, New Jersey 08540
In the United Kingdom: Princeton University Press, 6 Oxford Street,
Woodstock, Oxfordshire OX20 1TW

press.princeton.edu

ISBN 978-0-691-16191-4 (cloth)

ISBN 978-0-691-15974-4 (pbk.)

Library of Congress Control Number: 2013938974

British Library Cataloging-in-Publication Data is available

This book has been composed in Minion Pro

Printed on acid-free paper ∞

Printed in the United States of America

1 2 3 4 5 6 7 8 9 10

FOR JAMES NOHRNBERG

Satan, we would have to say, is the victim of a course
in "the Bible as Literature."
—Nohrnberg, "On Literature and the Bible"

Contents

Acknowledgments

I have been fortunate to have written this book in the company of many friends and scholars. I thank first of all my Yale University colleagues, a remarkable group of Miltonists to find in one place, and, much more, a group of exceptionally generous and caring people: Lawrence Manley, John Rogers, Annabel Patterson, Leslie Brisman, and Harold Bloom. They have read all or sizable parts of the book, including more than a few of its false starts. I am grateful for their incisive comments and encouragement, for the example of their own scholarship, and, above all, for their friendship. Other Yale friends, David Bromwich and Alexander Welsh, read and criticized the introduction and have helped me to make it more shapely.

Earlier versions of chapters and parts of chapters of this book have appeared in journal articles. They are reused here with the permission of the journals and their publishers. Chapter 1 appeared as "Milton's Book of Numbers: Book 1 of *Paradise Lost* and Its Catalogue," *International Journal of the Classical Tradition* 13.4 (2007): 528–49, copyright © 2004, Springer, with kind permission from Springer Science+Business Media; chapter 2 as "Ulysses and the Devils: The Unity of Book Two of *Paradise Lost*," *Milton Studies* 49 (2009): 20–48, copyright © 2008, University of Pittsburgh Press, by permission of the present publisher, Duquesne University Press; chapter 3 as "Fear of Falling: Icarus, Phaethon, and Lucretius in *Paradise Lost*," *Renaissance Quarterly* 57 (2004): 847–81, copyright © 2004, the Renaissance Society of America, Inc., by permission from the University of Chicago Press; chapter 4 as " 'Things Invisible to Mortal Sight:' Light, Vision and the Unity of Book 3 of *Paradise Lost*," *Modern Language Quarterly* 71.3 (2010): 249–69, copyright © 2010, University of Washington, by permission from the present publisher, Duke University Press; and parts of chapter 7 as "The Virgilian Coordinates of *Paradise Lost*," *Materiali e discussioni per l'analisi dei testi classici* 52 (2004): 177–97, copyright © Istituti Editoriali e Poligrafici Internazionali, by permission of the publisher. I am grateful to the journal readers—I wish to remember the late Richard DuRocher—and the journal editors, especially Paul Grendler, Marshall Brown, Glenn W. Most, and Sarah Spence. Their work improved my thought and writing.

I am also indebted to the larger community of Milton scholars in North America. I thank Gordon Braden and Joshua Scodel, who read the manuscript for Princeton University Press and offered me helpful and expert criticism. Charles Stanley Ross invited me to discuss parts of this book at the Newberry Library Romance and Epic Seminar; Regina Schwartz brought me to the Newberry Library Milton Seminar; Paul Stevens asked me to speak to the Canada Milton Seminar; and Jason Rosenblatt arranged for me to present my work at the Northeast Milton Seminar. I thank all four for their friendship and our ongoing conversations about Milton. I have other Miltonist friends to thank for reading earlier versions and more recent drafts. John Leonard's criticism was vital to getting this project started; Jason Rosenblatt and Mary Nyquist encouraged me to complete it. Stephen Fallon persuaded me that one of my chapters did indeed need to be reworked and helped me to clarify a different, crucial part of my argument. I have benefited from the comments of Victoria Kahn, Ronald Levao, and Michael Murrin on specific chapters; they are cherished friends. I thank a list of distinguished Miltonists and friends from whom I have been privileged to learn: John Archer, Andrew Barnaby, Carla Baricz, Chimene Bateman, David Currell, Samuel Fallon, Angus Fletcher, Natalka Freeland, Thomas Fulton, Beth Harper, Brad Holden, Blair Hoxby, Andrew Kau, Michael Komorowski, Benjamin LaBreche, Seth Lobis, James Ross Macdonald, Tanya Pollard, Ayesha Ramachandran, Rebecca Rush, Sarah van der Laan, Andrea Walkden, Anthony Welch, and Emily Wilson. I have had the pleasure over the last decade of attending meetings of the Northeast Milton Seminar, and learning from its members: they are too many to list, but I want to mention Joan Bennett, Ann Baynes Coiro, Achsah Guibbory, Dayton Haskin, Laura Knoppers, Barbara Lewalski, Thomas Luxon, Nicholas von Maltzahn, Stella Revard, William Shullenberger, Nigel Smith, Gordon Teskey, and the late Marshall Grossman. As this book was nearing completion, my thinking was enriched by Samuel Bendinelli, Radhika Koul, Drisana Misra, Ryan Pollock, Michael Rose, Maria Alexandra van Nievelt, Alex Werrell, and Madeline Wong. I thank Carla Baricz, who formatted the bibliography and assisted me in preparing the manuscript for publication. I am grateful for the work of my copyeditor, Cathy Slovensky, and to Ellen Foos and Alison MacKeen at Princeton University Press.

This book is dedicated to James Nohrnberg, my teacher and friend.

Inside *Paradise Lost*

Introduction

The message of *Paradise Lost* is: make love, not war. The poem that pretends to begin the epic tradition by retelling events that preceded those of all earlier epics would also end the epic genre by condemning its traditional subject matters, war and empire. The central human heroic act of the poem is Adam's choosing love for Eve, his wife and fellow human being, over obedience to God. In making us think twice at all about this choice, in appearing even to ratify it, *Paradise Lost* revises its biblical subject matter just as radically as it revises epic. The Fall is fortunate not only because it allows the Son of God to offer himself to save humanity, but because it already anticipates the supersession of the Law by the Love and Liberty the Son will bring about by his example. Its obverse in the poem is Satan's envious lust for power, his institution of monarchy in hell, and his readiness to enslave others. The Milton of *Paradise Lost* is a Christian humanist: his Christianity emphasizes the true empowerment of men and women as free moral agents.

These are the broad outlines of my reading of *Paradise Lost*, more and less familiar. In the broadest sense my argument has been anticipated by many commentators. Milton's God, however, is in the details, and this book goes inside the epic by examining some of its intricacies: how verbal design and allusive conceit together shape its units of meaning. These are poems within the poem. The generic expectations of Renaissance epic that looked back to the model of the *Aeneid* required *Paradise Lost* to maintain over its vast length not only the loftiness of the high style but the semantic density and unity of a lyric. For this reason, few great epics like Milton's were achieved, though many were attempted. This kind of epic was also expected to contain studied allusion in almost every verse, as Virgil was known to have imitated Homer, the Greek tragedians, and his own predecessors in Latin poetry. These expectations for the writer of the epic create expectations for the epic's reader, who will hold in his or her memory word-patterns that form and repeat themselves through the course of the entire poem: the rustling wings of the fallen angels in hell in book 1 make a "hiss" (1.768) that already anticipates their final transformation nine books later into hissing serpents in book 10. The reader will also be responsive to the allusions embedded in the verses and responsible for integrating them into the poem's meaning. That the outspoken angel Abdiel in book 5 is a version, via Girolamo Vida's *Christiad*, of the Bible's Nicodemus defending Jesus before the Sanhedrin characterizes Abdiel as a superior figure of zeal; it also allows us to grasp the larger analogy that Milton is drawing between Satan's and the rebel angels' refusal to acknowledge the Son and the understandable future skepticism and anger of the Jews with regard to the same Son. Such epic poems are preeminent examples of what Roland Barthes calls a "writerly" text, that is, a text that makes the reader do active and imaginative work in recomposing its meaning. Some assembly is required.[1]

The studies of *Paradise Lost* in this book show what such assembly can reveal about the poetic texture and pleasure of Milton's epic. They uncover verbal arrangements and thought structures that bind together—in widening configurations—episodes, individual books, motifs that run through the larger poem, and motifs running through Milton's still larger career. In many instances, I show how these designs are built *by and through* Milton's allusions—to the Bible, to previous literature, particularly to the epic tradition (classical and modern), and to his own earlier poetry.[2] Milton uses allusion to construct and unify the fictions of the poem: the discussion in chapter 2 of how allusions to the figure of Ulysses and to the myth of Scylla and Charybdis connect the various episodes of book 2 is perhaps the clearest, most systematic example. Such patterns have their own logic and tell their own stories, which complement and overlap with the larger narrative that embeds them. At times close to its surface, at others submerged, they can organize a whole book of the poem.[3] Five of the eight chapters of my book (1, 2, 4, 7, and 8) demonstrate the poetic unity of single books at either end of the epic (1, 2, 3, 10, and the composite 11–12, originally a single book 10 in 1667). The other three chapters (3, 5, and 6) cover much of the poem that lies in between, and the book as a whole follows the narrative arc of Milton's epic; I often return to its last books and ending. The second-order stories recounted through these designs—about poetry and idolatry, cosmology and materialism, envy and kingship, spiritual individualism versus loving community, death and choice, the status of women—turn out to be not secondary after all, but centrally constitutive to the meaning of *Paradise Lost*.

What is an allusion? In his classic essay on *Lycidas*, Northrop Frye writes that for a poet "the impulse to write can only come from previous contact with literature, and the formal inspiration, the poetic structure that crystallizes around the new event, can only be derived from other poems."[4] Poststructuralist thought, influenced by Barthes's "death of the author," conceives that a language or a tradition may write *through* a writer, and it labels this relationship with the catch-all term "intertextuality." But the words on the page did not get there by themselves. Cutting a theoretical Gordian knot, Stephen Hinds has distinguished allusion from seemingly infinite intertextual connections and the reduction of such connections to so many commonplaces. Instead, Hinds defines allusion as a reference, chosen by the author, to an earlier text or texts in order to produce an intended effect. Hinds accepts that the author's intentions are finally unknowable, and that "the alluding poet is ultimately and necessarily a figure whom we ourselves read out from the text" (50)—that is to say, allusion lies in the mind of the text's *interpreter*. The latter may be a version of Barthes's "writerly reader," but Hinds asks us to posit a poet whose "dialogue with the work of other poets can be a very private, self-reflexive, and almost solipsistic kind of dialogue" (49), an individual author who is alive and well.[5] The readings of Miltonic allusion that follow claim to recover the intentions of a poet who, in these specific cases, cites or imitates earlier texts for calculated purposes and results. My critical task is to persuade my readers that these *are* instances of allusion so defined. I also want to show how much of the power and thought of Milton's poetry can reside in its texture of allusions, how many of the challenges and pleasures of reading *Paradise Lost* derive from puzzling them out.

Let us begin with one complex but manageably brief example. In a passage in book 2 whose degree of irony is hard to determine, the fallen angels bow down and reverence Satan as a god for his volunteering to voyage through Chaos to earth to seduce Adam and Eve, putting himself at risk for their general safety and deliverance from hell. (When we realize in retrospect, in book 3, that Satan's presenting himself for the mission has parodied the Son's offer, through his future Passion, to deliver humanity from that mission's consequences, the irony or lack of irony becomes that much harder to pin down.) The narrator comments that the devils have not lost all their virtue, as this respect that they show for their leader's own virtue testifies. He then goes on to make a parenthetical aside:

> Oh shame to men! Devil with devil damned
> Firm concord holds, men only disagree
> Of creatures rational, though under hope
> Of heavenly grace: and God proclaiming peace,
> Yet live in hatred, enmity, and strife
> Among themselves, and levy cruel wars,
> Wasting the earth, each other to destroy:
> As if (which might induce us to accord)
> Man had not hellish foes enow besides,
> That day and night for his destruction wait.
>   *(2.496–505)*[6]

The sense of this grand invective seems clear enough. It is a paradox that human beings, who have hope of salvation, wage wars with each other while their real enemy is the devil, whose followers, though damned, live in concord with one another.

The passage, however, carefully looks back into the epic tradition, the tradition that, as Milton will complain in the invocation to book 9, has deemed wars to be its only heroic argument (9.28–29). In twelve stanzas (2–13) of book 7 of his *Os Lusíadas* (1571), the Portuguese epic poet Luís de Camões denounces Protestant schisms in Europe, but more generally inveighs against the wars that Christians—"Ó míseros Cristãos"—wage among themselves, sowing the teeth of Cadmus in internal strife (7.9), rather than coming together against their common Muslim enemy who, the poet notes, are completely united—"inteiros observantes"—on the score of waging war upon *them* (7.10). In Richard Fanshawe's 1655 translation, the poet enjoins Europeans to follow the example of his own crusading nation Portugal: "To scourge the arrogant Mahumetan / Your hands unite, your heads together lay" (7.13). The Camões passage, in turn, is modeled on an earlier, similar invective (17.73–79) in Ludovico Ariosto's 1532 version of the *Orlando furioso*, where the poet-narrator urges the European peoples—Spaniards, French, Swiss, and Germans—who are now fighting among themselves in Ariosto's war-ravaged Italy to turn their warfare against the infidel, to reconquer Jerusalem from the "renegades" who now possess it and recapture Constantinople from the Turks (17.75). If, he says to the kings of France and Spain, you want, respectively, to be called "most Christian" and "Catholic," why are you killing Christians—"Se Cristianissimi esser voi volete / e voi altri Catolici nomati / perché di Cristo gli uomini uccidete?" (17.75)—when you could go fight against the Muslim threat?[7] The heroes of the *Orlando furioso* are themselves engaged in such a war, the conflict fought by Charlemagne against Agramante, king of Biserta; Milton has already compared the devils to the latter's forces in book 1 (585–87). These epic forebears of Milton condemn contemporary war between Christians, but they are nevertheless sedulous to indite and glorify war that has the religious alibi of a crusade.

Milton's version of these earlier invectives substitutes the devil for the Mohammedan. It fits into a minor pattern in *Paradise Lost* that also finds Satan described as a Muslim potentate, labeled as a "sultan" (1.348; cf. "the soldan's chair" at 1.764), and the council of Pandaemonium a "dark divan" (10.457).[8] The most notable instance has appeared in the opening lines of the same book 2, again through the use of allusion:

> High on a throne of a royal state, which far
> Outshone the wealth of Ormus and of Ind,
> Or where the gorgeous East with richest hand
> Showers on her kings barbaric pearl and gold,
> Satan exalted sat …
> *(2.1–5)*

These lines echo the description of the Calyph of Egypt, the main power against whom the heroes of the First Crusade in Torquato Tasso's *Gerusalemme liberata* (*GL*; 1581) will fight for the conquest of the holy city.

Egli in *sublime soglio*, a cui per cento
gradi eburnei s'ascende, *altero siede*;
e sotto l'ombra d'un gran ciel d'argento
porpora intesta *d'or* preme co'l piede,
e *ricco* di *barbarico* ornamento
in *abito regal splender* si vede;
    (GL 17.10.1–6)

[He on a *high throne*, to which one climbs by a thousand ivory steps, *exalted* (proudly) *sits*; and beneath the shade of a great heavenly canopy of silver, presses his feet on purple cloth interwoven with *gold*, and is seen to *shine*, *rich* in *barbaric* ornament and *royal state* (attire).]

With a one-upmanship that is frequent in Miltonic allusion, Satan's pomp outshines the regal trappings of Tasso's Calyph, who incidentally numbers among his subject allies the kings of Hormuz (*GL* 17.25) and India (*GL* 17.28). One should not make too much of this orientalizing conceit: Satan and the devils are much more often described in terms of imperial and papal Rome and of the Stuart monarchy. Kingship, in fact, more than Islam, seems to be the real target here. Milton suggests that *all* earthly kings take their model from Satan, before whom their power in any case pales, and that there is no distinction between so-called Christian kings and Muslim despots to whom they may pretend to be opposed—they are all opposed to true Christianity.[9]

Another erasure of the difference between Christian and Muslim, but this time in the name of their common humanity, takes place in Milton's "O shame to men!" invective. These two allusive passages in book 2, which now appear linked to each other, group together Milton's three major sixteenth-century Christian epic predecessors, Ariosto, Camões, and Tasso, whose poems recount conflicts between European Christian and African and Asian, mostly Muslim, forces, and appeal to the model of crusader warfare. But Milton evokes these poets' alignment of the devil with the Mohammedan enemy in the book's opening verses only to correct it in his subsequent invective. His imitation of Ariosto and Camões includes rather than excludes Muslims among the human beings—"men"—who wage wars against each other instead of attending to their spiritual enemy, the devil. God, Milton writes in *On Christian Doctrine* (1.4), may ultimately reject the unbeliever, but he nonetheless bestows his grace on all (*Works* 14:146; *CPW* 6:192). In keeping with the general revision of epic in *Paradise Lost*, the book 2 passage condemns all human warfare, including crusades, and substitutes spiritual combat in its place: it is diabolic fraud rather than Muslim force of arms that we should fear. Nevertheless, the allusion itself makes the devil remind us of the Mohammedan and vice versa.

Allusion functions in *Paradise Lost* as another layer of metaphor, or perhaps the better analogy is to Milton's famous similes: it declares that a given description, action, whole scene is like, or just as often unlike, its counterpart in another text. This example demonstrates some features of Milton's technique: the imitation of a passage from a poet that itself alludes to an earlier poet (Camões to Ariosto); its linking to another allusion, often nearby or in a structurally prominent position (the initial allusion to Tasso), to suggest a continuing conceit and formal arrangement; a rewriting, at times to the point of inversion, of the meaning of the work alluded to. The application of these earlier texts to his Genesis or pre-Genesis story, whose plot, of course, precedes theirs by thousands of years, is an instance of Milton's frequent use of allusion to reverse his belatedness to his literary predecessors and to claim priority over them—a point well made by Harold Bloom.[10] But Milton's allusion, here as elsewhere, is more than a reaction of poetic anxiety. His address to contemporary men and women also brings the deep past up-to-date. By allusion, Milton places his poem within an ongoing literary history and a larger history, intellectual and political, in this case, the dilemma and contradictions that Christian thinkers, particularly sixteenth- and seventeenth-century Christians who inherited the pacifist tradition of Erasmus, faced in confronting militant Islam and their own crusading past.[11] This history seems, if anything, more timely at the moment of my writing this study than when Milton composed his epic. But without recognizing and taking account of the allusions—they are not noted in modern editions—we would miss it altogether.

To begin with, the subject of Milton's condemnation: *war*. War comes first, to get it out of the way for love. *Paradise Lost* tells the story of two falls, which its reader is asked to compare and contrast. There is the unending fall of Satan and his followers, and there is the Fall—and spiritual regeneration—of Adam and Eve. The fall of the rebel angels, noisy and full of the martial paraphernalia and heroics of earlier epic, is over and done with at the poem's beginning: the defeated devils themselves have no more thirst for fighting epic battles. The poet-narrator invokes a Muse who was present from the first, that is, from the first verses of Genesis and its account of the Creation, and then, surprisingly, asks the Spirit to "Say first" (1.27)—and tell what happened still earlier. His prequel to the Bible allows Milton to manufacture, through the contrast between the self-tempting devils and the man and woman whom Satan deceives, a theological safety valve for humanity, and to rehearse, in parodic form, scenes from the older epics his own poem supersedes. The first and last similes of book 1 note the similarity of its portrait of the devils to sailors' yarns and fairy tales, and Raphael's account weaves the War in Heaven—a subject that is not scripturally attested except in its anticipation/replay of the apocalyptic battles of Revelation—into the fables of Milton's epic predecessors. The inset, retrospective form of Raphael's narrative places the celestial war in a literary as well as a chronological past before the action of *Paradise Lost* begins. Raphael finishes the story of Satan's fall at the end of book 6 and halfway through the poem, leaving its second half to recount the fall of the first human couple, Milton's new epic subject, quieter if more talky. When Raphael recounts God's creation of the universe in book 7, and Adam recounts his and God's joint creation of Eve in book 8 (in 1667 these were both part of a single book 7), Milton's poem has caught up to the Muse and to Genesis at the poem's opening. By the end of *Paradise Lost*, however, when Michael tells of Eden's being swept away by the Flood, it may seem that its story of the human fall is itself receding into poetic fiction.

Satan's story is the old epic dispensation, the search for temporal power as a zero-sum game driven by envy and the desire for glory above one's peers. It can only culminate, if not be satisfied, in kingship, war, and destruction—*and* in alienation from God in a literal or mental hell, the latter identical to remorse, the "restless thoughts" that return to torment the despairing fallen angels as the hellhounds sired by Death return to torment Sin. It may imply, in Milton's century of astronomical revolution, the alienation from God of the universe itself, a destructive reversion to the infinite, random, and Babelic Chaos that surrounds but is kept outside the walls of God's new, orderly creation in *Paradise Lost*: epic warfare extended to a warring cosmos, to noise and non-meaning. The fall of Adam and Eve tells the story of the new dispensation of Milton's epic: of how love between human beings, here exemplified in marital love, enables (or is enabled by) the love of God; of the experience of spiritual goods that exceed finite temporal ones; of hope for an existence beyond the finitude of death, summed up by Adam as "peace of thought." Such love, in its fraternal, charitable form, also implies the political equality and liberty of a republic. In book 11, Milton's God takes credit for the reconciliation and renewal of their love that Adam and Eve have worked hard to achieve in book 10, and the Son's charity—his promise in book 3 of a future sacrifice for humanity repeated to the fallen couple in his book 10 oracle about the serpent and the woman's seed—appears to have made it possible. So, to the contrary, God hardens the heart of Satan, who refuses his grace.

The Christian God's new creative intervention and the poem's declared project of theodicy may provide the necessary conditions for, yet feel almost extraneous to, the foregrounded choices between power and love. (Or we could say that the theodicy itself depends on whether we see God as power or as love.) By their own exercise of charity, Adam and Eve can attain a paradise within in place of the one they have lost; and love seems to fulfill—and thus relegate to an older Law—the divine command of obedience. *Paradise Lost* restores to humans the freedom of the angels who obey God: "we freely love, as in our will / To love or not; in this we stand or fall." But this freedom and love are now directed first of all to relationships between human beings.

Even as the devil tries to draw God and the angels into the old epic battles, the human heroes engage in the new, more limited household world of their garden. The first couple fight, too, among themselves: the marital squabble of hurt feelings that leads Eve to separate herself from Adam and head for the groves (where Satan lies in wait); the more serious exchange of mutual recriminations after they have both fallen. The War in Heaven, the biggest battle ever fought—so big that it mocks earlier epic and becomes mock-epic—is succeeded by battles of the sexes: these have their comical moments, too, in spite of their fraught circumstances. Milton changes his notes for tragic in book 9 when he must narrate the Fall, but, in spite of the bite that Death and his remorse take out of human existence, in spite of the prophecies in the last two books of the poem about war, kingship, empire, and misery in store for human history, Adam and Eve leave *Paradise Lost* cheered, officially by the happy ending of Christian promise, dramatically by the comic solution of marriage.[12] No longer innocent, but now compromised human beings, they belong to the emergent world of the novel, the lower narrative genre of comic compromise that belongs to the subjected plain and domesticity to which they are headed, a literary world where small things must perforce stand in place of, and accomplish, great ones. Perhaps we are still in one kind of epic world after all: just as the Iliadic posturings of the devils in book 1 are replaced by their Odyssean fraud in book 2, so Milton's larger epic may at its halfway point replace the little *Iliad* of the War in Heaven with an *Odyssey* of marital reunion; but the *Odyssey*, as James Joyce understood and proved, is the prototype of the novel.

Paradise Lost starts with the devil. My first chapter shows how book 1 metapoetically depicts its own role in raising the rebel angels out of their "bottomless perdition" (1.46), an act of poetic creation analogous to the divine creation of the universe described in the invocation—"how the heavens and earth / Rose out of chaos" (1.9–10). Framed by its first and last similes, which suggest the devils are the unreliable figments of human tales, book 1 plays on perspective and size by reviewing, along with Satan, their "stature" and "number." After insisting on their gigantism, the similes, in order to count them, shrink the almost innumerable devils into infinitesimal units to make them fit into the human mind, no less than they themselves voluntarily shrink to enter their new home Pandaemonium. The profane temple Pandaemonium, raised by music that is hard to distinguish from the music of Milton's own verses, is a first idolatrous counterimage of the poetic edifice that will be *Paradise Lost*. Its fallen architect Mulciber is the poet's uncomfortably close double. The chief devils described in the catalog that occupies the center of book 1 and organizes its poetic figures and symbolic geography—Carthage, Sodom, Egypt, Babel-Babylon, Rome—are precisely those who will come to inhabit the pagan shrines that human idolatry will build next to or even inside the Jerusalem temple, profaning God's house. If not merely the products of the human imagination, the demons take on the face and names that the imagination has granted them. This catalog—whose traditional epic function is to size up military force—instead suggests the force of spiritual falsehood, and it corresponds to the defeated devils' own reluctance to pursue another direct war against God; they would rather resort to satanic fraud. Milton not-so-gently mocks their military posturing, which is going nowhere except to build their council hall in which to sit and talk, and the contrast to earlier epic appears to diminish the devils, much as does their shrinking themselves at the book's end. But the switch from swords to words, from open force to lies, may make them more dangerous, not less, to their human victims.

In book 2, Milton continues this story of the demilitarization of the fallen angels and of his epic more generally when he bases all of its action around the figure of Ulysses, the hero of eloquence and fraud, whose own epic comes in the aftermath of the Trojan War. Chapter 2 demonstrates that the *Odyssey*, imitated and parodied in Satan's voyage through Chaos to God's newly created universe in the book's last section, is just one of the classical stories about the career of Ulysses that Milton evokes as models for its different episodes. The various parts of book 2 are held together by this pattern of allusion, as well as by the Odyssean figures of Scylla and Charybdis, the emblem of bad choices, or of loss of choice itself. Unable to die, the devils have no real option but to experience the second death of endless remorse. Here the *Doloneia*, that unheroic, even spurious episode of the *Iliad*, in which volunteers are sought to go on spy errands from *both* Greek and Trojan camps, provides a central model in *Paradise Lost*, not only the model for Satan's mission but for the Son's subsequent offer to save humanity through his future incarnation and death. Thus, Milton's epic inverts the idea of heroism itself. The hell constructed by the devils—what civilization looks like in the absence of God—is matched in book 2 by the Chaos through which Satan travels. This is a nature from which God has withdrawn his creative hand.

The next two complementary chapters turn to the confrontation of Milton's poetry with cosmology in a century where earlier models of the universe had been exploded by a new science and astronomy. Chapter 3 shows how, through a complicated chain of intermediary texts, the depiction of Satan's fall through Chaos in book 2, which invokes the myth of Icarus, and the Son's successful ride in the paternal chariot of God at the end of the War in Heaven in book 6, which rewrites the story of Phaethon, both trace back to the *De rerum natura* of Lucretius. They counter the Roman poet's depiction of an Epicurean cosmos ordered by chance and in a constant state of falling through an infinite void— the "vast vacuity" of Chaos. Through allusion kept beneath the surface of the poem, I suggest, Milton here faces his own deepest skepticism. The myths of these highfliers who fall are further countered in *Paradise Lost* by the motif of *poetic* flight. The shaping power of poetry itself and the epic high style counteract the specter of a universe without bound and dimension, or of the shapelessness of Death ("If shape it might be called that shape had none"). Poetry raises the poet over his fallen human condition, the sinking feeling of a Serbonian bog or slough of despond.

To the hell and Chaos of book 2, book 3 opposes God's heaven and his new creation, the ordered universe, apparently presided over by the sun. But where the first two books describe their infernal realms by a kind of science fiction comparison to fallen human experience—here the epic tradition provided Milton with handy models—book 3 sets apart an invisible God and heaven from the visible universe, divine light from sunlight: "light" is the organizing term of the book. In doing so, my fourth chapter argues, book 3 points to a contrast between the internal illumination invoked by the blind poet and an Apollonian solar inspiration that motivates the poetry of paganism (reducible to the worship of a godless nature). It aligns the poet's opening prayer for light with the Son's faith that he will not be left in the dark of the loathsome grave when he offers to die for humanity. In the episode of the Paradise of Fools, the book further criticizes, with a particular eye toward Catholic practice, the tendency of men and women to read back through analogy from God's and their own visible works to the invisible Creator, and to confuse the two: it parodies, and admits the impossibility of, the book's own depiction of heaven. Yet, in distinguishing God's lower works from God and his heaven, "things invisible to mortal sight," Milton knows that he risks unlinking creation from Creator altogether, as do the book's alchemical philosophers, and as Satan does when he later suggests to Eve that the sun, not God, is the power source that gives life, as well as light, to the universe. The work of poetry in an age of astronomical revolution and uncertainty, Milton suggests, is both critical and constructive: to reveal what was too bookish and poetical, all too human—a Baconian Idol of the Theater—in earlier accounts of the cosmos; and to assert, through the model of its own bookishness, the order and divine authorship of the Book of Nature, however difficult that book may be to read and however invisible the author may be.

Chapter 5 applies this question of visibility to the political argument of *Paradise Lost* by focusing on Satan's envy, a condition associated with vision and first aroused, according to Raphael's account to Adam and Eve in book 5, by the *sight* of the Son elevated to vice-regency in heaven, an alteration in celestial affairs that also initiates the difference of linear time from the sameness of cyclical eternity. Satan's envy links vision to time, and to the finite goods of this world; at its end, the chapter suggests a scriptural parallel in Wisdom of Solomon 2–3. Satan's refusal to bow down before what he takes to be a temporal image of God corresponds to the later historical rejection of the incarnate Son by the incredulous and envious Jews—while his adversary, the zealous Abdiel, plays the role of a fearless Nicodemus before the Sanhedrin. Satan further argues backward, from the apparently secondary, temporal status of the Son, to assert that the Father, whom the Son visibly expresses, is equally secondary and a purely temporal power to be opposed by temporal force. In his envy, the devil invents worldly monarchy by misattributing it to God and wanting it for himself, inventing war, too, in the process. Milton ties Satan's envy to the proverbial envy of the early modern courtier in a royal court. In his meeting with Gabriel in book 4, where the two begin to fight a private duel, called off, as it happens, by God, Satan represents himself in the role of a feudal magnate, refusing to give up a former warrior existence for the cringing court servility to which he accuses Gabriel and the good angels of having subjected themselves. Loving Christian service and abject courtly servitude may indeed look alike. In the character of Gabriel, who briefly seems to rise to Satan's bait, Milton comments on how difficult it may be to reconcile aristocratic honor with Christianity. Earthly kingship and the royal-aristocratic social order, *Paradise Lost* thus suggests (guardedly for the Restoration censor, but nonetheless clearly enough), are incompatible with Christian brotherhood. The political form best suited to achieve brotherhood, Milton maintained in *The Readie and Easie Way*, is the "proportioned," that is, relative equality of a republican commonwealth. Michael's narrative in books 11–12 traces how Cain's fratricidal envy leads to kingship, which reproduces Satan's envy and monarchical ambition in human history.

Chapters 6 and 7 turn to the human heroes of the poem, to the Fall in book 9 and its aftermath in book 10. Chapter 6 almost stands apart, and it makes my largest claim. It relates the separate falls of Eve and Adam in book 9, respectively, to deeply held wishes that Milton reveals in other writings throughout his career. The fall of Eve grows out of the desire to make trial of an otherwise cloistered virtue and to stand approved in the eyes of God: individual recognition, which Milton uneasily assimilates with the wish for fame. The model in *Paradise Lost* is Abdiel, but the zealous angel has good company in the Lady in *Comus*, the poet-speakers of *Lycidas* and *Mansus*, and the hero Jesus, as well as his exemplar Job, in *Paradise Regained*. Abdiel, the lone dissenter who stands up to the rebel Satan after the latter accuses *him* of sedition, is a clear autobiographical stand-in for John Milton, and he introduces a distinctly Miltonic third term that complicates the alternatives of power and love that shape the poem's ethics and generic form: the imperative to prove oneself alone, to use one's talents like the good servant in the parable, and to receive divine applause: "Servant of God, well done." Such spiritual aspiration and the individual fame it wins in heaven may appear to be easily distinguished from the fame and renown sought by worldly conquerors and builders of Babels. It is harder to separate from the fame to which the Christian poet Milton aspires—to be equal in renown with Homer—a remainder, perhaps, of the will to power that lurks within piety and zeal.

Satan's tempting rhetoric to Eve criticizes this wish by turning it into a quest to be the object of universal admiration. Adam, on the other hand, falls in the name of marital love, which the fiction of books 5–8 has made analogous to the communion and joy that Raphael tells Adam and Eve the banqueting angels experience in heaven, and which is reproduced in the meal Raphael shares with them in Eden. This is the sociable joy, the personified Euphrosyne, of *L'Allegro* and the unifying charity that builds the church in *Areopagitica*. Adam's marital (and human) solidarity with Eve cuts him off from the larger community of God and his creatures. Both Eve and Adam have good reasons that go wrong when they disobey God, and their respective wishes—the proof, in Eve's case, of one's solitary spiritual worth and sufficiency, the remedying, in Adam's, of one's social deficiency through human love and companionship—survive and are ratified after the Fall when the couple appear to have switched positions. Adam at the poem's end asserts his vertical dependence on the only God, while Eve declares her love for and inseparability from Adam. Michael's supplement to Adam's profession of creed, enjoining him to add charity, seems to announce a new Christian liberty that aligns the poem's ending with Eve (who indeed gets its last word) and with the relationship of human marriage.

The restoration of the marriage of Adam and Eve in book 10, after their fall and mutual recriminations in book 9, is the dramatic climax of *Paradise Lost*, the event that brings them back both to each other and to God. Chapter 7 places this reconciliation of the first couple against the preceding first two-thirds of book 10, which have described the building by Sin and Death of their bridge over Chaos and Satan's return to hell. Each of these appears to be a "triumphal act," allusively associated with the triumph of Augustus depicted on the shield of Aeneas in *Aeneid* 8, the chronological "ending" of Virgil's poem. But allusion equally returns both demonic acts to the *beginning* of the *Aeneid*, the storm and shipwreck off of Carthage, and suggests the recursive shape of evil in the larger book 10, a book in which the narrative sequence of events seems to run in a loop. So these satanic acts of heroism are now understood as mock-triumphs that parody the real triumphs of the Son, true endings that foreshadow apocalyptic ones, at the respective ends of books 6 and 7. When the divine change of the earth's weather unleashes storm winds that match the turmoil of the despairing Adam, he, too, seems to have been returned to the landscape, outward and internal, of the opening scene of *Aeneid* 1. Book 10 places the reconciliation of Adam and Eve, the modest but true heroism of *Paradise Lost* that ensures a future for humanity, against the grand enterprises of the devils and of earlier epics—the *Aeneid*'s epic of Roman power in particular—that ultimately go nowhere. Satan is left behind in book 10 and out of Milton's poem, last seen in the same abject posture he was in at its opening. Eve raises Adam out of his despair, and he returns the favor, arguing Eve out of the course of suicide. But Eve's realization that she and Adam can opt to die restores choice to the human couple, one denied to the deathless fallen angels of book 2. Adam and Eve choose to live by choosing love.

Eve initiates their spiritual recovery, and in book 10 seems more sympathetic than her desperate husband, who exposes her at the Judgment Scene and bursts out into a rant against women when she first approaches him. Milton's celebration of marriage entails the rehabilitation of Eve as character and as representative woman, mother of mankind. The book rewrites other misogynistic myths and stories—Virgil's Dido, Pandora, and the concubine of Gibeah in Judges—in a systematic pattern of allusion that parallels and contributes to the countering of its own misogynistic biblical myth. These allusions, too, hint at not-so-concealed autobiography underlying Milton's depiction of the first human marriage.

A short coda to the book, chapter 8 examines the structure of the composite books 11 and 12, once the final book 10 of the 1667 edition, in which the prophesied destruction of Eden corresponds, antithetically, to the building of Pandaemonium at the beginning of *Paradise Lost* in book 1. After the Fall, Eden might become a temple, oracle site, a grove of pagan rites, goal of pilgrimage— it has already, at the moment that Satan invades it in book 4, been compared to the sheepfold of the Church, prey to thieves, a Church too rich to escape corruption. In books that predict the rise of empires, God dissociates his cult from power and wealth, closing down and eventually washing away Eden, lest it become another Pandaemonium, a haunt of foul spirits. Milton similarly closes down *Paradise Lost*, and the imaginative wealth of the epic tradition housed inside it, to exclude poetic successors. He turns against his own poetry the iconoclasm directed at Mulciber's idolatry; Adam's visions themselves cease shortly after Michael has predicted the Flood sweeping Paradise off its foundations.

Look for Eden now and you will only find living human temples containing a paradise within.

♦

By the end of *Paradise Lost*, the prospect of an up-to-date globe from the Mountain of Speculation shows the earth overrun by rising and falling empires and by kings, whether they go by the name of king, khan, czar, sultan, or negus. Human power has triumphed, and, beginning with Nimrod at Babel, it has reduced language and meaning to noise, to the "din" also shared by Satan's troops (first clashing swords against shields in hell, later hissing when they have been transformed into serpents), by the violence of the War in Heaven, and by the deafening roar of Chaos itself (12.61; 1.668; 10.521; 6.408; 2.1040). The same barbarous dissonance threatens to drown out the song of the poet-speaker, born perhaps into an age too late for poetry itself. He is surrounded, to transfer the terms that Satan will use in *Paradise Regained*, by a world that is all too "real" rather than "allegoric." The light of the sun seen through Galileo's telescope and the poem's verses is the harbinger of an enlightenment that consigns Adam, Eve, and Eden—and perhaps the grand narrative of Milton's religion itself—to "fables old." All of this is acknowledged by *Paradise Lost*. The epic already participates in a skeptical modernity.

Milton's new poem looks back on these old fables, however, not only with nostalgia but with hope. Its blind poet asserts that there is more to this finite "real" than the visible from which he is in any event excluded, and he provides the supplement of inner light and imagination. His poem's center, the defeat of Satan and the creation of a new heaven and earth, took place at the beginning of history, was repeated spiritually at the Incarnation, and will occur again at the apocalyptic end, giving God himself a chance at a do-over, to improve what he tried before. God may be biding his time, but humans, the poem tells us, can always start over, and the last lines show Adam and Eve with the world all before them. They carry with them the knowledge of Eden, of *Paradise Lost* itself, an Eden that is now for them as for us as much a recreation of the imagination as of memory, and they have learned that love is better than power. The world, Milton's great poem and all the fables of literature teach, need not be known to us, nor left by us, quite as it was given.

1

Milton's Book of Numbers: Book 1 and Its Catalog

A great deal and nothing happens in the first book of *Paradise Lost*. Satan and his fellow fallen angels rise from the burning lake of hell and assemble into what appears to be the greatest army ever summoned up by epic poetry. In full battle array, what do these devils do? Having already been defeated in the War in Heaven by an army that was, in fact, twice their own size and that possessed a secret weapon that God finally unleashed in the exploits of the Son, the fallen angels know better than to try again. The devils decide to talk things over, and construct a council hall for that purpose in Pandaemonium. Milton has pointedly reversed his epic model in the second book of the *Iliad*. The council of the Greeks, in which Odysseus dissuades Agamemnon from giving up the war against Troy, comes first and is then succeeded by Agamemnon's calling for a troop review to boost morale before marching on the city, the occasion, in turn, for Homer's famous catalog of the ships. In *Paradise Lost* the catalog of leading devils is followed by the troop muster and the promise of military action, a promise that fizzles out into talk and the ensuing council of book 2. Milton goes so far in this pattern of reversal as to place Homer's simile of the bees, which comes early in book 2 of the *Iliad*, describing the Greeks coming together for the council at verses 87–95, near the end, in verses 768–775, of book 1 of *Paradise Lost*. The order of *Iliad* 2—bee simile, assembly in council, muster, catalog—is repeated backward in *Paradise Lost* 1: catalog, muster, assembly in council, bee simile. Breaking their martial ranks, the fallen angels settle in to discuss their situation.

The anticlimax of Milton's book 1 suggests that the great speeches of Satan that run through it, pledging immortal hate and eternal war, will only lead to more speeches, that the devils are all talk. No sooner has Satan marshaled and counted up his troops than he dismisses the option of battle. Recalling their defeat in the War in Heaven, he asserts that God

> his regal state
> Put forth at full, but still his strength concealed,
> Which tempted our attempt, and wrought our fall.
> Henceforth his might we know, and know our own
> So as not either to provoke, or dread
> New war, provoked; our better part remains
> To work in close design, by fraud or guile
> What force effected not: that he no less
> At length from us may find, who overcomes
> By force, hath overcome but half his foe.
> Space may produce new worlds; whereof so rife
> There went a fame in heaven that he ere long
> Intended to create, and therein plant
> A generation, whom his choice regard
> Should favour equal to the sons of heaven:
> Thither, if but to pry, shall be perhaps
> Our first eruption, thither or elsewhere:
> . . . .
> But these thoughts
> Full counsel must mature: peace is despaired,
> For who can think submission? War then, war
> Open or understood must be resolved.
>   *(1.640–56, 1.659–62)*

As Satan spells out the subsequent plot of Milton's epic, he lets the air out of the preceding action that has raised up and mustered the "myriads of immortal spirits" (1.622) and "puissant legions" (1.632) whom he addresses.[1] From its very beginning *Paradise Lost* moves away from the epic of Iliadic warfare, which, we will find out subsequently in books 5 and 6, has already been staged in the War in Heaven and is over and done with before the action of the poem begins. Whereas in his first speech to Beelzebub Satan had seemed to consider the options of "force or guile" (1.121), he in fact already knows that force will not work: in spite of his protestations here, the devils *do* have something to dread from new war, as Belial will argue in book 2: "this would be worse" (2.186). For his post-Iliadic situation, Satan revises his earlier formulation and proposes instead the epic of Odyssean "fraud or guile"—which, of course, are not alternatives despite the "or," but the same thing.[2] It is a fraud, moreover, that Satan characteristically justifies by attributing it first to God, who he claims tricked the bad angels by holding the Son and his war chariot in reserve: Satan will fight fraud with fraud. The council in book 2 may debate whether this war is to be "Open or understood," but, in fact, Satan has already made his choice for the latter. It is Odysseus, the lying master of words, whom, as the next chapter demonstrates, Satan will repeatedly play in the pattern that unifies book 2.

By dressing up his devils for battle and then giving them no place to go, Milton at once imitates the representations of earthly military power in earlier epics and satirically belittles them: by the end of the book, the devils will have shrunk to the size of bees and fairy elves. He also redefines the nature of the epic that is to follow: all epic poems are, in the final analysis, wars of words, wars, that is, made up of the words we read on the page, but this one will be explicitly, self-consciously so, a battle for the hearts and minds of humanity. Action in this epic will be verbal, and conversely its poetry is a form of action.

The catalog of the chief demons from verses 376 to 521 at the center of the book illustrates this shift. It may appear to motivate the military muster that follows in the action, but, in fact, the weapons of these devils are not martial but the "falsities and lies" (1.367) by which they corrupted mankind to fall into idolatry. It is a catalog, not, as in earlier epics, of soldiers but of so many Odyssean liars. What had been the function of the traditional epic catalog, to number and measure the strength of contending armies and to give the epic poem its sense of grandeur, is taken up instead by the celebrated similes of book 1, which invoke vast military forces—the giants who warred on Jove, the Memphian chivalry of Pharaoh, the barbarian invaders of the Roman Empire, the armies of earlier epics and chivalric romances. The relationship of the similes is thus ironic to this catalog-which-is-not-a-catalog, a roll call of lying, noncombatant devils. Yet Milton also exploits the sense in which the ordering of the troops in the traditional epic catalog constitutes a miniature version of the epic poem's larger attempt to give form and intelligibility to the violence of war, where battle makes ordered ranks fall quickly into disarray. His centrally placed catalog corresponds to and determines much of the action of book 1, as well as the landscape of hell, both in Milton's physical descriptions and in the similes. It further controls the overall logic and sequence of these similes. The following discussion demonstrates the extraordinary symbolic unity of book 1, organized around its catalog, and of which the catalog, as an inset, organized unit, is a model and epitome. It suggests how the catalog of demons, whose idolatrous shrines abutted upon or even entered into the Jerusalem temple, relates to the construction of Pandaemonium, the temple-capital of the fallen angels built through music and poetry that is an anti-version of the poetic edifice of *Paradise Lost* itself. The book that gets the epic started is thus very much about its own writing: the Satan who first lifts himself and then his companions off the burning lake darkly mirrors his literary creator. In its consistent metapoetic argument, Milton's representation of the devils at once demystifies and may itself be complicit with the human making of idols.

The Shape of the Catalog

Demonstrating the spectrum of diabolic evil, the catalog, in fact, possesses its own intricate structure and logic.[3] "Say, Muse, their names then known, who first, who last" (1.376), the poet asks, and draws our attention specifically, self-consciously, to who stands first and last at either end of the catalog. It first lists "prime in order and in might" (1.506), beginning with Moloch and ending with Belial, the pagan gods of the ancient Near East who have biblical associations. They are followed almost as an afterthought by the classical Greek and Roman gods. The catalog thus ends *twice*: the first time with Belial, the second time with "Saturn old," who fled first to Italy and then, it seems, all the way to England, the "utmost isles." The analysis that follows considers different implications of the catalog's inner pairing of Moloch-Belial and its outer pairing of Moloch-Saturn.

MOLOCH AND BELIAL 1

The pairing of Moloch and Belial will be repeated in the council scene of book 2, where the two demons will propose the diametrically opposite courses of open war and possible self-annihilation on the one hand and ignoble ease and getting accustomed to hell on the other. (These alternatives will also be played out in the activities of the devils that Satan leaves behind in hell later in the book, between those who go mad with "vast Typhoean rage" [2.539], and the "others more mild" [2.546] who build a civilization of poetry and philosophy.) The opposition between Moloch and Belial, between a demon who demands human sacrifice in the form of children and a demon "than whom a spirit more lewd / Fell not from heaven" (1.490–91) and who is responsible for the demands to rape guests in Sodom and Gibeah, pits violence against lust, though the difference may disappear when we consider that the matron exposed at Gibeah (Judges 19) was raped to death.[4] This same opposition appears in the initial pairing of Moloch and Chemos, the Moabite god who was worshipped by "lustful orgies" (1.415). Chemos is, in fact, to be identified with Milton's old friend, the seducer Comus, as he is by Gerhard Vossius; Jerome identified Chemos as well with Priapus and thus made his lascivious nature clear.[5] His shrine in Jerusalem was, the poem tells us, next to "the grove / Of Moloch homicide, lust hard by hate" (1.416–17).

Chemos and Belial are also linked geographically, for the first extended his cult "to the Asphaltic Pool" (1.411), while the second was associated with Sodom: both, that is, are linked to the desolate region of the Dead Sea. This is one of the identities of the burning lake on which Satan is first discovered "Prone on the flood, extended long and large / Lay floating many a rood" (1.195–96). The "fiery deluge" (1.68) and "sulphurous hail" (1.171) that fall in hell recall the rain of fire and brimstone that destroyed Sodom and Gomorrah (Genesis 19:23–28) beside the Dead Sea. The saline Dead Sea was famous for keeping objects buoyant on its surface, and *this is why Satan and his cohorts lie floating*, "covering the flood" (1.312) of the lake of hell instead of sinking beneath its waves.

MOLOCH AND SATURN 1

The contrast of Moloch to Belial as first and last of the prime devils is succeeded by the contrast of Moloch to the last of the pagan gods, the Roman Saturn, the beginning and end of the entire catalog.

> First Moloch, horrid king besmeared with blood
> Of human sacrifice, and parents' tears,
> Though for the noise of drums and timbrels loud
> Their children's cries unheard, that passed through fire
> To his grim idol.
>   *(1.392–96)*

Moloch was a god of Carthage, the Phoenician deity Baal-Hammon, whose cult was brought by Punic colonists to the North African city. The ritual sacrifice to Moloch of children, immolated in fire, elicited horror among Greek and Roman writers.[6] The worship of this cruel god was also introduced, Milton goes on to record, into Israel under Solomon, then suppressed by Josiah (2 Kings 23:10): "And he defiled the Topheth, which is the valley of the children of Hinnom, that no man might make his son or his daughter to pass through the fire to Molech."[7] This cult site, "Tophet thence / And black Gehenna called," Milton comments was "the type of hell" itself (1.404–5), and we may understand the flames of hell as one giant holocaust to Moloch prepared for humanity. It is appropriate that Moloch comes foremost in the catalog.

The Saturn who is mentioned twice in verses 512 and 519 appears, by contrast, to have been a beneficent pagan deity.

>   who with Saturn old
> Fled over Adria to the Hesperian fields,
> And o'er the Celtic roamed the utmost isles.
>   *(1.519–21)*

The lines refer to Virgil's double version of Italian-Roman origins in the *Aeneid*: the Italian king Latinus is the descendant of Saturn in book 7 (45–49), while in book 8, in the passage primarily recalled here, Evander recounts to Aeneas how Saturn came as a fugitive to Italy, civilized its peoples, and founded a golden age (8.319–58). We are reminded of the glorious future Rome of its new founder Augustus, who, Anchises had predicted in the underworld of book 6, would establish a golden age again in place of Saturn: "aurea condet / saecula qui rursus latio regnata per arua / Saturno quondam" (6.792–94).

Is the evil, child-immolating Carthaginian god at the begining of the catalog thus contrasted to a civilizing, peaceful founding god of Rome at its end? No: whatever their appearances, everyone in this catalog is a devil, and these two are in fact *identical*. Saturn was also Cronos, the god who devoured his children, and it was the name that the Romans themselves gave to Moloch. The historian

Quintus Curtius writes that during the siege of Tyre by Alexander the Great, the Punic citizens considered "offering a freeborn boy to Saturn—this sacrilege rather than sacrifice, handed down from their fathers, the Carthaginians are said to have performed until the destruction of their city" (4.3.32).[8] Lactantius similarly pours down Christian indignation in the *Institutes*: "Or what will they do in profane places who commit the most extreme crimes around the altars of the gods? Pescennius Festus in his books of history recounts fully how 'the Carthaginians were accustomed to immolate human victims to Saturn, and when they were conquered by Agathocles, King of the Sicilians, they thought the god was angry with them; and so that they might more diligently make atonement, they immolated 200 of the sons of the nobles.'"[9] In a passage of the *City of God* that Milton appears explicitly to have in mind here, Augustine similarly identifies Saturn with the child-devouring Carthaginian god (7.26) while he cites Evander's speech in *Aeneid* 8 (7.27).[10] Moloch and Saturn are thus one and the same horrifying deity/devil. By lending his catalog the shape of a ring composition with Moloch and Saturn at either end, Milton suggests that there is little to choose between the great opponents of antiquity, Carthage and Rome, whose conflict is enshrined in the *Aeneid*. In this respect, he may have been anticipated by the *Aeneid* itself, for the first "Saturnia" we encounter there (1.23) is Juno, the patroness of Carthage; already in Virgil's poem it is difficult to determine the meaning of Rome's Saturnian inheritance.

MOLOCH AND SATURN 2: A MINIATURE *AENEID*

This conflation of Moloch and Saturn, of Carthage and Rome, governs or reflects the way that the topography and action of book 1 rewrites the opening of the *Aeneid*. As critics have pointed out, the scene that begins Milton's epic in medias res—its discovery of Satan and his fellow fallen angels dispersed on the storm-tossed burning lake of hell and seeking in the words of the archfiend to "tend / From off the tossing of these fiery waves / There rest, if any rest can harbour there" (1.183–85)—recalls the begining of the *Aeneid*, the storm sent by Juno and the finding by Aeneas and his Trojan followers of a harbor, "portum" (*Aen.* 1.159), near Carthage.[11] Like Aeneas struggling to the Punic shore, Satan manages to arrive at the "beach / Of that inflamed sea" (299–300). The hot sands of the Libyan desert, moreover, are suggested by the "burning marl" and "torrid clime" (1.296–97), the "burnt soil" of hell over which the devils march with "painful steps" (1.562), not so much marching as hotfooting it in a comic slap at their soldierly dignity. What ensues in book 1 is an *Aeneid* in miniature: by its end, the Aeneas-like Satan and the other devils have built their destined city Pandaemonium. Milton is probably making a joke on the proverb that "Rome was not built in one day." Putting to shame the builders "Of Babel, and the works of Memphian kings," his epic protagonists raise their city "in an hour / What in an age they with incessant toil / And hands innumerable scarce perform" (1.694, 1.697–99). The allusion to the Tower of Babel and to the pyramids, repeated at lines 717–18, "Not Babylon, / Nor great Alcairo," also identifies Pandaemonium with Rome: the biblical Rome as the Whore of Babylon of Revelation 17 accompanied by her seven-headed beast. This Rome was a new Babylon, as the Babylon that held the Israelites captive was another Egypt. It is the great city of Revelation 11:8, "which spiritually is called Sodom and Egypt," and thus it brings together the three locales of earthly sin that define the geography of Milton's hell. Satan and his cohorts have built a version of Rome where at the end of the book they will hold both a "consult" (1.798), a meeting of the ancient Roman senate, and a "conclave" (795), an assembly in modern, papal Rome. The Geneva Bible comments on the beast and the Whore of Babylon, "The Beast signifieth the ancient Rome: the woman that sitteth thereon, the new Rome which is the Papistrie, whose crueltie and blood sheding is declared by skarlat."[12] It has been suggested that the pilasters, pillars, and golden architrave of Pandaemonium recall the new Saint Peter's in Rome.[13] In this little *Aeneid*, the Church of Rome has been built in one day.

Just as Saturn and Moloch are one and the same, the demonic capital Pandaemonium conflates Virgil's Rome with his Carthage, the demonized double and opponent of Rome in the *Aeneid*—"Italiam contra Tiberinaque longe / ostia" (*Aen.* 1.13–14; cf. *PL* 2.296–98)—and makes the two indistinguishable.[14] Its roof of "fretted gold" (1.717) and the "starry lamps and blazing cressets" (7.728) that hang from it recall Virgil's description of the palace of Dido: "dependent lychni laquearibus aureis / incensi et noctem flammis funalia uincunt" (*Aen.* 1.726–27). The swarming of Milton's devils into their newly built capital, compared in simile to bees, evokes not only Homer's simile in *Iliad* 2 but recalls as well the famous simile in *Aeneid* 1 that compares the Carthaginians to bees when they are building their new city (430–36); how happy, Aeneas exclaims in the next line, are those whose city walls are already rising, wishing that he were already founding his own city. In *Paradise Lost*, however, Rome is being built in Pandaemonium simultaneously and inextricably with its enemy twin, Carthage, the city that lost out in history and was repeatedly defeated and sacked. But the Roman Empire celebrated by Virgil also fell, and the suggestion is that this infernal city and its newly hatched empire will be destroyed, too, in the long run: *Pandaemonium delendum est*. The point is brought home in a simile that compares the fallen angels to the barbarians who descended upon the Roman Empire, hordes that "Came like a deluge on the south, and spread / Beneath Gibraltar to *the Libyan sands*" (1.354–55). The devils seem to be the destroyers of the very Rome they are about to build, and the barbarians end up in Libya to destroy Carthage as well, sacked still another time by the Vandals in 439; the devils appear to be their own worst enemies. Later the devils constitute an army greater than any ever assembled in classical or chivalric epic, and here, too, the final figures alluded to return us to Libya: those "whom Biserta sent from Afric shore / When Charlemain with all his peerage fell / By Fontarabbia" (1.585–87). Milton refers to the doomed invasion of France by the Libyan king

Agramante in Boiardo's *Orlando innamorato* and Ariosto's *Orlando furioso*; his capital, Biserta, is sacked in the latter epic (*OF* 40.32–34). In this revised version of the story, the war also results in the fall of another Roman emperor, the Holy Roman emperor Charlemagne, an updating into Renaissance epic's fantasy Middle Ages of Virgil's opposition of Carthage and Rome. Once again, the destruction is shared and, in this case, mutual.

MOLOCH AND BELIAL 2: LIBYA AND SODOM

Let us return to the inner catalog, which begins with Moloch and ends with Belial. The pairing of Carthaginian Libya, represented by Moloch, with Sodom, represented by Belial, will return to describe our final vision of hell in book 10. Here Satan returns to Pandaemonium, invisible for a while before he appears to his followers "as from a cloud" (10.449) recalling the cloud that surrounded Homer's Odysseus when he entered into the city of Phaeacia, more pointedly, the cloud that concealed Virgil's Aeneas before he appeared to Dido in Carthage in book 1 of the *Aeneid*, and, perhaps most pointedly, the cloud that surrounds the Turkish sultan Solimano in canto 10 of Tasso's *Gerusalemme liberata*, when he enters invisibly into the royal council hall inside Muslim-held Jerusalem (*GL* 10.16–49): Satan finds his "great consulting peers, / Raised from their dark divan" (10.456–57) to congratulate him on his return. Satan comes back as an "emperor" (10.429) to his waiting "legions" (427), and anticipates a Roman-style triumph that would imitate the triumph of the Son after his victory in the War in Heaven. Instead, he and his fellow devils are transformed into serpents. "Not so thick swarmed once the soil / Bedropped with blood of Gorgon" (10.526–27), the poem tells us, referring to the *Libyan* desert described by Lucan in the *De bello civile* (9.619–937), where the snakes born from the blood of the Gorgon Medusa wreak gruesome havoc on the soldiers of Cato on their harrowing march across its sands. Satan and his now fellow serpents are constrained to reenact the original sin in Eden, and to eat and spit out a parodic form of the forbidden fruit that tastes of bitter ashes, "like that which grew / Near that bituminous lake where Sodom flamed" (10.561–62). Our last glimpse of Satan finds him in a hell that is a combination of Sodom and Libya.

But this will also be our last vision of Eden. The archangel Michael takes the lingering Adam and Eve by their hands and leads them out of Eden (12.637–38), in an action that recalls the angels who led the lingering Lot and his wife and daughters out of Sodom (Genesis 19:16), for God is destroying Eden much as he destroyed Sodom, turning it into a torrid, uninhabitable area.[15]

> The brandished sword of God before them blazed
> Fierce as a comet; which with torrid heat,
> And vapour as the Libyan air adust,

Began to parch that temperate clime.
    (12.633–36)

It is a very dark moment in the poem. Paradise is not only being lost; it is being transformed by human sin and divine anger into the landscape of hell, a hell that is part city of the plain, part Libyan desert in the region of a fallen Carthage.

EGYPT

Halfway through the catalog come the Egyptian gods Osiris, Isis, and Orus (1.478); these deities took the monstrous shapes of animals, the "birds, four-footed beasts, and creeping things" described by Paul in his definition of idolatry in Romans (1:23), a text that Milton paraphrases in verses 367–72. These bestial Egyptian gods had already aroused the skepticism of Cicero in his *De natura deorum* (3.19): "Then if the traditional gods we worship are really divine, what reason can you give why we should not include Serapis and Isis in the same category ... We shall therefore have to admit to the list of gods cattle and horses, ibises, hawks, asps, crocodiles, fishes, gods, wolves, cats and many beasts besides."[16] The cattle that Cicero mentions first are connected to his naming of Serapis, the incarnation of Osiris as a bull, whose "lowings loud" Milton describes in *On the Morning of Christ's Nativity* (215); Milton will further mention Serapis by name when comparing Pandaemonium to the pyramids and other grandiose buildings of ancient Egypt (1.720). John Selden links this Egyptian cult to the golden calf in the Exodus story and Milton goes on in the catalog to make a similar connection of Osiris to this first lapse of the Hebrews into idolatry, "the calf in Oreb" (1.484).[17] In another evocation of the Exodus, the poem relates how, in the last of the plagues visited on the Egyptians, the angel of death slew the firstborn not only of their children but also of their cattle (Exodus 12:29), and thus dispatched those of their "bleating gods" that the fifth plague (Exodus 9:6) had spared.

These Egyptian deities and their associations with the Exodus and its plagues correspond to the third symbolic complex that, in addition to Sodom and to Carthage/Rome, governs the geography of Milton's hell and the similes of book 1. Still another burning desert, and one neighboring the burning sands of Libya, Egypt was, in the words of Deuteronomy (4:20) and Jeremiah (11:4) a "furnace of iron," from which God delivered Israel, and hell is introduced to us from the very beginning, through the eyes of the fallen Satan, "As one great furnace" (1.62). When Satan manages to rise from the burning lake, and "on each hand the flames / Driven backward slope their pointing spires, and rolled / In billows leave i' the midst a horrid vale" (1.222–24), the scene suggests an infernal crossing through the Red Sea, where the "children of Israel went into the midst of the sea upon the dry land" (Exodus 14:22) and as the Song of Moses in Exodus 15:8 recounts, the "floods stood upright as an heap, and the depths were congealed in the heart of the sea." The poem already puts in place the scenario of the Exodus that Satan will subsequently parody in book 2, casting him as a diabolic Moses who promises his companions "Deliverance" (2.465) from their Egyptian-like bondage in hell and who crosses the wilderness of Chaos to the Promised Land of God's newly created earth and Eden.[18]

This Mosaic association is evoked, however, only to be belied by two similes of book 1 that, in rapid succession, compare the devils first to sedge afloat the Red Sea where the Pharaoh and his army once drowned as they pursued the fleeing Israelites, and implicitly to the Egyptians' own "floating carcasses" strewn on the waves (1.304–11), then, in the second simile, to the plague of locusts that Moses summoned against the same Egyptians (1.338–43). The devils are identified not with the delivered Israelites but with their Egyptian oppressors, and the combination of similes suggests that they are a plague upon themselves.[19] As is the case where the devils are depicted as Carthaginians, as the Carthaginians' mortal enemies, the Romans, and as the barbarians who sacked both Rome and Carthage, the poem also indicates here the self-defeating nature of their sin. The locusts anticipate the plagues of Egypt mentioned in the catalog, and through the prophet Joel they will represent in Revelation 9 the apocalyptic armies of Satan—in Hebrew Abaddon, in Greek Apollyon—who will rise out of the smoke of the bottomless pit, "as the smoke of a great furnace" (9:2). These same armies will be cast back again into "the lake of fire and brimstone" at the end of time in Revelation 20:9–10. In addition to resembling the Dead Sea and the stormy waves outside of Virgil's Carthage, Milton's lake is a kind of Red Sea from which Satan and his crew may make a temporary exodus, but to which they are destined to make a final return, like Pharaoh's army: "The depths have covered them: they sank into the bottom as a stone" (Exodus 15:5).

The Catalog and Pandaemonium

Papal apologists proclaimed that Saint Peter's Basilica on Vatican Hill was the successor and true version of Solomon's temple on Mount Zion in Jerusalem; this may partly explain why Pandaemonium, "Built like a temple" (1.713), with its "gates / And porches wide" (1.761–62) and its "infernal court" (1.792) bears a parodic resemblance to the Jerusalem temple.[20] But here, too, the catalog is closely connected to the action of book 1 and the ensuing construction of Pandaemonium. It lists the neighboring gods of the Israelites whose cults were introduced into Jerusalem itself. They

> durst fix
> Their seats long after next the seat of God,
> Their altars by his altar, gods adored
> Among the nations round, and durst abide
> Jehovah thundering out of Sion, throned

Between the cherubim; yea, often placed
Within his sanctuary itself their shrines,
Abominations; and with cursed things
His holy rites, and solemn feasts profaned.
    (1.382–90)

Moloch's temple was introduced by Solomon himself "right against the temple of God" (1.402) and the same "uxorious king" (1.444) built a temple of Astarte for his foreign wives (1 Kings 11:5–7). In one of his visions, Ezekiel sees women weeping for Thammuz "in the sacred porch" (1.454) of the temple (Ezek. 8:14) and views the abominations (Ezek. 8:17) taking place in its inner court. King Ahaz put up an altar to Rimmon in the temple (2 Kings 16:14–15), "God's altar to disparage and displace / For one of Syrian mode" (1.473–74).

    The fallen angels thus build in Pandaemonium an already profane version of the Jerusalem temple that the devils of the catalog will later infiltrate and defile. The ending of the catalog with Belial is again particulaly significant, for Belial, who lacks a temple, represents the spirit of ecclesiastical corruption itself.

        to him no temple stood
Or altar smoked; yet who more oft than he
In temples and at altars, when the priest
Turns atheist, as did Ely's sons, who filled
With lust and violence the house of God.
In courts and palaces he also reigns
And in luxurious cities …
    (1.492–98)

In Pandaemonium, both temple and city, Milton intimates not merely his revulsion at the Roman church, but his distrust of *any and all* established churches, too easily contaminated by pagan, carnal influences, by the world of kings and cities; his distrust, especially, of the physical buildings that house such churches. *Paradise Lost* begins by calling on the Spirit, "that dost prefer / Before all temples the upright heart and pure" (1.17–18), already replacing the earlier invoked "Sion hill" (1.10) before the ensuing fiction of book 1 builds the devils' temple. In book 11, Michael tells Adam that "God attributes to place / No sanctity" (11.836–37), as he shows him in a vision the washing away by the Flood of the mount of Paradise, which earlier in the same book he remarks might have been "Perhaps thy capital seat," a Jerusalem or a Rome with a temple at its center.[21]

    As the capital of hell, Pandaemonium is to be contrasted to Milton's heaven, where the angels described by Raphael in book 5 dwell camped in "pavilions" and "tabernacles" (5.653; 5.654) on the vast plain around the mountain of God, evoking the scenery of the wilderness around Sinai.[22] The contrast is scripturally inspired by Stephen's diatribe in Acts 7 against the temple after he has been accused of prophesying its destruction (Acts 6:14), the speech that earns him martyrdom. After mentioning the golden calf (7:41) and the tabernacle of Moloch (7:43), Stephen suggests the continuity of these idolatrous cults with the temple itself, opposing the worship of the Israelites in the wilderness to the subsequent cult center in Jerusalem.

> 44. Our fathers had the tabernacle of witness in the wilderness, as he had appointed, speaking unto Moses, that he should make it according to the fashion that he had seen.
> 47. But Solomon built him an house.
> 48. Howbeit the moste High dwelleth not in temples made with hands, as saith the prophet.

The Geneva Bible comments on verse 44, "They oght to have bene content with this couenant onely, & not to haue gone after their lewd fantasies," and on verse 48, "He reproveth the grosse dulnes of the people who abused the power of God in that they wolde haue conteined it within the temple."[23] Calvin's own commentary on Acts, translated into English by Christopher Fetherstone in 1585, notes that "This was almost a common error in all ages, because men thought that cold ceremonies were sufficient enough for the worship of God. The reason is, because forasmuch as they are carnal, and wholly set upon the world, they imagine that God is like to them."[24] The pastoral layout of Milton's heaven and the building project of Pandaemonium contrast the sojourn in the wilderness that the Israelites experienced close to their God to the institutionalization of their worship in the temple in Jerusalem, a temple that seems to have been *already* unsanctified by ritual religion and pomp before the devils cataloged by Milton would have their idolatrous cults placed alongside and within its spaces. The building of Pandaemonium is the beginning of priestcraft.

The Logic of the Similes in Book 1

The catalog at the center of the book also governs the sequential logic of Milton's similes in book 1. Milton's catalog, we have seen, is an anti-catalog that describes the spiritual force of falsities, lies, and idolatry, but it nonetheless bears the imprint of the traditional epic catalog that lists the size and strength of the contending army, and it thus *feels* connected to the ensuing muster of the devils who march in formation before their leader, Satan.

> he through the armed files
> Darts his experienced eye, and soon traverse
> The whole battalion views, their order due,
> Their visage and stature as of gods,
> Their number last he sums. And now his heart
> Distends with pride, and hardening in his strength

Glories: for never since created man,
Met such embodied force, as named with these
Could merit more than that small infantry
Warred on by cranes:
    (1.567–76)

Much of the ensuing epic will depict the progressive hardening of Satan's heart, which here takes pride in the "embodied force," the sheer physical violence that is at his disposal in this review of his troops. He first looks at their stature and then counts them up, and it appears to be this second act, his numbering them, that makes his heart swell. In so doing, Satan imitates—and the poem again self-consciously points to—the shape and sequence of book 1 itself. Its similes first look at *how big* the devils are, and then describe *how many* they are.

This army, the passage tells us, makes all human forces look like pygmies, whose war with the cranes is recorded by Homer in the *Iliad* (3.537). But book 1, which begins by comparing Satan to a Titan or a giant, and then to a sleeping whale (1.196–208), will end by likening the devils, who have shrunk themselves to fit into Pandaemonium, to those very pygmies or to fairy elves (1.780–88). Milton belittles the fallen angels—he allows us to watch them belittle themselves. But this change in his reader's perception of them is prepared for and integral to his book's moving from the question of "monstrous size" (1.197) to the question of number.

The distinction becomes clear in the similes that rapidly succeed one another between verses 287 and 311. Milton has continued the gigantism of his description of Satan by comparing his shield to the moon seen through Galileo's telescope and his spear, which would make a shipmast look like a mere "wand" (294), similes that also, as Harold Bloom has pointed out, seek to diminish earlier epics—Homer had compared the shield of Achilles to the moon and insisted on the weight of his spear that no other hero could handle (*Iliad* 19.374–88)—much as Satan's forces will later be said to dwarf those of Milton's epic predecessors, beginning with the giants of Claudian's *Gigantomachy* (576–87).[25] But then Satan calls on his fallen companions, and the perspective shifts from size to quantity, and the similes that follow compare them to "autumnal leaves" and the "sedge" of the Red Sea. I am less interested in how the first of these similes reaches back through the epic tradition to Dante, Virgil, and Homer than in the way in which they both suddenly diminish the size of the devils.[26]

When we think in numbers, and when the individual becomes a number without a name, the units become very small: leaves or sedges. The same thing happens in the ensuing simile that compares the fallen angels who rise and fly above the burning lake to a swarm of locusts: "So numberless were those bad angels seen" (1.344). The devils have, in fact, lost their individual identities through their sin: "Though of their names in heavenly records now / Be no memorial blotted out and razed / By their rebellion" (1.361–63). Evil is onto-logically privative, and the devils neither have names nor, as Satan will learn, a recognizable "shape" (4.835), and they are last seen in the poem in a state of metamorphosis in book 10. The catalog that follows in book 1 puts a literally human face upon them as they inhabit the idols that men and women have made. But the same diminishment returns in the book when the "multitude" (1.730) comes to pay a tourist visit to the newly completed Pandaemonium—"they anon / With hundreds and with thousands trooping" (1.759–60)—and are now compared to bees. When the devils, already shrunken to insects in the simile, now shrink themselves in order that all may fit "without num-ber" (1.791) into Pandaemonium, the action comments metapoetically upon the poem's own procedure and logic. At the same time, the poem itself self-consciously comments: "they but now who seemed / In bigness to surpass Earth's giant sons / Now less than smallest dwarfs, in narrow room / Throng numberless" (1.777–80). Milton made the devils big five hundred lines earlier, and now he makes them little, as if one has to think small in order to make the numberless fit into the confines of the imagination. The very greatness in num-bers that the traditional epic catalog counts up and celebrates only miniaturizes the devils, a sardonic enough deflation of the military subject of previous epic: "Wars, hitherto the only argument / Heroic deemed" (9.28–29). These devils, as we have noted, are not going to fight in any case: their shrinking to get into the council hall goes hand in hand with, and is the image of, their unheroic abandonment of force for fraud. But even in their former battle on the plains of heaven, the poem suggests here, the vastness of their army had already dimin-ished them. The infinite become the infinitesimal.

These issues, in fact, crop up again during Raphael's retrospective narration of the War in Heaven, at the very center of the poem in its original ten-book version of 1667. Raphael suggests the difficulty of retelling feats performed by "Army against army numberless" (6.224); he states that "deeds of eternal fame / Were done, but infinite" (6.240–41), and thus acknowledges that the mod-ern massed warfare of Milton's time, armed with the canonry whose satanic invention Raphael will subsequently recount, cannot be narrated in terms of individual heroes. It will take the Son's entrance into the battle on its third day, wielding a different kind of power, to end this melee and to reintroduce a kind of epic heroism: "Number to this day's work is not ordained / Nor multitude" (6.809–10), the Son tells the loyal angels.[27]

More pointedly, the Son's prowess has already been anticipated at the end of book 5 by the zealous witness borne by the lowly Abdiel against his aristocratic angelic betters and their vast numbers in Satan's camp:

Among the faithless, faithful only he;
Among innumerable false, unmoved,

Unshaken, unseduced, unterrified
His loyalty he kept, his love, his zeal;
Nor number, nor example with him wrought
To swerve from truth, or change his constant mind
Though single.
　　　(5.897–903)

Abdiel's keeping his faith in spite of the massive pressure of his peers has indi-viduated him and earned him a place in the story, and in the ensuing book 6 he will be acclaimed by God himself: "well hast thou fought / The better fight, who single hast maintained / Against revolted multitudes the cause / Of truth, in word mightier than they in arms" (6.29–32). Here, too, verbal combat, in this case the words of reasoned truth triumphing over devilish fraud, replaces tradi-tional epic warfare. Abdiel's fight is a very Miltonic combat in which the captain of the debate club triumphs over the football team. It is, nonetheless, the spiri-tual equivalent of the Son's victory and may be said to explain its true nature.

The poem parallels the two acts and places them at the end of their respec-tive books, lending the 1667 *Paradise Lost* two centers. Abdiel separates himself from the "revolted multitudes"; the Son separates and drives those multitudes out of heaven. In many respects, Abdiel's feat is more impressive, since he is not fitted out with the Chariot of Paternal Deity, and Abdiel, in fact, occupies and hinges the very center of the poem's original version, defeating Satan in debate at the end of book 5, striking Satan to his knees at the beginning of hostilities in book 6 (111–98): his spiritual heroism is paralleled not only to the Son's mili-tary heroism but to his own battlefield heroism as well. But it is the first kind of heroism, the spiritual one available to every man, that counts in this epic: the war of words and the interiorized, reasoned choice of faith, a choice that is necessarily individual and that resists being incorporated into the numbers of the epic catalog.

Raising Devils

Reduced to numbers without names, diminished in size, the devils become un-real in the final simile of book 1, a simile that makes them very little, into the little people, the fairies, just as the book's first simile had made them very big, like a sleeping whale, and perhaps no more real. The two similes frame the fic-tion and are meant to be paired and compared, "who first, who last."

　　　　　　　or that sea-beast
Leviathan, which God of all his works
Created hugest that swim the ocean stream:
Him haply slumbering on the Norway foam
The pilot of some small night-foundered skiff,
Deeming some island, oft, as seamen tell,

With fixed anchor in his scaly rind,
Moors by his side under the lea, while night
Invests the sea, and wished morn delays:
    (1.200–208)

                    or faerie elves,
Whose midnight revels, by a forest side
Or fountain some belated peasant sees,
Or dreams he sees, while overhead the moon
Sits arbitress, and nearer to the earth
Wheels her pale course, they on their mirth and dance
Intent, with jocund music charm his ear:
At once with joy and fear his heart rebounds.
    (1.781–88)

The best readings of these similes, by Geoffrey Hartman and Patricia Parker, emphasize their slowing down of the action and the figure of the onlooker, the pilot or the belated peasant, whose fate is suspended.[28] Will the dawn come up in time for the pilot to get his anchor out of the whale he mistakes for an island, or will the whale wake up first, dive, founder his ship, and drown him? Will the peasant be made a lunatic by his vision of the fairies? This suspense corresponds to the larger plot of the epic as it approaches the Fall of Adam and Eve, which it presents as anything but inevitable; at any moment their human choices might have turned out differently.

The onlooker, to push those readings further, is also a figure of Milton's reader confronting the satanic evil the poem represents. In both similes, the whale and the fairies are minding their own business, the former asleep, the latter "on their mirth and dance / Intent." The drama takes place in the onlooker's reaction: the failure to recognize the threat in the motionless, dormant whale; the potential fascination with the dancing fairy elves.

The similes have an additional dimension of demystification. The first is a sailor's yarn ("as seamen tell"), the second is a fairy tale, and possibly a dream; both are staged in the darkness and uncertainty of night. Framing book 1, the similes call into question the very reality of the devils it depicts—perhaps not the existence of the devil per se, attested to in scripture, but of the forms in which the human imagination has clothed him: the names by which the fallen angels now go in the catalog at the book's center.[29] The example of the myth of Mulciber—"Men called him Mulciber" (1.740)—which seems to contain its own etiological explanation of how a falling star might have been erringly converted by fable into a falling deity, fits into this pattern.

Book 1 already provides a generic home for the devils as make-believe fairies by means of two similes in its later section that evoke the romances of chivalry. The first, in verses 579–87, passes from epic precedents (Claudian, Statius,

Homer, Virgil) to invoke "what resounds / In fable or romance" (1.579–80) and refers to Arthur, "Uther's son" (1.580), as well as to the heroes of Carolingian romance who "Jousted in Aspramont or Montalban / Damasco, or Marocco, or Trebisond" (1.583–84); the second, in verses 763–66, picks up both this tournament figure and its switch between verses from Christian to pagan (Muslim) locales, and compares the spacious hall of Pandaemonium to "a covered field, where champions bold / Wont ride in armed, and at the soldan's chair / Defied the best of paynim chivalry / To mortal combat or career with lance." These are the "gorgeous knights / At joust and tournament" (9.36–37) that Milton, again conflating epic with romance, will reject as a heroic subject in his calling upon his Muse in book 9, the stuff of the poem on King Arthur he had himself once considered writing. Of course, there was already such a poem in English, Spenser's *Faerie Queene*, and fairies such as Morgan le Fay were protagonists of the chivalric legends. By the end of the book, the devils and their world seem to be consigned not only to the pagan, rather than Christian side of the romances, "at the soldan's chair," but to the romances themselves into which the book's epic fiction seems to be turning, or from which it may have never indeed been distinct: to the popular genre that Renaissance literary theorists routinely disparaged for its mere fictionality—"fabled knights / In battles feigned" (9.30–31), Milton dismissively comments.[30]

The final comparison of the devils to dancing fairies is an instance, moreover, of Miltonic self-citation. The ode *On the Morning of Christ's Nativity*, Milton's first major poem that opens the *Poems* of 1645, describes how the new light of truth at the birth of Christ drives out the pagan gods from their shrines and oracles. All but one are gods who reappear in the catalog of book 1, which is consciously rewriting the earlier poem. The *Nativity Ode* similarly concludes with the diminishment of these gods to fairies: "the yellow-skirted fays, / Fly after the night-steeds, leaving their moon-loved maze" (1.235–36). If there is something elegiac in Milton's vanishing fairies, whose maze refers to the patterns of their dance and the rings it leaves behind in the fields, they are not entirely innocuous, for they are part of a folk belief that Reformers tied to Catholicism. So the Anglican bishop and poet Richard Corbet (1582–1635) wrote in his ballad, "The Faeryes Farewell," which describes an expulsion similar to the one carried out in the *Nativity Ode*, and contains a similar hint of elegy or, in this case, nostalgia.

> Witnesse those Rings & Roundelayes
>   Of theirs, which yet remaine,
> Were footed in Queene *Maries* dayes
>   On many a Grassy Playne;
> But, since of late *Elizabeth*
>   And later *Iames*, came in,
> They never daunc'd on any heath

> As when the Time hath bin.
>
> By which we note the *Faries*
>   Were of the old Profession;
> Theyre Songs were *Ave Maryes*,
>   Their Daunces were *Procession*.
> But now, alas, they all are dead,
>   Or gone beyond the Seas,
> Or Farther for Religion fled,
>   Or elce they take theyre Ease.
>   *(25–40)* [31]

Milton's dancing fairy elves in *Paradise Lost* may thus carry with them the remnants of Catholic ritual and of the idolatry of the demonic pagan gods listed in the catalog with their "gay religions full of pomp and gold" (1.372). Their music could be associated with the same gods in the *Nativity Ode*—with the "dismal dance" around the idol of Moloch (210), the "anthems dark" that accompany the worshippers of Osiris (219)—as well as with the crypto-Catholic "rites" of Comus and of his "foundation" in Milton's *Comus*: "And on the tawny sands and shelves / Trip the pert fairies and the dapper elves" (117–18).

These associations with paganism or with a paganizing popery notwithstanding, the predominant idea of the endings both of book 1 of *Paradise Lost* and of the *Nativity Ode* seems to be the reduction of the face of the demonic to the level of fairies, that is, to unreal figments of the human imagination at its most vulgar level of ignorance and superstition. At this level, the fairies—precisely because they are make-believe—nonetheless have their charm: they are the stuff of poetry. "I may never believe / These antique fables, nor these fairy toys," says Shakespeare's rationalist Theseus in *A Midsummer Night's Dream* (5.1.2–3), as he goes on to discuss how the poet gives "airy nothing / A local habitation and a name" (5.1.16–17), turning airy into fairy.

The fairy elves of the last simile thus offer a final, skeptical comment on Milton's own fiction-making in book 1. The contrast between the inert whale of the first simile and these elves dancing to their jocund music adds another layer to this metapoetic argument. The action of the book has raised Satan and his fellow devils into action from their chains and immmobility. The poem has similarly animated them, and it has done so through the music of its verse. Beelzebub tells Satan that the fallen angels will respond to their leader's "voice, their liveliest pledge / Of hope in fears and dangers" (1.274–75), and it is in answer to "their general's voice" (1.337), reminiscent of the war-shouts of Agamemnon and Achilles in the *Iliad*, which calls on them to "Awake, *arise*, or be for ever fallen" (1.330), that the host of demons swarm up out of the burning lake; this invocation closely parallels the poet's own calling upon his Muse to catalog the chief devils, "*Roused* from the slumber" (1.377), those whose names have been "razed" (1.362) from heavenly memory, but who rise again here. The diabolic army begins to move through music, first when the imperial ensign is displayed "at the warlike sound / Of trumpets loud and clarions" (1.531–32), which occasions a collective "shout" (1.542), then "to the Dorian mood / Of flutes and soft recorders; such as *raised* / To highth of noblest temper heroes old" (1.550–52). We are told of "the soft pipes that charmed / Their painful steps o'er the burnt soil" (1.562–63): the commonplace Latinate pun on "charm" and "carmen," suggests that this music that propels them is a kind of poetry, perhaps identical to Milton's own poem that we are reading. Similarly, Pandaemonium is built to the sound of music: it "*Rose* like an exhalation, with the sound / Of dulcet symphonies and voices sweet" (1.711–12), and this recollection of the lyre of the poet Amphion that built Thebes also directs attention to the poem itself and its self-conscious fiction-making. The simile of the dancing fairies who "charm" the ear of the peasant onlooker completes and glances back upon the book's procedures: the power of its words and music has raised the devils into motion and raised their capital city, a poetic creation that parodies the work of Milton's Spirit-Muse, who is asked "what is low *raise* and support" (1.23) in the poet, and who taught Moses the story of the Creation itself: "how the heavens and earth / *Rose* out of chaos" (1.9–10).

Book 1 of *Paradise Lost* thus dramatizes the part its own poetry plays in creating the devils it places before the reader and suggests how idolatry itself is a kind of poetry. The demons of the catalog were "wandering o'er the earth" (1.365) before they became fixed in their cult sites as pagan gods, and the "falsities and lies" by which they corrupted the greatest part of mankind have originated as much with mankind as with them. The same chapter of the *City of God* in which Augustine discusses Virgil's Saturn concludes with his judgment that the whole of pagan polytheism "is occupied in inventing means for attracting wicked and most impure spirits, inviting them to visit senseless images, and through these to take possession of stupid hearts" (7.27).[32] The idea here seems to be that man proposes and the devil disposes: that real demons rush in when human belief creates imaginary gods. It is a critical take on the Middle Platonism expressed in such works as the Hermetic *Asclepius*, which Augustine cites and criticizes in the following book 8 of *The City of God*. The *Asclepius* piously describes how the Egyptian priests were able to attract benign demons to inhabit the statues of their gods: "they added a supernatural force whereby the images might have power to work good or hurt, and combined it with a material substance, that is to say, being unable to make souls, they invoked the souls of daemons, and implanted them in the statues by means of holy and sacred rites" (37).[33] Augustine seems to agree that the pagan idols were indeed animated, but by unholy devils who took advantage of human superstition and led it still further away from the true God: "For although man made gods, it did not follow that he who made them was not held captive by them, when, by worshipping them, he was drawn into fellowship with them—into the fellowship not of stolid idols, but of cunning demons" (8.24).[34] Milton's self-conscious poetic animation of his fictional devils points historically forward to, and seeks to denounce, the future inspiriting by real devils of the equally fictive human idols listed in the catalog, but the two are troublingly related: the imagination is the potential entry point for the diabolical into human experience.

Accordingly, Milton at once gives and denies a local habitation and a name to the devils of book 1. The insistent metapoetic reflection of the book reminds us that the face we put on the devil is our own, a fiction projected by the myth-making, human mind, and that the devils are similarly the product of the words of the poem itself. Milton must summon the devils into poetic being in order to warn a reader who, in the first simile of the pilot on the Norway foam, is figured as unaware of them. But he runs the risk of fascinating the reader with that very poetic creation, as the charmed peasant onlooker of the last simile attests: of making an idol that the devil can, in fact, inhabit. Milton shows himself aware of the difficulty of destroying idols, even or especially those that he has set up in order to pull down, aware that he may produce and perpetuate the very superstition, pagan and Catholic, he is trying to dispel. The raising of the devils of book 1 through the music of poetry is an object lesson in the origins of idolatry, but the power of Milton's poetry may nevertheless exceed its admonitory, demystifying purpose. In the peasant onlooker's heart, joy and fear redound together, but the joy of the fairy elves' charming music may outweigh the salutary fear that this music can lead to lunacy or demonic possession. Once raised, these devils are hard to put to rest or to return to airy nothing: back to the words on the page. For if *Paradise Lost* self-consciously reduces to a war of words, Milton's own words are at war with themselves.

Book 1 acknowledges that we really have no idea what the devil looks like, though the evidence of evil may be everywhere in the world. It thereby labels the fiction about Satan that follows in *Paradise Lost as* a fiction, a matter, we might say, of suspended belief. That the devils may not finally be reduced to poetry and written off, however, is suggested at the book's close. For all of its belittlement of Satan and the fallen angels, some residual part of them remains undiminished.[35]

> But far within
> And in their own dimensions like themselves
> The great seraphic lords and cherubim
> In close recess and secret conclave sat
> A thousand demigods on golden seats,
> Frequent and full. After short silence then
> And summons read, the great consult began.
> (1.792–98)

The deliberately short-circuited description, "in their own dimensions like themselves," gives no information about the shape or size of these devils, and they occupy the inner sanctum of this desanctified version of the Jerusalem temple where nothing was to be found behind the temple veil.[36] The book's skeptical wavering about the reality of its devils here seems to admit the possible existence—behind human fictions easy enough to expose if not entirely to strip away—of a demonic force that exists outside of mythopoesis itself, in the silence when its music stops. The silence is short-lived, quickly erased by enjambment. Then the poem's words begin again.

Appendix: Demonic Swashbucklers

The satirical depiction in book 1 of the fallen angels, mustered into arms only to settle down in council, is reinforced in verses 663–79, immediately preceding the building of Pandaemonium. Satan has just resolved on war, "Open or understood" (1.662), and his companions give a rousing cheer.

> He spake: and to confirm his words, out flew
> Millions of flaming swords, drawn from the thighs
> Of mighty cherubim; the sudden blaze
> Far round illumined hell: highly they raged
> Against the highest, and fierce with grasped arms
> Clashed on their sounding shields the din of war,
> Hurling defiance toward the vault of heaven.
> (1.663–69)

The devils thump their shields with their swords, and Milton's remarkable ear allows him to suggest a series of rhymes to match the din they make—grasped/clashed, arms/war, thighs/mighty/high/highest—as well as the snide put-down in his describing them raging highly against the highest divinity they cannot possibly affect. Their answer to Satan's words with their rhyming swords, as if it were now time to move from speeches to the real action of battle, will be belied by the book's ensuing action. But even here the swords are not put into combat use, but, as an extension of their leader's words, to make so much blustering, hollow noise, the "din" that in *Paradise Lost* will repeatedly characterize the reduction of language—and hence of the possibility of poetry itself—to nonsense: the din of Chaos (2.1040), the din of the War in Heaven (6.408), the din of the confused tongues of Babel (12.61), and the din of the hissing that Satan and his companions make in the last vision we have of them, transformed into serpents, in the halls of the Pandaemonium (10.521) they are here about to build.[37]

The devils' clashing of their swords against their shields invites, in fact, a double interpretation. Roman soldiers went into battle striking their spears or swords against their shields in order to frighten their enemy: so Polybius reports of the soldiers of Scipio Africanus in their victory over Carthage at the battle of Zama: "the Roman troops charged the enemy uttering their war-cry and clashing their shields as is their custom" (15.12).[38] Roman legions also clashed shields in approval of a commander: given Satan's identification as "the apostate angel" (1.125; see also 5.852 and 6.100), Milton may have in mind the response of the soldiers of the emperor Julian the Apostate to his speech urging them into combat against the Alamanni: "The soldiers did not allow him to finish what he was saying, but gnashed and ground their teeth and showed their eagerness for battle by striking their spears and shields together, and besought him that they might be led against an enemy who was already in sight."[39] The fallen angels similarly *appear* to confirm Satan's call for war and to be spoiling for a fight.

But clashing one's sword against one's shield had acquired a different possible meaning between Roman times and Milton's own. In his *The History of the Worthies of England*, published in 1662, Thomas Fuller explains the saying, "He is only fit for Ruffian's Hall."

> A *Ruffian* is the same with a Swaggerer, so called because endeavoring to make that Side to *swag* or weigh down, whereon he engageth. The same also with *Swash-Buckler*, that from *swashing*, or making a noise on Bucklers. *West-Smith-field* (now the *Horse-Markets*) was formerly called *Ruffian-Hall*, where such men met casually and otherwise, to try Masteries with the Sword and Buckler. More were frighted than hurt, hurt than killed therewith, it being accounted unmanly to strike beneath the Knee, because in effect it was as one armed against a naked man. But since that desperate Traitor *Rowland Yorke* first used thrusting with Rapiers, Swords and Bucklers are disused, and the Proverb only appliable to quarrelsome people (not tame, but wild garetters) who delight in brawls and blows.[40]

The swordplay at Smithfield of heavy broadswords against equally heavy shields is now out of use, Fuller notes, and it always was sword*play*, a relatively harmless kind of fray that was more noise than real fighting. Indeed, it is not clear whether Fuller's swashbuckler is beating the shields of opponents or upon his own shield—as an empty boaster and bully. The latter idea seems to be what we are to infer when Shakespeare's Justice Shallow refers to himself in *2 Henry IV* as having been one of a company of "swinge-bucklers" (*2 Henry IV*, 3.2.22), two scenes after the play introduces its "swaggerer," Ancient Pistol (2.4.70–211), the lower class, cowardly *miles gloriosus*. Nowadays, Fuller notes, this brawling behavior has migrated down to the lower stratum of society, to dwellers in garrets, and Shakespeare's Hotspur in *1 Henry IV* had sneered at Prince Hal consorting with such urban commoners as "that same sword-and-buckler prince," and implied that Hal lacked any real martial deeds (*1 Henry IV*, 1.3.228). Such figures, less harmless than Pistol, Milton wrote in *Eikonoklastes*, had accompanied King Charles when in 1642 he tried to arrest the five members of the House of Commons: "whose very dore he besett with Swords and Pistols cocked and menac'd in the hands of about three hundred Swaggerers and Ruffians, who but expected, nay audibly call'd for, the word of onset to beginn a slaughter" (*CPW* 3:377).

The joke is on Milton's fallen angels. As they clash their shields in book 1, they may look like Roman soldiers roused to battle, but they equally look ridiculous: like so many swashbuckling braggarts sounding defiance against a deity whom they, in fact, dare not fight. So the rest of the book will confirm. It makes a last sardonic comment on the draining away of the devils' fighting spirit in the simile that compares their next move, the building of Pandaemonium.

> As when bands
> Of pioneers with spade and pickaxe armed
> Forerun the royal camp, to trench a field,
> Or cast a rampart.
>   (1.675–78)

A vestige of military identity lingers in this image of army engineers setting out to prepare a battlefield. They are still armed, if only with their shovels. (We note, too, that these are royalist soldiers.) The simile recalls the epic actions of the *Iliad* (7.433–41), where the Greeks build ramparts to protect their ships, and of the *Aeneid* (7.157–59), which recalls the *Iliad* passage when Aeneas builds a Roman-style camp on the Italian coastline. The devils, however, are not building fortifications, but a council hall: talking and fraud, not fighting and force, are the order of the day.

2

Ulysses and the Devils: The Unity of Book 2

Book 2 of *Paradise Lost* is the book of Ulysses, the mythical hero whom it finally evokes by name near its end (2.1019), after Satan's voyage through Chaos has enacted a miniature *Odyssey*. Milton doubly organizes the book's fiction and ideas, first, around the figure of Ulysses himself, second, around one of the hazards Ulysses faces in the *Odyssey*, the paired monsters Scylla and Charybdis. The episodes of book 2 imitate a series of scenarios from the story of Ulysses, drawn not merely from the *Odyssey* but from different classical sources, and produce a number of Ulysses figures: the orator Belial and statesman Beelzebub, as well as the guileful Satan. These diabolic impersonations of Ulysses suggest how aspects of his heroism can be perverted toward evil; together they constitute a kind of anatomy of the ancient hero and a compendium of his career.[1] Milton's imitations of and allusions to Ulysses, some of which have been individually noted by earlier critics, thus form a systematic pattern, an extended poetic conceit, that provides book 2 with an underlying logic and coherence: they link the Ulyssean deliberation and fraud of the council scene that takes up the book's first part to Satan's *Odyssey*-like journey in its second half.[2] The fact that at nearly every turn in the book we are encountering a figure of Ulysses reinforces the repetition of the book's themes and motifs from episode to episode. These form a second, different anatomy: an exploration of the fallen angels' hopeless and unchanging existence. Milton additionally unifies these motifs by repeated evocations and versions of Scylla and Charybdis. Through these twinned and ultimately interchangeable alternatives, book 2 configures the devils' dilemma: their death that is not death, their loss of choice. The book's unity and repetition are thus part of its meaning: it tells the same sad story over and over again.

Milton picks up where book 1 leaves off and continues its ironic imitation of book 2 of the *Iliad*, which ran Homer's order of events backward—the catalog of the devils, the mustering of their troops, the calling of council in Pandaemonium—and thus saw Satan and his fellow devils, in their newfound cowardice, move not from council to assembly for war as in *Iliad* 2, but from assembled ranks to council debate, from Iliadic force to Odyssean guile. As if to reinforce the point and to note the obsolescence now of the Achillean heroism of the earlier War in Heaven, book 2 initially pairs the desperate, bellicose Moloch against the smooth-talking Belial: in doing so, it invokes the eloquent Ulysses, who defeated the warrior Ajax in debate in book 13 of Ovid's *Metamorphoses* and thereby obtained the arms and legacy of Achilles. The second pairing of Mammon and Beelzebub directly returns to the council scene of *Iliad* 2 itself, in which Ulysses took a central role. Beelzebub will initially play the part of that Homeric Ulysses, particularly in his countering the arguments of the Thersites-like Mammon. When Beelzebub subsequently proposes what we are later told was Satan's plan to send an explorer and spy to seek a route back to heaven and the newly created universe, the devils' council has changed Homeric venues. Milton's fiction is now modeled on another council scene of the *Iliad*, this time the one in book 10, where Nestor proposes the sending of spies into the Trojan camp. One of these will be Ulysses, who, along with Diomedes, practices subterfuge and murder against the Trojan counterspy Dolon in the nighttime episode referred to as the *Doloneia*. The counterspy to Satan will turn out in book 3 of *Paradise Lost* to be no one less than the Son of God himself. The echoes of the opening of the *Odyssey* in the heavenly council that rebegins *Paradise Lost* suggest a whole new model of heroism that supersedes all of the versions of Ulysses of book 2.

Satan's ensuing voyage is a version of the wanderings of Ulysses, and part of the point—and joke—of Milton's imitation is that what looks like the opening of the *Iliad* in *Paradise Lost* turns out to open an *Odyssey*. But before he sets out into the ocean of Chaos, Satan meets Sin and Death and rehearses the *Telegony*, the story of how Ulysses met his death at the hands of the son he never knew he had sired. Only in the last section of the book, when the devil journeys across Chaos to God's newly created universe, does Satan finally imitate the most famous Ulysses, the heroic wanderer who is the hero of his own epic poem. Book 2 thus flanks this Ulysses of the *Odyssey* with other versions of the same hero: the orator, the politician, the disreputable spy, the protagonist of an oedipal drama. The sequence of episodes and versions of Ulysses are charted in the following table.

43–227 Belial and Moloch	Ulysses and Ajax (Ovid, *Metamorphoses* 13; Quintus of Smyrna, *Posthomerica* 5)
228–389 Beelzebub and Mammon	Ulysses and Thersites (*Iliad* 2)
390–505 Satan volunteers	Ulysses and the *Doloneia* (*Iliad* 10)
648–889 Satan, Sin, and Death	Ulysses and Telegonus (*Telegony*)
890–1055 Satan's voyage through Chaos	Ulysses's voyage (*Odyssey* 5–13)

In addition to these versions of Ulysses, book 2 refers allusively to at least one more, the Ulysses who sails beyond Gibraltar in the modern fictions of Dante's *Inferno* and Tasso's *Gerusalemme liberata*; this Ulysses will be discussed in chapter 3.

Book 2 depicts multiple versions not only of Ulysses, but of the most formidable and final obstacle the hero encounters in the journey he narrates in *Odyssey* 9–12, Scylla and Charybdis, mentioned by name, respectively, at lines 660 and 1020. These are the figures of bad alternatives that, because they *are* bad, are no alternatives at all, in fact, versions of each other, and the poem's embodiments of the Homeric monsters—Sin and Death, the Chaos that swallows and then spits Satan back up—comment retrospectively on, and continue the logic of, the council scene that opens the book, where the devils can find no good solution to their condition. The paired speakers, Moloch and Belial, Mammon and Beelzebub, are themselves versions of Scylla and Charybdis. The lack of a real choice and the crucial quandary of the devils' situation are first realized by Belial in his exchange with Moloch at the beginning of the book: Moloch would like to be consumed by a Charybdis-like death, but Belial intuits that they cannot die. Satan later meets this very Death, but the *Telegony* battle in which son kills father never takes place. Book 2 thus prepares, by way of antithesis, the argument and paradox of *Paradise Lost*, that death, like divine grace, is the condition of human choice, the argument that is explored in book 10 (which, as book 9 in the 1667 ten-book structure of the epic, corresponded inversely to book 2). Knowing that they *will* and *can* die, Adam and Eve freely choose to go on living (I will analyze this episode in chapter 7). The first fall of the angels provides a model for the subsequent fall of mankind, but with an all-important difference: the deathless fallen angels are literally damned if they do and damned if they don't.

The insistence in book 2 that the devils' seeming alternatives are in fact identical, all versions of the same dilemma, runs ironically counter to its narrative. If book 1 rouses the fallen angels off the burning lake only to reseat them in the council of Pandaemonium where Belial would advise them in book 2 to stay seated and talking forever, in the ensuing action of the second book hell seems to break loose. Sin opens the doors of hell and Satan escapes and makes his way across Chaos to the newly created universe and eventually to earth. Milton repeatedly depicts the short-circuiting of this apparent narrative progress and satanic success story by indicating how its ultimate failure, the circular return of evil upon itself, is already built into it. Satan meets his Death in book 2 before he even sets out on his mission, but even before this meeting his Sin has already incorporated death in the unending torments of his remorseful conscience. Despite his seduction of mankind and its consequences for the poem's human reader, Satan's career is for him just as much a dead end and unviable alternative as the other options debated in the opening council scene and then tried out by the devils who remain behind to build a home and civilization in hell.

The figure of Ulysses, the common denominator of book 2, is a complicated model and ambivalent foil for Satan and his fellow devils. They misappropriate Ulysses's eloquence and fraud for their bad ends, and, in doing so, disclose and criticize some potentially unsavory aspects of the classical hero that had been noted since antiquity itself.[3] Milton demonstrates his bravura by imitating so many versions of the hero, following the Renaissance practice of *contaminatio*: he refuses to confine himself to the single, obvious model of the *Odyssey*.[4] Nonetheless, the Ulysses of the *Odyssey*, whom Milton saves for last, is not only the most important literary version of the hero, but the most important for the thought of book 2. This Ulysses chooses to exchange the sameness of immortality with Calypso for the adventures of mortal life and the ultimate goal of reunion with Penelope—and Milton's Adam will, in tragic circumstances, make a similar choice to die with Eve. As a human hero, Ulysses can choose a life bounded by death, and the further choices such a life affords, where the devils cannot. At the same time, the Ulysses of the *Odyssey*, for all the suffering he experiences in his wanderings, appears to have a taste for those adventures independent of his goal of wife, home, and family—his place in the succession of generations, which is also his acceptance of his own death—and the poem predicts the hero's further wanderings beyond its conclusion: his inexhaustible spirit of adventure has made Ulysses the life-affirming figure of a modern humanism.[5] This may all be very well, Milton suggests, and he incorporates adventuring into human experience in the "wandering steps and slow" of Adam and Eve setting forth into history in his epic's penultimate verse. But in the absence of a meaningful end, the poet also insists, such life becomes nothing but restless wandering—and this is also the pattern of the diabolic existence without hope, "in wandering mazes lost" (2.561).[6] The two-sided heroism of the *Odyssey*'s Ulysses can thus suggest both a human contrast with and human parallel to the devils' no-exit condition, the capacity on the one hand to choose and assent to the limitations (and possibilities) of mortal life, on the other to experience endless disquiet and remorse, which are a living death, a living hell.[7]

The Council

In chapter 1 we observed the fallen angels of book 1 muster into an epic army of vast proportions and then demonstrate their lack of stomach for war. They built the council hall of Pandaemonium to sit down and talk things over. This ironic inaction already indicated—here on the devils' own part—the general rejection by *Paradise Lost* of the traditional military heroism of epic. Satan tried to play Achilles, the hero of arms, in the War in Heaven, which the poem defers to Raphael's retrospective narrative in book 6. As the shift to the demonic council that opens book 2 suggests, it is now time to try on the role of Ulysses, the hero of words.

The council scene in book 2 is carefully, even intricately structured; a speech by Satan (2.11–42) introduces the council and sets its terms as a debate between the alternatives of force and fraud—"open war or covert guile" (2.41).[8] Similarly, Satan closes the council after it has approved Beelzebub's plan—"first devised / by Satan" (2.379–80) himself—to attempt the easier enterprise of attacking God's newly made universe and its creature, mankind; he does so by answering Beelzebub's call for a volunteer to find the way to the "new world" through the vast expanse of Chaos. In between, four speakers offer their counsel: the soldier Moloch, the rhetor and temporizer Belial, the accommodator Mammon, and the statesman Beelzebub. At either end of this sequence, Moloch as old-fashioned martial hero is contrasted with Beelzebub, the smooth strategist: open war will, in fact, be replaced by fraud and covert warfare, an Achilles by a Ulysses. Beelzebub's redirecting the devils to continue their hostility after they have been deflected by Belial's veiled appeasement and Mammon's outright rejection of war continues from book 1 the poem's imitation of the Greek council in the second book of the *Iliad*, and makes Beelzebub a type of the Ulysses who there dissuades the Greeks from making for their ships and sailing home from Troy (*Iliad* 2.244–332). Within the sequence of speakers, however, Moloch is also paired with Belial, as Mammon is paired with Beelzebub, and each of these pairings, too, produces a version of Ulysses: Belial, who plays Ulysses to Moloch's Ajax, and Beelzebub, who plays Ulysses to the Thersites of Mammon. Belial is, to be sure, a particularly degraded, ethically hollow kind of Ulysses, but then, so are Beelzebub and Satan as well in *their* Ulyssean guises—and so, finally, may be Homer's hero himself, measured against the new heroic standards of *Paradise Lost*.

Moloch and Belial Again: Ajax and Ulysses

In the council scene of book 2, Moloch and Belial repeat their pairing on either end of Milton's catalog of the chief devils in book 1, where they respectively embodied violent hate and insinuating lust. Now Moloch stands for the "open war" proposed by Satan, but Belial does not call for its alternative of "covert guile," but rather for further talk and inaction. Moloch the reckless warrior ("He recked not"; 2.50) and Belial the orator, whose lips "dropped" manna, are most clearly modeled on Virgil's Turnus and Drances in the council scene among the defeated Italians of book 11 of the *Aeneid* (11.336–444). Milton elegantly reverses Virgil's scenario, where the man of action Turnus sarcastically responded to the defeatism and appeasement of Drances, the Cicero-like man of words, echoing his adversary three times point by point, and led the Italians to further battle (and defeat). Here it is timorous Belial who speaks second and who refutes three arguments of the desperate Moloch in the reverse order to which Moloch put them forth. "First what revenge?" (2.129) Belial asks, and rejects both of Satan's options: "War therefore, open or concealed, alike / My voice dissuades" (2.187–88); he then refutes the possibility, even were it desirable, of the self-annihilation Moloch calls for (2.142–59); and third, notes that yes, things can get still worse for the devils (2.159–86). This reversal of the Virgilian model gives the last word to the talker and opponent of war, and it thus repeats in little the ironic action or inaction of book 1. Having been trounced in the War in Heaven, none of the fallen angels—except Moloch—wants to face God's army again. This includes Satan, whose initial posing of a choice between war and guile is, in fact, a sham. Already in his final speech of book 1, he had decided that the devils' "better part remains / To work in close design, by fraud or guile / What force effected not" (1.645–47) and to try his luck with God's new creation (1.650–56). The council of book 2 has been called and Pandaemonium built to discuss how to put this plan into effect. But Moloch does not appear to have gotten the agenda for the meeting; nor, for that matter, has Belial.

Beyond its more proximate Virgilian model, the opposition in Moloch and Belial of blunt, warloving soldier and wily orator also recalls the Ajax and Ulysses who publicly debate over who should receive the arms of Achilles; when the arms are awarded to Ulysses, Ajax goes mad and kills himself.[9] Modern scholars suggest that the exchange between Virgil's Turnus and Drances is, in fact, modeled upon earlier literary versions of the debate between Ulysses and Ajax, versions that Ovid would subsequently imitate as well in the major depiction of the dispute between the two Greek heroes that has come down to us in book 13 of the *Metamorphoses*.[10] Milton also seems to have intuited the relationship between these classical texts. He points to Ajax and Ulysses as epic types of force and guile when Belial responds to Moloch's assertion that the devils are already at the worst and have nothing to lose. Belial warns that God, incensed by their continual resistance, may punish the devils further and that they, "Caught in a fiery tempest shall be hurled / Each on his rock transfixed, the sport and prey / Of racking whirlwinds, or for ever sunk / Under yon boiling ocean" (2.180–83). Impalement on a storm-beaten crag was the fate, as Juno recalls at the opening of the *Aeneid*—"illum expirantem *transfixo* pectore flammas / *turbine* corripuit *scopulo infixit acuto*" (*Aen* 1.44–45)—not of Ulysses's opponent, Telamonian Ajax, but of his homonym, the lesser Oilean Ajax; the seer Proteus tells a version of the same event in book 4 of the *Odyssey* (4.500–11), a story that emphasizes the foolish defiance of the gods that earns this Ajax his death, in this case by drowning in the depths of the seething sea (*Od.* 4.510): Belial's alternatives allude to *both* versions of the hero's fate. Milton makes a learned joke at the indomitable Moloch's expense: as an Ajax figure, he can be not only a second-rate Achilles but a second-rate Ajax as well. The contrast between Belial's willingness "To *suffer*, as to do / ... to *endure* / Exile or ignominy, or bonds, or pain, / ... *sustain* and *bear*" (2.199; 206–9) versus the suicidal Moloch who "rather than be less / Cared not to be at all" (2.47–48) recalls Cicero's discussion of the two heroes (here it is the usual opposition between Ulysses and Telamonian Ajax that is in question) in the *De officiis*: "How much

Ulysses endured [*passus est*] on those long wanderings, when he submitted to the service even of women ... in order in the end to attain the object of his desire. But Ajax, with the temper he is represented as having, would have chosen to meet death a thousand times rather than suffer such indignities" (1.31).[11]

John Milton saw himself as an orator modeled on Ulysses in the two *Defenses* of the English people. In the prefatory section of the *First Defense*, he characterizes his adversary, Claude Saumaise or Salmacius, as an Ajax who, in his madness, flogged a ram under the delusion that it was Ulysses himself. "Your peroration is clearly tragic, drawn I suppose from Ajax the Lash-Wielder" (*CPW* 4:324),[12] Milton jeers, suggesting that Salmacius is an incompetent debater and has already lost the contest before he meets his Ulysses-like rival in John Milton. In the *Second Defense*, Milton assumes the role of Ulysses the orator in order to counter the aspersions of the writer of the *Regii Sanguinis Clamor* (*The Cry of Royal Blood*), whom Milton mistakenly identified as Alexander More. That pamphlet had called him "worse than Cromwell," and Milton takes it as a compliment. He cites the version of the debate between Ajax and Ulysses in the *Posthomerica*, the fourth-century AD Greek epic poem of Quintus of Smyrna: "Or do you not remember that when Ajax and Ulysses vied for the weapons of the dead Achilles, the poet chose as judges, on the advice of Nestor, not Greeks, their fellow-countrymen, but Trojans, their enemies?" (*CPW* 4:594).[13] To be taken by royalist foes as more dangerous to their cause than Cromwell himself is the highest form of praise, Milton argues, and then adds:

> For although I should like to be Ulysses—should like, that is, to have deserved well of my country—yet I do not covet the arms of Achilles. I do not seek to bear before me heaven painted on a shield, for others, not myself to see in battle, while I carry on my shoulders a burden, not painted, but real, for myself and not for others to perceive.[14] (*CPW* 4:595)

Already in the *Second Defense* Milton distinguishes between types of epic heroism; first between the soldier Achilles and the orator Ulysses, then, more radically, between public heroism and the heroism of private conscience. *Paradise Lost* opts for both of the latter alternatives, rejecting "Wars, hitherto the only argument / Heroic deemed" for "the better fortitude / Of patience and heroic martyrdom" (9.28–29, 9.31–32), choosing argument itself, the work of persuasion, instead of the force of arms, and emphasizing an inner life that is independent of and opaque to the external world. Maintaining that privacy has special urgency for a blind man, who may be scrutinized by those he cannot himself see.

The opposition of Moloch and Belial in the council scene of book 2 parodies this choice between heroic options. Moloch's case makes clear enough why Milton would reject martial heroism: Achillean warrior wrath and Ajax's thwarted pursuit of honor, which refuses to "Accept this dark opprobrious den of shame" (2.58), easily led into Moloch's suicidal despair and the desire that God "quite consume us" (2.96)—death before dishonor. But Belial depicts how the model of Ulysses that Milton *does* choose could itself degenerate into a vicious version of itself. Here, too, the reference is autobiographical. When Milton's narrator describes Belial as

> to nobler deeds
> *Timorous* and *slothful*, yet he pleased the ear
> *(2.116–17)*

he repeats, Annabel Patterson has pointed out to me, the charges that the young Milton in the prefatory section of the second book of *The Reason of Church Government* (1642) imagined his conscience might have leveled against him had he *not* embarked on his career as prose polemicist in the works of his "left hand," the works in which Milton thought himself reviving the role of an ancient orator.

> I foresee what stories I should heare within my selfe, all my life after, of discourage and reproach. *Timorous* and ingratefull, the Church of God is now again at the foot of her insulting enemies: and thou bewailst, what matters it for thee or thy bewailing? when time was, thou couldst not find a syllable of all thou hadst read, or studied, to utter in her behalfe. Yet ease and leasure was given thee for thy retired thoughts out of the sweat of other men ... Or else I should have heard on the other eare, *slothfull,* and ever to be set light by, the Church hath now overcom her late distresses after the unwearied labours of many her true servants that stood up in her defense; thou also wouldst take upon thee to share amongst them of their joy: but wherefore thou? where canst thou shew any word or deed of thine which might have hasten'd her peace; what ever thou dost now talke, or write, or look is the almes of other mens active prudence and zeale. (*CPW* 1:804–5; emphasis added)

Milton excuses his premature taking up of his pen, "thus out of mine own season when I have neither yet compleated to my minde the full circle of my private studies" (*CPW* 8:807), by the enforcement of his conscience that would otherwise upbraid him as fearful in the face of persecution, idle in prosperity. In Belial, Milton depicts a worst-case version of what his own career as rhetor-polemicist might have been, for Belial is the orator who speaks out and still manages to be timorous and slothful in his advocacy of doing nothing.

Belial's eloquence is that of a pure sophist and without heroic aim. It seeks only to obstruct decision making and stymie action: it "could make the worse appear / The better reason, to perplex and dash / Maturest counsels" (2.113–15). Similarly, Belial's actual advice to suffer, endure, sustain, and bear that makes him like Homer's Ulysses described by the repeated epithet, "much enduring" (*polytlas*), lacks the strategic goals for which Ulysses patiently suffered humiliation. Driven instead by Belial's fear of the death that Moloch craves (2.143–51), it is thus all the more a mock-version of the Christian patience and heroic martyrdom endured as a sign of obedience and love that *Paradise Lost* substitutes for Achillean military heroism, a Ulyssean endurance suffered for higher ends than Ulysses himself sought. Without such ends, Belial shows how a Ulysses must go bad. He answers Moloch's assertion that the devils are already at their worse (2.100) by arguing that their present situation is already an improvement over their fall from heaven ("That sure was worse").

> Is this then worst,
> Thus sitting, thus consulting, thus in arms?
> *(2.164–65)*

The wonderful irony of the line recapitulates again the situation of the devils: in arms, yes, but with no intention of using them, and instead sitting down and talking. But Belial would like nothing more than to keep on sitting, in hope of "what chance, what change / Worth waiting" (2.222–23) the future may bring— a parody of the true and effortful patience described by Milton's sonnet on his blindness in its injunction "to stand and wait" on God. Belial would sit and wait forever.[15] Words instead of action, suffering to no purpose can reduce to cowardice, both physical and spiritual, and to inertia: "ignoble ease, and peaceful sloth, / Not peace" (2.226–27).

Yet Belial is more clear-sighted than his peers about the nature of their condition, and the deepest irony of Milton's portrait is that Belial's craven passivity, however unacceptable in human behavior, may be the best that the devils can do, that his false patience is better than no patience at all.[16] The devils are damned if they do, damned if they don't—but if they do, their condition spirals further downward, the hardening of their already hardened hearts. Satan later admits in his soliloquy in book 9 that his vindictive urge to destroy washes back upon him: "though worse to me redound" (9.128), and echoes God's earlier prediction: "so bent he seems / On desperate revenge, that shall redound / Upon his own rebellious head" (3.84–86). Of the final transformation of the fallen angels into ash-chewing serpents, which is the poem's final view of them, Belial might drily comment, "this would be worse" (2.186). Belial's pagan categories of fate (197), chance (222), and of the devils' "present lot" (223) do not disguise his defeatist acknowledgment of God's omnipotence, and "what hope the never-ending flight / Of future days may bring" (2.221–22) is a mere pretext for the endless temporizing he advocates, identical to the "Ages of hopeless end" (2.186) he earlier fears. Milton's sly use of the indefinite "what" in "what hope … what chance, what change" similarly connects the end of Belial's speech back to his opening sarcastic rebuttal of Moloch, "First, what revenge?" (2.129), and suggests that this prospect of future change, too, is without foundation.

For Belial realizes that God has denied the fallen angels the only real change that might matter to them: death. To Moloch's desire to die fighting and to lose consciousness altogether, Belial responds with a version of Hamlet's "To be or not to be" speech.[17]

> And that must end us, that must be our cure,
> To be no more; sad cure; for who would lose,
> Though full of pain, this intellectual being,
> Those thoughts that wander through eternity,
> To perish rather, swallowed up and lost
> In the wide womb of uncreated night,
> Devoid of sense and motion? and who knows,
> Let this be good, whether our angry foe
> Can give it, or will ever? How he can
> Is doubtful; that he never will is sure.
> Will he, so wise, let loose at once his ire,
> Belike through impotence, or unaware,
> To give his enemies their wish, and end
> Them in his anger, whom his anger saves
> To punish endless?
>
> *(2.145–59)*

The devils, Belial suggests, cannot die even if they want to. He, for one, objects to being swallowed up by the death that Moloch seeks: he is a coward to start with and does not need conscience to make him one. But he also recognizes that God will not grant this cessation of being and sensation to the devils. Belial's alternative—"thoughts that wander through eternity"—initially sounds a note of humanistic admiration for the powers of the mind, and Fowler's note relates the phrase to Milton's assertion in *Areopagitica* that God "gives us minds that can wander beyond all limit and satiety" (*CPW* 2:528). But in the case of the devils who have misused divine gifts, this boundless mental energy condemns them to the eternal restlessness that is the bad conscience of the sinner who cannot repent, the remorse that is the condition of their torment: what Satan in his book 9 soliloquy calls "my relentless thoughts" (9.130). Milton collapses the difference between these alternatives. The fallen angels will not die, but the endless wandering of their thoughts is itself Milton's internalized form of death, the second death announced by the book of Revelation that awaits Satan and his associates at the end of history, but which has already begun now. By this contrasting portrait of the devils' situation, the poem already builds its subsequent case in book 10 that death for mankind after the Fall will be not merely God's justice but his mercy as the ground of free human choice: men and women can choose, above all, to live, the "better fortitude."[18]

The fallen angels have no such choice, no choice at all, and this initial opposition of Moloch and Belial already sets the terms of the rest of book 2. It casts irony on the whole diabolic council and its debate of alternatives. It looks forward to the Moloch-like and Belial-like pastimes that the devils invent to accommodate themselves to an unchanging and circular existence in hell (2.521–628), more false alternatives. It anticipates Satan's meeting with the Death that he has unknowingly sired, but who, pointedly, will not destroy him in Telegonic or oedipal battle. Death and Sin, too, embody the options that Moloch and Belial debate—death or living death—and collapse the difference between them. They incarnate and announce as well the book's Odyssean figure of Scylla and Charybdis, the figure of bad alternatives and impossible choice.

Mammon and Beelzebub: A Thersites Is Rebuked

After the appeasement of Belial, the next speaker in the council, Mammon, advocates outright peace, "dismissing quite / All thoughts of war" (2.282–83) at the conclusion of his speech. Here the epic, martial ambitions of Satan threaten to reach their dead end, and in the poem's continuation of its imitation of the council scene of *Iliad* 2, Mammon plays the role of the lowborn Thersites, who calls upon his fellow Greeks (*Il.* 2.225–42) to abandon the war at Troy and sail home.[19] Mammon, we have been told in book 1, was the "least erected spirit that fell / From heaven" (1.679–80) where he liked to contemplate the golden pavement rather than God. He represents, as Spenser's Mammon does in book 2 of the *Faerie Queene*, the materialism of a moneyed middle class; he advises the devils to give up on heaven and seek to build their own heaven down in hell out of its gems and gold; like Belial (2.215–19), he suggests that the devils will eventually get used to the heat (2.274–78). That Adam will so closely echo Mammon in his profession of Christian ethics near the end of *Paradise Lost* (compare 12.565–69 to 2.257–62) suggests, as Blair Hoxby has argued, the class shift that underlies Milton's redefinition of heroism: from aristocratic militarism and public glory to bourgeois pacifism and inward piety.[20] Mammon represents a complicated parody of that shift: in place of spiritual individualism, he urges self-reliance—"Our own good from ourselves" (2.253)—which boils down to the enjoyment of one's material well-being in apolitical liberty. He wants to build an independent realm in hell in order to be free from the feudal system, the "splendid vassalage" (2.252), of God's heaven, toward whose courtly rituals—"Forced hallelujahs" (2.243)—he expresses the citizen's distaste. In his rejection of the divine monarch, Mammon further resembles Homer's Thersites, who abuses his princely betters among the Greeks and who reduces the Trojan War to Agamemnon's greed for loot and gold, to the prizes of honor rather than to honor itself. [21]

"So the popular vote / Inclines" (2.313–14), sneers Beelzebub in response to Mammon's proposal of peace and to the loud applause it earns from the other devils, who have no inclination themselves for another battle against God's thunder and Michael's sword. Mammon, in fact, poses a threat not to God's monarchy but to the social order in hell. The optimate Beelzebub is a "pillar of state" (2.302) and of that social order as well. He plays out the role of the Homeric Ulysses who puts down Thersites in *Iliad* 2. Beelzebub admonishes the devils that they cannot transform their penal colony—for that is what the "dungeon" (2.317) of hell is, hot climate and all—into a new independent country as Mammon proposes. His warning that God "will with iron sceptre rule / Us here, as with his golden those in heaven" (2.327–28) recalls the golden scepter of Agamemnon that Homer's Ulysses uses to strike and silence Thersites (*Il.* 2.265–69) and his vox populi: a tip-off to the epic model behind the scene.[22] When Beelzebub puts forth Satan's own plan to continue the war, not against the feared armies of God, but against the easier target of earth and its "puny habitants" (2.367), he enables Satan to continue what was his monarchical ambition announced at the poem's very beginning: Satan wished "To set himself in glory above his peers" (1.39).

The narrator must step in here to remind us of the futility of Satan's plan

> to spite
> The great creator? But their spite still serves
> His glory to augment.
>   *(2.385–86)*

The theodicy of *Paradise Lost* aims to show how the redemption of humanity will counter the Fall and increase God's glory, that the devils will be hoisted on their own petard.[23] But the slight quibble on "His" of "His glory"—God's or Satan's?—is reinforced by the fiction. The immediate effect of the new war against mankind is indeed to glorify Satan—"whom now transcendent glory raised / Above his fellows, with monarchal pride" (2.427–28)—and he will emerge from the council to the general population of fallen angels no less "Than hell's dread emperor with pomp supreme" (2.510). It is the desire to be king that is the first cause of all our woe, king of no matter what kingdom.[24] Satan expressed the Caesarian sentiment in book 1 that "To reign is worth ambition though in hell: / Better to reign in hell, than serve in heaven" (1.262–63). It was only at this point that Satan turned his thought to raising his fellow fallen angels strewn on the burning lake. A king has need of subjects.

But already in hell, and included in its elite council, is a new class of capitalists, like Mammon, who both scorn courtly service in heaven and would seem unwilling to replace it in their new state, wishing instead to live "Free, and to none accountable, preferring / Hard liberty before the easy yoke / Of servile pomp" (2.255–57). Above all, they prefer peace to war, the traditional prerogative and reserve of king and nobility. Nonetheless, "pomp supreme" and monarchy is ironically just what Mammon and the devils get, and they bend down toward Satan with "awful reverence prone" (2.478), enslaving themselves to their infernal prince. Satan's and Beelzebub's tin-pot war plan can be understood as a last-ditch effort of an increasingly outmoded social and political order to prop itself up, a kind of Restoration after its own fall—and it is the

Restoration parliament, more than the Cromwellian one, that is the main satirical target here.[25] As Satan's agent, Beelzebub stands "With Atlantean shoulders fit to bear / The weight of mightiest monarchies" (2.306–7); here, too, we may compare Milton the spokesman for the Commonwealth in the *Second Defense* who wished to be a Ulysses, but who declined to hold up a shield of the heavens but rather the burden of conscience on his shoulders, while Atlas held up the heavens themselves on his. Atlas-like Beelzebub may offer a more heroic version of the orator Ulysses than the Belial who would "sustain and bear" to no end at all, but this patrician minister with his "princely counsel" (2.304)—a Clarendon or a Buckingham—deploys his Ulyssean eloquence and statesmanship on the wrong side: to shore up the monarchy Milton hated and opposed, as Ulysses, himself a lesser king, did for the tyrannical kingship of Agamemnon in the *Iliad* by keeping the Trojan War going and putting down the protests of the commoner Thersites.

Satan and the *Doloneia*

Beelzebub still leaves open the question of whether this war is to be accomplished "By force or subtlety" (2.358), whether "with hell fire / To waste his [God's] whole creation" (2.364–65)—which would return to and accommodate Moloch's opening exhortation to use "hell flames" (2.61) against the high towers of heaven—or to "Seduce" (2.370) the inhabitants of earth to the devil's party—the methods of Belial, both insidious rhetor and a demon "more lewd" (1.490) and of "fairer person" (2.110) than all the rest. Beelzebub leaves these alternatives open, but both he and the epic prototype he invokes tilt toward fraud—when he goes on to call for a volunteer to scout out God's creation.

> But first whom shall we send
> In search of this new world, whom shall we find
> Sufficient? Who shall tempt with wandering feet
> The dark unbottomed infinite abyss
> And through the palpable obscure find out
> His uncouth way, or spread his airy flight
> Upborne with indefatigable wings
> Over the vast abrupt, ere he arrive
> The happy isle; what strength, what art can then
> Suffice, or what evasion bear him safe
> Through the strict sentries and stations thick
> Of angels watching round?
>   *(2.402–13)*

The epic model has now shifted from the council of Homer's Greeks in *Iliad* 2 to their susbsequent nocturnal council in *Iliad* 10, where Nestor seeks out volunteers to spy on the Trojan camp; after fear strikes the assembly to silence

(*Iliad* 10.218), Diomedes comes forth and takes Ulysses with him—a coupling of what Beelzebub terms here "strength" with "art," another version of force and fraud.[26] In the ensuing nighttime episode of the *Doloneia* that takes up *Iliad* 10, Diomedes in fact does the dirty work, killing the Trojans and their allies in their sleep as well as the counterspy Dolon, who opted for his mission after an identical silence in the Trojan camp (*Il.* 10.313); Ulysses steals the horses of Rhesus and pumps Dolon for information with an assurance of mercy that turns out to be a lie. Dolon, the relatively lowborn son of a rich herald, is ugly and swift of foot and not very manly, as the odd fact that he is the only son in a family with five sisters would suggest (10.316–17). He has a passing resemblance to ugly Thersites, though Thersites is lame in one foot, while cowardly Dolon needs his speed in order to run away; when he is chased down by Ulysses and Diomedes, his teeth chatter in fear. As their Trojan counterspy and slightly comic foil who greedily asks to be rewarded with the horses of Achilles, foolish Dolon indicates the unheroic, déclassé nature of both spy missions—if killing sleeping men, breaking promises of mercy, and the sheer pursuit of loot were not enough. Ulysses and Diomedes, too, run away from the Trojans in the chariot of the slain Rhesus. "What evasion," Milton sardonically adds to "what strength" and "what art" will be required of Satan, the volunteer for Beelzebub's scouting mission after all his fellow devils sit mute and in dismay?

Milton would have been aware that ancient critics had regarded the *Doloneia* as a spurious interpolation; they were probably impressed as much by the spying episode's exposure of the shabby, nonheroic underside of war that is at odds with the prevailing ethos of the *Iliad*—the episode's depiction of force inseparable from fraud, of deeds done in the dark—as by its self-contained nature, apparently detachable from the larger narrative.[27] Beelzebub characterizes Satan's ensuing journey through the darkness of Chaos and through God's sentries—we will watch Satan evade, if only temporarily, the watchful eye of Uriel in book 3—as a version of this nighttime spy mission behind enemy lines. "I come no spy" (2.970), Satan tells Chaos in book 2; but when he is captured at night in book 4 by Zephon and Ithuriel in Eden and brought before Gabriel, he seems to admit that he came to "spy / This new created world" (4.936–37). Like Ulysses and Diomedes, Satan assaults a sleeping quarry, pouring his dream into Eve's ear. But Satan's capture by the angelic pair, one against two, in fact, places him no longer in the role of the spying Ulysses at all, but of that of Dolon, Ulysses's and Diomedes's unheroic victim. When Satan later responds to Gabriel that he has escaped hell to replace "Dole with delight" (4.894), there is, as Alastair Fowler points out, an ironic play on "Dole," which, in addition to its primary meaning of "pain, sorrow," can mean "fraud" or "trickery" from the Greek *dolos*. But this is also the name of Homer's character, the would-be trickster Dolon undone by the trickier Ulysses, and a sly wink at the episode's model.[28] Class issues play out here, too, for, in a reversal of Homer's model, to which we will return in chapter 5, Satan is abashed to be taken into custody by two plebeian angels so lowly that they apparently do not recognize him, though Gabriel, Satan's erstwhile fellow archangel, will shortly do so (4.869–71). "Not to know me argues your selves unknown" (4.830), Satan sneers, but the nature of his mission, as much as his sin, has placed him beneath his former social inferiors.

Meanwhile, Back in Hell...

While Satan is away on his voyage to God's new creation, the devils try out the other options advanced by Moloch (war and extinction), Belial (sedentary thoughts that wander through eternity), and Mammon (self-reliant building of a new environment in hell), only to find all of them wanting and ultimately alternatives without distinction. As the demonic council disperses the bad angels start

> wandering, each his several way
> Pursues, as inclination or sad choice
> Leads him perplexed, where he may likeliest find
> Truce to his restless thoughts, and entertain
> The irksome hours, till this great chief return.
> *(2.523–27)*

Wandering, perplexity, restless thoughts, to which one may at best find a truce, but not a lasting peace: these terms characterize the no-exit situation of the devils. The fallen angels seek entertainment, a diversion from having to face their predicament. Those inclined to lose themselves in physical action and force like the Ajax-like Moloch begin with sports competitions, "As at the Olympian games or Pythian fields" (2.530), and with war games, only to end in madness:

> Others with vast Typhoean rage more fell
> Rend up both rocks and hills, and ride the air
> In whirlwind; hell scarce holds the wild uproar.
> As when Alcides from Oechalia crowned
> With conquest, felt the evenomed robe, and tore
> Through pain up by the roots Thessalian pines,
> And Lichas from the top of Oeta threw
> Into the Euboic sea.
> *(2.539–46)*

These devils seem to enact the divine punishment that Belial had predicted for Moloch—"the sport and prey / Of racking whirlwinds" (2.182–83), the fate of Oilean Ajax—while they suffer the madness of a Hercules who was conventionally paired with the mad, suicidal Telamonian Ajax. In the same passage of the *Posthomerica* of Quintus Smyrnaeus that Milton cites in the *Second Defense*, and that he is recalling here, the burning funeral pyre of the latter Ajax is compared to Enceladus, imprisoned, like Typhoeus, beneath Etna—"vast Typhoean rage"[29]—and to Hercules, who, consumed alive by the flames of the poisoned robe of Nessus, committed suicide on Mount Oeta by placing himself on his own lit funeral pyre, his divine part rising to immortal life among the gods.

> as when
> Enceladus by Zeus' levin was consumed
> Beneath Sicily, when from all the isle
> Smoke of his burning rose—or like as when
> Hercules, trapped by Nessus' deadly guile,
> Gave to devouring fire his living limbs,
> What time he dared that awful deed, when groaned
> All Oeta, as he burned alive, and passed
> His soul into the air, leaving the man
> Far famous, to be numbered with the Gods,
> When earth closed o'er all his toil-tried mortal part.
> So huge amid the flames, all-armour clad,
> Lay Ajax …
> *(Posthomerica 5.639–49)*[30]

It is suicidal madness that the devils experience all right, but it cannot, in fact, result in the death that a Moloch desperately seeks, just as the war games are not the real war he craves and result in no casualties. This madness may seem to offer an ultimate distraction from the physical torture of hell, but Hercules, in fact, went mad from the *pain* of wearing the burning robe of Nessus, which seems indistinguishable here from hell's own everlasting fire (Matthew 25:41), a fire that never consumes its victim, nor leads to a higher form of existence.

Meanwhile, Belial's timorous and slothful eloquence, his counsel to sit pat, to endure and bear, finds its counterpart in the fallen angels who have "Retreated" (2.546) and who "*sat* on a hill retired" (2.557), the first turning to poetry, the others to a philosophy whose final goal is to "excite / Fallacious hope, or arm the obdured breast / With stubborn patience as with triple steel" (2.567–69). Such intermittent intellectual relief could suspend hell "for a while" (2.567), but it "found no end, in wandering mazes lost" (2.561). Belial's opposition between living thoughts that wander through eternity and death, the dreaded condition of being "lost" in the wide womb of night, becomes a distinction virtually without a difference when those thoughts are themselves lost, perplexed in wandering mazes without end.

Similarly the devils "found / No rest" (2.618) who sought, as Mammon counseled, to seek some "easier habitation" (2.573) in hell, only to discover a "universe of death" (2.622), which they cannot transform from evil. The hope expressed by both Belial and Mammon that the devils might get used to their new climate, like British penal colonists whose transportation to steamy Jamaica and Virginia was newly legislated in the first years of the Restoration,[31] will be similarly thwarted by these explorers' discovery of ice fields to which "At certain revolutions all the damned / Are brought: and feel by turns the bitter change / Of fierce extremes, extremes by change more fierce" (2.597–99). The ice is compared to the Serbonian bog, "Where armies whole have sunk" (2.592–94) and anticipates the Chaos through which Satan will first fall and then find himself in a "boggy Syrtis," a quicksand in which he is "nigh foundered" (2.939–40) and "swims or sinks, or wades" (2.950); both suggest the devouring "maw" of Death (2.847) in the intervening episode between them. These devils too, are tantalized by but denied the opportunity to drink from Lethe, available to the souls in Virgil's underworld in the *Aeneid* (6.703–51); they cannot obtain oblivion and start over again just as they cannot die. The whole episode concludes— as does the episode of Ulysses's consultation with the dead of the underworld in *Odyssey* 11 (633–35)—with the evocation of the monstrous, "worse / Than fables yet have feigned, or fear conceived, / Gorgons and Hydras, and Chimeras dire" (2.626–28). Fowler notes that Milton had earlier evoked Gorgons and Chimeras as figures of the torments of a guilty conscience in his university exercise, the first Latin prolusion, and it is the remorse of their own sin, a remorse no Lethean forgetfulness can remove, that is the true monster that haunts the inner life of the restless devils: so Satan's encounter that directly follows with the book's central monsters, Sin and Death, will spell out, an encounter that these final lines anticipate as they provide a link between the two episodes.[32]

There is a strong suggestion in all three cases—the physical culture devils, the poet-philosophers, the explorers of hell—of cyclical repetition. The first drive their chariots around the tracks and are carried by whirlwinds; the second reason in mazes forward and backward about "foreknowledge, will and fate, / Fixed fate, free will, foreknowledge absolute" (2.559–60); the last move "to and fro" (605) from cold to heat by "revolutions." They are going around in circles.

The devils freeze in the winter, fry in the summer. They invent a civilization: distracting themselves with sports, poetry, philosophy, exploitation of their environment. So they entertain the time while Satan is away, "till this great chief return" (2.527). They are not very different from humanity awaiting the Second Coming, especially from those human beings who are *not* standing and waiting for Christ, those living in Milton's increasingly secular world. Life without hope in a savior, life in which death makes no difference, is hell, the poet not so subtly tells us, and, in one of the epic's many striking moments of skeptical modernity, acknowledges that yes, there is a real possibility that this is all that human life may add up to: it is a matter of perspective and faith. This hell, on the surface, does not look so bad: the comforts of civilization. Better grin and bear it, says Milton's Belial, but Belial, discerning though he may be, knows how to "perplex" better counsels, and, as a result condemns himself to a circular existence of restless perplexity.

Milton's *Telegony*

That the counsels of Moloch, Belial, and Mammon turn into dead ends in hell augurs badly for the plan of Beelzebub and Satan as well. All the alternatives that the devils propose are bad alternatives, and they thus link the demonic council to the Odyssean figure that dominates the ensuing fiction of book 2, the choice between Scylla and Charybdis.

The pair of monsters are named, Scylla at verse 660, to whom Sin is compared, Charybdis in verses 1019–20, which also name for the first time the hero on whose career the entire book is shaped: the voyaging Satan is harder beset and more endangered than "when Ulysses on the larboard shunned / Charybdis, and by the other whirlpool steered." The other whirlpool is Scylla, here rationalized and reduced to an identical natural phenomenon; while Ulysses chose to steer by Scylla as the lesser of two evils, Milton insists upon the ultimate sameness of proverbially bad alternatives.[33] The circularity attributed to the options of the devils who stay behind in hell persists in the image of the whirlpool that replaces the earlier racking whirlwinds. The effect of the location of the two comparisons and the two names of the monsters at either end of Satan's journey through Chaos makes it into one long passage between Scylla and Charybdis. But already at the beginning of Satan's voyage Scylla-like Sin is coupled with her son Death and his hungry, insatiable "maw" (2.847), a version of the Charybdis that threatens to swallow down everything into its whirlpool.[34]

The Scylla and Charybdis figure here suggests that there is no real choice between Death and the experience of Sin and here, too, the book's opening opposition of Moloch's deathwish and Belial's wandering thoughts collapses. In Milton's double incest story, not only are Sin and Death both children of Satan—allegorically *they are his own sin and his own death*—but Sin has literally incorporated Death into herself, internalizing death in the hellhounds of remorse who gnaw at her bowels and "with conscious terrors vex me round, / That *rest* or intermission none I find" (2.801–2). Sin personifies and experiences—and retrospectively explains—the restlessness that afflicts all the guilty denizens of hell: a living death seated beside Death himself.

That they are all as good as dead—and will not die, nonetheless—is also the point when Satan's meeting with Sin and Death rewrites yet another, different myth concerning Ulysses, the *Telegony*, the subject of a lost cyclic epic known to the Renaissance through some later summaries.[35] Telegonus, the son whom Ulysses has unknowingly sired with Circe, arrives at Ithaca in search of his father. Unaware of each other's identity until it is too late, the two heroes fight and Telegonus mortally wounds Ulysses with a spear tipped with the sting from the tail of a stingray. Telegonus takes the body of his father, along with Penelope and Telemachus, back to Circe's island, where he marries Penelope, Telemachus marries Circe, and they live as immortals happily ever after. This mythic scenario is thwarted when Milton's Sin interposes to stop the impending duel between Satan and Death, the son Satan unwittingly conceived with her; the devil neither recognizes Death nor Sin herself. Death wields what Sin calls a "mortal dart," and this is presumably the "mortal sting" (3.253) of Death that the Son of God mentions in book 3 when he predicts his victory over death at his resurrection. It parallels the strange sting at the end of Telegonus's spear, and the Ulyssean subtext may also have suggested to Milton his invocation of 1 Kings 12:11 in Death's threat to use a "whip of scorpions" (2.701) as an alternative to his dart. But Sin herself is armed with a "mortal sting" (2.653), apparently, like a stingray or a scorpion, in her tail, for, as Paul writes in 1 Corinthians 15:56, "the sting of death is sin." These two persons of the infernal trinity are interchangeable, both physically and spiritually. With their stings, they anticipate the locustlike host of Revelation 9, who "had tails like unto scorpions, and there were stings in their tails" (Rev. 9:10) and who are sent to hurt

> only those men which have not the seal of God in their foreheads. And it was commanded them that they should not kill them, but that they should be tormented five months; and their torment was as the torment of a scorpion, when he striketh a man. And in those days shall men seek death, and shall not find it; and shall desire to die, and death shall flee from them. (Rev. 9:4–6)

On this deadly sting that does not kill, and the death that will not come for the sinner, the Geneva Bible comments: "Such is the terror of the unbelieving conscience, which hath no assurance of mercie, but feels the judgement of God against it, when men imbrace error and refuse the true simplicitie of God's word."[36] The sting of Milton's Sin is identical to her hellhounds who vex her with "conscious terrors": the sinner's remorseful conscience is already a form of death, that much deadlier when it cannot hope for an end in death. The physical ghastliness of these monsters, in which Milton indulges the full force of revulsion-inducing description, should not make us forget that he is describing an inner mental state—Satan's and more generally that of the hardened sinner—that is far more monstrous than allegory can tell.

The *Telegony* is closely related to the Oedipus story, the son who kills the father he has never known, and in Milton's oedipal scenario Death rapes his own mother Sin, while in the dizzying case with Telegonus and Telemachus the half brothers couple with each other's mothers. Satan finds Death athwart his way and tells him that he means to pass, much as Sophocles's Laius tried to thrust Oedipus out of the road by force (*Oedipus Tyrannos* 804–6). When Sin and Death meet Satan again in book 10 of the epic after the Fall, it is at a crossroads with the new highway that they have constructed across Chaos: "three several ways / In sight, to each of these three places led" (10.323–24). The setting recalls the place where three roads meet where Oedipus slew his father (*OT*, 716). But in neither scenario does Death overtake and kill Satan;

the poem's actions confirm Belial's retort to Moloch that God will not concede the devils a literal "coup de grâce" of extinction; rather, their state of unregenerate sin has already brought death to dwell inside them: they get to die forever.

Of course, were Milton to follow the scenario of the *Telegony* and have Death kill off his father, there would be no poem to follow. But Milton nonetheless evokes the myth to suggest the short-circuited nature of Satan's ensuing career, and he pointedly places his imitation of this last act of Ulysses's story *before* the devil even sets out on his own Odyssean voyage—in Death Satan meets his own foregone conclusion, as well as the condition he has already sired in himself: as Sin predicts, God's wrath "one day will destroy ye both" (2.734). Satan's apparent progress in the narrative of book 2, his escape from hell and his reaching the borders of heaven and the newly created universe that hangs beneath it, is only apparent, and, in reality, just as self-destructively recursive and circular as the activities of his fellow devils left behind in hell. God, we noted earlier, had declared that Satan's revenge would "redound" upon his own head, and Satan later acknowledges as much when he admits that revenge "back on it self recoils" (9.172) just before he steps into the circular coils of the serpent, a "labyrinth of many a round self rolled" (9.183). Sin and Death abet Satan on his jailbreak from hell, Sin turning the key to the prison gates that "open fly / With impetuous recoil" (2.879–80), in a parodic version of Christ's harrowing of hell: in the legendary account of the *Gospel of Nicodemus*, the gates fly off their hinges altogether.[37] But Satan the recidivist will return, and we will see him for the last time in the poem back in Pandaemonium undergoing punishment with the other devils as humbled serpents in book 10, completing a vicious circle. Like that burlesque episode, the failed *Telegony* in book 2 is proleptic of the end of history, when, according to Revelation 20, the devil will be first cast into the lake of fire (20:10), then death and hell itself will be cast there in the second death (20:14).

Commentary tradition tended to conflate these two moments and to identify death and hell with Satan.[38] It also conflated the fiery lake with the "abyss" or "bottomless pit" into which, earlier in Revelation 20, an angel casts "that old serpent, which is the Devil, and Satan" and sets a seal upon him (20:3), only for the devil to be released again after a thousand years. The abyss, in turn, was glossed as the open, devouring mouth of death, so that death seems to be thrown into another version of itself.[39] Milton exploits these homologies when his God describes these final events of history in book 10.

> till crammed and gorged, nigh burst
> With sucked and glutted offal, at one sling
> Of thy victorious arm, well-pleasing Son,
> Both Sin and Death, and yawning grave at last
> Through chaos hurled, obstruct the mouth of hell

For ever, and seal up his ravenous jaws.
    (10.632–37)

In what seems almost to be a mixed metaphor, Death, alternately conceived as bloated nigh to bursting with the life he has consumed and as a yawning, empty grave, becomes himself the seal that shuts up the abyss in Revelation 20, here stopping up the ravenous mouth of hell that resembles his own maw and returning both himself and Sin to their original function as hell's gatekeepers. Satan may break free of hell now, the poem suggests, just as he will be "loosed out of his prison" (Rev. 20:7) after the millennium, but only for "a little season" (Rev. 20:3), the end of history that Milton writes back into its beginning; then he will be swallowed up by hell, which is a version of the Death he has engendered. No one will get out this time.

Satan's *Odyssey*

The alternatives in Belial's answer to Moloch, "To perish, rather, swallowed up and lost / In the wide womb of uncreated night" and "this intellectual being, / Those thoughts that wander through eternity" are cast in recognizably Odyssean terms. The worst-case scenarios for the voyager Ulysses in the *Odyssey* are to be swallowed up and eaten—by the cyclops Polyphemus, by the Laestrygonians, by the whirlpool Charybdis—or of being cast into endless wandering, in his case physical rather than intellectual, not only the wandering of his storm-tossed adventures, but the further expiatory voyage to the ends of the earth that Teiresias imposes (*Od.* 11.121–31) on the hero after his return to Ithaca and that suggests the fate of the Flying Dutchman. As we have seen, Milton collapses the differences between these alternatives, and he does so once again in his staging of Satan's voyage across Chaos, an odyssey across an "Illimitable ocean" that dwarfs in dimensions the wanderings of Homer's Ulysses.

    Satan's meeting and escape from Death is doubled in the ensuing narrative when Satan begins to fall through the infinite reaches of space in Chaos, an episode that, together with Satan's larger voyage, we will look at again and more closely in chapter 3. Satan plummets through a "wild abyss / The womb of nature and perhaps her grave" (2.910–11), which, with its Lucretian void, "a vast vacuity" (2.932), presents a natural form of the bottomless grave pit of the hell that is Death; it looks, too, like the Serbonian bog that swallowed up whole armies sunk into its depths.

                and to this hour
Down had been falling, had not by ill chance
The strong rebuff of some tumultuous cloud
Instinct with fire and nitre hurried him
As many miles aloft.
    (2.934–38)

This had indeed been Belial's imagined vision of death, "swallowed up and lost / In the wide womb of uncreated night." But it is also an image of—rather than an alternative to—Satan's journey itself, the "wandering quest" through the "void immense" that he announces to his children Sin and Death (2.829–30). The voyager Satan is just as lost in the dimensionless sea of chance that is Chaos—not "half lost" (2.976) as he bluffingly tells the personified Chaos—and he might wander forever in its infinite space did he not stumble on the Babelic "hubbub wild" emanating from the movable pavilion and court of Chaos, the noncreative "spirit of the nethermost abyss" (2.956) with whom Satan will strike up an alliance.[40]

The unity of Milton's fiction becomes clear when we realize that Satan's fall through the "hoary deep" of space constitutes, like the figure of Death himself, another version of the *Odyssey*'s Charybdis.[41] Chaos is a natural minefield, and a chance explosion rockets Satan back up to where he started his fall. Similarly, the whirlpool Charybdis spews up what it sucks down three times a day (*Od.* 12.105–7), as it does to the keel and mast of Ulysses's ship while he clings to the fig tree over its maelstrom (*Od.* 12.431–42). Milton's Satan actually experiences a drowning "Ten thousand fathom deep" (2.934) in the illimitable ocean of Chaos, going down with the ship, only—by a very, very bad piece of luck for humanity—to be sent up again on his journey. Just as in his meeting with the Charybdis-like Death, Satan's heroic career again threatens to short-circuit, and he already acts out its predetermined end, his second-death-which-is-not-death in the bottomless pit of hell. Yet Satan's fall is but the physical enactment of the sinking feelings that he already suffers and admits to in book 4 when he declares that he himself is hell, and feels "in the lowest deep a lower deep / Still threatening to devour me" (4.76–77). Satan carries Charybdis inside him and these are also the sinner's self-tormenting "thoughts that wander through eternity." Through Milton's internalization of the Odyssean tropes of the fiction, his devil is a Ulysses who completes his voyage at the end of book 2, but never stops wandering, never escapes deathlike Charybdis.

Whose *Odyssey*?

Satan accomplishes his voyage, "like a weather-beaten vessel" (2.1043), at the end of book 2, having arrived in sight of heaven, "once his native seat" (2.1050). We feel the pathos when Satan, denied the homecoming of Ulysses, turns instead to God's new creation or appendix, "this pendent world" (2.1052). The devil's odyssey and this whole book of Ulysses have nonetheless reached their end. It comes as a surprise, then, to turn the page to book 3 and read God's speech that opens the action: irritated at the prospect of the impending Fall, the Deity takes us back to the *beginning* of the *Odyssey*. "Whose fault?" (3.96) will it be that Adam and Eve fall, God asks, and answers his own question.

Whose but his own? Ingrate, he had of me
All he could have; I made him just and right,
Sufficient to have stood, though free to fall.
    (3.97–99)

In these famous lines, which spell out the terms of the poem's theodicy, Milton's testy God repeats the opening words of Homer's equally irate Zeus that begin the *Odyssey*.[42]

"Oh for shame, how the mortals put the blame upon us
gods, for they say evils come from us, but it is they, rather,
who by their recklessness win sorrow beyond what is given ..."
    (*Od. 1.32–34*)[43]

Zeus complains specifically about the slaying of Agamemnon by Aegisthus; he had sent his messenger Hermes to warn Aegisthus not to commit the deed. So God in *Paradise Lost* will send the angel Raphael to forewarn Adam and Eve against disobeying the prohibition of the forbidden fruit, thus answering the narrator's own call for a "warning voice" in the opening verse of book 4. Milton, in fact, cites this passage of the *Odyssey* at the conclusion of his fourth chapter of book 1 of *De Doctrina Christiana* where he treats the question of predestination in order to defend the freedom of the human will (*CPW* 6:202; *Works* 14:174.) Beyond its importance for Milton's theodicy, this evocation of the beginning of the *Odyssey* underscores the sense that *Paradise Lost* is itself beginning again or beginning in earnest in book 3. The poet's invocation to holy Light, after he, as well as Satan, have escaped from the darkness of hell and Chaos, starts the epic anew and relegates the first two books to a kind of anti-masque. Up to now, what we have seen are perverse versions of Ulysses in the actions of Satan and his fellow devils. Now the real Odyssey of *Paradise Lost* will begin, and a true hero will emerge.

God goes on to ask the assembled host in heaven how a fallen humanity can be saved, and calls for a volunteer.

Which of ye will be mortal to redeem
Man's mortal crime, and just the unjust to save,
Dwells in all heaven charity so dear?
    (3.214–16)

We realize that not only have we returned to the beginning of the *Odyssey* but of the *Aeneid* as well; the last line inverts the Virgilian narrator's famous opening question about Juno—"tantaene animis caelestibus irae?" (*Aen.* 1.11; "can so much wrath exist in heavenly breasts?"). Milton's poem shows this divine wrath tempered by divine mercy, but not before a moment of suspense. The heavenly choir "stood mute" (3.217) and things look bad for mankind, until the Son of God offers to put off his glory and to suffer death. There is a clear parallel here to Satan's responding one book earlier to Beelzebub's call for a volunteer to undertake the dangerous mission to earth, while the rest of the demonic council "sat mute" (2.420). (The difference in posture is a constant in Milton's poetry where standing is all-important.) This parallel, moreover, fills out Milton's imitation of the Iliad's *Doloneia*, where, we remember, spies are sent out from *both* the Greek and the Trojan camp after both had fallen silent.

Now it is the Son who promises to undertake a version of the *Doloneia*. Milton places the Son's pledge in book 3 between Satan's own enactment of the Homeric scene at the beginning of book 2, where the devil volunteers for the mission, and the end of book 4, where he turns from the Ulysses he has hitherto seemed to be playing, into a version of the hapless Dolon, captured by Zephon and Ithuriel. What had been the most debased and nonheroic of epic episodes, repudiated by ancient critics, is now rehabilitated by the Son who will himself be despised and rejected by men. The ignominy of the Passion, described late in the poem by Michael as the Son's "coming in the flesh / To a reproachful life and cursed death" (12.405–6), is, of course, *the* paradigmatic instance of the better fortitude of patience and heroic martyrdom, and God insists here in book 3 not only that the Son will not "lessen or degrade" his divine nature (3.304) by descending to human form, but that he will, by this very descent and apparent abasement, promote himself—and humanity as well—to rule in his father's place: "Therefore thy humilation shall exalt / With thee thy manhood also to this throne / Here shall thou sit incarnate" (3.313–15). Again, the parallel to Satan is carefully worked out: Satan maintains his kingship over hell by setting out on his mission to defraud and seduce humanity; the son will be "Anointed universal king" (3.317) by suffering death to redeem humanity after the Fall.

Both Satan's fraud and the Son's humiliation and death stand in contrast to the conventional military heroism of epic. They can accordingly both fit the model of the *Doloneia*, and we might want to see Satan and the Son each taking on an aspect of Ulysses, the protagonist of Homer's episode: Satan carries the guile of Ulysses to its evil limit, and, when he is found by Zephon and Ithuriel, he has already begun to pour into the ear of Eve the dream that she will recount at the opening of book 5; the Son takes Ulysses's willingness to suffer—even, as Cicero points out, at the hands of servants and women—to its own extreme.

But this is not quite right, and it misses just how radically Milton's notion of Christian heroism has turned his classical epic models inside out, including the *Doloneia*. For if the captured Satan is revealed at the end of book 4 to be a Dolon rather than a Ulysses, so is the Son who volunteers for a literal suicide mission. The Iliadic model comes into play here, too, for there we first see Diomedes and Ulysses in the Greek camp, then the counterspy Dolon in the Trojan one, and Milton's sequence similarly places the Son's promise of self-sacrifice after Satan's offering to search out the way to earth. If Satan starts as Ulysses to end up as an unwilling and unwitting Dolon, the Son has designated himself as a victim from the beginning, and here, of course, he differs from the Homeric

Dolon who does not set off to die and who begs for his life when captured by Ulysses and Diomedes. But Milton's casting of the Son in the role of the epic fall guy Dolon, his asking his readers to identify through the Son with the ignoble dupe and abject prey of Ulysses—and we readers are more likely to be a common Dolon than the hero Ulysses in any case—inverts all norms of epic heroism, both Ulyssean cunning as well as Achillean force, and finds them wanting. It replaces them, in the words of Adam, who has learned his lesson at the end of the epic, with something entirely different: "by things deemed weak / Subverting worldly strong, and worldly wise / By simply meek" (12.567–69). Milton's Christian heroism performs a kind of jujitsu on the epic tradition, using apparent weakness to flip it over. Satan may very well continue in his Odyssean mode: when he approaches Eve as the serpent to tempt her to eat the forbidden fruit (9.532–48), he imitates Ulysses's ingratiating approach to Nausikaa in *Odyssey* 6 (148–69), with its overtones of potential rape. But the reopening of *Paradise Lost* in book 3 and the heroism of the Son announce a new *Odyssey* that no longer has room for Ulysses himself.

Fear of Falling: Icarus, Phaethon, and Lucretius

In his epic about the Fall, Milton includes versions of two famous characters of classical myth who fell from the heavens: Icarus, who fell when he ignored his father's warnings and flew too high on his wings of wax and feathers; and Phaethon, who fell, struck by Jupiter's thunderbolt, from the solar chariot of his father Apollo, the chariot he had unsuccessfully tried to drive through the sky, in spite of Apollo's plea that he forbear. Ovid tells the stories of the two highfliers as parallel myths in the *Metamorphoses* and twice couples Icarus and Phaethon as figures of his own fate in the *Tristia*; Renaissance poets would similarly juxtapose the two as figures of excessive pride and immaturity.[1] They thus provide analogues to the fallen offspring of Milton's epic, Satan and Adam and Eve, as well as contrasting foils to its good sons, the Son of God and Milton the poet himself. Milton further evokes these classical myths of falling in order to confront behind them the Epicurean doctrine of Lucretius's *De rerum natura*, the epic poem about an atomic universe that is in a state of free fall. At stake is nothing less than the cosmology and theodicy of *Paradise Lost*. Milton mentions neither Icarus nor Phaethon by name, however. The reworking of their myths needs to be excavated by patient philology from complicated, but coherent and deliberate systems of allusion to earlier epic poetry and to Milton's own youthful Latin poem, *Naturam non pati senium* (*NNPS*; Nature does not suffer old age), as well as to Lucretius. It will then become apparent how the epic poet who would justify the ways of God to men and explain the Fall that brought death into the world engages, beneath the surface of his text, the godless Roman poet and his doctrine of sheer contingency and purely natural mortality. Meanwhile, the myths of Icarus and Phaethon shape the metaphors of a poem in which falling is depicted as the failure of aspired flight. These metaphors will contrast to the soaring poet himself, a successful Icarus, lifted in spirit on the wings of verse.[2]

Icarus and Satan's Fall Through Chaos

Satan has scarcely taken off from the mouth of hell in book 2 when he begins to plummet through the unfathomed depths of Chaos.

> At last his sail-broad vans
> He spreads for flight, and in the surging smoke
> Uplifted spurns the ground, thence many a league
> As in a cloudy chair ascending rides
> Audacious, but that seat soon failing, meets
> A vast vacuity: all unawares
> Fluttering his pennons vain plumb down he drops
> Ten thousand fathom deep, and to this hour
> Down had been falling, had not by ill chance
> The strong rebuff of some tumultuous cloud
> Instinct with fire and nitre hurried him
> As many miles aloft:
> > (2.927–38)

The preceding chapter described Satan's fall and his rebound "As many miles aloft" (2.927–38) as a recollection of the whirlpool Charybdis that swallowed down and cast up the ship of Homer's Ulysses in the *Odyssey*. The scene of Satan's fall is also, as the present discussion demonstrates, Milton's version of the fall of Icarus. Through allusion, it reaches back and gathers together a whole series of epic predecessors who are themselves joined to one another in a continuous chain of allusion—Virgil, Ovid, Dante, Tasso, and, above and behind all of them, Lucretius. The series begins with Virgil's own submerged reference to Lucretius.

VIRGIL AND LUCRETIUS

The story of Icarus is present by its absence on the doors of the temple of Apollo at Cumae described by Virgil at the opening of the sixth book of the *Aeneid*. Positioned at the gates of the underworld (6.107) and in the groves of Avernus (6.19), the temple was built by Daedalus in order to commemorate his landing place after he had flown from Crete on his artificial wings of feathers and wax. He dedicated his "remigium alarum" to Apollo—the "oarage of his wings"; the wording suggests a mariner making a votive offering after surviving a stormy voyage or shipwreck, and Daedalus had indeed made a journey over the sea. Of course, we know that Daedalus was not alone: his son Icarus, the myth tells us, flew too close to the sun, fell into the waves, and drowned. The climax of Virgil's ekphrasis of the temple doors describes the scene that is not there. Daedalus, we are told, tried two times, but could not bring himself to depict his son's "casus" (6.32): Icarus's fall, which was also the accident that befell him.

What is this myth doing here? Virgilian critics have pointed to the way that the reference to the son who does not survive mirrors the end of book 6, the lament for Augustus's nephew and designated heir Marcellus. Daedalus's skill in fashioning the figures on the doors is comparable to Virgil's own artistry in depicting the procession of future Romans who later parade before Anchises, among whom Marcellus both does and does not take part.[3] As the survivor of a long sea journey, moreover, Daedalus is similar to Aeneas at this point in the poem: having reached his destination in Italy, Aeneas, too, has hung up his oars. True enough; but the myth of flying—and falling from the sky—has a particular resonance in this particular part of the world.

Avernus, we are told at verse 242, derives its name from the Greek "Aornum," that is, the place without birds, for no flying creature could safely wing their way there—"super haud ullae poterant impune uolantes / tendere iter pinnis" (*Aeneid* 6.239–40)—thanks to the sulfuric exhalations sent up from the earth and lake. Virgil's source is his great predecessor, Lucretius, who devotes a section of book 6 of his *De rerum natura* (*DRN*) to a description of the phenomenon.

> Nunc age, Averna tibi quae sint loca cumque lacusque
> expediam, quali natura praedita constent.
> principio, quod Averna vocantur nomine, id ab re
> impositumst, quia sunt avibus contraria cunctis,
> e regione ea, quod loca cum venere volantes,
> remigi oblitae pennarum vela remittunt
> praecipitesque cadunt molli cervice profusae
> in terram, si forte ita fert natura locorum,
> aut in aquam, si forte lacus substratus Avernist.
> is locus est Cumas aput, acri sulpure montes
> oppleti calidis ubi fumant fontibus aucti.
>   (*DRN* 6.738–48)

[Now listen, and I will explain what is the nature of those Avernian regions and their lakes. In the first place, they are given the name Avernian because of the fact that they are dangerous to all birds, because when they have come in flight to those places, forgetting the oarage of their wings they pull in their sails, and fall headlong with their soft neck outstretched to the earth, if that is the nature of the place, or into the water, if the lake of Avernus lies below. This place is near Cumae, where the mountains smoke, filled with bitter sulfur and rich with hot springs.]

Behind Virgil's Cumae and the "remigium alarum" that Daedalus dedicates at its temple lies Lucretius's Cumae and its surrounding sulfuric district of Avernus, a district fatal to birds and to their "remigi … pennarum": the textual echo is clear, and has been noted by earlier commentators.[4] Lucretius offers two naturalistic explanations for the birds dropping from the sky. The noxious fumes sent up from Avernus may simply poison them (*DRN* 6.818–29), or, as Lucretius returns to a favorite idea, they may create a vacuum or void.[5]

> Fit quoque ut interdum vis haec atque aestus Averni
> aera, qui inter avis cumquest terramque locatus,
> discutiat, prope uti locus hic linquatur inanis.
> cuius ubi e regione loci venere volantes,
> claudicat extemplo pinnarum nisus inanis
> et conamen utrimque alarum proditur omne.
> hic ubi nixari nequeunt insistereque alis,
> scilicet in terram delabi pondere cogit
> natura ...
>
>   *(DRN 6.830–38)*

[It happens at times that this power and effluence of Avernus disperses the air which lies between the birds and the earth so that an almost empty space is left. When they have come flying to this place, the flapping of their pinions suddenly goes halting and in vain, and all the effort of both wings is nullified. When they are unable to rest or persist upon their wings, nature assuredly compels them to fall to earth by their own weight.]

With no air on which to ride, Lucretius explains, the birds drop from the sky over Avernus. The repetition of "inanis" connects the void to the empty flapping of their wings. They thus look very much like the battling atoms that fall by their own weight through the void that Lucretius describes in books 1 and 2 of *De rerum natura*—"corpora cum deorsum rectum per inane feruntur / ponderibus propriis" (*DRN* 2.217–18).

Just why, in fact, does Virgil refer back to Lucretius's version of Avernus in the description of Daedalus's temple that frames Aeneas's descent into the underworld? He allows us to see a naturalistic explanation lurking behind the myth of Icarus. Birds drop from the sky around the lake of Avernus; eventually this somewhat freakish, if perfectly natural phenomenon produced a story of a winged boy who fell from the sky. Virgil's use of the periphrastic term "uolantes" at verse 239—which we assume refers to birds but connotes flying creatures more generally—nicely suggests how the mythic imagination could translate a falling bird into a falling birdman.

But Lucretius, we should remember, was not trying in his sixth book to demystify the story of Icarus. He was after bigger game. He wrote of Cumaean Avernus:

> ianua ne forte his Orci regionibus esse
> credatur, post hinc animas Acheruntis in oras

ducere forte deos manis inferne reamur ...
quod procul a vera quam sit ratione repulsum
percipe; nam de re nunc ipsa dicere conor.
    (DRN 6.762–64; 6.766–67)

[nor should it be thought that this perhaps is the gate to the kingdoms of
Hades, nor should we think that from here perhaps gods of the underworld lead souls down to the borders of Acheron ... for you perceive how
far that is removed from true reasoning; for I am trying now to speak of
the facts themselves.]

Lucretius is anxious in this passage to dispel the idea that Avernus is the gateway to an underworld that does not in fact exist but is a figment of the superstitious human imagination. Virgil, however, seems flatly to contradict Lucretius
by placing Aeneas's descent into Hades in book 6 hard by Cumae and its temple.
There is a tendency in the criticism of the *Aeneid* to see Virgil as a kind of anti-
Lucretius, to see his epic combating the Epicurean rationalism and godlessness
of his predecessor. But Virgil was himself, according to ancient testimony, a
student of Epicureanism, and it is possible that the *Aeneid*, by its allusions here
to book 6 of the *De rerum natura*, has it both ways.[6] It can produce an epic underworld scene along the lines of the *Odyssey* and, at the same time, tip off the
sophisticated and skeptical modern reader that this underworld at Cumaean
Avernus is not something to be believed literally. Like the myth of Icarus that
grows out of the local birdlessness that gives Avernus its name, so the whole
underworld episode that follows is a mythic imposition of the human imagination. In this respect the temple doors ("foribus" [20]) that open book 6 are the
counterparts of the doors of ivory that close the book and through which Aeneas leaves the underworld. These are the doors of false dreams that cast back
upon the whole episode an aura of unreality.[7]

DANTE, TASSO, OVID

If Virgil describes the flights of Daedalus and Icarus, using the oarage of their
wings, as a kind of sea voyage through the air, Dante, in turn, in *Inferno* 26
would describe the failed ocean voyage of his Ulysses as a kind of Icarian flight.

e volta nostra poppa nel mattino,
    dei remi facemmo ali al folle volo,
    sempre acquistando dal lato mancino.
    (Inferno 26.124–26)

[And turning our stern toward the morning in the east, we made wings
out of our oars for our mad flight, constantly gaining on the left] (i. e.,
going to the southwest)

Dante tells the story of a Ulysses who never made it home, but set off on a pure adventure beyond the Columns of Hercules at Gibraltar into the uncharted waters of the Southern Hemisphere where, in sight of the mountain of Purgatory, his boat capsized and he and his men drowned. It is the allegory, as John Freccero and others have demonstrated, of a proud, Platonic, contemplative flight, that, without the guidance of Christian revelation, is doomed never to reach the true celestial homeland of the soul: hence, it is a parodic counter-type to the poet-narrator's own journey, a descent into humility that will take him to Purgatory and finally to heaven.[8] It is contrasted in Dante's canto with the flight of the prophet Elijah on his chariot and his bodily assumption into heaven (26.34–39), and it is contrasted as well to the boat, piloted by an angel that Dante sees bringing the saved to the island mountain of Purgatory. His guide Virgil cries out to him:

> Vedi che sdegna li argomenti umani,
> sì che remo non vuol nè altro velo
> che l'ali sue tra liti sì lontani.
> Vedi come l'ha dritte verso il cielo,
> trattando l'aere con l'etterne penne,
> che non si mutan come mortal pelo.
>   (Purgatorio 2.31–36)

[See how he disdains human instruments, and wants no other oar or sail but his own wings to sail between such distant shores. See how he holds them straight toward heaven, cleaving the air with his eternal wings that never moult as does mortal plumage.]

Where Ulysses made his literal oars into wings, the angel, called an "uccel divino" (divine bird), two verses later (2.38), dispenses with oars and sails and propels the boat with the beating of his wings; he has, that is, an oarage of wings like the one that Daedalus successfully used to reach Cumae. There is a right way and a wrong way to get to Dante's heaven. Ulysses attempted to turn his oars into wings for a mad flight, and the verbal recollection of Virgil's book 6 makes him instead like that other mad flyer, Icarus, who similarly drowned when he fell into the sea.

Torquato Tasso would explicitly allude to the failed voyage of Dante's Ulysses and incorporate it into a whole complex of poetic meaning in canto 15 of his *Gerusalemme liberata* (1581), the epic that provided Milton with his most chronologically proximate model and that already did much of the synthesizing of earlier epic models for him. In this poem about the First Crusade in the year 1099, Tasso stages a sea journey through the Mediterranean and then beyond the gates of Gibraltar. A boat piloted by the personification of Fortune—here, like Dante's angel, the minister of divine providence and a kind of angel herself—conveys two knights, Carlo and Ubaldo, outside the known world to the Fortunate Isles (the Canaries). There they retrieve their companion, the poem's military hero Rinaldo, who is at the moment the erotic captive of the beautiful Syrian enchantress Armida. Armida has carried off Rinaldo in her flying chariot and keeps him sequestered in an enchanted garden perched atop a mountain that recalls Dante's island mountain of Purgatory on the top of which sits the original garden of Eden. In answer to Ubaldo's question about whether anyone else has ever sailed their course, Fortune both looks back on Ulysses and predicts the future voyage of Columbus. Of Ulysses, she says:

> Ei passò le Colonne, e per l'aperto
> mare spiegò de' remi il volo audace;
> ma non giovogli esser ne l'onde esperto,
> perché inghiottillo l'ocean vorace,
> e giacque co 'l suo corpo anco coperto
> il suo gran caso, ch'or tra voi si tace.
> (GL 15.26.1–4)

[He passed the Columns of Hercules, and spread the audacious flight of his oars through the open sea, but it did him no good to be skilled at seamanship, for the voracious ocean swallowed him up, and his great mischance still lies buried with his body, which now remains unsung among you.]

The fate of Ulysses is still unsung, Fortune says, because in the eleventh century Dante has not yet been born to sing it. The echo of Dante's Ulysses is clear— "dei remi facemmo ali al folle volo," and behind that passage lies Dante's own original in Virgil's story of Daedalus and Icarus. The sea voyage of Ulysses was a kind of flight, and the Virgilian "oarage of wings" is understood in the verb *spiegare*—"to spread"—which suggests the spreading of a bird's wings in flight. Tasso changes the "folle volo" into a "volo audace." He thereby only intensifies the recollection of Icarus, for, following a typical Renaissance practice of *contaminatio*, the imitation of several models at once, he has included a reference to another classical version of the story of Icarus, the one told by Ovid in book 8 of the *Metamorphoses.*

> cum puer *audaci* coepit gaudere *volatu*
> deseruitque ducem caelique cupidine tractus
> altius egit iter. rapidi vicinia solis
> mollit odoratas, pennarum vincula, ceras;
> tabuerant cerae: nudos quatit ille lacertos,
> *remigio* carens non ullas percipit auras,
> oraque caerulea patrium clamantia nomen
> excipiuntur aqua. . .
> (Metamorphoses 8.223–30)

[As the boy began to enjoy his *audacious* flight, he deserted his leader, and led by a desire for the sky, he took a higher path. The nearness of the consuming sun softened the fragrant wax that bound his wings together; the wax dissolved; he beat his bare arms, lacking *oarage*, they had no hold on the air, and his lips calling his father's name were engulfed in the blue waters of the sea.]

Tasso's "volo audace" translates the Ovidian "audaci ... volatu." We should note that Ovid's passage itself contains a tiny recollection of Virgil's book 6 in the "remigio," the oarage, that Icarus's now bare arms are said to lack.[9] Tasso imitates Dante as Dante imitates Virgil, and he similarly imitates Ovid as Ovid imitates Virgil. He also appears to echo Virgil directly: the "gran caso" of Ulysses recalls the "casus" of Icarus that Virgil's Daedalus could not bear to depict. Through the resulting Latinate pun, it is both a fall into the ocean that swallows him up and a surrendering to the chance that is sheer contingency—in contrast to Tasso's Fortune herself, subsumed into God's providential plan.

Tasso's fiction contrasts Dante's Icarian Ulysses not as Dante had done, with the individual soul on its pilgrimage to Purgatory and heaven, but with the boat of this Christianized Fortune, and, as Fortune goes on to prophesy, with Christopher Columbus, the navigator who will successfully sail out of Gibraltar and discover a whole New World.[10] The predicted voyage of Columbus is, however, no less divinely sanctioned than that of Dante in his poem, for it opens the way to the evangelization and civilization of the hitherto unknown continent—as Fortune tells Ubaldo and Carlo, "la fé di Piero / fiavi introdotta ed ogni civil arte" (*GL* 15.29.5–6; the faith of Peter and every art of civilization will be introduced there). She goes on to apostrophize the Genoese explorer.

> Tu *spiegherai*, Colombo, a un novo polo
> lontane sì le fortunate antenne,
> ch'a pena *seguirà con gli occhi* il volo
> la fama c'ha mille occhi e mille penne.
>   (GL 15.32.1–4)

[You *will spread* so far your fortunate sails to a new pole that Fame with its thousand eyes and thousand wings will hardly be able to *follow your flight with its eyes*.]

The passage echoes the earlier description of the ill-fated Ulysses. Where Ulysses "spread" his flight with oars, here Columbus spreads his fortunate sails—an acknowledgment of the new technology of the caravel. Columbus, too, achieves a kind of flight: the fiction refers, in a not very concealed way, to a common play on the explorer's name, "Colombo," which means "dove."[11] The contrast to Dante's Ulysses goes further, for when Fortune predicts that many-winged and many-eyed Fame will barely be able to follow Columbus's flight with her eyes—"ch'a pena seguirà con gli occhi il volo"—she again echoes *Inferno* 26. Here, in Dante's simile, it is Elisha whose eyes cannot follow the fiery chariot of his master Elijah as it rises to heaven.

> E qual colui che si vengiò con li orsi
>   vide 'l carro d'Elia al dipartire,
>   quando i cavalli al cielo erti levorsi;
> chè nol potea sì *con li occhi seguire*
>   ch'el vedesse altro che la fiamma sola,
>   sì come nuvoletta, in su salire:
>   (*Inferno 26.34–39*)

[And such as he who avenged himself by means of the bears saw the chariot of Elijah at its departure, when the horses reared up and rose toward heaven: for he could not so *follow it with his eyes* as to see anything but the flame alone, like a little cloud, ascending on high.]

The simile describes the tongues of flame that Dante sees in *Inferno* 26, each of which contains and endlessly consumes a sinner within it, including the double flame that holds Ulysses with his comrade Diomedes. Tasso appears to have understood how this reference to Elijah and his chariot contrasts in Dante's fiction to the voyage of Ulysses. If the "volo audace" assimilates Ulysses to the failed flight of Icarus, Tasso here aligns the "volo" of Columbus with the cloudy ascension of Elijah, both successful, transcendent flights, although the transcendence of Columbus is that of earthly fame, worthy of being memorialized in poetry and history—"di poema dignissima e d'istoria" (*GL* 15.32.8). Tasso's fiction, that is, opposes Ulysses/Icarus to Columbus, just as Dante's poem had opposed Ulysses/Icarus to Elijah.[12]

SATAN VOYAGER

The journey of Tasso's knights to the Fortunate Islands is one of the many models that lie behind the episode of Satan's journey across Chaos to the created universe in book 2 of *Paradise Lost*. Beelzebub has earlier in the book referred to "this new world" (2.403) as "the happy isle" (2.410), and later in book 3, Satan passes through stars that seemed "happy isles, / Like those Hesperian gardens famed of old, / Fortunate fields, and groves and flowery vales, / Thrice happy isles" (3.567–70), as he makes for earth and for Eden, a garden located atop a mountain like Dante's Eden and like Armida's garden in the Canaries on the future route of Columbus. After Satan has done his evil work with them, and they cover their nakedness, the fallen Adam and Eve will be compared to American natives whom "of late / Columbus found ... / Among the trees on isles and woody shores" (9.1115–18). At the end of book 2, as he reaches the boundaries of creation, the archfiend is likened to "a weather beaten vessel" that "holds / Gladly the port, though shrouds and tackle torn" (2.1043–44). Near the very

end of the episode, too, Milton finally names Ulysses (2.1019) the most prestigious epic voyager, to whom all subsequent maritime epic heroes are implicitly
compared. The devil's journey through Chaos, as we saw in the chapter 2, is a
little *Odyssey*, and Satan, we shall now see, recalls not only Homer's Ulysses, but
the failed Ulysses of Dante and Tasso as well.

But, in fact, Satan does not sail: he flies. At least he moves through the use
of his wings. Thus, an epic tradition that begins with the flying Daedalus and
Icarus as metaphorical sailors, traveling with the oarage of their wings, and
then describes sailors such as Ulysses and Columbus as metaphorical fliers who
make oars or sails into wings, now comes full circle with the Satan of *Paradise
Lost*. Milton's fiction, moreover, takes the tradition back even before Virgil's
Icarus to Virgil's own Lucretian subtext. The amount of poetic memory layered
into the passage is quite extraordinary.

> At last his sail-broad vans
> He spreads for flight, and in the surging smoke
> Uplifted spurns the ground, thence many a league
> As in a cloudy chair ascending rides
> Audacious, but that seat soon failing, meets
> A vast vacuity: all unawares
> Fluttering his pennons vain plumb down he drops
> Ten thousand fathom deep, and to this hour
> Down had been falling, had not by ill chance
> The strong rebuff of some tumultuous cloud
> Instinct with fire and nitre hurried him
> As many miles aloft:
> (2.927–38)

Satan's wings are sail-like, and, in fact, he needs an updraft from the mouth of
hell to get moving. Milton jokes at the devil's expense with the phrase "Uplifted
spurned the ground," where "spurned" suggests a proud act of will on Satan's
part, while it appears that he is being passively lifted up by the surging smoke.
The phrase will be echoed in Milton's account of the fifth day of the Creation
and the creation of the birds:

> They summed their pens, and soaring the air sublime
> With clang despised the ground ...
> (7.421–22)

The birds despise the ground as Satan spurns it, but they are real fliers, while
Satan seems here to be more of a literal "airship" (though elsewhere in the poem
he appears to fly under his own power). His wings are like sails that need a
favoring wind to keep him going. At first he meets with success and his flight
becomes "audacious"—the adjective, emphasized by a typical Miltonic inversion and by its placement at the beginning of the verse, recalls, faintly but

unmistakably, the "volo audace" of Tasso's Dantesque Ulysses and the "audaci … volatu" of Ovid's Icarus, and it already suggests the fall that is about to come: this is the pride before the fall. Moreover, the "cloudy chair ascending" makes of this proud flight a parodic version of the ascension of Elijah in his chariot: "chair" has the meaning of chariot in seventeenth-century English, and we may remember that Dante's Elisha sees his master rising to the heavens in his "carro" like a little cloud—a "nuvoletta." Thus Milton, no less than Tasso, is able to bring into play Dante's two contrasting figures in *Inferno* 26: the falling Icarus and the ascending Elijah; they are combined here and compressed into two lines, to denote both what Satan is and what he is not. The effect, moreover, is to moralize flight in a stark way in *Paradise Lost*: either one is on the way up to God and heaven, or one is condemned to a terrifying fall into untold, oceanic depths.

And Satan now does fall. He meets a "vast vacuity," a Lucretian void, and like one of the birds over Lake Avernus, he plummets downward through the infinite space of Chaos. We now realize that those exhalations that first carry him aloft rise from a hell that in its characterization as the "burning lake" (1.210) of Revelation 20:14–15 is also a kind of Avernus. The "surging smoke" is the sort of sulfuric exhalation that according to Lucretius creates pockets of vacuum above Avernus and causes birds to fall from the skies there, lending the place its name. We should note that in the phrase "Fluttering his pennons vain," Milton creates a new meaning for "pennons"—making it now signify "pinions / wings" instead of the normal "pennants / banners"—in order that we hear the "pinnarum" in Lucretius's Latin original behind this passage: "claudicat extemplo pinnarum nisus inanis" (*DRN* 6.834).

The "vast vacuity," however, is more than the local effect of the exhalations of the lake of hell, the kind of phenomenon that, as Virgil's allusion to Lucretius in *Aeneid* 6 would suggest, provides a naturalistic origin to the myth of Icarus. This void through which Satan, Milton's Icarus, plummets goes on forever and is to be identified with Chaos itself, with its endless reaches of space filled with randomly colliding atoms. This part of Milton's cosmos is also Lucretian in inspiration. As John Leonard has argued, the idea of a universe protected by its walls amid a sea of otherwise warring atoms derives from *De rerum natura*, and he properly suggests the terror, as well as the grandeur, of the vision, shared by Milton and Lucretius, of "the void profound / Of unessential night" (2.438–39)—"inane profundum" (*DRN* 1.1107)—the infinite, and possibly lightless universe.[13] Within this vast expanse of space, Satan is himself reduced to a Lucretian atom in free fall and subject to "high arbiter / Chance" (2.909–10). We remember Dante's and Tasso's Icarian Ulysses, who committed himself without divine guidance to the randomness of adventure and whose drowning is characterized by Tasso as an accident of chance—a "gran caso." Satan is saved from a metaphorical drowning in deep oceanic space only by a chance explosion of the nitrous particles of Chaos—possibly a parody of the Lucretian *clinamen*, the creative swerve of atoms—and hurtled back on track to earth and to the seduction of humanity. This "ill chance" is our bad luck, for otherwise Satan would still be falling.

The belittling of Satan is comic, and is shortly followed by a fall in poetic diction that anticipates the bathetic literary manner that Alexander Pope would satirize as the "Art of Sinking"—"half on foot, / Half flying; behoves him now both oar and sail ... With head, hands, wings or feet pursues his way / And swims or sinks, or wades, or creeps, or flies" (2.941–42, 2.949–50). The episode nonetheless engages seriously with Lucretius and with the implications of his godless universe. Milton combines Stoic and Lucretian-Epicurean cosmological models in order to cordon off the created world from the surrounding, infinitely extensive void of Chaos. Lucretius would have it that Chaos is the condition of the whole universe and that worlds created by accidents of chance within it are due in time to fall back through entropy into its disorder, as he declares at the end of book 1 of *De rerum natura*; Milton acknowledges this possibility when he calls Chaos, "The womb of nature and perhaps her grave" (2.911; cf. *DRN* 5.295). It is a possibility that would ultimately render the universe and human life absurd, and the poem sinks still further when it identifies Chaos with the nonmeaning of Babel—"a universal hubbub wild / Of stunning sounds and voices all confused" (2.951–52; cf. 12.60–62). But Milton resists this possibility by designating Chaos as that sector of the universe to which God has not put forth his "goodness" (7.171)—that is, his creativity— although he is careful to note in his *De Doctrina Christiana* (1.7) that such raw matter, in its potential to be shaped by God into creation, is good in itself and contains "the seeds of all subsequent good ... It was in a confused and disordered state at first, but afterwards God made it ordered and beautiful" (*CPW* 6:308; *Works* 15:22). Milton's Chaos is noncreative rather than entropic; it is the "world unborn" (7.220) or, more starkly, the "abortive gulf" (2.441), and its perpetually warring "embryon atoms" (2.900) can never combine long enough to reach elemental form. Its "high arbiter" (2.909) Chance cannot take the place of God's Spirit that sat "brooding on the vast abyss" (1.21) and create new worlds out of this Chaos. When Satan, attracted by the noise, looks for the "spirit of the nethermost abyss" (2.956; 2.969), he finds the personified "anarch" himself, old and faltering (2.988–89), who proves to be his merely passive ally.[14]

In this light, Satan's fall as a type of Icarus similarly corrects the Lucretian vision of a universe ruled by chance. Milton uses the Christianized Icarus-figure of Ulysses depicted by Dante and Tasso to counter the unbelief of Lucretius— and of Virgil, whose recollection of his Epicurean predecessor suggests that Icarus fell not because of any act of his own, but because it is the nature of things to fall. Like the mythic Icarus, Satan has disobeyed his father and aspired too high; his falling here repeats his nine-day fall through Chaos when he and his fellow rebel angels were rooted out of heaven (2.993–98, 6.871–77). Like the Dantesque Ulysses, Satan is on his own, without God, and hence gives himself up to chance. Having cut himself off from the divine source of meaning and creative order, Satan's fall into the confused meaninglessness and random disorder of Chaos is both the result and the emblem of his sin. So Satan internalizes his falling in his soliloquy in book 4.

> Which way shall I fly
> Infinite wrath, and infinite despair?
> Which way I fly is hell; my self am hell;
> And in the lowest deep a lower deep
> Still threatening to devour me opens wide,
> To which the hell I suffer seems a heaven.
>   *(4.73–78)*

When he speaks these words Satan is no longer in Chaos, but on the terra firma of the earth in the new, solidly built universe that God has created in his absence. But he still feels that he is falling. Miltonic wordplay transforms Satan's flight into a vain attempt to flee both from an angry God and, more powerfully, from his own inner torment. This Icarus is drowning in a despair as deep as the infinite reaches of Chaos itself. It is not the universe that is falling, then, Milton responds to Lucretius, but rather the hardened sinner, who, unable to repent, falls ever further away from his Creator. Moreover, Satan's interior state corresponds here not only to the Chaos into which he was falling earlier, but to hell, the bottomless pit: the hell that is his consciousness of falling itself, of having fallen and continuing to fall from a former state of happiness and goodness. Satan, that is, goes beyond the noncreative state of Chaos; his sin makes him positively *de*creative, both of himself and of God's other creations that he seeks to reduce back to Chaos: "only in destroying I find ease / To my relentless thoughts" (9.129–30), he ultimately confesses in his soliloquy in book 9, as he sets out to ruin God's greatest creation, Adam and Eve.

Phaethon, the Son, and the War in Heaven

Satan's decreative impulse comes into play in Milton's reworking of the myth of another would-be highflier who falls: Phaethon. Milton doubles his versions of the myth, however, in order to depict God's Son as a successful Phaethon, who drives the Chariot of Paternal Deity in the War in Heaven and restores the heavenly landscape that the warfare of Satan, the failed, falling Phaethon, has caused to go to rack and ruin. But Milton's target is once again the cosmology of Lucretius. His fiction not only refers back to Lucretius's own naturalistic discussion of the Phaethon myth, it also evokes the Latin university poem written toward the beginning of Milton's poetic career, *Naturam non pati senium*, itself a polemic against Lucretius. It thereby testifies to Milton's long-standing preoccupation with the Roman poet's dark view of a world that grows old and must fall eventually to pieces.

It has been noted by Barbara Lewalski that God's praise of his Son in the heavenly council of book 3,

Because thou hast, though throned in highest bliss
Equal to God, and equally enjoying
Godlike fruition, quitted all to save
A world from utter loss, and hast been found
By merit more than birthright Son of God,
Found worthiest to be so by being good,
Far more than great or high ...
    (3.305–11)

contains an echo of Apollo's reassurance of his paternity to Phaethon in Ovid's *Metamorphoses*:

        "nec tu meus esse negari
dignus es, et Clymene veros" ait "edidit ortus"
        (Metamorphoses 2.42–43)

["nor is to be denied that you are worthy to be my son, and Clymene," he said, "has proclaimed your true origins ..."]

It seems a rather odd recollection that Milton uses to hammer home an important point: that the Son is distinguished more by his merit than by his birthright, that his merit has earned or demonstrated his special birthright among God's other creatures, the angels. The Ovidian Phaethon goes on to show, in a spectacularly catastrophic way, that he is indeed *un*worthy of carrying out the work of his divine father. Lewalski does not develop the parallel much further.[15] But, in fact, the Son has demonstrated his merit once before, during the War in Heaven and the following Creation of the universe, and he has done so by playing the role of Phaethon. These events are narrated subsequently in the poem by Raphael in his conversation with Adam and Eve in books 6 and 7.

At first, it is Satan who seems to have cast himself in the role of Phaethon or Apollo in the War in Heaven. Already back in book 3, Satan's visit to the sun, as Davis Harding suggested, recalls the visit of Ovid's Phaethon to his father Apollo, the sun god: the "golden tiar" with its "beaming sunny rays" (3.625) of Milton's Uriel, the angel of the sun, echoes the crown of shining light that Apollo takes off —"circum caput omne micantes / deposuit radios" (*Met.* 2.40–41)—when he greets his son.[16] Satan's disguise as a "stripling cherub" (3.636), we may add, reinforces the resemblance of the two passages in which a youth approaches the resident divinity of the sun. Now this is the same Ovidian scene that Milton has just imitated in book 3 when God pronounced his Son worthy by merit. The juxtaposition within the same book of two versions of Ovid's fiction distinguishes a good Phaethon and good son of God from a bad one.

A similar juxtapostion takes place in book 6. Satan makes a grand entry into battle.

> High in the midst, exalted as a god
> The apostate in his sun-bright chariot sat
> Idol of majesty divine, enclosed
> With flaming cherubim, and golden shields;
>   (6.99–102)

Satan's war chariot bears an obviously imitative relationship to the Chariot of Paternal Deity with its "four cherubic shapes" that will appear later and that Milton derives from the vision of Ezekiel 1. It is, moreover, an Apollonian chariot—"sun-bright"—and already suggests that Satan will repeat the fate of Phaethon.[17] The war that Satan wages confirms the identification, for it begins to destroy the very foundations of heaven. Phaethon, as Ovid retells his story in the *Metamorphoses*, was unable to drive the sun god's chariot and, as a result, began to burn up the universe. The scorched, personified Earth called on Jupiter to come to the rescue.

> si freta, si terrae pereunt, si regia caeli,
> in chaos antiquum confundimur! eripe flammis,
> si quid adhuc superest, et rerum consule summae!
>   (*Metamorphoses. 2.298–300*)

> [if the seas, if the land and the realms of the sky perish, we will be confused in ancient Chaos! if anything yet remains, save it from the flames, and consult the sum of things!]

All parts of the world, including Jupiter's own heaven, are at stake, Earth warns, and they risk returning to the confusion of primeval Chaos from which, in Ovid's version of the Creation, they first came. Jupiter, the almighty father—"pater omnipotens" (304)—responds by striking Phaethon down with his thunderbolt and thereby saves the world from impending destruction. Phaethon is carried headlong with flames in hair—"At Phaethon rutilos *flamma* populante capillos / volvitur in *praeceps longoque per aera* tractu / *fertur*" (*Met.* 2.319–21). So *Paradise Lost* tells us of Satan at its beginning: "Him the almighty power / Hurled headlong flaming from the ethereal sky" (1.44–45). Now, through Raphael's narration, we see that Phaethon-like fall enacted.

Satan's warfare brings about a return to Chaos in at least three ways.[18] First, his invention of gunpowder involves digging up the raw materials of Chaos itself.

> materials dark and crude,
> Of spiritous and fiery spume, till touched
> With heaven's ray, and tempered they shoot forth

> So beauteous, opening to the ambient light.
> These in their dark nativity the deep
> Shall yield us pregnant with infernal flame ...
> (6.478–83)

Satan intuits that heaven, as will be the case of the created universe in book 7, is also made out of the stuff of Chaos, "the deep," confused matter that lies in darkness waiting to be shaped by the divine Creator. These are the "originals of nature in their crude / Conception; sulphurous and nitrous foam" (6.511–12) whose explosive properties Satan will himself experience still later in the chronology of the poem, when he is blown back upward from his fall through Chaos in book 2 by a "tumultuous cloud / Instinct with fire and nitre"; only now, retrospectively, do we recognize the poetic justice of that moment: Satan was hoisted by his own petard. In his attempt to find an equivalent to God's dreaded thunderbolt (6.491), Satan's gunpowder plot thus already brings Chaos back into creation.

Second, the war between the rebel and loyal angels is a civil, "Intestine war in heaven," and resembles the "intestine broils" (2.1001) of the warring atoms of Chaos. The atoms wage "endless wars" (2.897), and it is Satan's strategy to keep the War in Heaven going forever—"if one day, why not eternal days?" (6.424); God himself concedes that "in perpetual fight they needs must last / Endless" (6.693–94) unless he intervenes, and this eternal strife, too, would turn heaven into an image of the never-ending wars of Chaos.

Third, when the mountains that the good angels pluck up from their foundations to overwhelm Satan's cannons are met by similar mountains cast by the rebel angels in return—"So hills amid the air encountered hills" (6.664)—this version of the gigantomachy both verges on comic mock-epic and suggests cosmic decreation.

> Infernal noise; war seemed a civil game
> To this uproar; horrid confusion heaped
> Upon confusion rose: and now all heaven
> Had gone to wrack, with ruin overspread ...
> (6.667–70)

The initial emphasis is on unintelligible noise: "war" spreads acoustically into "uproar; horrid."[19] The gigantomachy and the piling of Pelion on Ossa were conventionally assimilated with the building of the Tower of Babel. Milton has already drawn on this association in his description of Satan's "royal seat" in book 5: "as a mount / Raised on a mount, with *pyramids* and *towers*" (5.757–58; cf. the coupling of "*Babel*, and the works of Memphian kings" applied to Satan's later temple-palace in Pandaemonium at 1.694). Here Babelic confusion rises on confusion like the unfinished tower itself and turns heaven into the "hubbub wild" and "voices all confused" of a meaningless Chaos.

The war that Satan brings to heaven would plunge God's creation back toward the confusion of Chaos, and it resembles the destruction wrought by Ovid's Phaethon—"in chaos antiquum confundimur," the Earth cries out in the *Metamorphoses*, imploring Jupiter to consult on the sum of things, to take care for his universe. It is to that destruction that Milton now alludes as God intervenes to end the war.

> and now all heaven
> Had gone to wrack, with ruin overspread,
> Had not the *almighty Father* where he sits
> Shrined in his sanctuary of heaven secure,
> *Consulting on the sum of things*, foreseen
> This tumult, and permitted all, advised:
> That his great purpose he might so fulfil,
> To honour his anointed Son avenged
> Upon his enemies, and to declare
> All power on him transferred:
> *(6.669–78)*

The echoes of Ovid's "pater omnipotens" and "rerum consule summae" are clear; God is in the position of the Ovidian Jupiter responding to the destruction wrought by Phaethon's unsuccessful attempt to drive his father's chariot.

But now Milton inverts the Phaethon story, for God tells *his* Son, "Ascend my chariot, guide the rapid wheels / That shake heaven's basis, bring forth all my war, / My bow and thunder" (6.711–13). God makes the Son into a good Phaethon, and his assertion that the Son will prove himself "worthiest to be heir / Of all things" (6.707–8) recalls (and in the poem's chronology anticipates) the declaration in book 3 of the Son's worthiness—"Found worthiest to be so by being good"—which, we have seen, echoes the words of Ovid's Apollo to Phaethon. There are Apollonian associations in the bow (6.763–64) that the Son employs together with his Jovian thunderbolts.

This is a Phaethon who restores rather than destroys the universe. The tone and action of the War in Heaven change after the mock-heroic mayhem of its first two days has threatened to spiral out of control. The Son's first act is to put heaven's landscape back into place.

> Before him power divine his way prepared;
> At his command the uprooted hills retired
> Each to his place, *they heard his voice* and went
> Obsequious, heaven his wonted face renewed,
> And with fresh flowerets hill and valley smiled.
> *(6.780–84)*

It was the Son—as by God's Word, Abdiel had reasoned and warned Satan back in book 5 (835–39)—who created all things in the first place, including heaven and the angels, and his return of heaven to the way it was repeats that original creative act. It also anticipates the Son's creation of the new universe in the following book 7, especially his command to Chaos that similarly prepares the way for his divine chariot.

> Silence, ye troubled waves, and thou deep, peace,
> Said then the omnific Word, your discord end:
> Nor stayed, but on the wings of cherubim
> Uplifted, in paternal glory rode
> Far into chaos, and the world unborn;
> For *chaos heard his voice*: him all his train
> Followed in bright procession to behold
> Creation, and the wonders of his might.
> *(7.216–23)*

Both of these moments show the creative Word at work, and Milton has carefully brought out their analogy. At the sound of its voice and fiat, both a chaotic heaven and Chaos itself are reduced to order. The Son's ensuing expulsion from heaven of Satan and the rebel angels is similar to his taking the chaos—the noise, violence, and discord—out of Chaos in order to extend that creativity into its reaches. The fulmination and fall of Satan and the bad angels through Chaos into hell completes Milton's reworking of the Phaethon myth. Satan, the bad, aspiring Phaethon who seeks to take the place of the divine Father and comes close to wrecking heaven, is finally *not* struck by divine "thunder" (6.854), for the Son, the good, obedient Phaethon and worthy driver of his father's chariot, holds back—"he meant / Not to destroy" (6.854–55)—and merely roots Satan and his crew out of the celestial precincts. They are indeed "thunderstruck" (6.858), but we should probably understand this adjective metaphorically: the Son's ten thousand thunders earlier "in their souls infixed / Plagues" (6.837–38)—it is warfare with literal psychological weapons—and here they are similarly driven by forces, "terrors" and "furies" (6.859), that are more inner and spiritual than external: panic terrors suitable to a "herd / Of goats" in stampede or to demonically possessed Gadarene swine tumbling over into the deep (Matt. 8:32).[20] Milton carefully cordons off the Son from the physical warfare of the first two days of the heavenly conflict.[21]

The confrontation of these two Phaethons in the War in Heaven constitutes a kind of cosmogonic struggle between divine creativity and the decreative force of Satanic evil that introduces war among things and makes them fall apart. It is at the same time a particular contest between Milton's Christian cosmology and the godless cosmology of Lucretius. For Lucretius, too, presents a version or understanding of the Phaethon story, one of the very few mythic references in *De rerum natura*. It appears at the climax of the section in book 5 (64–415) where Lucretius explains that while the universe and matter may be eternal and indestructible, the visible world within it that we inhabit is not: it is mortal just as we are, and someday the mechanism of this world will come crashing down: "multosque per annos / sustentata ruet moles et machina mundi" (*DRN* 5.95–96). The Roman poet rules out the possibility that the gods created the world for men and women (*DRN* 5.156–80). Having rather come into being by chance out of the rain of falling atoms, this world—the sum of things—can be battered and eventually destroyed by other groups of atoms coming out of the infinity of space like a violent storm, "corruere hanc *rerum* violento turbine *summam*" (*DRN* 5.368), a passage that Milton appears to remember when he describes the newly created world "with ever-threatening storms / Of Chaos blustering around, inclement sky" (3.425–26).[22] Lucretius continues to suggest that in the incessant battle among the four elements—which Milton translates into the battle in his Chaos of four elemental principles, "Hot, Cold, Moist, and Dry, four champions fierce" (2.898)—one can gain ascendance and bring about universal destruction. Indeed, this has already happened, and now Lucretius produces his clinching evidence.

> ignis enim superavit et lambens multa perussit,
> avia cum Phaethonta rapax vis solis equorum
> aethere raptavit toto terrasque per omnis.
> *at pater omnipotens* ira tum percitus acri
> magnanimum Phaethonta repenti fulminis ictu
> deturbavit equis in terram, solque cadenti
> obvius aeternam succepit lampada mundi
> disiectos redegit equos iunxitque trementis,
> inde suum per iter recreavit cuncta gubernans,
> scilicet ut veteres Graium cecinere poetae.
> quod procul a vera nimis est ratione repulsum.
> ignis enim superare potest ubi materiai
> ex infinito sunt corpora plura coorta;
> inde cadunt vires aliqua ratione revictae,
> aut pereunt res exustae torrentibus auris.
> umor item quondam coepit superare coortus...
>   (*DRN* 5.396–411)

[For fire once gained the upper hand and, spreading around, burned many things when the fierce might of the horses of the Sun carried Phaethon off course through the whole of heaven and all over the earth. *But the almighty father*, spurred then by harsh anger, cast down aspiring Phaethon with the sudden force of a thunderbolt from his horses to earth, and the Sun meeting him as he fell, took up the eternal lamp of the world, and brought back his scattered horses and yoked the trembling steeds; thereupon, driving them on their way, he created all anew. That is how the ancient poets of the Greeks have sung of it. But it is removed very far from true reason. For fire can dominate when the atoms of its matter gathered from the infinite are preponderant in number; thence its forces subside defeated by some reason or the world perishes, burned up in a firestorm.

Water also once, having gathered together, began to dominate ...]

Lucretius tells the story of Phaethon to discount it as myth—"thus they relate, / Erring"—at the same time that he argues, in euhemerist fashion, that it is poetic testimony to a real event: a catastrophic fire that once almost destroyed or did destroy the earth. If the fire subsided, as did a similarly ruinous deluge, which he goes on briefly to discuss, it did so because it was thwarted by other natural elements, not because some sun god, in whom Lucretius does not believe, restored creation ("recreavit"), and not because of the intervention of a "pater omnipotens," in whom he especially does not believe. Ovid takes this section of the *De rerum natura* to epitomize its dark message when he presents his history of Latin literature in the *Tristia*.

explicat ut causas rapidi Lucretius ignis,
    casurumque triplex vaticinatur opus.
        (Tristia 2.425–26)

[Lucretius explains the causes of devastating fire, and sings the fall of the threefold world] (i.e., earth, sea, and sky)

Lucretius, for Ovid, is the poet who sings the end of the world in conflagration, and we can note how Lucretius's language in this part of his poem—"hanc rerum ... summam" and "at pater omnipotens"—reappears in Ovid's retelling of the Phaethon story. Just as Virgil's depiction of Icarus suggests through allusion a naturalistic Lucretian explanation of the myth, so Ovid's version of Phaethon alludes to an explicit Lucretian explanation of the origins of this myth in a real natural disaster. And Milton is aware of the poetic operation going on in both cases and how they testify to an Epicurean vision of a world falling into entropy and toward its demise.

For Milton had already countered this vision and the Lucretian Phaethon in his early Latin poem, *Naturam non pati senium*, probably written between 1627 and 1630 while the young poet was at Cambridge. Lucretius is the obvious target of this poem, which attacks the belief of some blind and benighted thinkers who ascribe their own human mortality to nature (1–7). The first half of the poem consists of a series of sarcastic rhetorical questions and statements about this presumed aging of the earth and its eventual destruction. The passage reaches its rhetorical climax with a vision of the collapse of the universe onto itself (and then is immediately followed by the poem's second half, which rebuts this vision and the erroneous doctrine that stands behind it).

Tu quoque Phoebe tui *casus imitabere nati*
Praecipiti curru, subitaque ferere ruina
Pronus, et extincta fumabit lampade Nereus,
Et dabit attonito feralia sibila ponto.
Tunc etiam aerei divulsis sedibus Haemi
Dissultabit apex, imoque allisa barathro
Terrebunt Stygium deiecta Ceraunia Ditem
In superos quibus usus erat, fraternaque bella.
    At pater omnipotens fundatis fortius astris
Consuluit rerum summae, certoque peregit
Pondere fatorum lances, atque ordine summo
Singula perpetuum iussit servare tenorem ...
Floridus aeternum Phoebus iuvenile coruscat,
Nec fovet effoetas loca per declivia terras
Devexo temone deus; sed semper amica
Luce potens eadem currit per signa rotarum ...
    (NNPS 25–36, 41–44)

[And you, too, Phoebus, will be supposed to *imitate the fall of your son with a precipitous chariot*, and headfirst will be carried in your sudden fall, and Nereus will send up steam from your extinguished lamp, and will make a cadaverous hissing on the astonished sea. Then also with the uprooting of its foundations the peak of lofty Haemus would burst asunder, and the Ceraunian mountains, dashed down and striking the lowest underworld, will terrify Hades, who had used them against the gods in fraternal war.

    But the almighty father, who has set the stars more firmly in their place, *has taken care for the sum of things*, and he has fixed the scales of the fates with a sure balance, and commanded every individual thing to preserve its perpetual course in the universal order ... Phoebus shines with the bloom of eternal youth; the god does not veer his chariot downward to warm an exhausted earth, but always potent with cherishing light drives through the same tracks his wheels have made ...]

The Phaethon myth stands at the center of *Naturam non pati senium*, and Milton takes it, in its Lucretian sense, to stand for a once-and-future destruction of the earth by the aging and instability of its own elemental framework; the sun will fall from the sky, as Phaethon did once before, and this time take his chariot with him. Milton similarly understands the uprooted mountains of the gigantomachy, wielded here, it seems, in a kind of civil war among the gods, as figures of cosmic destruction. Both of these myths will shape the War in Heaven and turn it, too, into a test of the order of God's creation. The unmistakable

Lucretian-Ovidian tag, "At pater omnipotens ... / Consuluit rerum summae," which will also be reworked in the War in Heaven, already indicates here God's reassuring care for the universe he has made.[23] Milton throws back in Lucretius's face the Roman poet's own sarcasm about a supreme deity who cast Phaethon down.[24] Yes, the poem declares, just as the almighty father in the myth preserved the world when Phaethon was about to wreck it, so there is a God who keeps the sun and the rest of the universe running in its usual place. There will be no Phaethon-like destruction randomly visited on the earth as Lucretius teaches. Milton ends by conceding a final conflagration that will indeed destroy the earth, but only when God is ready for it at the Last Judgment—"Ingentique rogo flagrabit machina mundi" (*NNPS* 69). This is the true version and the poem's final correction of Lucretius's description of the "machina mundi" (*DRN* 5.96) falling by its own shaky elemental forces into ruin.

Milton thus rewrote Lucretius's version of the Phaethon myth twice, first in *Naturam non pati senium* and again in *Paradise Lost*, and the epic itself rewrites the early university poem. In both cases, he denies the Lucretian reading of the myth, which understands it as a story of inevitable cosmic decreation in a universe ruled by chance. He asserts instead the providential guidance of the Christian God who maintains his universe in rational running order and prevents it from disintegrating into Chaos. In *Paradise Lost*, this divine maintenance is enacted when the Son, playing the role of a good Phaethon in his father's chariot, returns the disordered scenery of heaven back into place, an act that is portrayed as one and the same thing as his defeat of Satan and the rebel angels, who are responsible for reintroducing Chaos into heaven. Satan falls from heaven through Chaos as a bad Phaethon, as earlier in the poem we have seen him fall as Icarus. There, too, Milton contested a Lucretian interpretation of the myth—the one that Virgil builds into the allusive texture of the *Aeneid*—which would have seen Icarus falling not from audacious aspiration in disobedience to his father's commands, but because falling is in the nature of things.

Milton's strategy is consistent in his anti-Lucretian treatment of these two myths of falling in *Paradise Lost*. He alludes to naturalizing readings of Icarus and Phaethon. But in their place, and in resistance to the Epicurean implications of such readings, Milton reaffirms their conventional, moral reading—these are stories about sons who want to be equal to or go beyond their fathers, but prove unable to sustain their ambitious flights. Milton renders this moral explicitly Christian. Sin makes Satan fall like Icarus into a Chaos ruled by chance, and he will still feel as if he is falling there even when he reaches the newly created world. Sin makes Satan begin, like Phaethon, to destroy heaven through his rebellion and warfare.

Nonetheless, the fact that Milton chooses to confront the Lucretian versions of these myths, and the poetic power, too, of his images of Satan's falling through Chaos and of the ruin and confusion of the War in Heaven, testify to an anxious preoccupation with *De rerum natura*. It was an anxiety that dated back to *Naturam non pati senium*, and suggests just how much of a challenge the Lucretian atomic universe of chance and entropy posed for his Christian belief. In *Naturam non pati senium*, Milton accused those who, like Lucretius, saw the universe aging and falling at last into dissolution, of daring to measure nature by their own mortal condition—"suis metiri facta deorum / Audet" (*NNPS* 4–5). If men die, nature dies, and Lucretius's own message is, reciprocally, that from the example of a dying nature human beings should accept the fact that death is the end. This was a conclusion that Milton as a Christian was bound to contest. The great subject of *Paradise Lost* may indeed be to depict how death came into the world through sin and thus to give death a meaning. The Son's defeat of Satan in the War in Heaven not only prevents God's creation from falling into ruin and keeps it ever new; the three days of warfare anticipate the Son's Passion, which is his victory over death. Yet by the time he came to write *Paradise Lost*, Milton had accepted the mortalist position that the human soul dies with the body: he had come close to conceding the central and most scandalous point of *De rerum natura* (*DRN* 3.417–829).[25] So Milton's doubts and fears may have run deeper, and he may have admitted the force of Lucretius's naturalistic arguments. We can only speculate. Perhaps his unease with the Epicurean doctrine he confutes is measured in the very indirectness of his approach to it: Milton buries his allusions to Icarus and Phaethon, neither mentioned by name, and to the Lucretian passages to which they further refer, as if they occupy a troubled poetic substratum of his epic, kept out of sight and out of mind.

Flight and Fall

The resonance of these episodes, and of the Icarus and Phaethon myths submerged beneath them, is nonetheless felt throughout *Paradise Lost* as it returns again and again to the opposition of flying and falling. Here, too, moralizing may help keep at bay the Lucretian prospect of a universe that is itself falling into non-meaning. It is not enough to portray the Fall: fallenness is measured by flightlessness or false attempts at flight. At the same time, the poet Milton, invoking his Muse, finds his personal relief or exemption from a fallen condition in the winged elevation of his verse.

Milton rewrites the low comedy of Satan's fall through Chaos into the still lower comedy of the anti-Catholic satire of the limbolike Paradise of Fools in book 3. "Up hither like aerial vapours flew" (3.445): the fools fly up through their own vanity and emptiness, an inversion of Satan and Lucretian atoms falling downward by their own weight through an empty void. When they think to arrive at Saint Peter's gate, a violent crosswind "Blows them transverse ten thousand leagues awry / Into the devious air" (3.488–89), echoing the "Ten thousand fathom deep" of Satan's earlier fall. The fools are the "sport of winds" blowing from Chaos, much as Satan was the plaything of its warring elements, and as they "Fly o'er the backside of the world" (3.494) to their fool's paradise, the scatological nature of these ill-winds is suggested.[26]

A few verses later, moreover, Milton describes the true gate of heaven, at whose foot

> a bright sea flowed
> Of jasper, or of liquid pearl, whereon
> Who after came from earth, sailing arrived,
> Wafted by angels, or flew o'er the lake
> Rapt in a chariot drawn by fiery steeds.
> (3.518–22)

The fools' unsuccessful ascent to heaven (3.486) is opposed, as was Satan's fall, to the flight of Elijah in his chariot and his assumption as one of the "Translated saints" (3.461), together with Enoch whose ascension, "Rapt in a balmy cloud with winged steeds," will be described in book 11 (706).[27] This flight is also a kind of sea voyage above heavenly waters, contrasted to the failed flight of the drowned Icarus. The passage, Fowler suggests, may also recall the angel who ferries the saved souls to Dante's Purgatory, a purgatory that the Paradise of Fools is satirizing.[28]

Delusory flight features in the dream that Satan pours into Eve's ear and that she describes in book 5. Her visitant, "shaped and winged like one of those from heaven" (5.55), tells her:

> Happier thou mayst be, worthier canst not be:
> Taste this, and be henceforth among the gods
> Thy self a goddess, not to earth confined,
> But sometimes in the air, as we, sometimes
> Ascend to heaven, by merit thine …
> (5.76–80)

The temptation is to flight and to the godhood that such flight would prove, and it is also colored with the vocabulary of worth and merit that has been associated with the Son as a new version of Phaethon. Earlier, Adam has observed that he and Eve "Have nothing merited" for their happiness (4.418). Now Satan is casting Eve in the role of Phaethon, and setting her up for a fall; he himself is earlier described high on his throne in hell at the opening of book 2, "Satan exalted sat, by merit raised / To that bad eminence; and from despair / Thus high uplifted beyond hope aspires / Beyond thus high" (2.5–8) in a parody of the Son's true merit, a passsage that will be echoed when Satan appears, Phaethon-like, in the War in Heaven: "High in the midst exalted as a god / The apostate in his sun-bright chariot sat" (6.99–100). No sooner has Eve in her dream eaten the forbidden fruit than

> Forthwith up to the clouds
> With him I flew, and underneath beheld
> The earth outstretched immense, a prospect wide
> And various: wondering at my flight and change
> To this high exaltation; suddenly
> My guide was gone, and I, me thought, sunk down,
> And fell asleep;
>> (5.86–92)

In her high, godlike exaltation, Eve echoes the aspiring Satan, while her sinking down suggests both a fall and a drowning in sleep. The satanic dream mimics Adam's true dream where a "shape divine" (8.295) brings him "over fields and waters, as in air / Smooth sliding without step" (8.301–2) to an Eden laden with tempting fruit. It also has its counterpart in the true heavenly ascent planned for human creatures, for it parodies in advance Raphael's subsequent speculation in the same book 5 that, through a process that includes a vegetarian diet, and thus also seems to involve eating fruit, although fruit of a different kind, the bodies of Adam and Eve "may at last turn all to spirit, / Improved by tract of time, and winged ascend / Ethereal …" (5.497–99). Man, as God first created him, Milton says, was indeed meant to fly—at least eventually as he became "worthier." But the Fall into original sin changed matters.

It is, ironically, such divine flight that Adam and Eve first imagine themselves experiencing when together they eat the fruit of the forbidden tree.

> They swim in mirth, and fancy that they feel
> Divinity within them breeding wings
> Wherewith to scorn the earth; but that false fruit
> Far other operation first displayed,
> Carnal desire inflaming, he on Eve
> Began to cast lascivious eyes, she him
> As wantonly repaid; in lust they burn:
>> (9.1009–15)

Satan spurns the ground; the birds at their creation despised the ground; Adam and Eve would scorn the earth. To the internal echoes of the poem Milton grafts a wicked parody of Plato's discussion of the wings of the soul in the *Phaedrus*. There Socrates explains to Phaedrus how the soul that descends into the body and into matter has lost the wings that "carry it aloft to the regions where gods dwell" (246e), and that these wings can be regrown through the experience of love kindled by the sight of the beautiful beloved.

> For by reason of the stream of beauty entering in through his eyes there comes a warmth, whereby his soul's plumage is fostered, and with that warmth the roots of the wings are melted, which for long had been so

hardened and closed up that nothing could grow; then as the nourishment is poured in, the stump of the wing swells and hastens to grow from
the root over the whole substance of the soul, for aforetime the whole
soul was furnished with wings. Meanwhile she throbs with ferment in
every part, and even as a teething child feels an aching and pain in its
gums when a tooth has just come through, so does the soul of him who
is beginning to grow his wings [*pterophuein*] feel a ferment and painful
irritation. (251b–c)

Although Socrates goes on to preach the chaste, sublimated, love of the philosopher (256b–d), it is clear that the throbbing wings of the soul that he describes
here bear a more than metaphorical relationship to the pangs of sexual desire
and to the male erection. Milton maliciously strips away the metaphor altogether as Adam and Eve fall into fornication. If they are preparing for Platonic
flight to the heavens, they crash and burn on takeoff. Their imagined wings
are glossed subsequently in the narrative, if at a chronologically prior point in
the plot, in book 10; Sin declares that she feels "Wings growing" (244) within
herself on the eve of the Fall, as she and Death hasten toward earth. There the
now fallen Adam finds himself in the same spiritual condition to which Satan
had earlier born witness.

> O conscience! into what abyss of fears
> And horror has thou driven me; out of which
> I find no way, from deep to deeper plunged!
>   *(10.842–44)*

There is no stopping once one begins to fall—unless, in the case of Adam, prevenient grace comes to the rescue in the person of the repentant Eve. The un-
redeemed and unredeemable Satan, on the other hand, felt "in the lowest deep
a lower deep" of torturing despair ready to devour him: the state of hell is an
endless free fall.

A Poetry Against Falling

Milton gives us another, more personal, version of the spiritual state of the rep-
robate in the words of his God in book 3. Of his grace the Deity says,

> They who neglect and scorn, shall never taste;
> But hard be hardened, blind be blinded more
> That they may stumble on, and deeper fall;
> And none but such from mercy I exclude.
>   *(3.199–202)*

Milton is paraphrasing Isaiah 6:10 and its later appearances in Matthew 13:14,
and at the very end of Acts in chapter 28:27: "Make the heart of this people fat,

and make their ears heavy, and shut their eyes; lest they see with eyes, and hear with their ears, and understand with their heart, and convert, and be healed." But as he spells out the relentless logic of perdition, Milton's intercalating of scriptural texts (see the ensuing Isaiah 8:14–15) allows us to feel the special resonance for the sightless poet in danger every day of stumbling and falling. It is as if Milton were trying to persuade himself that the physical affliction of his blindness is not to be confused with the spiritual affliction of despair for which it serves as a figure—that fearful state of falling ever deeper and farther from God. "This is not me," the poet says, even as his royalist enemies saw his blindness as a divine punishment and a sign of reprobation.[29] Or, instead, the blind Milton fights off his own dejection and projects it onto the character of his despairing devil.

For Milton the poet intends rather to fly, and he intends to do so precisely as a highflying *Icarus*, an Icarus who in this case will not fall. He characterizes his poetry in the opening invocation to the Muse of *Paradise Lost* as "adventurous song / That with no middle flight intends to soar / Above the Aonian mount" (1.13–15). This is poetry that will go beyond the middle course—"medio"— that both Ovid's Daedalus (*Met.* 8.203) and Apollo (*Met.* 2.137) counsel their sons Icarus and Phaethon to take. Milton is, in fact, revising the pledge that Guillaume Du Bartas (1544–90) makes at the beginning of *La Sepmaine* (1581) to maintain a middle course and to avoid the fate of an Icarus-like poetic over- reacher, seeking too curiously into divine mysteries.

Piqué d'un beau souci je veux qu'ore mon vers
Divinement humain se guinde entre deux airs:
De peur qu'allant trop haut, la cire de ses ailes
Ne se fonde aux rayons des celestes chandeles:[30]
    (*La Sepmaine 1.113–16*)

[My heedfull Muse, trained in true Religion,
Devinely-humane keepes the middle Region:
Least, if she too-high a pitch presume,
Heav'ns glowing flame should melt her waxen plume;][31]
    (*Sylvester, trans., The Divine Weeks 1.1.135–38*)

Where Milton depicted the Son as a successful Phaethon, he, Milton, claims to be a successful Icarus in his poetic flight, a claim that he repeats at the opening of book 3 when he speaks of revisiting the light "with bolder wing" (3.13), still bolder than the audacious flight—"audaci ... volatu"—of Ovid's Icarus. In the fiction of the *Metamorphoses*, Ovid doubled and rewrote the Phaethon story in the story of Daedalus and Icarus to suggest that the flight of the artist-poet is the mortal version of, or surrogate for, the experience of real divine flight.[32] Milton juxtaposes the mythical figures in a similar way to promise himself the godlike exaltation of poetry.

In the invocation to book 7, the figure shifts to an analogous myth. With half of the poem left to sing, the poet renews his claim to soar (7.3), and implores his heavenly Muse for a safe landing.

> with like safety guided down
> Return me to my native element:
> Lest from this flying steed unreined (as once
> Bellerophon, though from a lower clime)
> Dismounted, on the Aleian field I fall
> Erroneous there to wander and forlorn.
> (PL 7.15–20)

Flying on the winged Pegasean steed of poetry, Milton acknowledges the possible alternative of falling; having soared transgressively high on Pegasus, Bellerophon was thrown to earth and—with obvious resonance for Milton—was blinded.[33] His fate was similar to and already associated in antiquity with the falls of Phaethon and Icarus. Horace explicitly couples Bellerophon and Phaethon in *Odes* 4.11.25–28 as examples of overreachers. But it is Icarus that, as we shall see, the same Horace twice presents as a figure of failed *poetic* flight in the cluster of classical texts that lie behind this passage.

Milton is most directly rewriting the end of Pindar's seventh Isthmian ode, where the Greek lyric poet prescribes a moderate old age for himself: he will sing with his hair entwined with a garland, praying that he avoid the envy of the gods. Pindar invokes the counterexample of Bellerophon who sought to ride Pegasus up to the homes of the gods and of Zeus, and was thrown by his mount. As he asks the Muse to return him back safely to earth after recounting the War in Heaven, the epic poet Milton presents himself as having completed the sublime Pegasean flight that his lyric predecessor declined to make (and he has gone well above the transgressive Bellerophon, too). Milton's gesture is both doubly self-congratulatory and doubly aware of the potential risks he incurs, for even to emulate, not to overgo, Pindar's own sublimity can lead to a fall. So Horace had asserted in the *Odes*.

> Pindarum quisquis studet aemulari,
> Iule, ceratis ope Daedalea
> nititur pinnis vitreo daturus
>   nomina ponto.[34]
>   (*Odes* 4.2.1–4)

[Whoever tries to emulate Pindar, Iulus, attempts to fly on waxen wings of Daedalean workmanship and will give his name to a glassy sea.]

To venture the poetic flight of Pindar, the highflying Dircaean swan— "Dircaeum ... cycnum" (25)—is almost certainly to repeat the fate of Icarus, a failure to keep aloft, and we saw how Satan's fall in Chaos momentarily lowered the poetic register, a failure, too, of achieving a name for oneself as a poet.[35] In *Odes* 2.20 Horace had more confidently proclaimed his poetic immortality when he describes his own transformation into the swan of poetry; he feels downy feathers growing out of his arms and shoulders: "nascunturque leves / per digitos umerosque plumae" (11–12). The poet's fame will carry him, he says, in double form, half man, half bird, through the sky on no common or light plumage—"Non usitata nec tenui ferar / pinna biformis per liquidum ae-thera" (1–2)—and he is unworried lest he repeat the fate of Icarus, whose fame he has now, in any case, surpassed: "iam Daedaleo notior Icaro" (13).

The young Milton had this poem in mind when he wrote to Charles Diodati in September 1637.

> quid cogitem, quaeris? ita me, bonus Deus, immortalitem. Quid agam vero? πτεροφυω et volare meditor: sed tenellis admodum adhuc pennis evehit se noster Pegasus, humile sapiamus. (*Works*, 12:26)

> [Do you ask what I am meditating? by the help of heaven, immortality of fame. But what am I doing? *pterophuo* (I am letting my wings grow) and preparing to fly: but as yet our Pegasus raises himself on very tender pinions; let us be lowly wise.]

The Greek verb, we should note, is the same that Plato used in the *Phaedrus* to denote the growth of the wings of the soul, here transferred to the prepara-tion of the poet for flight, a poet who is also a Bellerophon on a still unfledged Pegasus.[36] His younger self could scarcely get off the ground, but the Milton of *Paradise Lost* has reached and maintained the sublime, and guaranteed his deathless fame. Where Satan, then Adam and Eve, sought to fly, only to fall and be plunged into depths of psychic affliction, Milton is uplifted and returned to earth by the miracle of poetry. The poet and the Son are the only characters of *Paradise Lost* to achieve successful flight.

Still, the poet of book 7 is anxious lest he himself fall, and he goes on to say that he is indeed "fallen on evil days / On evil days though fallen, and evil tongues" (7.25–26), the darkness of his blindness and of the political world of the Restoration, and he raises the specter of one more drowning: the "wild rout" whose "savage clamour drowned / Both harp and voice" of Orpheus (7.36–37). But the Muse returns each night to stop him from falling into despondency. In his last invocation in book 9, the trope of flight persists even as the poet worries that climate and an age too late "damp my intended wing / Depressed, and much they may, if all be mine, / Not hers who brings it nightly to my ear" (9.45–47). We should hear the modern meaning of "depressed," already cur-rent in the seventeenth century, in Milton's formulation: fallenness is a kind of dejection from which one can be rescued by the wings of poetry.[37] Milton's verse wishes to be sacred, and he claims that it could not succeed, or even exist, without divine prompting. But even for the devils left behind in book 2 to build a civilization without hope, song "suspended" hell (2.554), providing relief, however temporary, from their fallen state.[38]

To conclude with this personal application of the mythic figures of flying and falling to Milton and his poetry is not to reduce *Paradise Lost* to a battle against the poet's depression. But, in powerful way, it is that, too. In the world of both physical and spiritual death after the Fall, where it is impossible for the faithful to stand, much less ascend, unless upheld by grace (3.174–80), where, by the end of the poem, Adam and Eve are walking downhill toward the "subjected plain" (12.640), the only flight above the fallenness of things may be the imaginative flight of poetry. The soaring elevation of his verse approximates the Icarus-like Milton to the Phaethon-like heroism of the Son, and poetry offers him its own kind of salvation.

Milton conceives of his Muse as a special form of grace that keeps him and his poem aloft, a guarantor of the high style. Yet this therapy brings him closer in spirit to Lucretius than he might have wished to admit. It is after the Roman poet has presented his darkest doctrine—telling his readers to face the facts about individual extinction and to stop worrying about it—that he turns in the famous proemium to book 4 of *De rerum natura* to offer them the honeyed cup of poetry as a sugarcoating to his medicine. Perhaps the one constant consolation that Lucretius and Milton give us to hold on to against contingency is the epic poem itself, which, in the process of representing and giving form to a condition of falling, seeks in some measure to counteract and contain it. Another way of putting this is that the saving Christian myth depicted in *Paradise Lost* cannot be distinguished from the efficacy of mythopoesis itself. But Virgil's Daedalus, to end where we have started, suggests in stark terms one epic poet's knowledge that art may not be adequate to the task. Daedalus indeed knew how to fly. But as he seeks to sculpt the fall of his son Icarus—to give form to his grief and thus gain some degree of mastery over it—the hand of the artist father makes two attempts, and then itself falls away.

Light, Vision, and the Unity of Book 3

Milton begins book 2 of *Paradise Lost* with the adjective *High*, describing Satan's bad eminence on the royal throne of hell; he ends the book with the verb *hies* (2.1055), as Satan hastens toward God's new creation in his eagerness to take revenge. Something similar happens in book 3, where the invocation to Light ("Hail, holy *Light*") in the first verse is again matched in the book's last word, a verb describing Satan: "on Niphates's top he *lights*" (3.742). Both cases emphasize, through their very grammar, the devil's fall from his former height and brightness—this was Lucifer once upon a time, now reduced, in the derisive terms of book 10, to "false glitter" (10.452)—into motion and instability. The wordplay may seem overly precious, especially given the additional similarity in sound between "high" and "Light."[1]

In book 3, however, the placement of *Light* and *lights* at beginning and end is part of a much larger play on "light" that controls the book's elaborately worked-out structure and the unity of its fiction; the word occurs sixteen times in all. Perhaps nowhere else in *Paradise Lost* does such a semantic pattern count more, for here it shapes, and corresponds to, the questions that book 3 poses about the unity of the cosmos itself. Does the universe hold together in a meaningful coherence? In what way does it reflect, or even depend upon, a divine Creator? The action of the book moves from the colloquy in heaven between the Son and Father, whom the angels address as "Fountain of light, thy self invisible / Amidst the glorious brightness where thou sit'st" (3.375–76)—to the sun, the "great luminary" (3.576), which "Dispenses light" on the stars and earth of God's creation, where Satan pays a visit to the watchman angel Uriel. These likenesses, reinforced by allusion, distinguish and contrast a divine, ultimately inner light with physical sunlight, God with Apollo the pagan sun god, the invisible realm of heaven with the visible world. In doing so, Isabel MacCaffrey points out, they parallel and contrast different acts and kinds of vision.[2] Perhaps above all, the book contrasts the Son's offer to sacrifice himself and bestow eternal life on humanity to the sun that "gently warms" (3.583) and

"Shoots invisible virtue" (3.586) to each inward part of the universe, and that might be supposed to give it physical life.

Milton can thus appear in book 3 to rehearse older Platonic analogies and correspondences, particularly between God and the sun, the latter compared to, and sometimes identified in Hermetic thought with, an animating world-soul. Yet he does so only to suggest that such analogies no longer hold in an age of the New Science and Protestant iconoclasm. In his early treatise, *Of Education* (1644), Milton had written that the human imagination cannot "arrive so cleerly to the knowledge of God and things invisible, as by orderly conning over the visible and inferior creature" (*CPW* 2:368–69). Matters are more complicated in *Paradise Lost*. Raphael speculates in book 5: "What if earth / Be but a shadow of heaven, and things therein / Each to other like, more than on earth is thought?" What if, indeed?[3] Book 3 tests its reader by depicting first an invisible God beside his Son, "the radiant image of his glory" (3.63), and then two possible substitutes for that initial scene, the projected Paradise of Fools and the dazzling light of the sun, both of which the language of the book, in a scheme almost as insistent as its play on "light," describes in terms of "works," to distinguish them from their Creator, God the "great work-master" (3.696).

The distinction had been laid out by Francis Bacon in a passage from *The Advancement of Learning* (1605), which could serve as a virtual blueprint for the fiction and thought of book 3. Bacon describes

> the works of God, which do show the omnipotency and wisdom of the maker, but not his image. And therefore therein the heathen opinion differeth from the sacred truth; for they supposed the world to be the image of God, and man to be an extract or compendious image of the world; but the scriptures never vouchsafe to attribute to the world that honour, as to be the image of God, but only "the work of his hands"; neither do they speak of any other image of God, but man. Wherefore by the contemplation of nature to induce and enforce the acknowledgment of God, and to demonstrate his power, providence, and goodness, is an excellent argument, and hath been excellently handled by divers. But on the other side, out of the contemplation of nature, or ground of human knowledges, to induce any verity or persuasion concerning the points of faith, is in my judgement not safe: "Da fidei quae fidei sunt."[4] (2.6.1)

It is one thing to declare God's glory in his works; it is another—and a mistake—to read back from them to divine mysteries. Bacon goes on in the same passage to draw a similar moral about Homer's golden chain in *Iliad* 9.18–27, "'That men and gods were not able to draw Jupiter down to the earth; but contrariwise Jupiter was able to draw them up to heaven.' So as we ought not attempt to draw down or to submit the mysteries of God to our reason; but contrariwise to raise and advance our reason to the divine truth."[5] Milton transfers this golden chain into the fiction of *Paradise Lost* at the very end of book 2—the golden chain of being that Satan sees suspending the created universe, "this pendent world," from heaven (2.1051–53), and it is up and down this chain that the ensuing fiction of book 3 will run. Bacon concludes by warning against the commixture of religion and science (he terms the latter "philosophy"): it makes for "an heretical religion, and imaginary and fabulous philosophy."[6] Bacon is more concerned with the latter: he wants to set apart natural science as an independent realm of study; Milton worries about the former, a religion brought down to earth. God is to be known not through his works, but through his soon-to-be-human image and chosen mediation, the Son.

Paradise Lost separates the higher invisibilia—"things invisible to mortal sight" (3.55) in heaven—from "nature's works" (3.49), the lower, visible things of the Creation later narrated in book 7. At the same time, it enjoins us to believe that all depend on the same Creator, and in book 5 Raphael's "one first matter all" speech (5.472–505) will further expound Milton's monism: that all things, heavenly *and* earthly, partake of the same material being and substance (5.472).[7] Book 3 distinguishes two modes of error. The future denizens of the lightless Paradise of Fools, encountered between the heavenly light of the first half of the book and the light of the sun in the second, confuse the realms and project backward the visible upon the invisible; they make the Creator in the image of his and their *works*. Conversely, the equally foolish alchemist philosophers in verses 598–605 disjoin the created universe from a now dispensable Creator-God, and seek an alternative power source in the sun, the new center of a Copernican cosmos. The first course leads to idolatry, the second to godless materialism, even to a revival of paganism identified with solar worship. The logic of book 3 thus depends on the repeated drawing of likenesses that threaten to collapse into false identity or to split apart altogether.

Milton stakes out in book 3 a middle ground for poetry to occupy in the era of the New Science. Eve's innocent little question, which follows her love song to Adam in book 4—"But wherefore all night long shine these, for whom / This glorious sight, when sleep hath shut all eyes?" (4.657–58)—already suggests the challenge to traditional religious thought of a New Astronomy that displaced the earth and men and women from its center. Why are there stars in the sky? Eve asks. *Paradise Lost* has a series of answers for her: Adam essays—or, as a typical husband, bluffs—a response about stellar influences perfected by the sun (4.659–73), and he reminds Eve that they share the universe with spiritual creatures up all night around them (4.674–88). Adam then turns to Raphael at the opening of book 8 and asks the same question (8.15–38)—at which point Eve, ironically enough, leaves the two of them and does not stay around to hear the angel's abstruse exposition, which makes many of the same points. For in the meantime Satan has provided an answer of his own in the dream that he pours into Eve's ear and that she recounts in book 5: "heaven wakes with all his eyes / Whom to behold but thee, nature's desire / In whose sight all things joy" (5.44–45), flattery he will repeat when he seduces Eve to fall: "Thee all things living gaze on" (9.539). This is a more flattering version of Raphael's telling Adam that the bright luminaries of heaven are "Officious" not to the earth itself, "but to thee earth's habitant" (8.99), even as the universe is much bigger and complex: man "dwells not in his own; / An edifice too large for him to fill" (8.103–4). Raphael assures Adam that at least their part of the universe *is* made for humanity; at the same time the angel leaves open the possibility of other worlds within the universe with their own inhabitants equally served by their stars (8.153–58; 169–70). In his appeal to her vanity, Satan seems to be tempting Eve with the comforts of the old Ptolemaic system—or to put it another way, Milton discloses the element of human self-love, what Bacon refers to as idol-making and equates with theater and poetry, that went into the making of the geocentric model that Copernicus and Galileo had exploded. Like Raphael, Milton seeks to reassure his audience that they remain a focus of God's creation even if they may not reside at its spatial center; but he will not flatter them. Book 3 structures itself around tropes and analogies based on an older cosmology that, simultaneously and paradoxically, its poetry skeptically hollows out and labels as mental idols, fit for the Paradise of Fools placed near the book's center. Endowed with a new form of self-consciousness, Puritan and scientific, this poetry nonetheless preserves the habit of thought that animated those discarded images and that is constitutive of poetry itself: the making of comparisons and the building of structures of words and meaning. At a moment of cosmological uncertainty, poetry offers both an instrument of criticism vis-à-vis its own tradition and, in its own formal achievement, an idea or intuition of order. At issue in the carefully worked-out verbal patterns of book 3 are the bookishness and readability of God's creation; at stake in its semantic unity is the unity of Milton's universe itself.

Structure and Design

An initial cluster of occurrences of the "light" in lines 1, 3, and 4 is answered by a second cluster that corresponds shortly before the book's end (lines 713, 723, 724, and 730), and these, too, are arranged symmetrically to form a kind of frame. These correspondences are thematic as well as formal: the narrator invokes the divine fiat that brought forth light at the Creation "Before the sun" (3.1–11), while Uriel—whose name means "Light of God"—retells the creation of light and then of the heavenly luminaries (3.712–32). The larger book, moreover, divides into two parts, in the first the invocation to Light and the heavenly council that sees the Son volunteer to die for humanity (1–417), in the second the continuing voyage of Satan past the lightless site of the future Paradise of Fools to the sun, where he asks Uriel to direct him toward earth, and where his disguising himself as a cherub to fool the sharpsighted archangel (417–742) evokes Saint Paul's proverbial warning against false apostles, "And no marvel, for Satan himself is transformed into an angel of light" (2 Cor. 11:14).[8]

The structure of book 3 replicates the division of the preceding book 2, which now seems to have been a parody, in advance, of *it*: a council in hell that saw Satan volunteer for his mission to earth; his voyage toward God's new creation and stopping to ask directions from Chaos. In both books, Satan is attracted on his journey to possible substitutes for God: noise and hearing lead him to Chaos, the noncreative "spirit of the nethermost abyss" (2.956); light and vision draw him to the sun.

Each part of book 3 concludes as it begins. The first section in heaven begins with the poet's hymnic invocation of Light—"Hail, holy Light" and ends with the angels' hymn of praise to the Son (whom that initial "Light" may possibly have designated)—"Hail, Son of God" (3.412).[9] The second satanic section begins when the flying devil lands on the dark outside of the universe and "alighted walks" (3.422)—the Latinate pun suggests that he is deprived of light. In simile Satan is compared to a vulture who

> *lights* on the barren plains
> Of Sericana, where Chineses drive
> With sails and wind their cany wagons *light*. (3.437–39)

This second section ends when Satan "lights" in the book's final verse on Mount Niphates.

In the council in heaven an unseen God casts a light so dazzling that it can be viewed only as the outskirts of the clouds that sometimes cover it or as it is "impressed" (3.388) on the Son—"In whose conspicuous countenance, without cloud / Made visible, the almighty Father shines" (3.385–86; cf. 2 Cor. 4:6). The sequel moves to a substitute luminary, the visible sun, and then to the moon, which, Uriel tells Satan, reflects the sun and uses "borrowed light" to "enlighten the earth" (3.730–31). In between, the Paradise of Fools, lying "under the frown of Night / Starless exposed" (3.424–25), will later house denizens who will be the sport of winds like the light wagons of the Chinese. Milton's ecclesiastical satire in this passage picks up motifs from both the preceding vision of heavenly light and the later episode of the sun, and ironically mediates between the two.

To provide further symmetry between the two halves of book 3, Milton invokes the conventional pun in English religious writing between *Son* and *sun* and the interpretative tradition that identified the "Sun of righteousness" of Malachi 4:2 as Christ who, the gloss to the Geneva Bible explains, "with his wings or beames of his grace shulde lighten and comfort his Church."[10] The hinge between these two halves comes at the conclusion of the angels' hymn to the Son:

> Hail, Son of God, saviour of men, thy name
> Shall be the copious matter of my song
> Henceforth, and never shall my harp thy praise

Forget, nor from thy Father's praise disjoin.
> (3.412–15)

The verses repeat conventional formulas of the classical hymn, particularly the promises of a personified "Homer" in the *Homeric Hymn to Apollo*, whose first section, dedicated to the Apollo of Delos, begins, "I will remember and not be unmindful of Apollo who shoots from afar,"[11] and ends, "And I will never cease to praise far shooting Apollo, god of the silver bow, whom rich-haired Leto bare" (177–78).[12] Callimachus makes similar pledges in his *Hymn to Apollo*, imitating the Homeric prototype:

> for Apollo has power, for that he sits on the right hand of Zeus. Nor will the choir sing of Phoebus for one day only. He is a copious theme of song [εὔυμνος]; who would not sing of Phoebus? (29–31)[13]

By later antiquity Phoebus ("shining") Apollo was identified with Helios and had become the sun god. The angels of *Paradise Lost* praise the Son, whom both the Bible and Milton "seat at God's right hand" (Mark 16:19)—"on his right / The radiant image of his glory sat, / His only Son" (3.62–64; see also 6.892, 12.457)—in the language that had described the pagan solar deity, even as the division of the book insists on the difference between divine light and the created sun, between a God outside of nature, and a pagan god abstracted out of nature.

Yet who plays Apollo in book 3? Milton's double allusion to the myth of Phaethon, discussed in chapter 3, similarly divides the book into its two mirroring parts. The Father praises and further promotes his Son in the heavenly council—"By merit more than birthright Son of God" (3.309)—and recalls Apollo's reassurance to his son (Ovid, *Metamorphoses* 2.42–43). For the Son to be cast as Phaethon to God's Apollo is something like the later analogy implicit in Uriel's account of the Creation, which makes the Son like the moon to God's sun, the true "Fountain of light" (3.375).[14] Book 3 reinforces this analogy when it initially describes the "almighty Father" about whom "the sanctities of heaven / Stood thick as stars" (3.60–61) and subsequently literalizes the simile in its first description of the sun, "the great luminary / Aloof the vulgar constellations thick" (3.576–77). In the uncertainty about who plays the sun, Father or Son—a revision of traditional Christ-centered typology—there is more of a hint of Milton's Arianism, his view of the created, subordinate nature of the Son.

The same Ovidian episode of Phaethon's visit to Apollo the sun god is recalled in the second half of book 3 when Satan, in his disguise as stripling cherub, pays a visit to the sun and to its presiding angel, Uriel, wearing his crown "Of beaming sunny rays" (3.625). The doubling of the Phaethon story, repeated as we have seen in the War in Heaven in book 6, here reinforces the symmetry between the two halves of book 3 and its structuring contrast between the holy, divine light of God invoked in the first and the light of the physical sun in the second. It is to the latter, what would become the object of pagan worship in the form of Apollo, that Satan is symptomatically attracted. For if the first half of book 3 argues for the internalization of spiritual light, the second portrays light as one of Bacon's created "works," from which fools may make their paradise.

Universal Blank

The inspiration sought by the poet in the invocation to Light in book 3 is pointedly nonsolar and non-Apollonian. In its asking to see the invisible, in identifying poetic inspiration with inner light, the invocation already spells out the separation of God's heaven from his earthly creation, divine illumination from sunlight. It argues that the eye of faith compensates the poet for his physical blindness: faith analogous to and based on the example of the Son's faith, recounted in the ensuing heavenly dialogue, in his victory over the gloomy power of death. The book ties the invocation at all points to its subsequent fiction.

The nightly visitations of the Muse besought by the poet are compared to, but distinct from, the seasonal and daily movement of the sun:

> Thus with the year
> Seasons return, but not to me returns
> Day, or the sweet approach of even or morn,
> Or sight of vernal bloom, or summer's rose,
> Or flocks or herds, or human face divine.
> *(3.40–44)*

So Milton had described his blindess in his sonnet to Cyriack Skinner:

> Nor to their idle orbs doth sight appear
> Of sun or moon or star throughout the year,
> Or man or woman.
> *(4–6)*

The poet of the book 3 invocation not only refers, with mounting pathos, to the affliction of his blindness, but also, at the moment when he is about to depict the eternal, invisible realm of God and his light, he distinguishes his inspiration from the mediation of the temporal, physical world and finally of the human body, made in God's image—mediation that Milton's thought assimilates with a more traditional appeal for inspiration from Phoebus Apollo as the leader of the Muses, the sun as the source of seasonal, springtime growth ("vernal bloom"), as well as of poetic creativity.[15]

In fact, the invocation to book 3 rewrites—by pointedly rejecting—Milton's own earlier version of such a scene of solar inspiration and the coming of spring, his fifth Latin elegy, *Elegia Quinta: In adventum veris*, composed long before in 1629.

Fallor? an et nobis redeunt carmina vires,
    Ingeniumque mihi munere veris adest?
Munere veris adest, iterumque vigescit ab illo
    (Quis putet) atque aliquod iam sibi poscit opus.
Castalis ante oculos, bifidumque cacumen oberrat
    Et mihi Pyrenen somnia nocte ferunt.
Concitaque arcano fervent mihi pectora motu,
    Et furor, et sonitus me sacer intus agit.
Delius ipse venit, video Peneide lauro
    Implicitos crines, Delius ipse venit.
Iam mihi mens liquidi raptatur in ardua coeli,
    Perque vagas nubes corpore liber eo.
Perque umbras, perque antra feror penetralia vatum,
    Et mihi fana patent interiora Deum.
Intuitur animus toto quid agatur Olympo,
    Nec fugiunt oculos Tartara caeca meos.
Quid tam grande sonat distento spiritus ore?
    Quid parit haec rabies, quic sacer iste furor?
Ver mihi, quod dedit ingenium, cantabitur illo;
    Profuerint isto reddita dona modo.
      (Elegy V 5–24)

[Am I deluded? or are my powers of song returning as well? Is inspiration at hand by the gift of spring? It is at hand by the gift of spring, and again (who would think it?) it already seeks some work from me. The Castalian spring and the forked peak of Parnassus float before my eyes, and my nighttime dreams bring Pirene to me. My breast is stirred and burns with a mysterious impulse, and inner frenzy and sacred sound goad me on. Delian Apollo himself comes—I see his locks entwined with Penean laurel—Delian Apollo himself comes. Now my mind is rapt into the heights of the liquid heavens, and I go, freed from my body, through the wandering clouds. Through the shadows and caves I am borne, through the secret sanctuaries of the poets and the innermost temples of the Gods. My spirit looks on what is taking place all over Olympus, nor does the darkness of Tartarus escape my eyes. What does my spirit sing so mightily with full throat? To what does this madness, this sacred furor give birth? Spring, which gives me inspiration, will be the subject of the song; in this way her gifts will be repaid to her profit.]

The rebirth brought by the springtime sun—Apollo is invoked by the name of *his* birthplace, Delos—starts a new round of poetic activity. Like the narrator of book 3, the sunstruck poet of *Elegy V* appears ready for an initiation into the divine: all the precincts of the pagan heaven on Olympus come into view.[16] But this heavenly vision is never realized and instead—in a kind of short-circuit or self-referential logic—the poet settles on the subject of springtime creation itself, what begins as a cosmic procreation between the sun and the personified earth (Tellus), who sings a love song to Phoebus and offers him all of the treasures that their union will produce (75–78), then extends to lovemaking among humans and among the gods, who by its end have become assimilated with fauns, satyrs, and nymphs, the deities of nature. The inspiration of the sun god Apollo never raises the poet above the world of a sexualized, pagan nature of which it reveals itself to be a part.

The young poet Milton had already realized that such inspiration would not do for the higher, Christian poetry to which he aspired. He anticipated the invocation to book 3 when, later in the same year of 1629 he composed in English his first great sacred poem, *On the Morning of Christ's Nativity*: he looked back and disavowed the Apollonian terms of his elegy. In its opening stanzas, Nature, awestruck by the birth of Jesus, knows that in wintry December, it is "no season then for her / To wanton with the sun her lusty paramour" (35–36); later in the poem the sun itself "saw a greater sun appear" (83), and hides his own light, and, still later, Apollo will be the first of a series of pagan gods expelled from their shrines (176), nearly all of whom were ancient sun gods: Milton structured the ode straightforwardly on the typology of Christ as the Sun of righteousness.[17] Nature hides her guilty front and shame with "innocent snow" (39), as if to make herself pristine again, clearing the poem's visual field in preparation for "the globe of circular light" (110) of angels that will subsequently appear in place of the absent sun. The snow cover or blank page is an earlier version of the "universal blank" that the poet of book 3 suffers from his blindness and that cuts him off from the returning seasons. This blank is similarly a precondition for divine illumination.[18]

> or human face divine;
> But cloud in stead, and ever-during dark
> Surrounds me, from the cheerful ways of men
> Cut off, and for the book of knowledge fair
> Presented with a universal blank
> Of nature's works to me expunged and razed,
> And wisdom at one entrance quite shut out.
> So much the rather thou celestial Light
> Shine inward, and the mind through all her powers
> Irradiate, there plant eyes, all mist from thence
> Purge and disperse, that I may see and tell
> Of things invisible to mortal sight.
> (3.44–55)

The separation of the poet's inspiration in the invocation to book 3 from "nature's works" and especially from the creative agency and temporal movement and cycles of the sun thus retells an old Miltonic story. It rejects Apollo once again. If the life of Milton by his nephew Edward Phillips is to be trusted, more-over, Milton's actual poetic creativity while writing *Paradise Lost* ran directly counter to the natural, springtime generation he had first celebrated in *Elegy V*: "his vein never happily flowed but from the autumnal equinoctial to the vernal, and that whatever he attempted [otherwise] was never to his satisfac-tion, though he courted his fancy never so much, so that in all the years he was about this poem, he may be said to have spent but half his time therein."[19] The year might very well return with the spring, but Milton would not have profited from it even without his loss of sight, for he was bent on a different kind of poetry whose dictates did not come from the regenerative rhythms of nature.

Still, it was one thing for the young poet to have willed an imaginative blank-ness and the rejection of Apollo in order to be initiated into timeless divine mysteries; it was another for the Milton of *Paradise Lost* to have these imposed upon him by blindness. In compensation, the poet would tell of "things in-visible to mortal sight." This is not only an appeal for poetic power, with the uncertainty left open whether he will prove a new blind Homer or rather a failed, blind Thamyris (3.35). Nor is it simply occasioned by the present task of depicting God in his heaven, although Milton, distinguishing between God's visible and invisible creations, does, in fact, specify in chapter 7 of book 1 of *On Christian Doctrine* that "THINGS INVISIBLE, at least to us, are the high-est heaven, the throne and dwelling place of God, and the heavenly beings or angels" (*CPW* 6:311).[20] The capacity to see "things invisible to mortal sight" is the basis of Christian faith itself.

Paul declares in Hebrews 11:1, "Now faith is the substance of things hoped for, the evidence of things not seen." Paul elaborates, in the context of bearing earthly afflictions, such as Milton's blindness, in 2 Corinthians 4:18, "While we look not at the things which are seen, but at the things which are not seen: for the things which are seen are temporal, but the things which are not seen are eternal," and 5:7, "For we walk by faith, not by sight." Milton aligns these two verses in his concluding chapter 20 on faith in the same book of *On Chris-tian Doctrine* (*CPW* 6:473). His contemporary Richard Baxter, the moderate Calvinist theologian with whom Milton would have disagreed on many tenets, nonetheless brings the poetic subject of book 3 together with larger, common-place doctrine in a passage from *The Life of Faith* (1670): "Remember therefore that God and Heaven, the unseen things, are the final object of true Faith; and that final object is the noblest; and that the principal use of Faith is to carry up the whole heart and life from things visible and temporal, to things invisible and eternal."[21] Milton's invocation to Light is an explicit prayer for—as well as an act of—faith.

The poet intimates at the same time that his blindness is an actual help to this faith, that because the distraction of "nature's works" is wiped clean—"expunged and razed" (3.49)—from a mind that is now a "universal blank" page

(3.48) or tabula rasa, he can more readily exercise his faith in the vision of invisible things. His blindness, that is, seems to have caused him to revise the idea suggested in *Of Education* that knowledge can move smoothly from the visible to the invisible. The ensuing fiction bears out the terms of the invocation, for the God Milton depicts is himself invisible, hidden either in his own light or behind the "cloud / Drawn round about thee like a radiant shrine" (3.378–79) that the angels describe in their hymn; the dazzled seraphim must "with both wings veil their eyes" (3.382).[22] This glory cloud bears an inverse relationship to the "cloud ... and ever during dark" that surround the blind poet: blindness may be the best condition from which to describe a blinding God. Milton repeats here the arguments of his *Second Defense of the English People* (1654), in which he had also defended himself against the charges made by his royalist enemies that his blindness was divine retribution for his part in the regicide. He had invoked the example of the prophet Phineus, also recalled in the invocation to book 3 (3.35), whose blindness was "recompensed with far more potent gifts" (*CPW* 4:584) and should not be considered punishment for any crime. He goes on to claim that "we blind men are not the least of God's concerns, for the less able we are to perceive anything other than himself, the more mercifully and graciously does he deign to look on us," and that "divine favor not infrequently is wont to lighten these shadows again, once made, by an inner and far more enduring light" (*CPW* 4:590). His physical blindness initiates him to the vision of God and the light of faith, and is all the more preferable to the moral blindness that so afflicts his royalist adversaries, "that you may see nothing whole or real" (*CPW* 4:589).

This argument is subsequently taken up in book 3 by Milton's God, who authoritatively redefines the terms of light and blindness as he spells out the terms of his grace.

And I will place within them as a guide
My umpire conscience, whom if they will hear,
Light after *light* well used they shall attain,
And to the end persisting, safe arrive.
This my long sufferance and my day of grace
They who neglect and scorn, shall never taste;
But hard be hardened more, blind be blinded more,
That they may stumble on, and deeper fall;
And none but such from mercy I exclude.
     (3.194–202)

The first part of the passage recasts light as the inner light within the human individual, here described as a kind of spiritual progress, while the second paraphrases Isaiah 6:9–10 to describe the blindness of those who refuse the gift of grace, this too progressive, a spiraling downward into greater blindness and hardening of their hearts: the process the poem depicts in the career of Satan and the devils.[23] This inner light is characteristic of the general internalization of tropes in *Paradise Lost*, which will end by compensating the loss of Eden with the "paradise within thee, happier far" (12.587). Just as the invocation to book 1 tells us that God's Spirit prefers, "Before all temples, the upright heart and pure" (1.18), before the book goes on to criticize temples through its catalog of devils and the building of Pandaemonium, so here the light of the invocation to book 3 is resituated in the individual believer. It is also the light of poetic inspiration, and the poem that we read, especially the scenes in heaven, presents itself both as an act of ordinary faith and as the pledge of extraordinary calling: the two cannot be separated.

The faith that the blind poet asserts in things unseen in the invocation is doubled *inside* the fiction by the Son's faith in the most unseen of all things in which the Christian believes. His heroic volunteering to die to save humanity is followed by a confident declaration.

> on me let Death wreak all his rage;
> Under his gloomy power I shall not long
> Lie vanquished; thou hast given me to possess
> Life in my self for ever, by thee I live,
> Though now to Death I yield, and am his due
> All that of me can die; yet that debt paid,
> Thou wilt not leave me in the loathsome grave
> His prey, nor suffer my unspotted soul
> For ever with corruption there to dwell;
> But I shall rise victorious, and subdue
> My vanquisher, spoiled of his vaunted spoil;
>   *(3.241–51)*

There is no more moving passage in *Paradise Lost* than this one, whose tone Milton so superbly controls. The Son is confident, and it turns out he has reason to be. He knows that he has already twice triumphed in glory, after the War in Heaven and after the Creation—as he will triumph again when these events that correspond typologically to the Son's Passion are repeated at the apocalyptic end of history. But the epic's readers do not yet know about these chronologically earlier events that Raphael will later recount to Adam and Eve in books 6 and 7; the angels' ensuing hymn gives only a summary version (3.390–98). By deferring knowledge of these previous glorifications, Milton invites the reader of book 3 to hear a quiet question and appeal lurking beneath the Son's confidence: surely God will not leave him in the loathsome grave, will he? No creature, not even the Son, can *know* that he or she will rise from death and the corruption of the body: all visible evidence points to the contrary.[24] Part of the pathos lies in the suggestion that death, far from the occasion for victorious triumph, may be the ultimate defeat—"lie vanquished," "I yield," "his prey"—imagined by a poet who has suffered political defeat and lies as well under the "gloomy power" of his own blindness. The confident Son shares his faith directly with the Father, but it is still the same act of faith in which every Christian partakes against doubt before the physical fact of death. If there is no resurrection, Saint Paul admits, "then is our preaching vain, and your faith is also vain" (1 Cor. 15:14).

Book 3 aligns these two assertions of faith, the claim of the blind poet to inner light, the claim of the Son to escape the loathsome grave. The complaint of the despairing, blind Samson that climaxes his opening speech in *Samson Agonistes* (*SA*) allows us to see how closely they may be related.

> As in the land of darkness yet in light,
> To live a life half dead, a living death,
> And buried; but O yet more miserable!
> Myself my sepulchre, a moving grave,
> Buried, yet not exempt
> By privilege of death and burial
> From worst of other evils, pains and wrongs,
> But made hereby obnoxious more
> To all the miseries of life,
> Life in captivity
> Among inhuman foes.
> (*SA* 99–109)

The passage has a clear autobiographical cast, a portrait of John Milton at the Restoration suffering the double captivity of blindness and of thralldom to his political enemies; a second version in the invocation to book 7 of *Paradise Lost* describes the poet "On evil days though fallen, and evil tongues; / In darkness, and with dangers compassed round" (7.26–27). It suggests a very different mood from Milton's defiant response to his royalist foes in the *Second Defense*, where he wears his blindness as a badge of honor and special, divine election. Here blindness feels as if one were already buried alive in the "loathsome grave," the fate that the despairing Adam contemplates in book 10: "then in the grave, / Or in some other dismal place who knows / But I shall die a living death?" (10.786–88).[25] Samson may free himself from this despondency at the end of the tragedy, if we are to believe the pronouncement of the Chorus, when, "With inward eyes illuminated" (*SA* 1689), he rouses himself to the heroic action of which no one thought him still capable: what corresponds in Milton's biography to the heroic action of writing *Paradise Lost* itself. Book 3 aligns the invisible light of faith with faith in the central Christian mystery: the final, still invisible, deliverance from death. Milton's epic, on more than one occasion, suggests that the first is the token of, even a present substitute for, the second—a paradise within—and already begins that deliverance in life itself. In Milton's own case, this deliverance is felt in the inward illumination that his blind narrator invokes at the book's opening and that enables his sacred song.

Vision

There is a self-evident sense in which the irradiation of divine light that would allow the poet to see "things invisible to mortal sight" anticipates as a foretaste or stand-in for the triumph over death that the Son promises to achieve and make possible for humanity: these are the same things that the poet, too, will see on rising from the loathsome grave, and which the Son reassures himself he, too, will look upon after death when he "Shall enter heaven long absent, and return, / Father, to see thy face, wherein no cloud / Of anger shall remain" (3.261–63). Paul speaks of eschatological knowledge in terms of seeing God "face to face" (1 Cor. 13:12), and here the removal of the cloud appears to promise not only the appeasement of God's wrath but a new level of beatific vision, God seen without his interposing cloud, what would correspond, too, to a definitive purging of the mist and cloud of the poet's blindness, permitting him once again to see a face divine.

The Son's sight of the Father is one in a series of parallel or contrasting acts of seeing in book 3, generated out of the poet's initial declaration of blindness and prayer for special inner light. These constitute another carefully constructed pattern of meaning in the book. Light, divine or physical, is the condition of sight. No sooner has the poet asked for the vision of "things invisible to mortal sight" (3.55) in place of "nature's works" (3.49) than that vision portrays a God whose initial act is to bend "down his eye, / His own works and their works at once to view" (3.58–59).[26] The inversion of perspective—God has nowhere to look but down and all that he sees is his creation—nicely plots out in advance the book's ensuing division between its depiction of an invisible God and heaven and the visible universe, God's "works" (as Bacon distinguishes them from God's image), works that produce their own works and secondary effects, whether the generative warmth of the sun or the works of angels, men, and women. The book repeatedly contrasts humans, including the Son who will become human, looking up toward the higher heaven with God and the angels, including Satan, looking down on God's lower works, works that, Uriel says, "glorify / The great work-master" (3.695–96). In the same verses in which the Son predicts his seeing the unclouded face of God after his conquest of death and his restoration of those "works" (3.277), he also foretells the repetition of God's initial bending downward of his eye in a reciprocal gesture of paternal approval—"Thou at the sight / Pleased, out of heaven shalt look down and smile" (3.256–57). As the fiction of book 3 moves with Satan away from heaven to the visible creation lit by the sun, the upshot of this extended conceit will be, however, to suggest the asymmetry of these downward and upward modes of sight: it opposes God's perfect vision of his works to the difficulty that human beings experience, in return, in seeing an invisible God through and beyond those works.

The downward glances of God are subject to diabolic parody when Satan subsequently gets *his* first look at God's new creation. Arriving at the trapdoor that opens beneath the stairs of heaven through which the eyes of God would later regard the Promised Land of Palestine (3.534), Satan

> Looks down with wonder at the sudden view
> Of all this world at once. As when a scout
> Through dark and desert ways with peril gone
> All night; at last by break of cheerful dawn
> Obtains the brow of some high-climbing hill,
> Which to his eye discovers unaware
> The goodly prospect of some foreign land
> First-seen, or some renowned metropolis
> With glistering spires and pinnacles adorned,
> Which now the rising sun gilds with all his beams.
> Such wonder seized, though after heaven seen,
> The spirit malign, but much more envy seized,
> At sight of all this world beheld so fair.
>   (3.542–54)

Satan's survey is doubly parodic, and he does more than play God. The simile that expands and enriches the implications of this moment continues a pattern that has made Satan's journey from the Egypt that is hell across the "darksome desert" (2.973) of Chaos to the newly created universe a version of the Exodus and Satan himself a Moses figure; the simile evokes the Israelites' desert wandering ("dark and desert ways") and now identifies Satan with the scouts Caleb and Joshua, sent out by Moses in Numbers 13 to reconnoiter the Promised Land, the land that they will subsequently conquer. Satan's career thus perversely charts the central biblical story that establishes the typology for the salvation that the Son has earlier offered to humanity. The simile, too, reminds us of the spy-mission nature of the voyage of Satan who, when he finally reaches Eden in book 4, declares "with narrow search I must walk round / This garden, and no corner leave unspied" (4.528–29).[27] This is a particularly instrumental mode of seeing, a prelude to conquest and ultimate destruction, and it triggers envy, Satan's typical, sinful reaction to the sight of God's works, both here and subsequently in the poem: this envy is the subject of chapter 5. It is the opposite of the benevolent glance of God who seeks, through the sacrifice of the Son, to preserve his creation: "thou know'st," he responds to the Son's offer, "how dear, / To me are all my works, nor man the least" (3.276–77).

The correspondences do not end here. The dawn vision of the city gilded by the sun in the simile looks both backward and forward in the book. Satan has just been attracted from the darkness of the outer side of the firmament by "a gleam / of dawning light" (3.499–500), which turns out to be the stairs to the outside of the wall of heaven and "The *work* as of a kingly palace gate" (3.505), while he will now enter into the realm of light and visibility provided by the sun, which will similarly allure his eye and determine his course (3.572–73). The Janus-like simile suggests an equivalence between heaven and the created universe as God's works—both Promised Lands—and the latter arouses wonder in a Satan who has known but is now excluded from the former, even as it repeats the book's separation of divine from earthly light. Satan's downward glance toward earth from the stairs of heaven, moreover, contrasts with Jacob's upward dream vision of those stairs (Gen. 28:12) described shortly before: "The stairs were such as whereon Jacob *saw* / Angels ascending and descending" (3.510–11)—the movement of the angels mirroring the two-way, up-and-down modes of vision depicted in book 3. The acts of seeing and knowledge are *not* comparable and reciprocal, however, for Jacob does not see with his own eyes but through the special revelation and divine accommodation of the dream.

The blind poet points to the scriptural passage that authorizes not only his fiction here of the outside of heaven but of the extraordinary vision that he invokes at the book's beginning, a vision that would overgo Jacob's by peering still more intimately inside of heaven's walls and into "things invisible to mortal sight": what had seemed to be promised to the Apollonian Milton of *Elegy V*, and has now been granted to his sacred alter ego in *Paradise Lost*.

The poet's and Jacob's glimpses into the invisible heavens are paralleled by a still third example of mortal visionary experience, the identification of the angel Uriel as "The same whom John *saw* also in the sun" (3.623; cf. Rev. 19:17). Uriel himself reverses the trajectory of vision, for he is one of the seven archangels who are God's "eyes / That run through all the heavens, or down to the earth" (3.650–51), and it is Uriel who was an eyewitness at the Creation from its very beginning: "I *saw* when at his word the formless mass, / This world's material mould, came to a heap" (3.708–9), those "wondrous works," which Satan, in his disguise as a stripling cherub and sightseeing tourist or pilgrim, professes an "Unspeakable desire to *see*, and know" (3.662–63). Uriel, who saw the creation of the sun itself, in effect, takes over the sun's position as eye of the universe, as the sun was called in the Orphic hymns and as Adam and Eve will address it in their morning prayer in book 5: "Thou sun, of this great world both eye and soul" (5.171).[28]

Uriel, as his name declares, is the true "angel of light" in the book, whereas we are meant to feel the pathos as well as the irony of the fallen Satan, the erstwhile Lucifer, transforming himself into an angel of light once again, this time in the disguise of a cherub—a member of the angelic order that was itself associated by Pseudo-Dionysius the Areopagite in his vastly influential *Celestial Hierarchy* (1.1, 205c), with "the power to know and to see God, to receive the greatest gifts of his light, to contemplate the divine splendor in primordial power."[29] Satan attempts to recover a youthful, more innocent-seeming, as well as more diminutive and socially reduced, version of his former self—"the shape of a meaner angel," says the Argument to book 3. This transformation anticipates the wistful desire that Satan expresses in his immediately ensuing soliloquy in book 4: had God's "powerful destiny ordained / Me some inferior angel, I had stood / Then happy" (4.58–60). Satan utters these words, we want to remember, *while he is disguised as just such an inferior angel.* When that mask momentarily drops while he rejects the course of true remorse and submission to God and Uriel can now see him "disfigured" (4.127), the loss of face physically enacts Satan's inner failure to humble and spiritually regenerate himself.

Yet, "sharpest sighted spirit of all in heaven" (3.691) as he may be, Uriel cannot initially see through Satan's dissembling.

> For neither man nor angel can discern
> Hypocrisy, the only evil that walks
> Invisible, except to God alone.
> *(3.682–84)*

In the terms that book 3 has set out from its invocation, hypocrisy also turns out to be one of the "things invisible to mortal sight."[30]

The Sun

In one further parallel and contrast of acts of seeing, book 3 juxtaposes John's apocalyptic vision of the angel in the sun with a very different way of looking at the sun mentioned a few verses earlier. On his arrival on the sun, Satan is likened to "a spot like which perhaps / Astronomer in the sun's lucent orb / Through his glazed optic tube yet never *saw*" (3.588–90). Unlike the author of Revelation, Galileo's telescope does not see any angel in the sun, but only the spots on or just above its surface. The news of moving and transient sunspots dismayed conservative seventeenth-century thinkers, for they attested, against Aristotle's idea of the sun as an incorruptible and flawless sphere, to the temporal "corruption" and "generation" of matter in the heavens—Galileo preferred the less-loaded term "mutation." Galileo described the sunspots as "produced and dissolved" on the sun "in a manner not unlike that of clouds and vapours on earth."[31] Until this recent discovery, these spots had been invisible to mortal sight, and the astronomer, who uses the telescope to get a closer look at the light of the sun, is a foil not only to John but to the poet himself, who begins the book by asking to see the invisible heavens.

Sunlight is another matter. For the Sun *is* created matter for Milton, even if it is matter of the lightest—in both senses of the word—kind. Even as he cites Galileo, Milton still works within the terms of Aristotelian science and describes the sun and other heavenly bodies as made up of Aristotle's ether, the fifth element or quintessence that is without weight: they flew upward at the

Creation, Uriel tells Satan, while the four other weighty, "cumbrous" elements each found their place in the new universe.

> Swift to their several quarters hasted then
> The cumbrous elements, earth, flood, air, fire
> And this ethereal quintessence of heaven
> Flew upward, spirited with various forms,
> That rolled orbicular, and turned to stars
> Numberless, as thou seest.
>   *(3.714–19)*

Light is "light," and defies gravity. Nonetheless, the visible sun is the external, temporal counterpart to the invisible divine light sought by the inner eye of faith; sunlight gives the carnal imagination something to work upon and by which to confuse creation with Creator.[32]

This imagination, in fact, produces its own carnal version of faith's quest for things unseen: the reduction of this fiery quintessence, the likeness of divine light, to the still lower—in fact, lowest—earthly element that is *its* likeness.

> The place he found beyond expression bright,
> Compared with aught on earth, metal or stone;
> Not all parts like, but all alike informed
> With radiant light, as glowing iron with fire;
> If metal, part seemed gold, part silver clear;
> If stone, carbuncle most or chrysolite,
> Ruby or topaz, to the twelve that shone
> In Aaron's breastplate, and a stone besides
> Imagined rather oft than elsewhere seen,
> That stone, or like to that which here below
> Philosophers in vain so long have sought,
> In vain, though by their powerful art they bind
> Volatile Hermes, and call up unbound
> In various shapes old Proteus from the sea,
> Drained through a limbeck to his native form.
>   *(3.591–605)*

"Not all parts like": Milton acknowledges and declares his allegiance with Galileo's new observations that had called into question the uniformity and incorruptibility of the sun; his narrator's ensuing, ambiguous remarks that "here"—on the sun? on earth?—there might be fields, regions, and rivers (3.606–7) may even go Galileo one step better and transfer to the sun the astronomer's hardly less unsettling discoveries, announced in the widely distributed *Starry Messenger*, of "heights and chasms" on the moon.[33] But the emphasis of the passage shifts from one kind of scientific endeavor to another, however Milton may suggest their possible interrelation: from the astronomer's peering into the sun to the alchemist's attempt to bring the sun and its power down to earth. It begins as a poetic comparison; the shining sun is brighter than any shiny metal or stone seen on earth; it glows *as* fiery iron does in a forge or crucible. The ensuing lines continue this comparison, but as they do so, they introduce likenesses—gold and silver, the precious stones on Aaron's breastplate—that alchemy *literally* connected to the sun's quintessence and its operations, a connection that Milton may partly concede in vv. 608–12, where the "arch-chemic sun" produces metals and gems in the earth, though he has already qualified the sun's actions upon the universe as "unseen" (3.585; cf. 5.300–302).[34] But the alchemists go further, and want to capture this invisible solar power in the philosopher's stone, "Imagined rather oft than elsewhere seen." The stone is another thing invisible to mortal sight, but the opposite of the things the poet has asked his Muse to reveal. Rather than move from the visible sun to the invisible light of God in the manner of a good Christian or, for that matter, Platonic contemplative, the philosophers seek, in a downward inversion and parody of that act of faith, to find something equally invisible, because, in this case, it is non-nonexistent: an earthly distillation of the sun's light and quintessence, perhaps of the supposed world-soul itself, residing in their metals.[35] Their "powerful art" seeks to increase human power over God's creation, but they are on a fool's errand.

The Paradise of Fools

The philosophers seek the stone "in vain ... / In vain." The repetition emphasizes their connection, even if it is an inverse and symmetrical one, to the Paradise of Fools that is still a future prospect when, earlier in the book, Satan stands on the lightless, windswept outside of the firmament.[36]

> Alone, for other creature in this place
> Living or lifeless to be found was none,
> None yet, but store hereafter from the earth
> Up hither like aerial vapours flew
> Of all things transitory and *vain*, when sin
> With *vanity* had filled the works of men:
> Both all things *vain*, all who in *vain* things
> Built their fond hopes of glory or lasting fame,
> Or happiness in this or the other life;
> All who have their reward on earth, the fruits
> Of painful superstition and blind zeal,
> Nought seeking but the praise of men, here find
> Fit retribution, empty as their deeds;
>   *(3.442–54)*

"Vain" appears still three more times in the passage (3.457, 465, 467) that satirizes the "empty ... deeds" of the fools. Earlier in the book God had promised salvation to "them who renounce / Their own both righteous and unrighteous deeds" (3.291–92), but the fools have sought to make their way to heaven, like the giants among them, "With many a vain exploit" (3.465). Their error is apparently the opposite, and yet bears underlying similarity and relationship to that of the philosophers, who fix their art exclusively on this world. The fools not only seek earthly glory and happiness but confuse them with the glory of heaven and the happiness of the afterlife, as if they could take it all with them. The ultimate target is the carnal ceremonialism of Catholicism and its system of works ("the *works* of men")—the "relics, beads, / Indulgences, dispenses" (3.491–92)—by which its adherents seek to buy their way to salvation in place of the faith that Protestantism and Milton's God uphold as the sole justification of the saved. Empty deeds are coupled in the next verse with the "unaccomplished *works* of nature's hand" (3.455) and, in both cases, the satire suggests the futility and ultimate monstrosity of a secondary creativity, human or natural —what God sees when he looks down on "His own works and *their works*"— should it become autonomous from the divine Creator and substitute itself for him. Among such "unkindly mixed" (3.456) works of nature are the mixed-race giants themselves, often assimilated with the builders of Babel who follow them in this catalog of fools (3.463–67): vanity is a form of pride, the sin traditionally ascribed to both. Catholic ritualists are the builders of "New Babels" (3.468), those who would use human and earthly means to gain heaven, and it is they and the other fools who are truly blind in their superstitious zeal, one further recasting of the physical sightlessness of the poet onto others in the form of spiritual blindness. That poet's faith in things invisible is contrasted to the fools' trust in their all too visible works; those who vainly seek "to pass disguised" (3.480) into heaven in Dominican or Franciscan attire anticipate Satan's subsequent hypocrisy, his putting on the garb and appearance of a stripling cherub.

Behind this passage, it is often noted, is the episode of the moon in Ariosto's *Orlando furioso* 34–35, which also attacks ecclesiastical abuses, and to which Milton alludes in verse 459 when he relocates his Paradise of Fools—"Not in the neighboring moon, as some have dreamed." Less noted is that Ariosto's episode is itself a satirical parody of Dante's *Divine Comedy* and so is Milton's. Like the flight of Dante through the old Ptolemaic universe of the *Paradiso*, the fools, briefly allowed to fulfill their fantasy, "pass the planets seven, and pass the fixed, / And that crystalline sphere" (3.481–82) and seem to be about to meet Saint Peter at the satirically reduced "wicket" (3.484) of heaven, when they encounter the winds that here batter the outside of the universe and cause them to "fly o'er the backside of the world": an ill wind and a kind of cosmic flatulence.[37] So much for Milton's great Catholic predecessor poet. "Then *might ye see*" (3.489), says the narrator of the windblown fools in another reprise of book 3's insistent thematics of vision, pointing to the special, allegorical, and tongue-in-cheek nature of the episode. This alternative way of imagining things invisible to mortal sight describes a "Limbo of Vanity," as the Argument to book 3 puts it, that does not yet exist and that may exist only in the future minds of the fools themselves, and then exists only to be whirled away, leaving darkness and emptiness in its place, a universal blank. It is a literal mise en abyme that implicates all attempts to represent an invisible heaven: these include Dante's poem and finally must include Milton's own fiction that has opened book 3.

The episode of the Paradise of Fools, which some critics have found to be an indecorous excrescence in the poem, isolated from the rest of book 3 both in its content and low tone, is thus very much a piece of the book's whole.[38] Book 3 charts a progress in the imagination itself: from the poet's vision of faith of an invisible world of heavenly light, to the fools' creating a heaven in the image of their own works and earthly reward, to the astronomer and philosophers who ignore the invisible heaven for the visible sun and who would reduce an already material sunlight to an even more material and earthly stone. The whole book has become an exercise for the reader, who learns—the poet's blindness has made it easier for *him* to do so—to separate a higher world beheld only in spirit from a lower, physical one and, nonetheless, to understand and believe in the continuity between them.

Moreover, the vanity of the fools connects them to the book's semantics of light and lightness. Like the "cany wagons light" that the Chinese drive with sails and wind, the fools and their works become "the sport of winds." Thus they fly upward—"*Up* hither like aerial vapours *flew*"—in a parody of the upward flight of light itself at the Creation to form the sun and stars—"And this ethereal quintessence of heaven / *Flew upward*." The fools are "light"—that is, they are full of vanity—but they are compared not to physical light but to the terrestrial vapors that were thought, in the science of Milton's time that followed Aristotle's *Meteorology* (1.4), to explain the phenomenon of shooting stars. When Uriel subsequently descends on a sunbeam in book 4, he is likened to "a shooting star / In autumn thwart the night, when vapours fired / Impress the air" (4.556–58). Such vapors rise from the earth until they are ignited by the atmosphere, and then fall back from whence they came, much as the fools ascend toward heaven before they and their earthly works are blown aside. Their lightness neither brings them to the light of heaven nor achieves the qualities of physical light. The starless limbo on the outside of the universe in which they are to wander until the "final dissolution" (3.458) cuts them off equally from both.

This lightness is a judgment on the fools. The association with vapors and shooting stars links them with the greatest star that has fallen from heaven and lost its light, Satan or Lucifer, who is subsequently compared to one of the sunspots that Galileo similarly compared to rising and dissolving vapors. Satan will be balanced in God's scales at the end of book 4:

> in these he put two weights
> The sequel each of parting and of fight;

The latter quick *up flew*, and kicked the beam;
Which Gabriel spying, thus bespake the fiend.
. . . .
And read thy lot in yon celestial sign
Where thou art weighed, and shown how *light*, how weak
If thou resist.
    (4.1002–5, 4.1011–13)

The passage combines a Homeric-Virgilian scene of divine weighing on the battlefield with the handwriting on the wall that judges Belshazzar in Daniel 5:27—"TEKEL, thou art wayed in the balance and *art founde too light*" reads the passage in the Geneva Bible. Satan's lightness causes the scale to fly upward much as the fools do in their vanity; both are condemned to an unbearable lightness of being, to the loss of the light within, and to wandering in the dark.

Sun Worshippers

The sun in book 3 has acquired a prominence that is both old and new. "In splendor likest heaven" (3.572), "the great luminary / Aloof the vulgar constellations thick" (3.576–77), the "all-cheering lamp" (3.581): the sun already *looks*, as Satan will describe it in his soliloquy that opens book 4 "like the God / Of this new world; at whose sight all the stars / Hide their diminished heads" (4.33–35). The terms are Platonic, indebted particularly to the late Neoplatonism of Iamblichus that described the sun as the visible symbol and emanation of an intellectual light that itself was the emanation of the divine. "The sun regulates and guides all things celestial, like a veritable lord of the sky ... it gives light to all the stars," wrote Marsilio Ficino in the fifteenth century when he sums up this Platonic tradition and seeks to Christianize it in his treatise *De sole*.[39] "Very many Platonists place the soul of the world in the Sun which, filling the entire sphere of the Sun, radiates is own rays through the fiery globe as through a heart," Ficino notes, although five chapters later he is careful to dissociate himself from this view.[40] At the same time, book 3 alludes to a new understanding of the sun made possible by the telescope, the glazed optic tube through which the astronomer looks on the sun's lucent orb. The allusion is one of three that *Paradise Lost* makes to Galileo (see also 1.287–91 and 5.261–63), and that acknowledge the new astronomy that had changed the shape of the cosmos and placed the sun at its center—"By centre, or eccentric, hard to tell" (3.575), the poet remarks of Satan's approach to the sun, anticipating Raphael's heliocentric explanation of the planetary system in book 8. Catherine Gimelli Martin has noted the juxtaposition of this passage to the earlier consignment of the Dantesque-Ptolemaic universe to the Paradise of Fools; it suggests, she argues, Milton's allegiance to the new heliocentrism.[41]

These two languages by which the sun is addressed in book 3, of the old Neo-platonism and of the New Science, were historically interrelated. In the tenth chapter of book 1 of *De revolutionibus*, Copernicus invoked the language of *De sole* and the metaphors of Neoplatonic esotericism to support his hypothesis.

In the middle of all sits Sun enthroned. In this most beautiful temple could we place this luminary in any better position from which he can illuminate the whole at once? He is rightly called the Lamp, the Mind, the Ruler of the Universe; Hermes Trismegistus names him the Visible God.[42]

Galileo himself repeated the passage in his *Dialogue Concerning the Two Chief World Systems*: "Copernicus admires the arrangements of the parts of the universe because of God's having placed the great luminary which must give off its mighty splendor to the whole temple right in the center of it, and not off to one side." But Galileo adds the caveat that such metaphors did not constitute science: "Please let us not entangle these little flowers of rhetoric in the rigors of demonstration. Let us rather leave them to the orators, or better to the poets."[43] Nonetheless, Kepler continued to clothe his discoveries in the solar mysticism of Neoplatonism, while Milton's contemporary poet Henry More enthusiastically embraced Copernicanism in order to demonstrate the compatibility of heliocentrism with the hoary Neoplatonic teaching that More Christianized: "The sunnes the type of that eternall light / Which we call God, a fair dilineament / Of that which Good in Plato's school is hight."[44]

As he explores the implications of a new heliocentrism, Milton the poet takes up these metaphors but in a spirit that shares something of the scientific outlook of a Galileo but owes even more to Protestantism. Milton evokes, in order to reject, a Platonic way of thinking where analogy (sunlight is our best image of divine light and the Good) becomes direct cosmic correspondence (the sun is created *as* the model of divine light and the Good). The latter idea argues for the human capacity to read back from God's visible works in nature to God's invisible supernatural being, the capacity that Milton had optimistically described in *Of Education*, but that he now calls into question in *Paradise Lost*. The idea could lead to the error of the fools in their Limbo of Vanity. It could also lead to the divinization of nature and, in particular, to the worship of the sun, which Milton, following John Selden, saw at the heart of paganism and which could devolve into a sheerly materialist conception of nature, if a nature still imbued with quasi-magical solar power.[45] The alchemists in pursuit of the philosopher's stone seek to harness that power for human ends. And the astronomer, newly placing the sun at the center of things, could be complicit with them.

The heliocentric model joins materialist and Neoplatonic discourses. Each is problematic in its own way to Milton's religion, and his fiction seeks to pry them apart. J. B. Broadbent found one of Milton's likely sources for his episode of the sun in the first century BCE *Universal History* of Diodorus Siculus, where Diodorus accounts for why Arabia and other regions "directly under the Meridian" should produce "by the power and virtue of the Sun … a world of pretious [*sic*] stones of different natures as well as colour and splendor."

> Truly it is very apparent, that colours, odors, fruits, different savours, greatness of creatures, forms of things, and varietie of kindes produced by the earth, are made and procreated by heat of the Sunne, which, warming the moisture of the earth, is the true and only cause of those productions.[46]

The passage appears to be echoed in book 3:

> The arch-chemic sun so far from us remote
> Produces with terrestrial humour mixed
> Here in the dark so many precious things
> Of colour glorious and effect so rare …
>   (3.609–12)

Diodorus gives a straightforward naturalistic or scientific account of solar generativity, and it corresponds to Milton's depiction of the sun as a purely material celestial orb. Diodorus may consider the processes of creation to be hidden and marvelous, but there are no grounds here for Broadbent's suggestion that he turns the sun into a divinity or object of cult, the "Visible God" of Hermes Trismegistus cited by Copernicus.

Milton knew, however, that there had been a historical attempt to overthrow Christianity itself in the name of a solar religion. Its leader, the emperor Julian the Apostate, addressed the Alexandrians in a letter in 362 CE:

> Are you alone insensible to the beams that descend from Helios? Are you alone ignorant that summer and winter are from him? Or that all kinds of animal and plant life proceed from him? And do you not perceive what great blessings the city derives from her who is generated from and by him, even Selene who is the creator of the whole universe? Yet you have the audacity not to adore any one of these gods; and you think that one whom neither you nor your fathers have ever seen, even Jesus, ought to rank as God the Word? But the god whom time immemorial the whole race of mankind has beheld and looked up to and worshipped, and from that worship prospered, I mean mighty Helios, [is] his intelligible father's living image, endowed with soul and intelligence, cause of all good.[47]

Julian's religion imposes late Neoplatonism on the Mithraic cult of Sol Invictus that had been the religion of the Roman army; he consciously substitutes the sun for Jesus-as-Logos. In a different scheme, Selene the moon, generated from Helios, is the maker of the universe. Milton's alignment of the Son with the reflected light of the moon in book 3 may even owe something to this latter pattern.[48] Julian might worship the sun in Platonic fashion as the visible sign of an invisible, intelligible deity, but his appeal to the Alexandrians rests on a more literal cult of the visible sun, the creative power of nature worshipped in and of itself. This is what pagan religion had conduced to for Milton, as early as his *Elegy V*, a substitution of God's works, headed by the sun, for their creator, a universe that seems to work perfectly well without him. When Milton next echoes Diodorus, in the words of Satan tempting Eve to distrust God and to fall in book 9, the devil sounds very much like Julian as well.

> The gods are first, and that advantage use
> On our belief, that all from them proceeds;
> I question it, for this fair earth I see,
> Warmed by the sun, producing every kind,
> Them nothing.
> > (9.718–22)

It is not clear whether Satan is anticipating/repeating a pagan apostasy from true religion or merely fostering a godless materialism, but these are two sides of the same coin.[49]

It is a signal irony of book 3 that it should be the same Satan, who, in his disguise as a pious cherub, spells out the correct response of the worshipper to beholding God's works, the "shining orbs" (3.668; 670) of heaven. He tells the unsuspecting Uriel that he has been driven by

> Unspeakable desire to see, and know
> All these his wondrous works, but chiefly man,
> His chief delight and favour, him for whom
> All these his works so wondrous he ordained,
> . . . .
> On whom the great creator hath bestowed
> Worlds, and on whom hath all these graces poured;
> That both in him and all things, as is meet,
> The universal maker we may praise;
> > (3.662–65, 3.673–76)

Although Satan can barely contain his envy of mankind, the doctrine is sound: sun and stars have been created for God's chief creature, and sun and stars and human beings alike attest to and render praise to their "universal maker." So Adam and Eve will later confirm in their morning prayer in book 5:

> These are thy glorious works, parent of good,
> Almighty, thine this universal frame,
> Thus wondrous fair; thy self how wondrous then!
> Unspeakable, who sit'st above these heavens

To us invisible or dimly seen
In these thy lowest works, yet these declare
Thy goodness beyond thought, and power divine ...
    (5.153–59)

In their spontaneous, unmeditated hymn "to praise / Their maker" (5.147–48), the first human beings anticipate the psalmist—"The heavens declare the glorie of God; and the firmament sheweth the work of his hands" (Psalm 19:1). The God who is invisible to mortal sight may possibly—the "or" conveys some uncertainty—be seen in his works, but the operative word is the adverb "dimly." The universe is a "work" that, as Bacon granted, implies a benign creator. But Adam and Eve, like Bacon, know perfectly well not to argue back from the work to, and thus confuse it *with* the Creator, even as they go on to address the sun in Orphic and Neoplatonic language: "Thou sun, of this great world both eye and soul, / Acknowledge him thy greater" (5.171–72). This is not, as Broadbent suggested, "a qualified worship" of the sun but quite the opposite.[50] Adam and Eve use the anthropomorphic and psychic analogies as analogies: they do not invest the material sun with its own reasoning being as if it *could* acknowledge the greater God—this is also the pointed effect of placing Uriel in the sun, not as a Platonic planetary intelligence or daemon but as a divine watchman and God's eye. The sun is not an animated world-soul that in turn creates and animates the universe. Later pagan error might lead one to take these analogies literally, divinize the sun as the model of a higher godhood, and worship nature itself—or rather worship the idol that human thought has made out of nature. Milton's portrait of an original pure religion in Eden breaks those future idols in advance.

Poetry and Science

Such Protestant iconoclasm, it has been pointed out, could be historically allied to the New Science.[51] Bacon combines the two in the extract from *The Advancement of Learning* cited at the opening of this chapter. In a parallel passage in the *The New Organon* (1620), where Bacon distinguishes four types of idols that stand in the way of an objective study of nature, the confusion of scientific doctrine and religious truth is a subset of what he calls Idols of the Theater, the tendency of the human mind to arrange the data of the natural world into aesthetically pleasing systems. Bacon has the Aristotelian dramatic unities in mind when he objects to stories that are "more compact and elegant" (*concinniores sint et elegantiores*) than the histories, human and natural, they describe.[52] The old science, Bacon observes, was too bookish in its very form—it was a kind of poetry—and when systems are extracted out of readings of the Bible, they are apt to turn both science and religion into poetic fictions: Bacon repeats his charge that "from this unwholesome mixture of things divine and human there arises not only a fantastic philosophy but also a heretical religion" (*Philosophia phantastica sed etiam Religio haeretica*).[53] Bacon consigns the old science to the realm of literature where it always belonged, its superseded truths now suitable for "ornaments of discourse" (*sermones ornent*).[54] Galileo similarly wished to relegate Copernicus's Hermetic language to the poets.

Where does this leave the poet of *Paradise Lost*? With whatever lingering nostalgia—"what if earth / Be but the shadow of heaven … ?"—Milton stands on this side of the divide in human thought, described by Michel Foucault as the end of the analogical universe, and by Eugenio Garin as the incipient separation of the Book of Nature from the Book of God. Garin writes, "The book of Nature is not an extrinsic and fleshly introduction to the *invisibilia Dei*, to intrinsic and spiritual foundations, a return to a mysterious and hidden source; it is to the contrary, the point of departure for a discourse that is ever more simple, evident and accessible—ever less *visual, allusive, emotive*, and ever more *rational*."[55] One can feel the two books being pulled apart in the juxtaposition in book 3 of John's vision of an angel and Galileo's vision of spots in the sun.

Yet Milton, Christian and poet, is not ready to relinquish the link between the two books or the metaphor of the book itself. The narrative sequence of book 3 and its frame of light descend from God's invisible heaven to the visible universe only to reconnect the latter back to God: it culminates in Uriel's eyewitness description of the making of the universe—first the Creation of light itself, then of the stars, sun, and moon—by its divine Creator (3.713–32). With its own carefully wrought semantic unity, its neat division and parallels between heavenly and solar domains of visibility, its play on the word "light" itself, book 3 embodies the compromise that Milton finds for poetry with the New Science. One half of poetry's task, its *via negativa*, rehearses the analogies of the older cosmology in order to disclose them *as* outmoded poetic fictions, to remove their demonic half-life and to turn them into dead metaphors, ornaments for discourse. But Milton's book nonetheless organizes itself around the very analogy, the correspondence between God and sun, which it criticizes and discards: the old glosses, however beautiful, no longer work, but it is still possible to derive from them, and to posit in turn, an intimation of deeper structure, the universe as a divinely authored book. The too tidy patterns of poetry elicit a habit of mind that, Bacon warns, stands between the human observer and nature; by that very token, Milton counters, they can offer an idea of order and divine presence now that the new philosophy calls all in doubt. In wake of the depiction of the Lucretian Chaos of book 2, the poetic unity of book 3 may be as reassuring as the appearance in it of the character of God himself. It anticipates Raphael's assertion to Adam in book 8 that "heaven / Is as the book of God before thee set, / Wherein to read his wondrous works" (8.66–68). Yet here, too, the book is hard to decipher, even when the Baconian interpreter reads it on its own terms as God's work rather than as his image. The angel then adds that the divine architect "Did wisely to conceal, and not divulge / His secrets to be scanned by them who ought / Rather admire" (8.73–75). Read this book, know that it *is* a book, admire its author with wonder; but don't expect to master it.

Paradise Lost dramatizes the hazards of this strategy. In repudiating false links that the human mind has forged between the works of nature and their Creator, Milton risks breaking the connection between them altogether. God may himself disappear—"invisible or dimly seen"—from a nature that has been disenchanted for the sake of properly worshipping him *and* in order to allow nature to be read on a new empirical basis. Like Raphael, Uriel declares that the maker of the heavens and earth "hid their causes deep" (3.707). The hidden first cause is Satan's opening to insinuate doubt and distrust—"I question it"—and propose the sun as universal power source and incubator of creation, a materialist alternative that gained new resonance as Milton's century came to recognize the sun as the center around which the earth moved. *Paradise Lost* subsequently echoes and corrects Satan's science and that of Diodorus. In book 11, Michael tells Adam, distraught at being ejected from Eden, that God is everywhere.

> Adam, thou know'st heaven his, and all the earth.
> Not this rock only; his omnipresence fills
> Land, sea, and air, and every kind that lives,
> Fomented by his virtual power and warmed.
> *(11.335–38)*

The passage also carefully echoes the first description of the sun in book 3,

> that gently warms
> The universe, and to each inward part
> With gentle penetration, though unseen,
> Shoots invisible virtue even to the deep.
> *(3.583–86)*

And it still more carefully echoes Adam's first attempt at science, his explanation to Eve in book 4 of the cooperation of stars and sun in the earth's generative processes:

> these soft fires
> Not only enlighten, but with kindly heat
> Of various influence foment and warm,
> Temper or nourish, or in part shed down
> Their stellar virtue on all kinds that grow
> On earth, made hereby apter to receive
> Perfection from the sun's more potent ray.
> *(4.667–73)*

Never mind how God's works work, Michael now tells Adam (cf. 12.576–79): God is the true giver of life to his creation, the maker of "every kind." You know this, the angel insists, and reminds him of what he and Eve knew in their book 5 prayer and what Adam himself knew instinctively at the moment of his creation as he recounts it to Raphael in book 8: his first words were directed to the sun, but only to ask about their mutual "great maker" (8.273–78.) Now the doctrine is repeated as the revealed truth, through the mouth of an angel. Yet this knowledge is not obvious. The invisible God works invisibly to fill and foment his creation, and the sun itself, Milton's language insists ("unseen," "invisible"), imitates its maker. So Satan had doubly lied when he earlier based his case on visible evidence:

> for this fair earth *I see*,
> Warmed by the sun, producing every kind,
> Them nothing.

The playing off against each other of Michael's doctrine and Satan's skepticism repeats the division in book 3 between invisible light and the light of the sun, between the eye of faith and mortal sight. Seeing, the blind poet argues, is not believing.

5

The Politics of Envy

The third verse of *Paradise Lost* echoes the Wisdom of Solomon in the biblical Apocrypha: "For God created man to be immortal, and made him to be an image of his own eternity. Nevertheless *through the envy of the devil came death into the world*: and they that do hold of his side do find it" (2:23–24). So the Fall that Satan engineered "Brought death into the world, and all our woe" (*PL* 1.3). The first thing we learn in the poem after its invocation is that "envy and revenge" (1.35) stirred Satan into action.[1] Envy, as much if not more than pride, triggers the original sin against God in *Paradise Lost* (before the Fall of Adam and Eve that bequeathed Original Sin to humanity).[2] The envy that Satan experiences for the Son whom God has anointed (5.605) drives him into disobedience and rebellion; he will then envy Adam and Eve in Paradise. And it is the original political sin as well, through which *Paradise Lost* will examine and lay out its political ideas about kingship, class, and equality—and about its own historical moment. Satan's envy is triggered by the begetting/exaltation of the Son *in time*, out of a seemingly undifferentiated eternity, and as a *visible image* of God: Satan interprets the evidence of his eyes and understands the Son and God himself in sheerly temporal terms. Like the unbelieving Jews at the later incarnation of the Son, which also starts a new era in history, he refuses to bow down to a fellow temporal creature. By the same logic he infers that the Son's and God's rulership is merely a matter of temporal power, and Satan thus invents worldly kingship by misattributing it to God and then by trying to obtain it—by force—for himself. Carnal kingship inspires Satan's envy, and, as the last two books of *Paradise Lost* recount, envy, the sin and legacy of Cain, conversely produces earthly monarchy in human history.

Cain's violent crime, like the kingship to which it leads, is a crime against brotherhood, and the envy at the basis of both Satan's revolt against God and his attempt "To set himself in glory above his peers" is a response to what Satan perceives as an unbearable situation of equality. As Satan misrecognizes God as a worldly monarch, so he misrecognizes the spiritual equality of the angels before God—"as sons of one great sire" (6.95)—as the political leveling of a royal court. Milton aligns Satan's envy to his own historical world, where the demise of feudal relationships—which appear still to be glimpsed in the hierarchy of the angels—has produced new political forms of equality. Rather than speak for the free equality of a republican commonwealth, the form of human government that Milton, in his political tracts, argued could most nearly approximate and foster Christian brotherhood, Satan speaks against republicanism's perverse, demonic double, the enforced equality of court society beneath a monarch, even as he creates such a society by himself becoming king of hell. Satan regards the equality of heaven as common servitude to God the temporal king rather than as the parity and communion produced by loving service to God the Deity-Creator and to one's fellow creatures, a communion that, the loyal angel Abdiel will argue, has been promoted and enhanced by the new anointment of the Son. By turning down equality on the latter terms that God offers, Satan is left with the alternatives to be all or nothing. Envy, which Milton defines in *De Doctrina Christiana* (2:11; *CPW* 6:746) as begrudging of one's happiness to others (the prospect of shared equality) as much as resentment of the happiness of others that one does not possess (the sense of being lesser or indebted), thus informs Satan's remaining, monarchical option to be more than others: to make himself the worldly, temporal king that he takes God to be, to make others envy *him*. Satan's violent reaction—his resort to violence itself—is as inventive as it is regressive, for even if it seems to signal a backward turn to a warrior society like the one that obtained before the state-building monarchy in British and European history, it instead discovers a new martial identity and occupation for angels who have heretofore lived as peaceful attendants and servants to God. Satan invents war itself: his Minerva-like Sin emerged from his head as "a goddesss armed" (2.757). By understanding spiritual equality under God as mere political subjection, Satan traps himself and his followers, angels and human, in the vicious cycle of monarchy and war—the subject of earlier epics that Milton is not sedulous to indite. The "servile pomp" (2.257) that Mammon begrudges to God in book 2 is shortly transferred to "hell's dread emperor with pomp supreme" (2.510), and the fallen angels exchange one supposed temporal king for another real one. For a while, too, Satan seems to turn even the good angels into fighters, his antagonists in the War in Heaven. The interrupted duel of Satan and Gabriel at the end of book 4 puts an end, however, to this military, epic option, and the discovery of Satan by Zephon and Ithuriel, mere foot soldiers in God's new model army, suggests an equality of goodness in which Satan refuses to participate and which he finds intolerable to endure.

The following consideration of these issues falls into three sections. The first deals with envy as a spiritual sin, and traces how Satan's envy leads him through his career in *Paradise Lost* to his ironically unenviable fate. The blind poet Milton emphasizes the visible nature of the exalted Son, God's image, as a source of envy, in analogy to the incarnate Jesus of the New Testament. This iconicity, as well as the unprecedented newness of the Son—the eruption of time into eternity—helps explain, and even makes a good case for, the apostasy of the fallen angels. The second section locates envy in the political world and in Milton's politico-historical moment. The anointment of the Son represents something new in history, an egalitarian society governed, as the exaltation of the Son suggests, "By merit more than birthright" (3.309). Envy is a particularly modern response to this new equality, which Satan characterizes as servitude in a royal court, the proverbial site of envy. Against what he understands in carnal, political terms as enforced equality, Satan in turn appeals to bodily force—"our own right hand" (5.864)—the most carnal form of politics of all. Its historical dead end—here *before* human history can properly begin and before *Paradise Lost* will retrospectively depict the angels fighting their still earlier War in Heaven in book 6—is suggested in the duel that fails to take place between Satan and Gabriel at the end of book 4, the ritual combat that kept the old-style ethos of honor and violence alive in the face of a pacified courtly society. Like early modern monarchs and states, God bans dueling between his creatures and calls this fight off. But God should not be confused with an earthly king, nor vice versa. The third section, however, looks at how Satan's error is repeated and inverted in the attempts of human conquerors and kings to play God in books 11 and 12. They bring into earthly being the royal-aristocratic regime, so many versions of Nimrod and his crew, including Charles II and his court. In this critique of monarchy, the old regicide Milton is at it again.

Envy and the New Dispensation

Milton opposes the devil's envy to the Son's loving-kindness in three separate echoes of one passage of Virgil's *Aeneid*.[3] As chapter 2 already mentioned, when Milton's God asks in heaven for a volunteer to sacrifice himself to redeem humanity, his last words before the ominous silence that the Son alone will break are "Dwells in all heaven charity so dear?" (3.216). This is Milton's answer to the anxious and unresolved question that Virgil's narrator poses at the opening of the *Aeneid* with reference to the anger of Juno that persecutes the exiled Trojans: "Tantaene animis caelestibus irae?" (*Aen.* 1.11)—can there be such great wrath in the breasts of the heavenly gods? It is not the wrath of Homer's hero Achilles that is in question in the great Roman epic, but that of the divinity. Yes, Milton replies, the Christian God can be angry, but he can also be mollified by the charity that he knows the Son will offer.[4]

But Satan will pose the question differently when he tempts Eve to eat the forbidden fruit in book 9, echoing both Virgil and the earlier words of God. How can your knowledge hurt God? Satan asks.

> Or is it envy, and can envy dwell
> In heavenly breasts?
> *(9.729–30)*

The answer is, in fact, no, or at least not in heavenly breasts that will stick around in heaven.[5] The envy that Satan projects upon God, both here and earlier in the dream he sends to Eve—"Or envy, or what reserve forbids to taste" (5.61)—is his own. This process of projection is depicted in book 4, when Satan first turns "For envy" (4.503) from the sight of Adam and Eve embracing and kissing, then, in soliloquy, asks of the knowledge of the forbidden tree, "Why should their Lord / Envy them that?" (4.516–17) and characterizes the prohibition as "Envious commands" (524).

When the Son makes his appearance in the War in Heaven in book 6 and restores the heavenly landscape that the contending angels, bad and good, have uprooted and cast about, this act of creation should have made the rebel angels think twice and repent. But it has an opposite effect on them.

> This saw his hapless foes but stood obdured,
> And to rebellious fight rallied their powers
> Insensate, hope conceiving from despair.
> In heavenly spirits could such perverseness dwell?
> But to convince the proud what signs avail,
> Or wonders move the obdurate to relent?
> They hardened more by what might most reclaim,
> Grieving to see his glory, at the sight
> Took envy, and aspiring to his highth,
> Stood re-embattled fierce …
> *(6.785–94)*

In heavenly spirits could such perverseness dwell? This is the clearest of all of the echoes of *Aeneid* 1, both grammatically and because it is expressed in the voice of the epic narrator, here Raphael. What is a "heavenly breast" in Satan's words to Eve has become the hardened heart of the sinner that, as it is described by Isaiah 6:10 and also by Milton's God in book 3 (199–201), only hardens more before the word or signs of God that might reclaim it. A biblical example that Milton recalls here is the hardening of the heart of Pharaoh before the plagues that are God's signs and wonders in Exodus 7:3 and of Pharaoh and his fellow Egyptians in Exodus 14:8 and 14:17 just before they are overthrown into the Red Sea (cf. the "stubborn heart" [12.193], softened and then hardened again, of Pharaoh, "the obdurate king" [12.205] in Michael's account of the Exodus itself in book 12); so the bad angels will topple out of heaven.[6]

These three echoes of *Aeneid* 1.11, which also echo one another—notice the use of "dwell" in each of them—contrast the Son's charity to the envy of Satan and of his fellow fallen angels. Envy initiates and continues their perverse, downward spiral. Depending on the etymological relation in Latin that gives the word "invidere" the meanings both "to envy" and "to look askance" or even "to cast an evil eye on another,"[7] Milton depicts this envy as a particularly visual condition: "Grieving to see his glory, at the sight / Took envy." The Geneva Bible says that Saul "had an eye on David" (1 Sam. 18:9) and explains in its gloss: "Because he bare him envie & hatred." It glosses the "wicked eye" of Mark 7:22 as envy. Noting some of these scriptural passages, Bacon writes in his essay, "Of envy," that "there seemeth to be acknowledged, in the act of envy, an ejaculation or irradiation of the eye."[8] In Alciati's emblem, Envy is represented as a woman whose eyes give her pain.[9] "O hell! What do mine eyes with grief behold" (4.358), "Sight hateful, sight tormenting!" (4.505), Satan exclaims as he "turned / For envy, yet with jealous leer malign / Eyed them askance" (4.502–4) when he beholds Adam and Eve in Eden in book 4. He and his evil eye must be removed from the scene before the book can depict the happiness of the first couple's nuptial bower. In the War in Heaven Satan and all the rebel angels literally cannot stand the sight of the Son of God. The divine eyes of the paternal chariot, in return, leave them "Exhausted, spiritless, afflicted, fallen" (6.852).

Satan and his bad companions thus end the War in Heaven as they had first begun it. Gabriel has earlier narrated how Satan,

> he of the first,
> If not the first archangel, great in power,
> In favour and pre-eminence, yet fraught
> With envy against the Son of God, that day
> Honoured by his great Father, and proclaimed
> Messiah king anointed, could not bear
> Through pride that sight and thought himself impaired.
> (5.659–65)

It is the sight of the newly begotten Son, as much as the promotion to divine vice-regent, that triggers Satan's malice. God makes his glory visible in the Son—"in whose face invisible is beheld / Visibly, what by deity I am" (6.681–82)—and this manifestation produces envy in the great archangel and starts his fall.[10]

This new revelation, with what Satan repeatedly calls its "New laws" (5.679; 680), enacts at the beginning of history a first version of the Incarnation that will subsequently separate Christianity from Judaism and its Law, and that similarly evokes skepticism from celebrants of the older, iconoclastic religion.[11] In *De Doctrina Christiana* (2.11), Milton opposes envy to charity and particularly to goodwill to all one's fellow men.

> For example, a man may find it unbearable that another should share his good fortune. The first lot of laborers of the parable, Matt. xx.1, etc., are an instance of this: so, too, are the Jews who envied the Gentiles salvation

(see Acts, *passim*). Or a man may be envious that another should have what he cannot obtain himself: thus Satan envies man's salvation, and Cain was jealous that his brother should be favored by God more than he was, Gen. iv. (*CPW* 6:746)

The first two of these examples—and we shall see that they are *all* coordinated by Milton in *Paradise Lost*—are one and the same, for the laborers in the vineyard who complained about the latecomers symbolize the Jews, purportedly envious of the Gentiles in the new dispensation of Christianity. In the Gospels, Pilate thinks that the Jewish priests have turned the new Messiah over to the Romans for crucifixion out of envy (Mark 15:10; Matt. 27:18). The Jews extend their envy of Christ to the apostles and the other nations to whom they preach in the passages of Acts (13:45 and 17:5) to which Milton refers. "Thei disdained that the Gentiles shulde be made equal to them," says the Geneva Bible, glossing Acts 13:45, about the chosen people who saw themselves deprived of their ancient favor and privilege. Paul, in Romans 10:19, cites the Moses of Deuteronomy 32:21 against his own people, "I wil provoke you to envie by a nation that is not my nation, and by a foolish nation I will anger you" (Geneva Bible). So, too, Satan and the devils will envy and expend their malice on the new, to their eyes lesser, human creatures who have displaced them: "Into our room of bliss thus high advanced" (4.359).

The analogy between the envy of the angels and the envy of the Jews, both of whom reject the Son, governs the choice of Milton's model for the episode of Abdiel in book 5. Milton bases this central moment of his poem, in which Abdiel, the one faithful angel among Satan's host, rises up to oppose their rebellion against the Son and Father, on an episode in Girolamo Vida's *Christiad* (1535), a Neo-Latin epic poem on the Passion of Christ. In book 2 (135–215) of Vida's poem, Nicodemus, alone in the council of priests in the Jerusalem temple, tries to convince his fellow Jews to worship Jesus. He succeeds only in kindling the hostility of his listeners, who expel him from their assembly and exile him from Jerusalem. So Satan and the incensed rebel angels scornfully thrust Abdiel from their midst. Milton, who admired the *Christiad* and praises it in his early, unfinished poem, *The Passion*, understood that Vida was here radically revising the conventional understanding of the biblical Nicodemus, who in the Gospel of John (7:51) manages only to voice a one-sentence objection about legal procedure during the temple council.[12] Although later tradition recorded his exile from the city and accorded him quasi-sanctity for his part in the burial of Jesus (John 19:39), Nicodemus was also taxed for his failure to bear testimony to his faith—"he did not allow the faith that was in him to show itself in its nakedness, but wrapped it with simulation as if in a dark cloak," comments Cyril of Alexandria.[13] Milton cites Nicodemus in *De Doctrina Christiana* in his chapter on zeal (2.6), among those who fall short of the supreme profession of martyrdom: "Opposed to this is concealment of our religion exemplified by Nicodemus"

(*CPW* 6:702).[14] The biblical character gave his name to Nicodemism, the practice of timid or prudent believers who hide their faith when faced with persecution. In the apocryphal, widely diffused fourth-century CE *Gospel of Nicodemus*, however, the character protests against the prosecution of Jesus directly to Pilate, and Vida draws on this extracanonical material in his portrait of an outspoken Nicodemus.[15]

Vida's Nicodemus is initially fearful and unwilling to speak alone against all the others—"sed non / Audebat dictis contra omnes tendere solus" (2.153–54)—but he overcomes his qualms to bear witness to the miracles and godhead of Jesus: "vera dei patuit soboles, verus deus" (*Christiad* 2.168; he is revealed as the true offspring of God, the true God).[16] He thus becomes an appropriate model for Milton's Abdiel, "Among the faithless faithful only he" (5.897), who has no inhibitions about standing up and "in a flame of zeal severe" (5.807), voicing his faith in the Son and his dissent from Satan. Abdiel is a still further improved version of Vida's Nicodemus, himself an improved version of the Nicodemus of the Bible. Each speaker concludes his speech with the advice of repentance. Abdiel's counsel to "hasten to appease / The incensed father, and the incensed Son, / While pardon may be found in time besought" (5.846–48) appears to be modeled on Nicodemus's exhorting his fellow Jews "una omnes adeamus, ab ipso / Suppliciter pacem oremus, commissa fatentes" (*Christiad* 2.194–95; let us one and all go and beseech pardon with supplication from Him, confessing the wrongs we have done). The echo becomes clearer when Satan punningly rejects Abdiel's and Nicodemus's suggestions —"thou shalt behold / Whether by supplication we intend / Address, and to begirt the almighty throne / Beseeching or besieging" (5.866–69). We should note, however, that Adam and Eve will successfully use these terms in book 10: following Eve's earlier cue, Adam urges that they "prostrate fall / Before him reverent, and there confess / Humbly our faults, and pardon beg" (10.1087–89).

God's initial act of accommodation starts the problems and actions of *Paradise Lost*. It begins the narrative of salvation history out of a heretofore undifferentiated eternity, the ever returning cosmic cycles of the "great year" (5.583). The begetting and anointing of the Son places divine mediation within creaturely time, and identifies the visible with the temporal.[17] The Arian, anti-Trinitarian Milton, who asserts in *De Doctrina Christiana* (1.5) that "it is as plain as it could possibly be that God voluntarily created or generated or produced the Son before all things" (*CPW* 6:211), also insists on the temporal, created nature of the Son: "So God begot the Son as a result of his own decree. Therefore it took place within the bounds of time" (*CPW* 6:209).[18] Abdiel intuits, on seemingly little evidence, that the newly begotten Son has been around all along as the creative Word that created the angels themselves; but Satan reads the visible evidence another way: "who saw / When this creation was?" (5.856–57), he pointedly asks Abdiel, who has faith in things unseen. Given the first opportunity to think in temporal terms, Satan can think only in terms of what he has or has not seen.

At issue is the very iconic and incarnational status, as well as the historically latecomer status, of the Christian deity and religion. Judaism forbade the making and worship of images. John Chrysostom insists upon the role of *seeing* Christ in arousing the envy of the Jews in his homily on Matthew 2:4–5, where the temple priests truthfully testify to Herod that the king of the Jews will be born in Bethelehem: "Seest how all things are done to convict the Jews? how, as long as He was out of their sight, the envy had not yet laid hold of them, and they rehearsed the testimonies *of Him* with truth; but when they saw the glory that arose from his miracles, a grudging spirit possessed them, and thereafter they betrayed the truth."[19] So, too, in Milton's retrojection of the envy of the Jews back upon the envy of the fallen angels: as long, it appears, as God remained an invisible voice on his holy mountain, everything functioned as usual in heaven, as eternity rolled through the cycles of the great Platonic year.[20] Only when the Son expresses the deity in visual, *created* form do problems ensue—for envy physically depends on seeing—and the linear history of fall and salvation begins. The Son appears to join divine and angelic nature as he will later join divine to human, and God proclaims that the angels will benefit from a new communion through the Son, "United as one individual soul" (5.610), Milton's angelic version of the Pauline human body of Christ. Abdiel asserts that as their head, the Son "One of our number thus reduced becomes" (5.843): it is a divine gift to the angels, Abdiel maintains, a promotion of them, from a deity who is known to be provident of their good and dignity. The bad angels, at Satan's lead, read this reduction of the divine to the angelic literally and in reverse: Why worship a creature, one of our own?[21] The same complaint might be lodged by supposedly envious Jews against a later religion established by a human son of God: "Strange point and new!" indeed.

Satan's defense of the status quo contains a criticism of idolatry and the worship of images: he objects to

> Knee-tribute yet unpaid, prostration vile,
> Too much to one, but double how endured,
> To one and to his image now proclaimed?
>   (5.782–84)

This is a logic shared by John Milton, author of *Eikonoklastes*, reforming Protestant, and a poet who cites his blindness as a privileged condition of internal, spiritual vision. Manmade images of divinity, he writes in book 1, caused idolaters "to forsake / God their creator, and the invisible / Glory of him who made them" (1.368–70). It locates, however, an unsolvable problem: How can we distinguish such idols from the one genuine case of divine accommodation, the Son of God made visible creature? How can Xenophanes's ancient criticism of anthropomorphic polytheism—if a horse or oxen could draw, he supposes that their God would look like a horse or an oxen, and so in this case an angel's God would look like an angel—avoid including the one Christian exception to the rule?[22]

Because God has said it is so: this is a partial, but insufficient answer in Milton's poetic representation. The divine proclamation removes the issue from the field of vision to the higher plain of hearing the divine word as it issues from behind God's glory cloud. But the poem depicts this problem as a test of faith and obedience for the angels akin to the command for Adam and Eve not to eat the forbidden fruit. Satan spectacularly fails the test by reasoning recursively that not only does the Son share the same temporal nature as the angels—a belief that had been attributed to the Arian heresy[23]—but that, like Son, like Father, God must share this nature too. "We know no time when we were not as now" (5.859) says Satan, and concludes that God, Son, and all the angels, including himself, came into being out of refined sky stuff, out of literal thin air—"the birth mature / Of this our native heaven, ethereal sons" (5.862–63)— in one of those eternal, natural cycles like the great year by their own "quickening power, when fatal course / Had circled his full orb" (5.861–62). Satan denies his Creator, who is now reduced to Satan's own ontological standing, as merely one more of the "Natives and sons of heaven" (5.790), abstracted, like a pagan god, out of nature, rather than above and outside of nature.[24] If we are to worship one of our own, why not me and in God's own place? Satan wants to be king.[25]

Milton describes envy as the seeing in another a more perfect mirror image that reflects back a lack in one's own self-image: Satan thought himself "impaired." There may be a quibble here that suggests that Satan feels that he cannot, or can no longer be paired with the Son; from the outset of the epic we learn that Satan not only aspired to set himself in glory above his "peers," a position he mostly already enjoyed, but "trusted to have equalled the most high" (1.40). In his speech to his fellow rebel angels in book 5, Satan wishes to use force "to try / Who is our equal" (5.865–66). In his narratively prior but chronologically later encounter in book 4 with Zephon and Ithuriel, who fail to recognize him and where he is now *below* those former inferiors among his peers, Satan pines not only at the sight of their goodness—note the repetition of "saw" in verses 847–48—but "chiefly to find here observed / His lustre visibly *impaired*" after his fall (4.849–50). That Satan's sense of self-impairment should be so largely visual—concerned with how he appears in the eyes of others as well as how he feels he measures up to what he himself sees—attests to its vanity and idolatry, its concern with externals rather than with inner spirituality. Because he is a creature and not the Creator, Satan cannot conceive of being greater than God or the Son, but of equaling them, of occupying their position and being seen to do so. In book 5, he makes his assembly on his own diamond and gold Mountain of the Congregation, "Affecting all equality with God, / In imitation of that mount whereon / Messiah was declared *in sight of heaven*" (5.763–65). Satan the iconoclast wishes, in fact, to make *himself* an "Idol of majesty divine" (6.101).

Instead, when Satan fails to equal what he envies, he destroys.[26] In his soliloquy that opens book 9, the mirror of envy has been reversed.

> Nor hope to be my self less miserable
> By what I seek, but others to make such
> As I, though thereby worse to me redound:
> For only in destroying I find ease
> To my relentless thoughts;
>   *(9.126–30)*

Rather than take the place of those whose power or happiness he envies, Satan will try to make them take *his* place. In a perverse parody of the Son's charity, Satan shares his misery with others. The despairing, fallen Adam will indeed conclude himself "miserable / Beyond all past example and future, / To Satan only like both crime and doom" (10.839–41).

Yet Adam is wrong. No one can be *as* miserable as Satan—"such / As I." So Satan earlier asserts when he seeks to confirm his kingship in hell. The bright side of losing the War in Heaven, Satan tells his fellow devils, is that it finds him

>   much more
> Established in a safe unenvied throne
> Yielded with full consent. The happier state
> In heaven, which follows dignity, might draw
> Envy from each inferior; but who here
> Will envy whom the highest place exposes
> Foremost to stand against the thunderer's aim
> Your bulwark, and condemns to greatest share
> Of endless pain?
>   *(2.22–30)*

Satan aims here to discourage any possible rivals to his infernal throne: no one will "claim in hell / Precedence" (2.32–33) if the only reward of ambition is more pain. But this blatant, politically motivated sophistry happens ironically to be true. Satan wants to be envied by others, and he appears here to view the envy that brought about his fall as the normal motive of all creatures: another instance of projection, as will also be the lying tale he later tells to Eve in his disguise as a serpent about his attainment of the forbidden fruit: "round the tree / All other beasts that saw, with like desire / Longing and envying stood, but could not reach" (9.591–93). In this tale, Satan describes himself as the object of universal envy, the way he would wish to see himself and the motive of his seeking kingship over his peers.[27] In fact, the inverse is the case: he only succeeds, as he tells his fellow devils in book 2, in making himself the *only being whom no one will envy.*

In a passage of his book 4 soliloquy that looks back on the book 2 speech, Satan admits that while he is adored on the throne of hell, "The lower still I fall, only supreme / In misery" (4.91–92). If the nihilistic impulse of Satan's envy—and of envy more generally—is to destroy rather than to enjoy the happiness of others, the fact that everyone is going to be happier, at least less miserable, than he is condemns Satan to a self-defeating and circular existence. Unable to make others entirely "such / As I," since in the very process of destroying them "worse to me redounds," Satan is caught in a vicious cycle that is also a downward spiral, falling still lower. His relentless thoughts find no ease, but go on and on.

> Revenge, at first though sweet,
> Bitter ere long back on itself recoils;
> Let it; I reck not, so it light well aimed,
> Since higher I fall short, on him who next
> Provokes my envy, this new favourite
> Of heaven, this man of clay, son of despite,
> Whom us the more to spite his maker raised
> From dust: spite then with spite is best repaid.
>   *(9.171–78)*

In these closing words of his soliloquy, Satan discloses both his unhappy consciousness of his situation of envy and the pride and narcissism that makes him unable to escape from it. The unusual moment of rhyming "favourite" with "despite," and the continuing internal echoing of "spite" in the last two verses, suggests the recoiling that he describes. God creates mankind, he claims, as a direct affront to him and his fellow fallen angels: it is all about me, the devil asserts. Even though he knows that his revenge will circle back upon himself and make him more miserable, he cannot give up the envious spite that has become his own negative identity and selfhood. Dostoevsky will later depict characters who cling to their own abjection and nihilism: "Save what is in destroying, other joy / To me is lost" (9.478–79), says Satan in his final soliloquy of the poem, just before he undertakes the seduction of Eve.

Angels and Courtiers

Milton's envious Satan depicts himself in *what looks like* an explicit seventeenth-century social setting, a royal court. The envious Jews of the New Testament, who purportedly resented the loss of their privileged state as chosen people, which they now had to share with gentile followers of Jesus, are one analogue for Satan and his followers. A second analogue is more up-to-date: Satan's terms suggest the rebel angels' likeness to a contemporary European nobility, jealous of its old feudal privileges and local autonomy, now forced by early-modern state-building monarchs to serve at court and rub shoulders with newly promoted upstarts and favorites as their fellow courtiers. Envy was regarded as the particular vice of princely courts. "The stinging and poisonous stimulus of pestiferous envy," wrote Matteo Bandello in the first and therefore emblematic story of his *Novelle* (1554), "continuously weighs the favors of the prince, and in one moment raises one who was lowly and lowers another who stood high, in such a manner that in courts there is no malady more pernicious nor more harmful than the disease of envy."[28] In his dialogue *Il Malpiglio* (1585), Torquato Tasso argued that the double aims announced in the first chapter of Baldassarre Castiglione's classic *Book of the Courtier* (1528)—to obtain the favor of princes and the praise of one's fellow courtiers—were simply incompatible: "those very things that win goodwill from princes cause envy in courtiers."[29]

Paradise Lost picks up on this language of courtiership and disappointed favorites. Milton had portrayed God and his angels *as* a kind of court in the famous Sonnet 16 on his blindness; there, God's "state / Is kingly" and "They also serve who only stand and wait," waiting upon God as well as for the Second Coming. In *Paradise Lost* he carefully analogizes the worship that the angels proffer to God both to Jerusalem temple ceremonies—"this high temple to frequent / With ministeries due and solemn rites" (7.148–49), as Milton's God himself puts it—and to a kind of court service: "those who in their course / Melodious hymns about the sovereign throne / Alternate all night long" (5.655–57). Among these servants of God, Satan had been "great in power, / In favour and pre-eminence." But the archangel now finds himself demoted, first here by the promotion of the Son, then later by "this new favourite / Of heaven," man (cf. 3.664). Feeling like Macbeth after Duncan has elevated Malcolm as his heir and Prince of Cumberland, Satan suggests to his fellow angels that their own "magnific titles" (5.773) have been emptied and cheapened by this new act of royal capriciousness and nepotism: they are now all equally subordinates of the Son.[30] Satan misunderstands the new religious dispensation brought about by the anointment of the Son as a new political dispensation, and it provokes his envy. At the same time, Satan describes his rebellion as a revolt against his situation as a nobleman-courtier.

Satan's envy is a response to the leveling of court society: as Georg Simmel puts it, "Insofar as a number of people are equally subject to one individual they are themselves equal."[31] Simmel's description of this situation of despot and equalized subjects directly follows his sociological explanation of Christian equality.

> The Christian religion is praised for making its adherents "peaceful." The sociological reason for this is very probably the feeling that all beings alike are subordinate to the divine principle. The faithful Christian is convinced that above him and above each of his adversaries, whether Christian or not, there exists this "highest tribunal"—and this frees him

from the temptation to measure his strength by violence. It is precisely because he stands immeasurably high above each individual Christian that the Christian God can be a bond among very large circles, all of which, by definition, are included in his "peace."[32]

The sense of being subordinated and judged alike in the sight of a transcendent God, Simmel asserts, imparts to the Christian a sense of equality with one's fellow beings and a peace that is both inner and social. But when this equality is felt, in Satan's case, to be the outcome of subordination to a prince of this world, the result is envy and the resort, in the hitherto peaceful society of heaven, to violence. As Bacon observes, thinking of the case of Cain and Abel, "near kinsfolks and fellows in office and those that have been bred together are more apt to envy their equals when they are raised. For it doth upbraid them their own fortunes, and pointeth at them, and cometh oftener into their remembrance, and incurreth likewise more into the note of others."[33] When the playing field is indeed even, the elevation of another can seem all the more an affront to oneself and one's own worldly fortunes, apt to be ascribed by envy to fortune, to an act of royal whim. Somebody else, but not I, has all the luck.

But the likeness of heaven to a royal court may be *only* an analogy. That God is a king is a standard biblical metaphor (see Psalms 24, 47, 93, 96, 99, 145.) It is Satan who insists upon literalizing the metaphor. The fiction and political thought of *Paradise Lost* both depend on preserving the gap between divine mysteries and the language of earthly accommodation that describes them. If heaven is indeed a metaphorical court, it is the only true one, just as God is the only true, equally metaphorical king: a king, moreover, who, through the Son, will at the end of time explicitly get rid of kingship itself and reveal the liberty, equality, and fraternity that has been the nature of the Christian heaven all along: "For regal scepter then no more shall need, / God shall be all in all" (3.340–41; cf. 6.730–33).[34] Earthly monarchs are God's idolatrous imitators, but we nonetheless think of God in *their* terms.[35]

Satan, in fact, *invents* worldly monarchy by ascribing it to God.[36] Just as he and the fallen angels understand as carnal literalists the accommodation offered to them in the visible person of the Son, a temporal creature whose mediation points, so Satan suggests, to the temporal and creaturely, rather than divine, nature of the Father—so they take the royal analogy literally and carnally, as if they were indeed courtiers in a human Renaissance court: this is the "servile pomp" to which Mammon objected in book 2: "to celebrate his throne / With warbled hymns, and to his Godhead sing / Forced hallelujahs" (2.241–43). The republican Milton has no use himself for such royal courts on earth that would make the monarch into an "Idol of majesty divine," a king who would, in the words of *The Readie and Easie Way to Establish a Free Commonwealth* (1660), "set a pompous face upon the superficial actings of State, to pageant himself up and down in progress, among the perpetual bowings and cringings of an abject people, on either side deifying and adoring him" (*CPW* 7:426). His narrator describes the naked Adam greeting Raphael in book 5, "More solemn than the tedious pomp that waits / On princes, when their rich retinue long / Of horses led, and grooms besmeared with gold / Dazzles the crowd, and sets them all agape" (5.354–57). His human emperor has no clothes and is all the better for it.

Milton hated both kings and the "splendid vassalage" (2.252), as Mammon puts it, to which they subject their courtiers and minions. But Satan and his companions—and some readers of *Paradise Lost*, from William Blake on—make a category error when they portray God as a tyrant king who has made courtiers out of them, and this temporal, political understanding of a spiritual relationship is the essence of the fallen angels' irreligion and sin. Milton explores the implications of their pretense in order to explain their envy and their fall. He also, not so surreptitiously, continues in his Restoration poetry the earlier attacks on monarchy he had made in his Commonwealth prose. In this sense, Blake was right to understand Milton as being of the devil's party, but Milton is so always between brackets or within quotation marks: God is like and not like an earthly king, heaven is like and not like an earthly royal court, while, inversely, kings and courts are blasphemous attempts to play God on earth.

Furthermore, Milton uses his devils to satirize false ideas of liberty and alternatives to kingship of his particular historical moment, caught between a capitalist future and a feudal past. Even were they rebels against a worldly king, as John Milton himself was, Mammon and Satan do not get it. Their perspectives are fleshly. Mammon, the "least erected" of the angels, is fixed on the material riches of heaven, its golden pavement, and then on those in the soil of hell (1.679–92; 2.270–71). Satan, who would conquer by brute force and, in the last analysis, simply destroy, is no less intent on exploiting the substrate of heaven, its "materials dark and crude" (6.478), to invent the gunpowder that will give him his temporary military advantage. Despising the pomp of kingship, Mammon wishes simply to be left alone in order to enjoy his pursuit of wealth and material well-being, to "Live to ourselves, though in this vast recess, / Free, and to none accountable" (2.254–55), and suggests a selfish, Ayn Rand-ish bourgeoisie not yet politically mature enough to inherit the role of republican citizenship.[37] Satan for his part adapts the pose of an outmoded magnate asserting his autonomous military power and local lordship—the angels' titles, he says, "assert / Our being ordained to govern, not to serve" (5.801–2)—against a central monarchy and a court where his king would make him his dependent. Satan, that is, imagines what Lawrence Stone called "the crisis of the aristocracy."

The conflict between overmighty noble subject and king, and the role of court society in taming the former's violent ways and rendering him a docile royal servant, is a common story in early-modern state-building, described not only by Stone's resonant "crisis of the aristocracy," but also by Norbert Elias's "civilizing process."[38] In the War in Heaven in book 6, Satan derides Abdiel and the faithful angels as just such courtiers of God.

> At first I thought that liberty and heaven
> To heavenly souls had been all one; but now
> I see that most through sloth had rather serve,
> Ministering spirits, trained up in feast and song;
> Such hast thou armed, the minstrelsy of heaven,
> Servility with freedom to contend,
> As both their deeds compared this day shall prove.
> *(6.164–70)*

In Satan's punning taunt, the heavenly ministers have become effeminate minstrels: he is about to find out, as he plays Goliath to Abdiel's David, that such harpists can still pack a wallop.[39] Their hymns of praise and "mystical dance" described in book 5 (618–27), Satan suggests, are so many court entertainments of feast and song, the latter related to the "court amours / Mixed dance, or wanton mask, or midnight ball" (4.767–68) earlier denounced by the narrator in book 4, the former to chivalric "marshalled feast / Served up in hall with sewers and seneschals; / The skill of artifice or office mean" (9.37–39) rejected by the same narrator as a matter for his heroic poem in the invocation of book 9. Satan suggests that the good angels have been reduced to the "office mean" of just such sewers and seneschals, court servants who carry out the literal tasks of servants. They who also serve by only standing and waiting have become waiters. Or something still more abject, if we align these passages with Milton's nasty description in *The Readie and Easie Way to Establish a Free Commonwealth* of "a servile crew, not of servants only, but of nobility and gentry, bred up then to the hopes not of public, but of court offices; to be stewards, chamberlains, ushers, grooms, even of the close stool" (*CPW* 7:425). One cannot make an army out of such soft creatures. So Satan contends in the role he has just invented for himself as champion of feudal liberty and as tough old soldier who refuses to be civilized and tamed at court.

This role of overmighty warrior-vassal appears to be a newfound discovery of Satan, as much as his and Mammon's charge that he and his angels have been reduced to servile courtiers around an arbitrary monarch, although *Paradise Lost* may show some inconsistency on the issue. We have learned in book 1 that Mulciber built palaces in heaven for "sceptred angels" who "sat as princes, whom the supreme king / Exalted to such power, and gave to rule, / Each in his hierarchy, the orders bright" (1.734–37). In book 5, the rebellious angels pass "the mighty regencies / Of seraphim and potentates and thrones" (5.748–49) to reach Satan's seat in the north. So heaven does indeed seem to be laid out in a series of feudal fiefdoms. But these are not yet militarized. The angels whom Raphael describes in book 5 are organized according to a hierarchy and muster in what seems to be a military organization under "Ten thousand thousand ensigns high advanced, / Standards, and gonfalons" (5.588–89); numbers of them wave their banners beneath the command of Satan, who claims, with a "we" that may or may not be royal, to "possess / The quarters of the north" as a local fief (5.687–89).[40] There is, however, something of an optical illusion here, for, on closer examination, these banners suggest a hierarchy based on merit.

> and gonfalons twixt van and rear
> Stream in the air, and for distinction serve
> Of hierarchies, of orders, and degrees;
> Or in their glittering tissues bear imblazed
> Holy memorials, acts of zeal and love
> Recorded eminent.
> *(5.589–94)*

The characteristic Miltonic "Or" in verse 592 revises the idea of what we have been watching. It is not a martial muster at all, and no one is apparently in the armor that will subsequently encumber the angels, good as well as bad.[41] The orders and degrees are organized by their capacity to love, in accordance with the traditional description of the celestial hierarchy deriving from Pseudo-Dionysius the Areopagite. Their standards are a series of merit badges, earned by their pious zeal and love. The career of the zealous Abdiel later in book 5 shows how such badges and divine recognition might be earned. In this context, too, the begetting and anointment of the Son is more logical than Satan would allow, although the Son is being rewarded in advance, in the *chronology* of the poem, for the supreme love that he has already demonstrated in its *narrative sequence* by offering himself as a willing sacrifice to redeem humanity, "By merit more than birthright Son of God" (3.309).

The good angels comment on the novelty of the warfare that Satan introduces into heaven. The narrating Raphael notes: "strange to us it seemed / At first, that angel should with angel war, / And in fierce hosting meet, who wont to meet / So oft in festivals of joy and love" (6.91–94). Abdiel at the beginning of the book may be as much surprised to find chariots and flaming arms, "war in procinct" (6.19), in heaven as he is to find his news of Satan's rebellion already known. Michael describes Satan's sin and resulting evil as formerly "unknown," "unnamed," "uncreated," and asserts that "Heaven the seat of bliss / Brooks not the works of violence and war" (6.273–74). It is as if Satan reverses the historical process that Milton's Europe had experienced, and invents a military identity for angels created in the first place as a pacified nobility—or he discloses an aggression that has been repressed all along beneath their civility.

This identity—Satan as the overmighty feudal subject—proves to be illusory and short-lived in the ensuing War in Heaven, in part because of the very canonry that Satan invents. Artillery made the individual warrior and the feudal culture that had grown up around him into anachronisms, just as it spelled the end to the epic poetry that had celebrated that culture. By the opening two books of the poem, the fallen angels, licking their wounds in hell, know better than to persist in the warfare that only the suicidal Moloch advocates, and shift from force to fraud.

Paradise Lost has *already* depicted the last gasp of this noble, martial culture and effectively said good-bye to it at the end of book 4, in the episode of the duel that fails to materialize between Satan and Gabriel. Here, too, Satan renews his charge that the good angels are God's servile courtiers. Because of Raphael's inset, retrospective storytelling, the episode narratively precedes Satan's chronologically earlier histrionics as old-fashioned aristocratic rebel. Feudalism, with its open violence, is over before it begins in the poem, and this, like Satan's meeting his own Death in book 2, is another instance of the way that his career short-circuits upon itself, his defeat a foregone conclusion.

The duel is the ritual par excellence of the older warrior ethos, the subject of innumerable sixteenth- and seventeenth-century treatises and arguments about honor, a literature that arose in counterpoint to handbooks on courtiership and civility.[42] In fact, the dueling nobleman could be seen as the opposite of the tame courtier (even if the same aristocratic individual could occupy both roles). Through the duel's formalized violence, the nobleman could assert his individual claim to honor outside of the jurisdiction of his prince. In doing so, moreover, nobles could recreate the idealized chivalric and epic situation of one-on-one combat. Milton's Satan and Gabriel square off to fight in pointed contrast to their etiquette in God's heaven, each accusing the other of courtly abjection. But God lets down his golden scales from heaven (4.990–1004), and calls their combat off. So seventeenth-century monarchs enacted ordinances against dueling.

Issues of nobility and class hierarchy immediately arise when Zephon and Ithuriel capture Satan crouched down beside the ear of Eve in book 4. In a reversal of the *Doloneia* episode in *Iliad* 10, where the heroes Ulysses and Diomedes capture the lower-class Dolon, here the haughty Satan is apprehended by two subordinate angels. The pointed inversion of the Homeric model inaugurates the criticism of aristocratic epic heroism in the passage that follows. Zephon and Ithuriel fail to recognize their former social superior in his now "faded splendour wan" (4.870), and occasion Satan's noble disdain.

> Know ye not then said Satan, filled with scorn,
> Know ye not me? Ye knew me once no mate
> For you, there sitting where ye durst not soar;
> Not to know me argues your selves unknown,
> The lowest of your throng;
>   *(4.827–31)*

These limitary cherubs are mere nobodies, Satan sniffs, so far down the celestial hierarchy that they do not know with whom they are dealing. Yet deal with them he must, nonetheless: he's under arrest. The book has begun with Satan himself disguised as a stripling cherub and imagining himself as "some inferior angel" (4.59), and now he has to come to terms with what appears to be a real fall in social status. He is "abashed" before the "awful goodness" (4.846–47) of Zephon, a goodness that levels social ranks and makes its sharers spiritual equals.

It should come as a relief to Satan that in the ensuing action Gabriel immediately *does* recognize him as "the prince of hell" (4.871), and addresses him by name (4.878), even if it is not his former name in heaven (5.658–59). Satan appears to have been right all along in his insistence to deal "Best with the best" (4.852), with Gabriel, his counterpart on the side of the good angels, rather than with the lowly star troopers who have brought him in. These two angel grandees understand each other and appear to operate according to the same aristocratic code of private honor. Gabriel affords Satan the ultimate form of mutual, noble recognition by first goading him into a duel and then preparing to fight one out with him.

Milton shapes this quarrel according to the traditional formulas of the aristocratic duel, and subjects those formulas to a parody verging on burlesque. He incorporates equally traditional criticism of the duel advanced in his own century by absolutist states eager to curb noble violence and the autonomous power of local magnates. At the heart of the episode lies a polemic against the very code of aristocratic honor that both Satan and Gabriel appear to uphold. Gabriel chides Satan

> To say and straight unsay, pretending first
> Wise to fly pain, professing next the spy,
> Argues no leader, but a liar traced …
>   (4.947–49)

Gabriel has given Satan the lie, as well one might to the father of lies. But this is the "lie direct," the verbal insult up to, but just short of, which Shakespeare's clown Touchstone is willing to go in the stages of a quarrel in *As You Like It*, in the play's mockery of dueling treatises and their casuistry of honor. Unconditionally to call your adversary a liar obligates him to fight a duel to remove the stain upon his honor. Cromwell's colonel and correspondent Robert Hammond had killed a brother officer, a Major Gray, in a sudden duel, "for giving him the lie" in 1644; he was tried but acquitted, "the provocation being great."[43] In Milton's portrait of the duel, hardly less satirical than Shakespeare's, Satan duly responds with a challenge: "Far heavier load thyself expect to feel / From my prevailing arm" (4.972–73).

Yet the "warlike angel" (4.902) Gabriel seems incensed here less by Satan's prevarication than by Satan's insulting description of him as one of God's courtiers; Satan sneers that Gabriel has come

> to try once more
> What thou and thy gay legions dare against;
> Whose easier business were to serve their Lord
> High up in heaven, with songs to hymn his throne,
> And practised distances to cringe, not fight.
> *(4.941–45)*

As one of those "gay" legions, Gabriel is, according to Satan, a gorgeously outfit-
ted courtier—like the effeminate royal "popingay" whom Shakespeare's feudal
magnate Hotspur derides in *1 Henry IV* (1.3.50)—one of those demilitarized
noblemen who have found a new social identity in court ceremonies and service to the Throne, a cringer, not a soldier. Gabriel's reply is striking in that
he does not deny Satan's charge. Worshipping God—and Milton has in mind
the prostrations before God's throne and in front of the Lamb in Revelation
7:9–12—can *look like* such cringing courtly abasement, which is conversely, as
The Readie and Easie Way argues, an idolatrous and blasphemous making of an
earthly monarch into a god—"the perpetual bowings and cringings of an abject
people, on either side deifying and adoring him." Instead, Gabriel accuses Satan
himself of having been the real archcourtier before his fall, and one who prac-
ticed the dissimulating courtly art of hypocrisy.

> who more than thou
> Once fawned, and cringed, and servilely adored
> Heaven's awful monarch? Wherefore but in hope
> To dispossess him, and thy self to reign?
> *(4.958–61)*

You cringed as much, even more, than we did, says Gabriel, who further contends that it is Satan, not he, who was servile, because Satan's service to God
was insincere and not freely given, merely outward in gesture and under com-
pulsion, and this hypocrisy turns him from devout angel into envious courtier and would-be usurper.[44] The upshot of the exchange between Gabriel and
Satan is that worshipping the Christian God in his heaven is formally similar
but diametrically opposed to serving a carnal, profane king in his royal court.
"Freely we serve, / Because we freely love" (5.538–39), Raphael will describe the
"voluntary" rather than "necessitated" service (5.529–30) of the angels to God
in the ensuing book 5. Christians love to serve their God; courtiers, who must
serve their prince, envy.

But serving and cringing is the lot of those who have undergone the crisis
of the aristocracy—and, the republican Milton suggests, of all royalists, whatever their professions to aristocratic honor or to Christian piety. It is to prove
that they are not merely docile creatures of their lord, but still possess fighting
spirit and an honor that is both hereditary and individual, that nobles conduct
duels. Milton deliberately leaves ambiguous, however, just how Gabriel intends

to respond to Satan's challenge, whether in single combat or with his entire angelic squadron, which begins to hem Satan round in a crescent formation (4.977–80). If Gabriel is ganging up with his fellow angels—using the unfair advantage unworthy of a gentleman that in the language of dueling and chivalry is called *supercherie*—he might seem to confirm Satan's taunt that God's servant angels have lost the stomach for fighting that can only be truly manifested in the one-on-one duel. But Gabriel, for his part, may have deduced even before God interrupts their quarrel by hanging out his heavenly scales, a sign that puts Satan to cowardly flight, that the private duel is a diabolic temptation, an assertion through violence that one has an individual existence and identity independent of God. The operation of his squadron, archangel and lesser angels united as one, indicates the equality of its members in God's service.

At the sight of the scales, Gabriel correctly spells out the moral.

> Satan, I know thy strength, and thou knows't mine,
> Neither our own but given; what folly then
> To boast what arms can do, since thine no more
> Than heaven permits, nor mine, though doubled now
> To trample thee as mire.
> *(4.1006–10)*

The moral is as much political as theological. Milton takes up conventional legal arguments advanced by state authorities against the duel that, using the analogy to religious arguments against suicide that forbid one to take the life that God has created into one's hands, claim that this life belongs to the state. One version of this argument is nicely summed up in the *Discorsi* (1586) of Annibale Romei, translated as the *Courtiers Academie* in 1598.

> Combate to kill and destroy: it is contrary to lawes divine and civill, because neither by the one, or the other law is it permitted, that a particular man shuld dispose, either of his own, or of another mans life: considering that the law respecteth a particular man, not as of himselfe, but as belonging to the country & Prince, under whose dominion he is subject.[45]

Gabriel similarly acknowledges that neither he nor Satan have anything that they can call their own, including the force and valor of their own arms: these belong to God and one's lord. In the case of the angels, these are one and the same. Gabriel narratively discounts in advance (if ex post facto) Satan's claim at his rebellion to rely on "our own right hand" (5.864)—the rugged individualism of creaturely force.[46]

Gabriel, whose case is perhaps the more interesting of the two adversaries, cannot resist getting in one last jab about trampling Satan as mire. He rose to Satan's bait and has some lingering desire to fight it out, angel to angel. True individual heroism in Milton's antimartial epic is demonstrated by Abdiel, the "servant of God" who, at the corresponding moment at the end of book 5, is

allowed only a *verbal* duel with Satan in which he testifies to the truth and endures the scorn of the rebel angels. Abdiel is a secondary reflection of the Son,
the Suffering Servant. At the end of the poem Adam is explicitly cautioned by
Michael *not* to dream of the Son's fight with Satan "As of a duel" (12.387).

Yet Abdiel was subsequently given a chance to bring Satan to one knee in
the War in Heaven, asserting that it is only just "That he who in the debate of
truth hath won, / Should win in arms" (6.122–23), even though Milton and the
reader know that such justice is rarely enough evidenced on earth. There, too,
Gabriel had his good at bats, cleaving the violent Moloch from head to waist
(6.354–62). Satan's rebellion briefly turned the good angels, too, into soldiers,
but that lasted only for two days of the heavenly battle. By the second day, the
faithful angels have not only been given the chance to experience Christian
humiliation and heroic martyrdom by Satan's artillery and derision, but also
in their own righteous anger turned into "Rage" (6.635) had, as Gabriel nearly
does now, left patience behind and become nearly interchangeable with their
demonic foes. "They stood / A while in trouble; but they stood not long" (6.633–
34), before they reached for mountains to throw down on Satan's canonry, and
their leaving the posture of standing suggests a criticism of their retaliatory
action. In their conflict "all heaven / Had gone to wrack" (6.669–70) as now in
the impending duel of Gabriel and Satan "all the elements / At least had gone to
wrack" (4.993–94), taking God's new creation with them. Both Abdiel and Gabriel were required to "Stand still" (6.801) as bystanders—a spiritual attitude of
perseverance as well as a physical stance—while the Son single-handedly took
on and cast the rebel angel forces out of heaven.[47] Such combat as they were allowed is now in the past or reserved for an apocalyptic final battle, and Gabriel
must henceforth put up his sword.

In Gabriel's renunciation of the combat he would like to fight, Milton indicates, *pace* Simmel, with what difficulty an angel or any Christian gives up
private aggression and accepts that one's proper role is to be a servant—which
to a profane, external observer may seem like servility. Milton suggests how
especially hard it is for an aristocrat of his own time to follow the Christian
injunction to submit to insult—what amounts to submitting the adjudication
of his honor to the eyes of God. John Milton, son of a scrivener and moneylender, had himself adapted noble airs. In the autobiographical passage of the
Second Defense of the English People, he tells us that he wore a sword in the seeing days of his youth and knew how to use it, "and I was fearless of any injury
that one man could inflict on another" (*CPW* 4:583). This episode of *Paradise
Lost* asserts, however, the incompatibility of this aristocratic ethos of individual
martial honor with Christianity. It suggests, furthermore, the difficulty that the
nobleman may have in giving that ethos up when his Christian humility may so
closely resemble a tameness enforced upon him by a modern prince: he'll look
like a courtier sissy. Let us return to those court waiters, the "sewers and seneschals" whom Milton's narrator scorns. In a passage of Luke 22:25–26 that we

shall shortly see Milton cite in *The Readie and Easie Way*, where Jesus enjoins his apostles to be Christian servants, he adds, in a passage that Milton elects *not* to cite, his own example at the table of the Last Supper: "For whether is greater, he that sitteth at meat, or he that serveth? Is not he that sitteth at meat? But I am among you as he that serveth" (Luke 22:27). Just how *does* a nobleman distinguish such service from literal waiting on tables at court, which marks his subservience to a prince who would strip him of his former feudal power and prerogative, especially the prerogative of violence?[48] Satan's insults to Gabriel's fighting angelhood, with their innuendo of effeminacy and faintheartedness, hit a nerve because they reflect a moment of historical transition.

This transition has generic consequences. Colin Burrow and Michael Putnam have noted that the final verse of book 4 describing Satan's flight from the scene, "Murmuring, and with him fled the shades of night" (4.1015), echoes the final verse of the entire *Aeneid*, "uita *cum gemitu fugit* indignata *sub umbras*" (*Aen.* 12.952), the flight to the shades of the underworld of the indignant, murmuring (in the sense of complaining) soul of the Italian hero Turnus after he has been slain by Aeneas in the duel that climaxes Virgil's epic.[49] In that final scene of the *Aeneid*, Virgil's Jupiter suspends his scales in heaven to determine which of the heroes will die (*Aen.* 12.725–27). Milton's God hangs forth in heaven his golden scales, conflating Virgilian and Homeric models with the judgment of Belshazzar on God's scales in Daniel 5:27. He does so in order to stop the impending duel, and Satan gets the message and flees the scene. Had they fought, Milton's epic might have come to an end then and there, as Virgil's concluded with a final duel. As it is, this scene puts an end to the first third of *Paradise Lost* and opens the space of books 5–8, where Satan is absent (if, nonetheless, very much present in Raphael's narrative in books 5 and 6), before his return in book 9, dividing the poem into three four-book-long parts; a similar pattern obtained in the 4-3-3 structure of the first version of the epic in ten books (1667). But the recollection of Virgil's ending here points out one more time that nothing in Milton's poem will be settled by the contest of arms that has heretofore been the stuff of epic—"Wars, hitherto, the only argument / Heroic deemed" (9.28–29). So Milton's narrator declares as his poem enters into its decisive final third in book 9. Not only does *Paradise Lost* continue for another eight books after Satan's confrontation with Gabriel, but their impending duel, a final opportunity for traditional epic combat, is not allowed to take place in the poem's narrative present: such fighting is relegated to the past when Raphael recounts the heavenly war to an enthralled Adam and Eve, to a *literary* as well as chronological past. If Milton's epic does not end here, an older martial epic does. Its military subject is no longer viable for the epic of Adam and Eve's and Milton's own time, either because heroic poetry will henceforth explore the better Christian heroism or because the nobleman soldier, the protagonist of that earlier epic, has now become a pacified courtly servant.

Paradise Lost thus offers two explanations, one sacred (the celebration of a Christian ethos), one profane and class-driven (the political demise of the old ethos of military honor) for its own generic shift, and these also inform the alternatives between the Son's spiritual charity and Satan's temporal envy. Gabriel's contention that Satan was himself a hypocritical courtier even before the anointment of the Son made him fall in envy indicates just how regressive are the rebellion and civil war that Satan introduces into heaven: the tame and civil archangel invents a violent and anarchic past into which he and his confederates claim to return. In doing so, Satan suggests the particularly modern quality and genealogy of his envy: it is the vice of a society in which open violence between rivals is no longer tolerated and in which equality prevails over traditional class hierarchy. Milton acknowledges the role that absolutism and the royal court have played in pacifying feudal violence and the leveling of classes, even as he satirizes both historical phenomena. Monarchical institutions produce an equality based on unwilling servitude, and are a false alternative to the republican parity and meritocracy—"By merit more than birthright Son of God" (3.309)—the true equality that Milton the Commonwealth man envisions as the proper successor to feudalism. Yet, by taming and civilizing a warrior nobility, king and court may have functioned historically to prepare for the egalitarian republic, whose citizens freely agree to live as political equals, just as the kingship of the Son prepares for his eventual abdication. This second perspective on the monarchy that Milton otherwise unequivocally opposed may account for some ambivalence in his portrait of a divine monarch, and of a peaceful heaven that is and is not like a royal court: it is Satan's sin to reduce this accommodating analogy to its earthly terms, the terms of Milton's own times, but there may still be something to the analogy itself. The new equality—whether of God's transcendent kingship, of court society, or of republican commonwealth—weakens traditional markers of individual identity: titles, Satan complains, have become "merely titular" (5.774). It raises on the one hand the opportunity of a compensating Christian community among spiritual equals, the incorporation into "one soul." On the other hand, a sense of impaired selfhood and the frustration of armed aggression can fester into envy. It is the vice of Milton's time and of our own.

Brotherhood versus Kingship in Books 11–12

For all his posing as rebel magnate, we are not allowed to forget that Satan wants to be king himself, in glory above his peers. He tells his fellow rebel angels that they are "if not equal all, yet free, / Equally free; for orders and degrees / Jar not with liberty, but well consist" (5.791–93), lest they take up a true egalitarianism and refuse to serve him in place of God. Milton may equivocate here along with his devil. The refutation of Satan's assertion is assigned in the poem to Eve, who *after* her fall, thinks that she would like, in relation to Adam, to be "more equal, and perhaps, / A thing not undesirable, sometime / Superior; for inferior who is free?" (9.823–25). *Paradise Lost* raises the question of whether freedom can be reconciled with hierarchy, but deliberately puts *both* the positive and negative answers in the mouths of impeachable sources, the devil and the first human sinner at the moment of her sin, in order to leave it undecided. But Milton's epic makes it plain that if liberty may consist with some degrees of inequality, it is ruled out entirely by the worldly kingship that Satan is the first to establish in hell.

The Readie and Easie Way argues that a republican Commonwealth is the form of government that comes closest to bringing together "due libertie and proportiond equalitie" (*CPW* 7.424)—the latter term suggests unequal equals— and contrasts it to the abjection of monarchy and its attendant institution, court society. Only in a republic, he argues, can state institutions further the aspirations of human beings to a life of Christian charity. He cites the words of Jesus in Luke 22:25–26.

> *the kings of the gentiles,* saith he, *exercises lordship over them;* and they that *exercise authoritie upon them, are call'd benefactors: but ye shall not be so; but he that is greatest among you, let him be as the younger; and he that is chief, as he that serveth.* The occasion of these his words was the ambitious desire of *Zebede's* two sons, to be exalted above thir brethren in his kingdom, which they thought was to be ere long upon earth ... And what government coms neerer to this precept of Christ, then a free Commonwealth; wherin they who are greatest are perpetual servants and drudges to the public at thir own cost and charges, neglect thir own affairs; yet are not elevated above thir brethren; live soberly in thir families, walk the streets as other men, may be spoken to freely, familiarly, friendly without adoration. Wheras a king must be ador'd like a Demigod, with a dissolute and haughtie court about him of vast expense and luxurie, masks and revels, to the debaushing of our prime gentry, both male and female; not in thir passetimes only, but in earnest, by the loos imploiments of court service, which will be then thought honorable. (*CPW* 7:424–25)

The error of the sons of Zebedee is very similar to that of Satan and his fellow fallen angels, the imagining of God's kingdom as an earthly monarchy in which they, brothers themselves, would "be exalted above thir brethren." In the virtuous republic, Milton maintains, the officers of government are not "elevated above thir brethren," and follow the injunction of Jesus that the greatest should instead be as servants. The Commonwealth thus provides a positive, earthly model of service for the public good that captures something of the angels' willing service to God in heaven in *Paradise Lost*. The false double of both is the degrading servitude that courtiers, the "servile crew," pay to an earthly king, a form of idolatry and the pursuit of false honor. The prospect of being a perpetual drudge may not seem that much more appealing than the courtier's "perpetual bowings and cringings" that *The Readie and Easie Way* describes a few sentences later. Perhaps this is how Milton sometimes felt about his position as Secretary for the Foreign Tongues in the Commonwealth government. But Milton equates such public service with a Christian willingness to act as a loving servant to one's fellow men and women. The Commonwealth's "proportiond equalitie," whereby state servants remain on the same level as the public they serve, conditions a true Christian brotherhood that Milton declares in *De Doctrina Christiana* to be the highest form of charity: "BROTHERLY OR CHRISTIAN CHARITY [*CHARITAS FRATERNA, seu CHRISTIANA*] is the greatest of all. It is what makes fellow-Christians love and help one another, as members of Christ. It makes them all of one mind [*unanimes*] so far as is possible" (*CPW* 6:748; *Works* 17:270). As we have noted above, this human brotherhood, described in the Pauline terms of the body of Christ, has its equivalent in *Paradise Lost* in the new communion that the Son, according to God's proclamation, offers to the angels in heaven, "United as one individual soul" (5.610), and a version of which, Raphael narrates, the angels already enjoyed, "Unanimous, as sons of one great sire" (6.95).

An equivalent perhaps—one might well assume that sons of one great sire are all brothers—yet *Paradise Lost* reserves the relationship of brotherhood to human beings. "Brethren" only appears once outside of books 11 and 12 and their depiction of human history, and it does so to describe the central event of that history, the prophecy in book 3 of the Son's future passion, when he will "be judged and die, / And dying rise, and rising with him *raise / His brethren*, ransomed with his own dear life" (3.295–97). Rather than be elevated above his human brothers, the Son, in his unmatched charity, will descend to their mortality and raise them with him to his own divinity.

It is the opposite with the earthly conquerors and kings in books 11 and 12, whose crimes, in the terms that the poem insistently repeats, are, above all, crimes against brotherhood. They repeat over and over again the initial deed of human history that Michael displays to the appalled Adam, Cain's killing of Abel. And the cause of this first crime ensuing on the Fall is envy.

> These two are brethren, Adam, and to come
> Out of thy loins; the unjust the just has slain,
> For envy that his brother's offering found
> From heaven acceptance;
>   (11.454–57)

Here envy is quite literally pitted against the brotherhood it destroys. Cain's envy of Abel repeats Satan's envy of the Son, preferred for his true service by God, and this original fratricide has a political legacy in the last two books of *Paradise Lost*: monarchy. First come the antediluvian "conquerors / Patrons of mankind, gods, and sons of gods, / Destroyers rightlier called and plagues of men" (11.695–97) in book 11. They are not identified as kings, but these "patrons" are, differently translated, the same "benefactors" of the Luke 22:25 passage cited in *The Readie and Easie Way*: the kings of the Gentiles. Their claims of divinity and divine sonship—Milton has Alexander the Great and Augustus Caesar particularly in mind in these, their antediluvian antitypes—squarely oppose them to the charity of the true Son.[50] After the Flood, in book 12, Nimrod, tyrant king and builder of the Tower of Babel, will inherit what the poem depicts as the true curse of Cain.

In a vicious cycle of luxury and war, the daughters of the race of Cain—"his race / Who slew his brother" (11.608–9)—mix on the plain with the sons of Seth, "Just men" (11.577), like Abel the just, men who hitherto had known how to preserve "Freedom and peace to men" (11.580) in their high hills. Their descent and intermarriage, in turn, produces the conquerors, who, Adam protests,

> multiply
> Ten thousand fold the sin of him who slew
> His brother: for of whom such massacre
> Make they but of their brethren, men of men?
> But who was that just man ... ?
> *(11.677–81)*

Mass warfare escalates Cain's original crime. As is well known, the model for the fourth vision that Michael presents to Adam, and on which he is commenting here (11.638–73), is Homer's depiction of a city at peace and a city at war on the shield of Achilles in *Iliad* 18 (490–540). The vision reverses the order of the two cities in the *Iliad*, so that the one at war is succeeded by the one at peace as the fourth vision of conquest is itself succeeded by the fifth vision of a luxurious and decadent peace—"All now was turned to jollity and game, / To luxury and riot" (11.714–15)—that leads to the universal destruction of the Flood. It shows the city of peace not in peace at all, but in "factious opposition" (11.664) that the intervention of the one just man, Enoch, can do nothing to stop.

The Homeric model, in fact, is ironically superimposed upon another scheme of two cities, the city of man and the city of God, in Augustine's *The City of God*, particularly as it was laid out in the commentary on the early stories of Genesis in books 15 and 16, which Milton is closely following here.[51] In this case, *both* of the fourth vision's cities are versions of the earthly human city of sin, and the one denizen of the heavenly city, Enoch (see *City of God* 15.19), has to be snatched from the violent hands of his fellow men and translated to heaven itself. The factional strife he seeks to mediate already anticipates the "civil broils" (11.718) and "hostile deeds in peace" (11.796) of the fifth vision where the conquerors have ceased warring in order to luxuriate in their spoils, only, it is suggested, to turn on each other in civil strife.

Milton is thinking of the Roman republic's first-century BCE descent into civil war when it became too rich from its conquests—the story that is classically outlined at the beginning of Sallust's *Conspiracy of Catiline*, with its emphasis on "luxuria" and "luxus" (10–13).[52] This is the Rome that Augustine in *The City of God* calls the head of the earthly city, and which, he notes, repeats the founding act of the earthly city, Cain's murder of Abel, with its own founding fratricide, Romulus's killing of Remus. On Rome's decline Augustine refers his readers directly to Sallust's history, in which "he shows how the profligate manners which were propagated by prosperity resulted at last even in civil wars" (2.18).[53] The translation of Enoch out of this city of man, in fact, performs an ironic, epic variation, not only on the *Iliad* but on a famous passage in the *Aeneid*, the poem's first simile in book 1 that, we shall see in chapter 7, Milton reworks in other places in *Paradise Lost*. The calming of the stormy seas by Virgil's Neptune is compared to an outbreak of disorder and mob violence in a great nation that is calmed by the speech of a man revered for his piety and merits—"pietate gravem ac meritis" (*Aeneid* 1.151). When "grave" Enoch, "eminent / In wise deport," similarly tried to quell faction, speaking "much of right and wrong, / Of justice, of religion, truth, and peace, / And judgement from above," the crowd "exploded" him, that is, it hooted him down (see *PL* 10.546), and would have done worse (11.662–69); we are reminded of the bad angels' reaction to Abdiel's arguments and exhortations. There is no real peace to be had in the city of sin, founded on war and luxury, Milton suggests, and that would especially include Virgil's Rome for all of that poet's wishful thinking. Like that Rome, the human history that began in fratricide is heading for fratricidal internal conflict again when it is interrupted by the Flood. But, as Adam has understood, foreign conquest of other human beings is no less a violation of brotherhood than civil war.

After the Flood, the sad story of decline repeats itself in book 12. Noah's descendants enjoy a period of God-fearing peace under "paternal rule," but then Nimrod rises, whose kingdom at Babel (Genesis 10:10) is the first to be mentioned in the Bible, "a cruel oppressor and tyrant" says the Geneva Bible, following a long tradition that also makes him the builder of the Tower of Babel. Like the race of Cain, Nimrod, too, seeks out a plain, the plain of Shinar and site of the tower. Like Cain's crime, the monarch Nimrod offends against brotherhood.

> Under paternal rule; till one shall rise
> Of proud ambitious heart, who not content
> With fair equality, fraternal state
> Will arrogate dominion undeserved
> Over his brethren ...
>   (12.24–28)

The language here directly recalls *The Readie and Easie Way*, where the sons of Zebedee were scolded by Jesus for wishing "to be exalted above thir brethren," where the servants of the republic "are not elevated above thir brethren," and where Milton had also wondered: "Considering these things, so plane, so rational, I cannot but yet further admire on the other side, how any man who hath the true principles of justice and religion in him, can presume or take upon him to be a king and lord over his brethren, whom he cannot but know, whether as men or Christians, to be for the most part every way equal or superiour to himself" (*CPW* 7:364). What were Charles Stuart, father and son, thinking, and what does it say about them? The pamphlet is echoed again in Adam's comment on the scene:

> O execrable son so to aspire
> Above his brethren, to himself assuming
> Authority usurped, from God not given;
> *(12.64–66)*

So much for the divine right of kings, who would overthrow the fraternal state of political equality, a state, moreover, that the poem, in its internal rhyming, makes equivalent to the paternal rule that followed the Flood. So much, too, then, for the idea that patriarchy implies kingship, that kings enjoy a father's absolute and "natural" rule over their subjects.[54] The two passages neatly and pointedly refute both pillars of the royalist doctrine of Sir Robert Filmer, who penned in 1652 a refutation of Milton's first *Defense of the English People*, and who, four years earlier in *The Anarchy of a Limited or Mixed Monarchy*, had derived divinely sanctioned monarchy from the patriarchal rule of Noah and his sons.[55] Milton dismisses Filmer in the space of forty verses.

The antediluvian sequence of conquest and peacetime luxury, moreover, repeats itself even among the best of kings, where one might not expect it. David, in Michael's subsequent telling, is

> for piety renowned
> And puissant deeds,
> *(12.321–22)*

succeeded by his son Solomon:

> for wealth and wisdom famed
> *(12.332)*

The careful chiastic construction places the good traits of these renowned biblical kings on the outside, but nonetheless leaves the sins of monarchy with which they are alliteratively coupled in plain sight as a rotten core: "puissant deeds" and "wealth." These are the same empire and riches that will spread, like the disease of the human body-politic that is monarchy, until they encompass the globe that Adam has beheld from the top of the mount of speculation; the tempter Satan will offer their kingdoms and glory to Jesus, the second Adam (11.381–411). The coupling avoids the censor. Kings who appeal to the Davidic model—the Stuarts were routinely compared or compared themselves to both David and Solomon—stand on slippery ground.[56]

Adam's words spell out the resemblance of Nimrod to Satan, "aspiring / To set himself in glory above his peers" (1.38–39) at the beginning of Milton's epic. The resemblance is underscored by Nimrod's companions, "a crew, whom like ambition joins / With him or under him to tyrannize" (12.38–39). The word "crew" appears eleven times earlier in *Paradise Lost*, in all but one case referring to the rebel angels who are Satan's associates: "thy rebellious crew," as Gabriel describes them to Satan (4.952), "that godless crew / Rebellious," as the divine voice calls them at the beginning of the War in Heaven (6.50). Milton derives Nimrod's own name etymologically from rebellion (12.36–37): the attempt of Nimrod and his associates to impose a carnal, earthly kingship is another version of the rebellion of the fallen angels.[57] God holds both "in derision" (5.736; 12.52; see Psalm 2:4). Milton's withering description presents a retrospective gloss on those angels and all similar royalist cronies and courtiers willing to abrogate the relationship of brotherly equality. They are even willing, as the "or" phrase suggests, to subject themselves *under* a satanic tyrant in order to subject others to themselves: such are the "servile crew," the court nobility of the Stuart kings, in *The Readie and Easie Way*. Each attempt to establish monarchy, diabolic and human, ends in an alienating "din" (10.521; 12.61): Satan and his crew transformed into serpents, "hiss for hiss returned with forked tongue / To forked tongue" (10.518–19), Nimrod and his followers afflicted by the confusion of tongues at Babel.[58] *Paradise Lost* depicts its own travesty or reduction to noise and nonsense in these Orwellian visions of how the princes of this world empty language of reason. Satan's metamorphosis into the biggest snake of all ironically grants him his initial wish: "his power no less he seemed / *Above the rest* still to retain" (10.531–32). Satan's monarchical ambition, inseparable from his envy—both the antithesis of the brotherly charity of the Son—replicates itself in human history in Cain's envy and fratricide and in the conquerors and kings who are Cain's heirs. The drive to worldly kingship is both the cause that leads to the Fall in *Paradise Lost*, and, as Michael will explain to Adam in psychological terms, the effect of that Fall: "Since thy original lapse, true liberty / Is lost" (12.83–84). The political polemic of the epic, not only of its last two books, should now be clear: within the limits of his post-Restoration situation and censorship, Milton repeats the arguments of his tracts against kingship.

A passage that has already been mentioned in Augustine's *The City of God*—and the biblical passage that lies behind it, in turn—offer one more gloss on Milton's fiction and perhaps allow us to bring together its disparate depictions of envy and of envy's opposite, charity. Augustine compares the different reasons behind the envy that caused Romulus to kill his brother Remus, both of them already inhabitants of the earthly city, and the envy that prompted Cain, founder of that earthly city, to kill Abel, citizen of the heavenly one.

> Romulus and Remus ... both desired to have the glory of founding the Roman republic, but both could not have as much glory as if one only claimed it; for he who wished to have the glory of ruling would certainly rule less if his power were shared by a living consort. In order, therefore, that the whole glory might be enjoyed by one, his consort was removed; and by this crime the empire was made larger indeed, but inferior, while otherwise it would have been less, but better. Now these brothers Cain and Abel were not animated by the same earthly desires, nor did the murderer envy the other because he feared that, by both ruling, his own dominion would be curtailed—for Abel was not solicitous to rule in that city which his brother built—he was moved by that diabolical envious hatred with which the evil regard the good, for no other reason than because they are good while themselves are evil. For possession of goodness is by no means diminished by being shared with a partner either permanent or temporarily assumed; on the contrary the possession of goodness is increased in proportion to the concord and charity of each of those who share it. In short, he who is unwilling to share this possession cannot have it; and he who is most willing to admit others to a share of it will have the greatest abundance to himself. The quarrel, then, between Romulus and Remus shows how the earthly city is divided against itself; that which fell out between Cain and Abel illustrated the hatred that subsists between the two cities, that of God and that of men.[59] (15.5)

Augustine asserts that the evil hate the good simply because they are good, but he also suggests why this should be so. For those who think in temporal, earthly terms, like Romulus and Remus, he argues, the goods of the world are finite. Human brothers envy and struggle against each other to possess as many temporal goods as possible, in a zero-sum game of politics, where one's gain is the other's loss.[60] Such a world without charity must lead to kingship, the domination of one alone. The citizens of the city of God, by contrast, realize that spiritual goods—love of God, love for one's fellow human beings—are superabundant and multiply through being charitably shared, and such communion makes its partakers willing equals, true brothers. In *Paradise Lost*, this doctrine of charity ironically turns up in the mouth of Satan in the dream that he inspires in Eve, urging her to eat the forbidden fruit, and that Eve cites at the beginning of book 5: "since good, the more / Communicated, more abundant grows, / The author not impaired" (5.71–73). The same Satan, we have seen, in Raphael's retrospective narrative at the end of the book, earlier thought himself "impaired" (5.665) as the *recipient* of God's good when offered the chance of greater communion through the Son: Satan rejects Abdiel's pious contention that this new dispensation will not "make us less" but rather "exalt / Our happy state."[61] The envious and evil, Augustine implies, cannot abide the happiness of the charitable and good, because they cannot recognize or enter into its terms: they cannot see spiritual opportunities—equality, community—in a temporal world.

When Augustine described the hatred that the wicked bear to the good on account of their very goodness, he almost surely had in mind Wisdom of Solomon 2–3, the passage with which this chapter started: Milton, too, clearly meditated upon this section of Wisdom.[62] Here the primary temporal good that the ungodly find finite is human life itself: "For our time is a very shadow that passeth away; and after our end there is no returning: for it is fast sealed, so that no man cometh again. Come on therefore let us enjoy the good things that are present" (Wis. 2:5–6). With time running out, the ungodly seek to "crown ourselves with rosebuds, before they be withered" (2:8) and cheerfully oppress the weak: the poor, the widow, and the aged. And they persecute the good who "upbraideth us with our offending the law" (2:12), and whose righteousness is a reproof to them: "Let us condemn him with a shameful death" (2:20). Milton's Michael echoes this last passage when he narrates to Adam the killing of the most righteous of all: Jesus will be "to death condemned / A shameful and accurst, nailed to the cross" (12.412–13). The wicked behave this way because they do not know the mysteries of God; that is, "the hope full of immortality" that the good share (3:4). The superabundance of charity that Augustine attributes to the members of the City of God is thus based on faith in something beyond death (or, less mystically, on an *acceptance* of human finitude). For the same Wisdom passage continues in the verses we began by citing: "God created man to be immortal and to be an image of his own eternity. Nevertheless, through the envy of the devil death came into the world: and they that do hold of his side do find it." Milton traces this envy back to Satan's initial misrecognition of the anointed Son. It is the moment when time and change first differentiate themselves out of eternity and become a problem for consciousness. Satan understands God's image, an image that Milton insists *was* created in time, in exclusively temporal and political terms when it is presented before his eyes, and the sight simultaneously rouses his envy and his monarchical ambition: Satan's own spiritual death is the first that his envy brings into the world. The rest is history.

6

Getting What You Wish For: A Reading of the Fall

It takes two, Adam and Eve, to fall in book 9 of *Paradise Lost*, just as it takes both of them to reconcile with each other and accept the gift of God's grace in book 10. Eve falls deceived by the wiles of Satan, failing the test she sets for herself to confront and withstand temptation as a lone individual. Adam knowingly falls with Eve, an act that combines marital love, human solidarity, and Adam's fear of repeating his earlier loneliness before Eve's creation: "To live again in these wild woods forlorn" (9.910). Adam's choice—the choice of death—aligns him with the second Adam, the Son, who will die for and in the place of humanity, and might seem to place Adam on a higher ground, heroic and moral, than his wife, "much *deceived*, much failing, hapless Eve" (9.404). Milton provides a version of the Genesis story that accords with 1 Timothy 2:14: "And Adam was not deceived, but the woman being deceived was in the transgression." Paul glosses the divine judgment of Genesis 3:16—"thy desire shall be subject to thy husband, and he shall rule over thee"—and notoriously uses the deceived and transgressing Eve to subordinate not only wives to husbands but women to male authority, and to ordain their silence. "Deceived," a word used sparingly in *Paradise Lost* in any case, reappears in the second of its only two uses in book 9 at the moment when Adam falls, an explicit echo of the Pauline passage: "he scrupled not to eat / Against his better knowledge, *not deceived*, / But fondly overcome with female charm" (9.997–99). One may begin to suspect a pun, especially in light of the privative "dis-" words that open the book "distrust, disloyal, disobedience, distance, distaste" (9.6–9): by falling alongside his wife, Adam was not "dis-Eve-d."[1]

Earlier in the poem, however, Milton's God gives the 1 Timothy passage a striking twist. He explains in book 3 the difference between the fallen angels, who fell on their own and are beyond redemption, and the case of Adam and Eve and their human descendants.

> The first sort by their own suggestion fell,
> Self-tempted, self-depraved: man falls *deceived*
> By the other first: man therefore shall find grace,
> The other none:
> > (3.129–32)

No scriptural foundation underlies this enunciation of the theological escape clause of *Paradise Lost*. Because "man" falls through the deceit of Satan, humanity can be redeemed through the Son and, as God goes on to say, his mercy will outshine even his glory. But in this corporate "man," it was Eve, not Adam, whom Satan deceived, as the opening of the poem declares: "he it was, whose guile / Stirred up with envy and revenge, deceived / The mother of mankind" (1.34–36). Adam's decision to transgress together with Eve may fit into a category all its own, but in this light his knowing what he is doing aligns him as much with the devil as with the Son: "To Satan only like both crime and doom" (10.841), Adam himself comments on his condition after the Fall in book 10. Thus, in his fall, Adam can appear both less and more culpable than Eve. Milton both works with 1 Timothy and works changes upon it when he allots blame for the first sin, as well as credit for God's grace, between the first husband and wife. In doing so, he qualifies Paul's foundational misogyny. To fall deceived may not, the word of the apostle notwithstanding, have been the worst thing. It is to the nature of Eve's fall, in fact, that human beings owe their chance to be saved.[2]

Eve's and Adam's respective falls, and the way that they are assigned the gender attributes of the first woman and man, each correspond to deeply held, if sometimes opposed, wishes that Milton entertained throughout his writing career.[3] To put them in bald terms, the first wish imagines a solitary, virtually self-sufficient human being undefiled by worldly temptation and approved in faith by God, an individual described in feminized, largely passive terms—the Lady in *Comus*, the Jesus of *Paradise Regained*—who holds out against a seducer. It is a wish, too, uneasily intertwined with the poet's hope for fame: fame is an individual and individualizing attainment. The second wish is gregarious and sociable, envisioning the individual interacting with others in relationships of human love and with a fallen world more generally, and it is characterized as masculine—aggressively so in the Samson of *Samson Agonistes*. In *Paradise Lost*, these dual wishes are built into the actions of the first couple from the beginning. Eve first awakes into being beside a pool of Narcissus; Adam asks his Creator for a partner and, however gently, seizes Eve when she turns back toward her watery image.

These wishes are also spelled out by *Paradise Lost* in contrasting terms of human *sufficiency* and *deficiency*. Milton's God pronounces that he has created human individuals "Sufficient to have stood" (3.99) and that, even after the Fall, divine grace will provide them "What may suffice" (3.189) for regeneration;

Adam tells Eve as she goes off on her own in book 9 that God has "Nothing imperfect or deficient left" in them (9.345). Yet one book earlier Adam recalls telling God: "Thou in thyself art perfect, and in thee / Is no deficience found; not so is man" (8.415–16). Adam's sense of a lack in his lone self—"In unity defective" (8.425)—makes him request from his "absolute" (8.421) Creator a "like" to "solace his defects" (8.418–19).[4] The countervailing ideas that human beings are spiritually self-sufficient in relation to God and socially dependent on one another—it is "not good for man to be alone" (8.445)—generate the problems and drama of the epic. They correspond to the double imperatives of Milton's Protestant Christianity, the obligation of the human individual to establish a personal faith in God and the demand that humans love one another in the relation of charity and in the community of a church, however invisible or mystical that church may be. So the first part of *Areopagitica* would foster "the growth and compleating of one vertuous person" (*CPW* 2:528), while its second half projects a super Church in which "all the Lords people are become Prophets" (*CPW* 2:556), held together by Paul's "*unity of Spirit*" and "*bond of peace*" (Eph. 4:3) (*CPW* 2:565). The two wishes are already in tension in Milton's poetry in the vatic solitude of the *Penseroso* and the sociability of the *Allegro*, in the individual fame the speaker of *Lycidas* seeks from the witness of Jove and the solemn troops and sweet societies envisioned for the dead Lycidas that replace their earlier pastoral fellowship, the bright college years at Cambridge.

The studies of William Kerrigan have identified these wishes as psychic drives in a classical Freudian narrative that describes the overcoming of the younger Milton's quest for chaste purity and denial of death by his entrance into adult sexuality and marriage, and his acceptance of (the Father's law that decrees) his mortality.[5] So, already predicting this narrative, "wisest Fate" or Father says "no" to the fantasies of a purity now and forever, of time running backward away from death, in Milton's first great poem, the *Ode on the Morning of Christ's Nativity*. This was indeed the story of Milton's life, a story he told over and over again in his poetry. His poetic career itself divided between the 1645 *Poems*, largely the product of his period of chaste "retirement" and study in the 1630s, and the 1667 *Paradise Lost* and 1671 *Paradise Regained* and *Samson Agonistes*, the long works that followed his almost twenty years of public engagement as pamphleteer in the 1640s and as Commonwealth bureaucrat in the 1650s, and in the wake of his first two marriages. The succession of life stages did not cancel out Milton's first wish by the second, but, by a conservation or layering of inner life, kept them *both* in play, and they are still present and in competition in the 1671 volume that followed his great epic. Both *Paradise Regained* and *Samson Agonistes* plot out retrospective versions of Milton's life story that led to the great action of his life: the writing of *Paradise Lost*. But the Jesus of the brief epic lives out this story as Milton had originally, ideally projected it in the first wish of individual perfection; Samson in the tragedy lives it out as the life that Milton had actually led in accord with the second: marriage and disappointment, political engagement and defeat, blindness.[6]

The following discussion reads the double fall in *Paradise Lost* inside this larger Miltonic career—we shall see how book 9 echoes Milton's earlier writings and is echoed in turn by the 1671 poems: the chapter contains an excursus on *Paradise Regained*. Eve's fall stages and, of necessity, criticizes the first wish of spiritual self-sufficiency and quest for recognition; Adam's fall does the same for the second of human love and codependency. They each seem to tip, to one side or the other, the equilibrium that *Paradise Lost* explores between the vertical relationship of proving oneself in the sight of God and the collateral relationship of love and community, between going it alone and going it together. Each wish maps out a sphere for the exercise of human freedom and will that is initially divinely sanctioned—to make a trial of oneself, to choose a loving relationship with another. In each case disobedience would make that sphere autonomous from God. But, at the same time, these wishes lend heroic dignity to the tragedy of the Fall: their respective impulses—to affirm faith, to share charity—are good and already proto-Christian, and thus can still be understood as expressions of prelapsarian innocence, up to the very point of the Fall.[7] And they will be vindicated after the Fall, when human beings, particularly in the affective realms of marriage and love, appear, in fact, to have gained an increased Christian liberty and independence: they have outgrown the divine tutelage in Eden for whose loss the poem simultaneously mourns. In the formal resolution of the epic, Adam and Eve appear to have exchanged the two wishes, he now to obey the only God, she now to stay at his side; it implies a new sense of the relationship between male and female roles. How the poem makes us *feel* about this realignment is another question. Eve gets the last word in *Paradise Lost*.

The Seduction of Eve

Masculinist though he may be, Milton invests a large part of himself in the character of Eve. Her temptation and fall in book 9 recapitulates Milton's earlier dramatizations of individuals tested by the world and its evils and confirmed in their spiritual purity by divine approbation. Her feelings hurt by what she takes to be Adam's questioning of her ability to resist the temptation of Satan—"Less attributed to her faith sincere" (9.320)—Eve, according to the prose argument of book 9, was "the rather desirous to make trial of her strength."[8] We may be reminded of the Lady of *Comus* who asks Providence to "square my trial / To my proportioned strength" (328–29). Eve could be a reader of *Comus*, *Areopagitica*, and *Lycidas*, when she justifies facing their enemy on her own.

> If this be our condition, thus to dwell
> In narrow circuit straitened by a foe,

Subtle or violent, we not endued
Single with like defense, wherever met,
How are we happy, still in fear of harm?
But harm precedes not sin: only our foe
Tempting affronts us with his foul esteem
Of our integrity: his foul esteem
Sticks no dishonour on our front, but turns
Foul on himself; then wherefore shunned or feared
By us? Who rather double honour gain
From his surmise proved false, find peace within,
Favour from heaven, our witness from the event.
And what is faith, love, virtue unassayed
Alone, without exterior help sustained?
Let us not then suspect our happy state
Left so imperfect by the maker wise,
As not secure to single or combined;
Frail is our happiness, if this be so,
And Eden were no Eden thus exposed.
        (9.322–41)

Eve is right to assert that God has created Adam and Eve "Sufficient to have stood": yes, Adam admits even as he cautions her, God left nothing "deficient" in his creation. Eve underestimates, however, the "hap" or contingency in Adam's and her happiness, for they are also "free to fall" (3.99). It is in the name of individual freedom that she asks what is the good of her faith, love, and virtue if it is "unassayed / Alone." Critics have discussed how Eve echoes Milton's call for the reading of uncensored, even evil books in *Areopagitica*, the testing of virtue by its opposite:[9]

> I cannot praise a fugitive and cloister'd vertue, unexercised & unbreath'd, that never sallies out and sees her adversary, but slinks out of the race where that immortall garland is to be run for, not without dust and heat. Assuredly we bring not innocence into the world, we bring impurity much rather: that which purifies us is triall, and triall is by what is contrary. That vertue, therefore which is but a youngling in contemplation of evill, and knows not the utmost that vice promises to her followers, and rejects it, is but a blank vertue, not a pure; her whiteness is but an excrementall whiteness; Which was the reason why our sage and serious Poet *Spencer*, whom I dare be known to think a better teacher then *Scotus* or *Aquinas*, describing true temperance under the person of *Guion*, brings him in with his palmer through the cave of Mammon and the bowr of earthly blisse, that he might see and know, and yet abstain. (*CPW* 2:515–16)

Virtue has no use unless it is tested, Eve asserts, and emphasizes the test's solitary nature: "Single," "Alone," each adjective emphasized by enjambment and placement at the beginning of the verse, the first additionally by metrical inversion. Faith, Milton's Protestantism insists, has to be established by each individual believer.[10] Adam and Eve have just heard, moreover, from Raphael the story of Abdiel, who resisted the temptation of Satan and the pressure of his peers, "Though single" (5.903; cf. 6.30), his only care "To stand approved in sight of God" (6.36). So Eve similarly aspires.[11]

In the famous *Areopagitica* passage cited above, "virtue" is already gendered, as are most personifications in Latin, as feminine. Her cloistering, which in Eve's words are the "narrow circuit" that turns the enclosed garden of Eden into a fortress-prison, suggests the nunnery that protects young women (a "youngling") from sexual knowledge. Milton depicts Satan's temptation of Eve as a kind of erotic seduction, in terms that echo Comus's attempts to make the Lady drink his cup of concupiscence: "you are but young yet" (*Comus* 754), he tells her, suggesting both that she grow up in sophistication and that youth itself will run out: seize the day. Milton thinks of pure faith and virtue as a kind of spiritual chastity that not only depends on the typology of Hosea, where an apostasizing Israel is figured as God's wife whoring after strange gods, but on Milton's own cultivation of physical chastity with its accompanying fantasy of bodily inviolability and transformation into undying soul—"Till all be made immortal" (*Comus* 462)—that the Elder Brother describes in *Comus*. Such abstinence, Milton acknowledged in his sixth prolusion at Cambridge, had earned him the epithet of "the Lady" (*domina*), the "lady of Christ's College" according to John Aubrey. It is a femininity he does not entirely reject in the prolusion— the similarly clean-living Virgil had been dubbed a maiden (*parthenias*) during *his* student days in Naples.[12] The college nickname only connects Milton more closely with the Lady of *Comus* and the female type that she establishes for lonely virtue put to the test.

The cloistering of virtue in *Areopagitica* also evokes the protective walls and courtyards of the university, of Milton's Cambridge. In this light, and in the context of other passages in *Areopagitica* that compare believers reliant on others to children still under the discipline of their schoolteachers, there may indeed be something peculiar about the "error" attributed to Milton here of forgetting that Spenser's Palmer is not present with Guyon during the latter's visit to and temptation in the cave of Mammon (*Faerie Queene* [FQ] 2.7; the Palmer *is* present with Guyon in the Bower of Blisse in 2.12). However it may be feminized as the passive virtue of just saying no, this youngling virtue needs to graduate, to escape (or internalize) its tutors, to leave its confinement and confront the world in order to know just what it is turning down; and it needs to do so by itself. Guyon is able to resist, "Alone, without exterior help sustained," Mammon's invitation for him to eat the golden fruit of Proserpina's garden and sit on its enchanted silver stool, a version of the chair that kept Theseus seated forever in Virgil's underworld (*Aen.* 6.617–18)—although he will need to be rescued by divine grace and a guardian angel, by the returning Palmer and Arthur, at the beginning of the following canto. The fruit of this Spenserian garden—apparently the fruit that Proserpina herself ate and that brought death into the world in pagan myth—already suggests a similarity to the forbidden fruit of Eden, and the episode of the cave of Mammon lies at the basis of Milton's scenes of temptation in both *Paradise Lost* and *Comus*, where the Lady has in fact sat down into immobility while she continues to refuse Comus's cup and similarly needs heavenly rescue through the Attendant Spirit and Sabrina. The last words that Comus speaks to the Lady, "Be wise and, taste" are echoed in Satan's last words to Eve in book 9: "Goddess humane, reach then, and freely taste" (*PL* 9.732).

These last words of Satan, "Goddess humane," echo his first words to Eve, and culminate a second evocation and imitation of the same book 2 of the *Faerie Queene*, mediated, in this case too, by a previous imitation of that Spenserian episode in *Comus*. Satan begins with flattery and already suggests that Eve is made for better things.

> Wonder not, sovereign mistress, if perhaps
> Thou canst, who art sole wonder, must less arm
> Thy looks, the heaven of mildness, with disdain …
> . . . .
> Fairest resemblance of thy maker fair,
> Thee all things living gaze on, all things thine
> By gift, and thy celestial beauty adore
> With ravishment beheld, there best beheld
> Where universally admired; but here
> In this enclosure wild, these beasts among,
> Beholders rude, and shallow to discern
> Half what in thee is fair, one man except,
> Who sees thee? (And what is one?) Who shouldst be seen
> A goddess among gods, adored and served
> By angels numberless, thy daily train.
>   (9.532–34; 9.538–48)

What is a beautiful girl like you doing in a place like this? The provincial "enclosure wild" that Satan describes reminds us of Eve's own feeling of being confined in the "narrow circuit" of Eden, and behind it the cloister that confines the inexperienced virtue in *Areopagitica*. In spite of his assertion that all living things already gaze with wonder on her, "The cynosure of neighbouring eyes," as Milton's speaker commented of a beauty in her hidden rural tower in *L'Allegro* (80), Satan suggests that Eve should be seen by a better class of beings, like one of the city and court ladies at the end of that early poem, whose "bright eyes / Rain influence" (121–22) on their knights and barons. These ladies of *L'Allegro*, as the metaphors suggest, are stars—"cynosure" refers to the fixed North Star and celestial center of attention. Eve, Satan proposes, should be taken to a heavenly Hollywood from her small-town drugstore counter in Eden and turned into a star or goddess at a truly universal studio. She could leave behind her rube of a husband—one man—who, the serpent insinuates, doesn't appreciate the half of her any more than the beasts do: Satan the snake's over-the-top flattery already suggests as much. The facetiousness and updating of my critical description matches the tone of the passage and of its models: the encounter of the roué with the innocent to whom he promises a higher life and social standing, Milton knows, is a hackneyed, repeated story. He takes it back to the beginning of history at the Fall itself.

Behind Satan's first words are the first words that Comus addresses to the Lady who has lost her way in the woods:

> Hail foreign wonder
> Whom certain these rough shades did never breed
> Unless the goddess that in rural shrine
> Dwell'st here with Pan or Sylvan ...
> *(Comus 264–67)*

The Lady, like Eve, is a wonder, and in this case Comus is right: the aristocrat Alice Egerton who plays her *doesn't* belong out in the countryside. But neither is she a goddess. *O dea certe!*, says Aeneas to his mother Venus in the first book of the *Aeneid* (*Aen.* 1.328), a real goddess of love in ironic disguise as a follower of chaste Artemis. The Virgilian episode inverts the flattery of Odysseus to the young, virginal Nausikaa, whom the Greek trickster compares to Artemis in book 6 of the *Odyssey* (6.149–52). Homer's narrator also compares Nausikaa to Artemis in an extended simile (6.102–9) that Milton has just imitated when he compares Eve, at her departing from Adam, to "a wood-nymph light / Oread or dryad, or of Delia's train, / ... but Delia's self / In gait surpassed and goddess-like deport" (9.386–89), to a follower of Artemis or Artemis herself. It is one thing for Homeric and Miltonic narrators to liken Nausikaa or Eve to goddesses, another for the wily Odysseus and Satan to tell them that they are goddesses indeed.

The roots of Milton's scene return to the beginnings of epic—once again, it's an old story—but his primary literary source is a more proximate, degraded parody: the approach of the lowborn, impostor knight Braggadocchio and his equally spurious squire Trompart to Belphoebe in the third canto of book 2 of the *Faerie Queene*. Belphoebe is the *Faerie Queene*'s human figure of the virgin Queen Elizabeth, and she is attired appropriately in the buskins of Artemis (2.3.27), to whom she is subsequently compared with the same *Odyssey* 6 simile (2.3.31): the "Phoebe" in her name already identifies her with the chaste goddess. "O Goddesse (for such I thee take to bee)," says Trompart to Belphoebe as he now introduces her to Braggadocchio, whose first reaction at her coming was to run away and hide. Braggadocchio now tries out his own pitch to Belphoebe.

> But what are thou, O Lady, which doest raunge
> In this wilde forest, where no pleasure is,
> And doest not it for ioyous court exchaunge,
> Emongst thine equall peres, where happy blis
> And all delight does raigne, much more then this?
> There thou maist loue, and dearely loued be,
> And swim in pleasure, which thou here doest mis;
> There maist thou be seene, and best maist see:
> The wood is fit for beasts, the court is fitt for thee.
>   *(FQ 2.3.39)*

Comus takes up the same argument later in the masque; he tells the Lady

> Beauty is Nature's brag, and must be shown
> In courts, at feasts, and high solemnities
> Where most may wonder at the workmanship;
> It is for homely features to keep home,
> They had their name thence.
>   *(Comus 744–48)*

The seducer returns to the rhetoric of wonder, the response to the Lady's beauty, which, as "Nature's brag," offers a tip-off to the speech's Spenserian model. Both passages lie behind Satan's enjoining Eve to get out more and be seen. Satan and Comus are both aligned with Spenser's posturing *miles gloriosus* and his attempt to convince Belphoebe/Elizabeth to leave her rural haunts and come to an erotically licentious court—to the "marshalled feast" (9.37) that the invocation of book 9 has just rejected, the "courts and palaces" (1.497) of book 1 where the lustful Belial reigns, and, most pointedly, the "court amours" that book 4 directly opposes to the homely marriage of Adam and Eve in Eden.

> court amours
> Mixed dance, or wanton mask, or midnight ball,
> Or serenade, which the starved lover sings
> To his proud fair, best quitted by disdain.
>   *(4.767–70)*

The court is the place to be seen, Braggadocchio and Comus insist, and the "occhio" in the former's name helps make the point. It is the home of superficial, rather than true, nobility and virtue, and therefore a fitting milieu for Spenser's cowardly faux knight.

Court society is both itself theatrical and the place of eroticized theatrical performances—the Hollywood analogy is apt enough. Comus addresses a Lady who is in fact being shown off in the courtly masque in which she is participating, and to that extent seems already to have won much of his point. Satan invites Eve to enter such a society of publicity as its queen and goddess—Satan will shortly address her as "Empress" (9.568; 9.626), "Sovereign of creatures, universal dame" (9.612), "Queen of this universe" (9.684)—where she will be "adored and served / By angels numberless, thy daily train." Milton ironically inverts his Spenserian model that tells of a queen who in real life as Elizabeth I was already surrounded by the kind of splendid court that the *Faerie Queene* has satirized in the court of Lucifera in book 1 (*FQ* 1.4) and will satirize again four cantos later in its bourgeois replication around Mammon's daughter, Philotime (2.7)—a queen who nonetheless allegorically, that is, spiritually, resides in the lonely woods and cultivates her chastity.[13] Satan, to the contrary, tempts the sylvan Eve to aspire to royalty, transferring to her his own monarchical ambition: here, too, desire for worldly monarchy motivates a Fall. Spenser's Belphoebe appears to be about to disparage the goings-on "In Princes court," when Braggadocchio cuts short their colloquy by attempting to embrace her.

Spenser's episode not only adapts Homeric-Virgilian precedents but also the medieval subgenre of the *pastourelle*, where a knight meets and engages a country girl in a dialogue that ends, alternatively, with her acquiescence to his sexual invitation, her rejection and repulse of his advances, often with a witty deflation, or with the knight's raping her by force.[14] Milton read a condensed example of the last version in Chaucer's *The Wife of Bath's Tale*, which opens when one of King Arthur's knights "saugh a mayde walkinge him biforn, / Of which mayde anon, maugree hir heed, / By verray force he rafte hire maydenheed," and thence must be educated in the true meaning of nobility ("gentillesse") and not to disdain poverty—as Milton comments in two different entries in his commonplace book (*CPW* 1:472, 1:416). Milton has in fact framed the scene of the temptation with a modernized version of the pastourelle in the simile that describes Satan's first view of Eve in her flowery plat.

> As one who long in populous city pent,
> Where houses thick and sewers annoy the air,
> Forth issuing on a summer's morn to breathe
> Among the pleasant villages and farms
> Adjoined, from each thing met conceives delight,
> The smell of grain, or tedded grass, or kine,
> Or dairy, each rural sight, each rural sound;
> If chance with nymph-like step fair virgin pass,
> What pleasing seemed, for her now pleases more,
> She most, and in her look sums all delight.
>   *(9.445–54)*

Spenser's Braggadocchio was already an impostor knight, a degraded courtier, and here the chivalry that is dead—both historically and in the character of Satan—is cast out of the genre, in favor of a Londoner's typical outing into the countryside. The story is updated for the modern bourgeois, for whom the city with its crowds and stench may be a living hell and the suburbs an Eden.[15] The pastourelle's class-inflected mix of sexual suspense and danger remains, but now it has become the story—itself to be worn-out in succeeding centuries—of the city slicker and the farmer's daughter. After comparing Eve to Delia-Artemis, Milton's narrator seems to correct himself: "Though not as she with bow and quiver armed / But with such gardening tools as art yet rude, / Guiltless of fire had formed" (9.390–92), and there is some pathos in Eve's being an unarmed rustic as she goes to be found by Satan. Spenser's Belphoebe had warded off Braggadocchio with her huntress's spear and fled into the woods, leaving her suitor-rapist to complain: "that Ladie should agayne / Depart to woods vntoucht, and leaue so proud disdayne" (*FQ* 2.3.43.8–9). "Best quitted with disdain": but Eve will succumb to Satan's assault on her spiritual purity— "much less arm / Thy looks, the heaven of mildness, with disdain," the serpent pleads with courtly accent—that makes Eve, wedded matron though she may be, virginal like the country maid in the simile.

Satan's inviting Eve to appear before a heavenly audience ironically reworks, and thereby criticizes, Eve's own terms in the Separation Scene: it suggests how the wish to prove one's faith and "To stand approved in sight of God" like the loyal Abdiel can turn too easily into a narcissistic quest for approval. To be seen by all eyes is an invitation to worldly *fame*, and a substitution for that celestial recognition earlier accorded Abdiel:

> They led him high applauded, and present
> Before the seat supreme; from whence a voice
> From midst a golden cloud thus mild was heard.
>   Servant of God, well done ...
>   (6.26–29)

The acclamation of Abdiel recalls the exaltation of the Son (5.596–615), and it defines the aspiration to divine recognition and applause of John Milton, for whom Abdiel is a fairly transparent biographical stand-in. The phrase "Servant of God, well done" derives from Matthew 25:21, "Well done, thou good and faithful servant," the response of the master to his servant in the parable of the talents, a text that Milton explicitly invokes in his prose and his famous Sonnet 16 on his blindness, where he is bent on offering his true account to his maker, only to be reminded that he need do nothing more than stand and wait.[16] The Jesus of *Paradise Regained* (*PR*) takes up the issue, invoking the example of Job:

> This is true glory and renown, when God,
> Looking on the earth, with approbation marks
> The just man, and divulges him through heaven
> To all his angels, who with true applause
> Recount his praises; thus he did to Job,

When to extend his fame through heaven and earth,
As thou to thy reproach may'st well remember,
He asked thee, Hast thou seen my servant Job?
Famous he was in heaven, on earth less known;
Where glory is false glory.
    (*PR* 3.60–69)

More heavenly applause: accorded here to the man "who dares be *singularly good*" (*PR* 3.57), like the single Abdiel, and whom God in return singles out for praise. Jesus distinguishes this true heavenly glory from the worldly fame that Satan is tempting him to attain, but the distinction, we shall see below, is unstable: Job may be less famous on earth than in heaven, but his fame has been extended in heaven *and* on earth, nonetheless.

Milton had already explored in his writings prior to *Paradise Lost* this uneasy relationship of God's approbation and fame in the eyes of men, specifically the fame that Milton hoped for his own poetry. Eve's declaration of her spiritual ambition and desire for divine recognition in the Separation Scene hearkens back not only to *Areopagitica* but to *Lycidas* as well. Adam tells Eve that he is trying to avoid Satan's affronting or dishonoring her by the act of temptation, and adds that he is made stronger when she is looking on.

Why should not thou like sense within thee feel
When I am present, and thy trial choose
With me, best witness of thy virtue tried.
    (*9.315–17*)

We should do this together, Adam argues, but Eve claims a still better witness than her husband, and argues that the devil's assault provides them with a spiritual opportunity:

        Who rather double honour gain
From his surmise proved false, find peace within,
Favour from heaven, our witness from the event.
    (*9.332–34*)

Like a very good student of the kind that John Milton undoubtedly was, Eve wants to be tested, and she chooses God as her witness and as the giver of his extra credit—redoubled honor and favor. So Phoebus assured the speaker of *Lycidas* that God, the "perfect witness," was looking on and prepared to reward him.

Fame is no plant that grows on mortal soil,
Nor in the glistering foil
Set off to the world, nor in broad rumour lies,
But lives and spreads aloft by those pure eyes,
And perfect witness of all-judging Jove;

As he pronounces lastly on each deed,
Of so much fame in heaven expect thy meed.
    (Lycidas 78–84)

The words of Phoebus correct the pastoral speaker's anxious worry that he might suffer an early death like that of Lycidas before he could fulfill his poetic career; the young Milton had been preparing for this career and its attendant fame—"That last infirmity of noble mind" (71)—by his studies at his father's house at Horton ("the *homely* slighted shepherd's trade"), and his erotic self-denial: no Amaryllis or Neaera for him.

Phoebus also corrects the tradition of pastoral elegy in which Milton is writing, where the apotheosis of the dead shepherd is a figure for the earthly fame that the poem itself is conferring on him.[17] Fame is reidentified as the apocalyptic ("pronounces lastly") judgment of salvation that will place the speaker along with Lycidas, in the Christian afterlife, and we might presume that the deeds such Protestant fame rewards are acts of faith above good works. But alongside this orthodox sense there lingers the idea that the perfect witness of heaven extends to literary judgment as well, that God would acknowledge the poetic works that the speaker *would* have written should he, like Lycidas, not live to accomplish them. "Servant of God, well done": your use of your talent is rewarded. Each individual receives a quota of divine recognition for specific deeds that may be qualitatively different, but nonetheless hard to distinguish from worldly fame, leaving a residue in the elegy that is similar to the double placement of Lycidas, not only in heaven among the solemn troops and sweet societies of heavenly saints but also as "genius of the shore," still exerting a personal presence on earth.

Just how far Milton's imagination could confuse the rewards of virtue in the Christian heaven with the personal fame won by poetry appears in the striking ending of his Latin poem, *Mansus* (1639), addressed to the Neapolitan patron Giovanni Battista Manso whom Milton had met in Italy. *Mansus* is in dialogue with both *Lycidas*, published a year earlier, and with Milton's second great pastoral elegy, *Epitaphium Damonis*, composed in Latin later in 1639 to mourn the death of his great friend Charles Diodati. In *Mansus* the awarding of heavenly approval described in *Lycidas* has been transferred from God to Milton himself. He imagines himself, following a career as an epic poet singing the deeds of King Arthur and—after a distinguished earthly funeral—in his heavenly home.

Tum quoque, si qua fides, si praemia certa bonorum,
Ipse ego caelicolum semotus in aethera divum,
Quo labor et mens pura vehunt, atque ignea virtus
Secreti haec aliqua mundi de parte videbo
(Quantum fata sinunt) et tota mente serenum
Ridens purpureo suffundar lumine vultus

Et simul aethereo plaudam mihi laetus Olympo.
   (Mansus 94–100)

[Then, too, if there is such a thing as faith, and assured rewards for the
good, I myself, far away in the ethereal realm of the heaven-dwelling
gods, conveyed thither by labor and a pure mind and fiery virtue, will
from some part of that secret world look down (as much as the Fates
allow) on these things on earth, and smiling with my whole mind, my
face suffused with a rosy light, I will happily applaud myself on heavenly
Olympus.]

So *Mansus* concludes. It is an odd passage, possibly more revealing than the
poet is ready to admit. Unlike Lycidas and Damon-Diodati, who partake in the
sweet societies and, in the latter's case, festive orgies of heaven, Milton imagines
himself in some place in heaven that is set apart (*semotus*) and solitary (*secreti*).
In this literally splendid isolation, he will be his own best witness. God hardly
enters the picture. The pure eyes of the all-judging Jove of *Lycidas* are replaced
by the poet's own pure mind and fiery virtue, which seem to raise him on his
own to heaven. It is such burning virtue (*ardens … virtus*), which, the sibyl
announces to Aeneas in book 6 of the *Aeneid*, raises a very few, those loved by
just Jupiter, out of the realm of the underworld to the heavens (*Aen.* 6.129–31),
here too, a classical, euhemerist figure for the fame that will survive death. Milton's self-apotheosis blurs fame and things down on earth (*haec*) with celestial
beatitude. Such confusion may result from the strict classical vocabulary of the
Mansus, the common ground that Milton found to write to his Catholic ad-
dressee—though the play on the Virgilian tag *si qua fides* (*Aen.* 3.434, 6.459)
and *labor* nonetheless allow him to present a version of Christian faith and
works. But the passage also invokes the optimism and spiritual agency that ends
Comus, "Love Virtue, she alone is free, / She can teach ye how to climb / Higher
than the sphery chime" (1017–19), and is only partly qualified by the subjunc-
tive acknowledgment of grace that follows: "Or if Virtue feeble were, / Heaven
itself would stoop to her."[18] In the *Mansus*, this virtue looks upon and applauds
itself. Milton seems aware here that God's apocalyptic witness and reward of
fame imagined by *Lycidas*—or the rewards of Abdiel and Job later depicted in
Paradise Lost and *Paradise Regained*, "high applauded" in heaven and attested
by divine proclamation—are not available in this world, equally aware that the
substitute for such longed-for divine recognition is inevitably a form of self-
approval: perhaps not so unlike the "answering looks / Of sympathy and love"
(4.464–65) that please Eve from her reflection in the pool.[19]
   It is Satan who redescribes Eve's similarly high spiritual ambition and thereby
discloses the element of human autonomy and self-regard that the *Mansus* suggests may have been potentially present all along in Milton's semi-Pelagian wish
for a spiritual purity able to withstand temptation (and to write great poetry).

The serpent transforms Eve's seeking to assay her virtue and be approved and witnessed by God into a more general, heroic quest—God should, Satan perversely argues, "praise / Rather your dauntless virtue" (9.693–94)—to become the (divinized) object of a universal regard: "Thee all living things gaze on." So the models behind Satan, Spenser's Braggadocchio and Milton's own Comus, had respectively promised Belphoebe and the Lady. The word "gaze" clusters six times in the scene of Eve's temptation. The serpent, who has first approached Eve, "as in gaze admiring," and who expresses his desire to "gaze / Insatiate" (9.535–36), "to come / And gaze" (9.610–11) on her, claims to transfer this gaze to her from the tree of the forbidden fruit itself—"I nearer drew to gaze" (9.578)—a tree that is feminized by its breastlike "fair apples"(9.581; 9.585) and as the "Mother of science" (9.680), and which is already in the Genesis account "pleasant to the eyes" (Gen. 3:6). The pattern is deliberate: Milton has used it before in the corresponding scene of the dream that Satan has sent to Eve in book 5, where Eve is first told that all of heaven's eyes "gaze" on her (5.47), and then sees an angelic figure standing before the forbidden fruit: "on that tree he also gazed" (5.57). It now becomes Eve's turn in book 9: "Fixed on the fruit she gazed, which to behold / Might tempt alone" (9.735–36); she looks upon a tree that has somehow in Satan's terms become a double or mirror of herself. Eve is tempted not only to return to the narcissism of the pool of book 4, but also to a further regression to a mother whom she has never had, figured now in the tree and earlier in the womblike cave (4.454) from which that pool issued.[20] A similar identification is suggested by means of verbal quibble, when, *after* eating the fruit, Eve speaks inwardly to herself and addresses the tree at the same time: "Thus to herself she pleasingly began. / O sovereign, virtuous, precious of all trees" (9.794–95). By the end of the scene, she has bowed down to the tree as a substitute for God (9.835–37), an anticipation of Canaanite tree worship (Deut. 12:2; Hosea 4:13; Ezek. 6:13), and like all idolatry, a worship of, or confusion with, the idol-making self. Satan's terms suggest how the individual's testing of his or her faith in God, central to the poet's Protestantism, can devolve into a form of pride, a self-idolatry that here, as elsewhere in *Paradise Lost*, the blind poet describes as a particularly visual condition, of seeing and wishing to being seen.

Adam's increasingly exasperated recriminations of Eve in books 9 and 10 *after* the Fall spell out the moral. "Let none, henceforth seek needless cause to approve / The faith they owe" (9.1140–41). In retrospect, Adam asserts, Eve's desire to test her faith was a form of overreaching, an unnecessary spiritual ambition and overconfidence that led to her fall. So, in his next exchange, he accuses Eve of having wished "to find / Matter of glorious trial" (9.1176–77): Adam had earlier warned her that "trial will come unsought" (9.366). Ambition to prove her faith has now become a quest for the glory that God might confer on her, and it becomes difficult to distinguish from the pride that Adam will go on reductively to ascribe to Eve in his misogynistic outburst in book 10.

> *thy pride*
> *And wandering vanity,* when least was safe,
> Rejected my forewarning, and disdained
> Not to be trusted, *longing to be seen*
> Though by the devil himself …
> *(10.874–78)*

It was Eve's hurt pride in the first place, Adam asserts, that triggered her arguments, with their echo of *Areopagitica*, to exercise her lonely virtue, and one can see where *that* got the both of them. A particularly feminine vanity was the real motive of her desire for divine recognition: not content to have Adam be her witness, she claimed God as her witness, but any onlooker, in fact, would do. You would have thrown yourself at the devil, this outraged husband says. The immediate irony is that Adam has not yet come to the realization (10.1033–35) that the serpent *was*, in fact, the devil. But Adam is also wrong to ascribe these motives to Eve before her temptation and fall, and he belies the very progression and gradual transformation that has been implied in his mounting indictment of her. He is making her out to be fallen before the Fall, as if Eve had *already* been infected by Satan's persuasion before her encounter with him, before, that is, Satan has turned Eve's (and Milton's) wish to exercise an individual virtue and faith "sufficient to have stood" into Godless self-sufficiency, her (and Milton's) longing for God's approbation into vainglory, and, finally, into self-regard.

This account cannot adequately explain Eve's fall, whose causes Milton keeps many and irreducible. Her soliloquy before she eats the forbidden fruit does not indicate how much force Satan's temptation to promote her to be queen of heaven and the cynosure of all eyes may have had with her; he *has* succeeded in making her feel her "want" (9.755) in her present condition of incomplete knowledge, to distrust God, and to debate her freedom. Only *after* she eats do Satan's arguments come flooding back: "nor was godhead from her thought" (9.790). At that point the divine witness that Eve had earlier sought has ironically changed for her into the "continual watch" of "Our great forbidder," which she seeks to avoid, together "with all his spies" (9.814–15): after the Fall, both Adam and Eve will know that they are naked and wish to hide from God and each other. The quest for fame has turned into the discovery of shame. Nonetheless, the process of temptation the poem depicts, and that Adam's accusations of his wife progressively rechart, indicates how deeply Eve's fall is implicated in a larger, repeated Miltonic scenario of individual virtue triumphant over temptation and rewarded by divine approval. Eve fails where Abdiel in *Paradise Lost*, where earlier in Milton's writings the Lady of *Comus* and the personified Virtue of *Areopagitica*, where later the Jesus of *Paradise Regained* and his model Job succeed; and, for all that, her fall retains something of their heroism, of purity that knows itself only through trial and, in her case, knows itself all too well in its own loss.

When Adam accuses Eve of having sought "matter of glorious trial," he echoes her own words, "O glorious trial of exceeding love" (9.961), with which Eve had admired—and egged on—his own decision to fall beside her, an act that contained its own heroism. The phrase also echoes the Son's words, "Matter to me of glory" (5.738), with which he characterizes Satan's rebellion as the occasion for his own glorification: "thou always seek'st / To glorify thy Son, I always thee," he declares to the Father in the corresponding passage in book 6 (724–25), after the Father has "on his Son with rays direct / Shone full" (6.719–20), the poem's highest depiction of divine recognition.[21] The Son, the divine hero of *Paradise Lost*, will reappear as the human hero Jesus of *Paradise Regained*, resisting allurements by Satan that, as the next section of this chapter will discuss, resemble the temptation of Eve rather than the choice of Adam in the earlier epic. In so doing, this Jesus carries out Milton's wish, which had gone so wrong in Eve's case—the wish that virtue and purity be sufficient to withstand trial and earn God's approval. Jesus, the ideal man/God, might seem to be the exception that proves the rule that Eve's failure, and the original sin that had resulted from it, have imposed on humanity. But in the Miltonic imagination and career, the opposite—that *Eve* is the exception who reaffirms the rightness of the wish—may be closer to the mark.

The Second Adam as Second Eve

In *Paradise Regained*, the act of divine approval and recognition begins the action of the poem. At the baptizing of Jesus by John the Baptist at the Jordan, the skies open, the likeness of a dove appeared—"what'er it meant" (1.83), Satan later wryly comments about the Holy Spirit, which Milton himself did not accept as a person of the Trinity—"while the Father's voice / From heaven pronounced him his beloved Son" (*PR* 1.32–33). The scene is repeatedly, almost obsessively recalled over the course of *Paradise Regained* by Satan to the demonic council (1.81–85), by Jesus himself in his meditations (1.280–86), by Satan again to Jesus (1.327–30), where Satan significantly already links it to "fame" (1.334), by the bereft disciples (2.50–52) and Mary (2.83–85), and by Satan still again near the poem's end (4.510–13). Similarly, the first chronological action of *Paradise Lost* is the exaltation of the Son, and in both poems the preapproved Son of God must live up to his advanced billing, and in both cases the conclusion is foregone. In *Paradise Regained*, the divine Father's plan to "exercise" Jesus in the wilderness (1.156)—like the Milton of *Areopagitica*, he cannot praise a virtue that is unexercised—is seconded by the human mother Mary, who urges her son to let his thoughts "soar / To what highth sacred virtue and true worth / Can raise them" (1.230–32). She sees to it that Jesus's thoughts and ambition are nothing less than Messianic, to "sit on David's throne" (1.240), a kingdom without end.

Satan aims in *Paradise Regained*, as he had with Eve in *Paradise Lost*, to turn such high aspirations into self-serving ones: above all, to substitute the quest of worldly fame and glory for Jesus's self-sacrificing mission—or, even more insidiously, to reveal fame and glory to be the real motives of that mission. Jesus may be the new Adam and new Israel in the typological scheme of Milton's brief epic, but it is the temptation of Eve in the predecessor poem that Satan's persuasion repeatedly imitates and quite explicitly invokes.[22]

An example of how Jesus is associated with Eve rather than with Adam is the banquet temptation in book 2 that, with the corresponding Athens temptation and storm scene in book 4, are Milton's primary additions to his gospel sources. The temptation begins, in fact, with Belial urging the devils to "Set women in his eye" (2.153), as if Jesus were indeed the new Adam and subject to the uxoriousness that contributed to Adam's falling beside Eve and that Belial goes on to typify in Solomon bowing before the gods of his wives (2.169–71). Satan rejects the idea out of hand, and argues that Jesus is made of sterner stuff, unlike the sensualist Belial himself.

> Have we not seen, or by relation heard,
> In courts and regal chambers how thou lurk'st
> In wood or grove by mossy fountain-side,
> In valley or green meadow to waylay
> Some beauty rare, Calisto, Clymene,
> Daphne, or Semele, Antiopa,
> Or Amymone, Syrinx, many more
> Too long, then lay'st thy scapes on names adored,
> Apollo, Neptune, Jupiter, or Pan,
> Satyr, or Faun, or Sylvan?
>   *(PR 2.182–91)*

The passage changes the demonic menace from women set before Jesus's eyes to a threat *to* women as objects of potential rape. Here are pagan, demonic versions of the very virgin birth that produced the Son of God, discussed by Mary herself only a hundred verses earlier, a series of offspring of rape passed off as children of gods who are themselves as much bestial hybrids (satyr, faun, sylvan) as deities—Jupiter disguised himself *as* a satyr to pursue Antiopa; Pan fits somewhere in between as his position at the end of the verse and the ambiguity of "or" suggest. Belial's haunt in the courts and regal chambers—so he is also described in *Paradise Lost*: "In courts and palaces he also reigns / And in luxurious cities" (*PL* 1.497–98)—seems to lend these encounters something of the shape of the pastourelle that Milton invokes for Satan's approach to Eve, and when Satan approaches Jesus at the banquet, "As one in city, or court, or palace bred" (*PR* 2.300), we hear an echo of that passage, "As one who long in populous city pent" (*PL* 9.445). Jesus is placed in the feminized position of Eve before a seductive seducer, like the Lady of *Comus* in her courtly masque.

The banquet temptation takes the form of such a masque. Satan has told Belial that a woman would fail to move the severely virtuous Jesus, even should she

> As sitting queen adored on beauty's throne
> Descend with all her winning charms begirt
> To enamour, as the zone of Venus once
> Wrought that effect on Jove, so fables tell.
>   (*PR* 2.212–15)

Here again, the initial idea is that Jesus will not be fondly overcome with female charms as a second Adam. The model of Jupiter's and Juno's sexual dalliance in *Iliad* 14, during which Juno wore the irresistible girdle ("zone") she has borrowed from Venus, had been twice invoked to describe the lovemaking of Adam and Eve in *Paradise Lost*, both in their sanctified marriage bed before the Fall in book 4 (697–702) and in their lascivious coupling after the Fall in book 9 (1029–42).[23] The chaste Jesus will not repeat Adam's sexual love for his wife, holy or unholy. But the image suggests a throned figure descending at a masque, and it seems to cue Satan into action. He gathers a troupe of fellow spirit-actors "To be at hand, and at his beck appear, / If cause were to unfold some active scene / Of various persons each to know his part" (*PR* 2.238–40). Satan puts on another version of the masque presented at Ludlow Castle in the ensuing banquet in a "woody scene" (2.294) that is pointedly "Not rustic as before" (2.299), but urbane and courtly, and the final vanishing of the banqueting table (2.401–403) smacks not only of *The Tempest* (3.3.183), but of the magical scene changes of the court masque to which Shakespeare's play is itself indebted. Satan/Milton has recourse to the same models that had formed the backdrop of the temptation of Eve in *Paradise Lost*. The devil invokes the attempted seduction of the Lady in *Comus*, and behind it, of Spenser's Mammon episode; the banquet will be immediately followed by Satan's Mammon-like offer to Jesus of the riches of the world: "Get riches first, get wealth and treasures heap" (2.427; cf. *FQ* 2.7.9–66). Comus's command, "Nay lady sit" (658) to the Lady already seated in an enchanted chair—which itself recalls Mammon's urging Guyon, "Why takest not of that same fruite of gold, / Ne sittest downe on that same siluer stoole" (*FQ* 2.7.63.7–8)—is repeated *three* times by Satan in *Paradise Regained* to Jesus: "only deign to sit and eat" (2.336), "What doubts the Son of God to sit and eat?" (2.368) "Sit down and eat" (2.377). The seated immobility of the Lady in *Comus* is the common aim and imagistic thread of all of Satan's temptations in *Paradise Regained*, to turn "David's throne" into a paralyzing earthly end in itself, whether it be "beauty's throne," a seat at the banqueting table, "the seats of mightiest monarchs" (3.262), the "two thrones" (4.85) of Parthia and Rome, or "Moses' chair" (4.219) in the learning temptation of Athens. (The sightless, incapacitated Milton would have found himself sitting for long stretches, nearly in the position of the Lady: the "sedentary numbness" that the blind Samson fears will be his fate in *Samson Agonistes*.)[24] Jesus's ability figuratively to stand—"stoodst" (4.420)—*and* sit—"thou / Satst" (4.425)—simultaneously in the storm scene of book 4 anticipates his even more difficult test to stand on the pinnacle of the temple at the book's end: to be active in apparent passivity.

"Alas how simple, to these cates compared, / Was that crude apple that diverted Eve!" (2.348–49), the narrator comments. To note the reappearance of the Comus/Mammon motifs that link the banquet temptation to the temptation of Eve in *Paradise Lost* may belabor a point that *Paradise Regained* itself spells out. The brief epic continues explicitly to link Jesus with Eve after Satan's failure to interest Jesus in the throne of Parthia, the first of the temptations of the kingdoms:

> the persuasive rhetoric
> That sleeked his tongue, and won so much on Eve,
> So little here, nay lost; but Eve was Eve,
> This far his over-match ...
> > *(PR 4.4–7)*

Jesus himself evokes the parallel after Rome has been added to the offer and Satan calls on Jesus to fall down and worship him, "this attempt bolder than that on Eve / And more blasphemous" (4.180–81). That Satan is repeating himself and restaging his earlier temptation of Eve *does* explain how the masquelike banquet is connected to the ensuing temptation of the kingdoms. In the first Satan brings city, court, and palace into the wilderness; in the second he brings Jesus, in turn, to them. As he had asked of the beautiful Eve in her "wild enclosure," Satan asks the talented Jesus what he is doing in the desert.

> These godlike virtues wherefore does thou hide?
> Affecting private life, or more obscure
> In savage wilderness, wherefore deprive
> All earth her wonder at thy acts, thyself
> The fame and glory ... ?
> > *(PR 3.21–25)*

Eve, Satan had told her in *Paradise Lost*, was the sole wonder of the world—"Wonder not, sovereign mistress, if perhaps / Thou canst, who art sole wonder"—and now he similarly urges Jesus to get out of the wilderness and be wondered at. The devil offers Jesus the same temptation to earthly fame—to be seen and admired by other creatures instead of being approved in the sight of God—that he had dangled before Eve; so in the later temptation of classical learning in Athens, he will enjoin Jesus to "Be famous then / By wisdom" (*PR* 4.221–22).

The place for such fame, Satan had suggested to Eve, Comus to the Lady, and Spenser's Braggadocchio to Belphoebe, is a royal court. With the temptation of the kingdoms, Satan offers a similar visit to the court to Jesus, but under the guise of an educational field trip. Jesus will apparently go to see rather than be seen, as the mountaintop perspective and the mentions of telescope (4.42) and microscope (4.57) insist.

> The world thou hast not seen, much less her glory,
> Empires and monarchs, and their radiant courts,
> Best school of best experience, quickest in sight
> In all things that to greatest actions lead.
> The wisest, unexperienced, will be ever
> Timorous and loth, with novice modesty,
> (As he who seeking asses found a kingdom)
> Irresolute, unhardy, unadventurous:
> But I will bring thee where thou soon shalt quit
> Those rudiments, and see before thine eyes
> The monarchies of the earth, their pomp and state,
> Sufficient introduction to inform
> Thee, of thyself so apt, in regal arts,
> And regal mysteries; that thou may'st know
> How best their opposition to withstand.
>   (PR 3.236–50)

Satan presents the kingdoms temptation as a course in worldliness for the raw beginner Jesus. With his "novice modesty," Satan suggests, Jesus is like the personified Virtue of *Areopagitica*, cloistered and ignorant of the world. God's plan for Jesus was "To exercise him in the wilderness" (1.156) as a new Israel repeating the Exodus wandering. Satan's strategy is to get Jesus out of the wilderness into a false, worldly Promised Land: the vision of the kingdoms is a kind of Pisgah view. Without Satan's "introduction," which both suggests admission to a royal court that would make the devil his sponsor and an introductory course of study that picks up the idea that such courts are a kind of school (and so links the temptation of the kingdoms to the ensuing temptation of learning in Athens), Jesus will never venture out of his remote, politically and culturally insignificant Palestine. He will be "Timorous and loth," a phrase that recalls the "Timorous and slothful" Belial of book 2 of *Paradise Lost* (2.117), terms that echo in turn, as we noted in chapter 2, the reproaches—"Timorous," "slothful"—that Milton imagines for himself had he *not* engaged in religious controversy in *The Reason of Church Government*, had he not contributed "those few talents which God at present had lent me" (*CPW* 1:804–5).[25] Satan presents another version of his appeal to zeal—urging Jesus to get moving and show his stuff—that Jesus has just rejected (*PR* 3.171–202), and at the end of the speech he cunningly echoes the arguments of *Areopagitica* that Virtue must know in order to withstand her adversary. The guileful double meaning lies in Satan's suggestion that Jesus might learn how to resist the kings of the world by becoming such a king himself. He shows him the opposing monarchies of Parthia and Rome and asks him to choose one or the other; these are the "Means" to David's throne that Jesus goes on to reject (4.152). By the end of the mountain temptations, the disgusted Satan is willing to return Jesus to the wilderness: "What dost thou in this world?" (4.372).

The likenesses of the temptations to the temptation of Eve continue. The Athens temptation is to knowledge: the groves of academe, with their "studious walks and shades" (4.243), recall "the shade / High roofed and walks beneath" (2.292–93) of the earlier banquet temptation, and both recall the tree of knowledge and forbidden fruit in Eden. The temple temptation is to godhead itself. Jesus overcomes them in Eve's place, and in the wake of Jesus's angry response, "Get thee behind me" (4.193) to the offer of the kingdoms, the frightened Satan tries to absolve his own part as tempter:

> The trial hath endamaged thee no way
> Rather more honour left and more esteem;
> Me naught advantaged, missing what I aimed.
> (PR 4.206–8)

The devil's conclusion echoes what the overconfident Eve had predicted for herself, answering Adam's objection that the very act of being tempted would dishonor her, in the Separation Scene in book 9.[26]

>   only our foe
> Tempting affronts us with his foul esteem
> Of our integrity: his foul esteem
> Sticks no dishonour on our front, but turns
> Foul on himself; then wherefore shunned or feared
> By us? Who rather double honour gain
> From his surmise proved false, find peace within,
> Favour from heaven, our witness from the event.
> And what is faith, love, virtue unassayed
> Alone, without exterior help sustained?
> (PL 9.327–36)

Jesus, Satan tells him, has only gained honor and esteem from the trials he has undergone. Such honor and esteem won by the individual may *still* contain an element of vainglory: I have helped to make you famous, the devil insinuates even as he exculpates himself. Satan had diverted Eve's spiritual ambition, the honor and favor she sought from God's witness, into a self-seeking, worldly desire for recognition. Jesus has avoided this trap, dismissing earthly fame: "Yet if for fame and glory aught be done ... / The deed becomes unpraised, the man at least, / And loses, though but verbal his reward" (*PR* 3.100–104).

But Jesus and his poet-creator at the same time find a special dispensation that might resolve the either/or of finding approval in the eyes of God and fame in the mouths of men: a way to have one's forbidden fruit and not to eat it too.

> Yet so much bounty is in God, such grace,
> That who advance his glory, not their own,
> Them he himself to glory will advance.
>   *(PR 3.142–44)*

The individual who acts selflessly for the glory of God will be granted glory in turn.[27] So Eve had correctly believed that God would acknowledge her spiritual victory, a double honor—had she succeeded. Insofar as this glory cited by Jesus apparently includes a divinely sanctioned fame on earth, it seems more Miltonic than Christian, an attempt to reconcile the contradictory impulses for divine and human recognition that risk confusion in Milton's poetry and whose confusion prompted Eve's fall. Jesus's words rework famous passages in the Gospel of John.[28] Jesus has just a few lines earlier disowned personal glory, "I seek not mine, but his / Who sent me" (*PR* 3.106–7), echoing his future sayings in John 8:50 and John 7:18, and his prayer in John's account of the Last Supper "I have glorified thee on earth ... And now glorifie me, thou Father, with thine owne self, with the glory which I had with thee before the worlde was" (17:4–5; Geneva Bible), a passage we have seen the Son echo to the Father during the War in Heaven in *Paradise Lost*: "thou always seeks't / To glorifie thy Son, I always thee" (6.724–25). Milton's hopes for a return on the glorification of God also rest on the much-cited passage of 1 Samuel 2:30: "for them that honour me, I wil honour" (Geneva). For the Calvinist editors of the Geneva Bible, the Samuel passage seemed to grant liberty to the individual will and elicited a nervous gloss and qualification: "God's promises are onely effectual to suche as he giveth constancie vnto, to feare and obey him." In *On Christian Doctrine*, Milton cites the 1 Samuel passage to confirm the contrary, that "men have freedom of action" (*CPW* 6:155). The Geneva gloss makes clear, however, that the honor in question is salvation itself, and the constancy that God provides is the "perseverance," the binding, irresistible grace that will see the believer through to a new glorious life in heaven. So, too, the Johannine Jesus seemingly aspires to a heavenly glory that is not only outside but prior to the world. But Milton wants more, and Jesus's opposition of unworldly and worldly glory is disrupted by his evocation once again of the exemplary good man, Job, whom God allowed Satan to tempt *in order* "to extend his fame through heaven and earth" (3.65), especially *on earth*, where he was "less known" (3.68):

>   I mention still
> Him whom thy wrongs with saintly patience borne,

> Made famous in a land and times obscure,
> Who names not now with honour patient Job?
>> (PR 3.92–95)

Job won applause among the angels (3.63), but now he enjoys earthly fame and honor as well, the hero of his own book of the Bible. Milton attributes this honor from God as a gift of grace, an Arminian prevenient grace that requires individual virtue to cooperate with it in order to earn the ultimate reward in heaven, but also, as something less doctrinally normative, a terrestrial bonus of renown for being "singularly good" (3.57). Like Eve, Jesus also thinks of virtue alone, without exterior help. At the very end of *Paradise Regained*, such help finally comes as the angels lift Jesus from the uneasy station he has maintained on top of the temple pinnacle—"Or if Virtue feeble were / Heaven itself would stoop to her," in the words of *Comus*—feast him, and honor his divinity with hymns: "Hail, Son of the Most High" (4.633). The poem's initial act of divine recognition at the baptism of Jesus exponentially amplifies at its end, as the gratification that has been deferred through its course now gets full rein. Such glorification is not exclusively heavenly. The angels' song looks back to the hymn in book 8 of the *Aeneid* to Hercules, another divine son raised to divinity—"salue, uera Iouis proles, decus addite diuis" (*Aen.* 8.301)—with whom Christ was conventionally paralleled and to whom, battling with the earthborn Antaeus, Jesus has just been compared in simile (4.563–68).[29] The angels are making Jesus a new object of earthly cult, superseding pagan altars and oracles. From his Palestinian backwater, Jesus has become, until the advent of the Beatles, the most famous man on earth. So, too, his model Job: "Made famous in a land and times obscure; / Who names not now with honour patient Job?" And so, John Milton, writing in far-off, obscure England and in "our native language" (4.333) of modern rather than classical times, has glorified God in *Paradise Lost* and expects his own glorious reward as Christian and epic poet. One wish is fulfilled, and then some.

Adam's Choice: "One flesh"

James Nohrnberg has correlated the temptations of *Paradise Regained* to Milton's biography: anti-Roman Parthia to his writings on church reform in the 1640s, bureaucratic Rome to his work as Latin secretary and on affairs of state during the Protectorate, learned Athens to his classical scholarship and literary ambition. From the retrospect of *Paradise Regained*, all of these worldly engagements contained temptations that might have—but did not ultimately—distract Milton-Jesus from his true mission: the writing of *Paradise Lost*. The great epic is Milton's version of the secret that Jesus has withheld and then revealed on the temple pinnacle to Satan, "smitten with amazement" (4.562) at the end of *Paradise Regained*, just as it is Milton's version of the trial of strength that Samson displays, "As with amaze shall strike all who behold" (1645), at the conclusion of *Samson Agonistes*. Both of the 1671 poems are in some sense *about* how *Paradise Lost* came into being in spite of the contingencies of Milton's life. The contingencies overcome in *Samson Agonistes* are different in kind: inimical marriage, political defeat and captivity, the affliction of blindness. As he sets out on his mission to deliver humanity, the virginal Jesus of *Paradise Regained* abstains from worldly impurity to the point of appearing uncharitable. He refuses when Satan first asks him, in an addition to the accounts of the temptation in Matthew (4:2) and Luke (5:3), to change stones into bread not only for his own hunger but also for the poor: "So shalt thou save thyself and us relieve / With food, whereof we wretched seldom taste" (1.344–45). Similarly, he refuses to rescue the ten lost tribes of Israel (3.414–32) or to restore Roman republicanism (4.131–45), both figures for the fallen English Commonwealth. But Samson would deliver both himself and Israel, and to do so he must engage with the world. The virtue of Jesus still remains partly in the cloister and wilderness. Samson, "Against his vow of strictest purity" (319), gets married.

In *Paradise Lost* Adam asks God to make him a wife. As opposed to the Miltonic wish or imperative to be approved "single" by God, which Abdiel fulfills (6.30) and to which Eve aspires (9.339), Adam argues with his Creator that the "single imperfection" of the human being is the basis for marriage: so he recalls to Raphael in book 8.

> But man by number is to manifest
> His single imperfection, and beget
> Like of his like, his image multiplied,
> In unity defective, which requires
> Collateral love, and dearest amity.
> Thou in thy secrecy although alone,
> Best with thyself accompanied, seek'st not
> Social communication, yet so pleased,
> Canst raise thy creature to what highth thou wilt
> Of union or communion, deified;
> I by conversing cannot these erect
> From prone, nor in their ways complacence find.
> (8.422–33)

"In unity defective": the other side of the aspiration to spiritual self-sufficiency is a sense of human incompleteness and Adam's desire for a "like" to "solace his defects" (8.419), the wish for "Social communication" and conversation that Adam cannot find with the prone animals. The ensuing creation of Eve from Adam's side seems to be a punning literalization of the "*Collateral* love and dearest amity" that is required of a human species that will reproduce itself. A similar literalization inheres in the marriage formula of Genesis 2:23–24, "bone of my bones, flesh of my flesh," that Eve recalls Adam paraphrasing at their first meeting:

> Whom fly'st thou? Whom thou fly'st, of him thou art,
> His flesh, his bone; to give thee being I lent
> Out of my side to thee, nearest my heart
> Substantial life, to have thee by my side
> Henceforth an individual solace dear;
> Part of my soul I seek thee ...
>   *(4.482–87)*

Adam is the first and only husband whose wife is literally made of his own flesh, but he already expands the idea by asking Eve to return to his side in collateral love and as an "individual solace." The adjective "individual" denotes the indivisibility of their relationship, but the phrase equally suggests, according to more modern usage already present in Milton's writing, that Eve is to be a solace just for Adam as an individual and that she is herself an individual, separate being, a part of his soul that is also apart from him.[30] Adam subsequently repeats the terms of this passage that add "heart" and "soul" to the Genesis formula in his recollection of the meeting to Raphael, "And they shall be one flesh, one heart, one soul" (8.499). After Eve falls, the force of his love causes Adam to stay by her side: he restates the formula at the end of his internal monologue, in which he resolves to fall with Eve, and again at the end of his vocal declaration of his choice to her.

>   yet loss of thee
> Would never from my heart; no no, I feel
> The link of nature draw me: flesh of flesh,
> Bone of my bone thou art, and from thy state
> Mine never shall be parted, bliss or woe.
>   *(9.912–16)*

> Our state cannot be severed, we are one,
> One flesh; to lose thee were to lose my self.
>   *(9.958–59)*

"Not deceived, / But fondly overcome with female charm" (9.998–99), remarks the censorious narrator.[31] Adam has left "soul" out of these inner and outward speeches. Given his admission to Raphael one book earlier of the "Commotion strange" that Eve arouses in him, critics have suggested that Adam may be taking the figure of "one flesh" too literally and carnally; Milton complicates his hero's motives.[32] But Eve quickly supplies the missing terms in her response "And gladly of our union hear thee speak, / One heart, one soul in both" (9.966–67). In his silent soliloquy, moreover, Adam has himself stated that he cannot live without Eve's "sweet converse and love so dearly joined / To live again in these wild woods forlorn" (9.909–10), and thus restated both Milton's assertion in *The Doctrine and Discipline of Divorce* that "in Gods intention a meet and happy conversation is the chiefest and noblest end of marriage" (*CPW* 2:246) and his own assertion of that idea in his half-abashed reply to Raphael that he loves Eve above all for "her words and actions mixed with love / And sweet compliance" (8.602–3)—the repetition of "sweet," we shall see below, is part of a larger pattern.

"One flesh" is a figure—rather than a literal state—both in *Paradise Lost* and in Milton's other writings for human marriage that both participates in and is itself a figure for an expanding body of love and community, of which Raphael, the "sociable spirit" (5.221) is himself an embodiment, the spirit of sociability. From its first enunciation in the narrator's praise—"Hail wedded love"—marriage is both the model and the foundation that first makes known "Relations dear, and all the charities / Of father, son, and brother" (4.756–57). In the exchange in which Adam asks God for a mate, cited shortly above, marriage is a human equivalent of—if also, importantly, an alternative to—the "union or communion" (8.431) to which God can raise his creatures: in effect it is an equivalent of the very conversation that Adam is having with God at that moment and of the very conversation with Raphael in which he now reports it. It is the equivalent, too, of the communion that he, Eve, and Raphael share over their luncheon, or love feast, in Eden.

In the divorce tract *Tetrachordon*, Milton recalls Paul's own application in Ephesians 5:30–32 of the "one flesh" of human marriage to Christ's love for the Church, which is his body and which is similarly one in its unity.

> Why did *Moses* then set down thir uniting into one flesh? And I again ask, why the Gospel so oft repeats the eating of our Saviours flesh, the drinking of his blood? *That wee are one body with him, the members of his body, flesh of his flesh, and bone of his bone. Ephes.* 5 (*CPW* 2:606; emphasis in original)

We are one body in marriage, Milton argues, in much the same way that we are with Christ in his Church, particularly in the communion that is symbolized by the Lord's Supper, a sacrament, he asserts in *De Doctrina Christiana* (1.28), that does not require a minister to perform it, nor is necessary to salvation (6:552–60). He implies here that a too literal reading of marriage as the indissoluble union of two bodies (a physical impossibility, too) would be the equivalent of a literal, that is, Catholic reading of the Lord's Supper as a real uniting with the physical body of Christ: both marriage and communion with God are spiritual unions that have no meaning without "love and peace" (2:606), and the first is the token for the second. So, conversely in book 1, chapter 24 of *De Doctrina Christiana*, titled "Of Union and Communion with Christ and His Members, also of the Mystic or Invisible Church" (De Unione et communione cum Christo eiusque membris, ubi de ecclesia mystica sive invisibili), Milton notes that "Christ's love for this invisible and immaculate church of his is figured by the love of husband for wife" (*CPW* 6:500; *Works* 16:64; Amor Christi in hanc suam ecclesiam invisibilem et immaculatam illustrator simili amore conjugali). His Adam says as much in *Paradise Lost* about this larger union or communion with God when he requests a wife from his Creator. When Adam subsequently tells Raphael about the "Union of mind, or in us both one soul" (8.604) that characterizes his marriage with Eve, he echoes Paul's injunction in Philippians 2:2 to the members of the Church, a scriptural verse that Milton included and translated in his discussion of Christian charity in book 1, chapter 11 of *De Doctrina Christiana*: "that you may be of the same mind, having the same charity, unanimous and of one opinion" (*CPW* 6:749)—"ut eodem sitis affectu, eandem charitatem habentes, unanimes, et unum sentientes" (*Works* 17:270). Milton asserts in his treatise that charity makes the members of Christ, as far as possible, of one mind or soul—"qua fideles ut membra Christi ... quantum fieri potest unanimes plane sunt" (*Works* 17:270). Adam and Eve are said to be "unanimous," in one of the three moments where the word appears in *Paradise Lost*, in their nightly prayer of thanksgiving to God—"This said unanimous" (4.736)—just before they turn to lovemaking in their nuptial bed, the seal of a marital union of mind that mirrors, and will turn out to depend upon, their shared devotion to their Creator.

The middle books, 4–8, of *Paradise Lost* depict the marriage of Adam and Eve as one version of communion within a church that expands to take in both humans and angels. Milton connects marital union to the cohesion of a larger community, not only through the Pauline metaphor of Ephesians 5 but through the terms of the *Odyssey*, which provides the primary *epic* model of these books: the epic banquet with its inset storytelling. When Adam describes to Raphael the happiness of companionate wedded life that goes beyond sexual happiness,

> Union of mind, or in us both one soul;
> Harmony to behold in wedded pair
> More grateful than harmonious sound to the ear
> (8.604–6)

he echoes not only Paul writing on charity and the being of one mind (*auto phronete ... hen phronountes*) in the church in Philippians 2:2—what Milton translates into Latin with *unanimes*—but the words of Homer's Odysseus talking about marriage itself. In book 6 of the *Odyssey*, its hero tells Nausikaa that the best of things is marital concord: "may the gods grant you a husband and a house and sweet agreement [*homophrosyne*] / in all things, for nothing is better than this, more steadfast / than when two people, a man and his wife, keep a harmonious [*homophroneonte*] / household" (*Odys.* 6.181–84). The Greek original is best translated as "unanimity" and "unanimous," the like-mindedness and one soul that Milton's Adam ascribes to his marriage with Eve.[33] In the edition of Homer that we know Milton consulted, the Renaissance translator

Jean de Sponde rendered it as *concordia* in Latin, which Milton picks up in "harmony"; in his index, however, Sponde refers to the passage: "Coniuges sint *unanimes* et *concordes*" (Spouses should be of one mind and in concord).[34]

Three books later, Odysseus opens book 9 of the *Odyssey* by telling Nausikaa's father, King Alcinous, that the best or fairest of things is something else: the gathering together to banquet and to listen to the stories of a singer, when a resulting "festivity ["euphrosyne"; translated by Sponde as "laetitia" or "joy"] holds sway among all the populace" (*Odys.* 9.6). Odysseus will now himself occupy the role of singer and storyteller for the next four books of the *Odyssey*: the hero and the poet Homer are complimenting themselves in advance on the pleasure their poetry will provide Alcinous and the Phaeacians inside and the reader outside the poem. The two Homeric passages are probably meant to parallel each other and to contrast the domestic "homophrosyne" between Odysseus and Penelope that awaits Odysseus in Ithaca with the public, communal "euphrosyne" that he finds in Phaeacia and which the suitors have meanwhile violated at home—the hero's task is to restore and bring the two together.

It is clear that *Milton* read the passages this way: he had written *L'Allegro*, devoted to the personification of the latter sociable mirth or joy, "In heaven yclept Euphrosyne" (*L'Allegro* 12). When invoking Odysseus's ideal of "homophrosyne" to describe the first marriage of Adam and Eve, he would have connected the two Greek words and the mental states they describe. And he draws his own parallel in *Paradise Lost* between wedded concord and the experience of conviviality and listening to poetry. When Adam says that marital harmony is even better than "harmonious sound to the ear," he refers back to the earlier compliment he has paid in book 8 to Raphael's storytelling. The angel has occupied the same position at the meal Adam and Eve have been hosting as that of the storytelling guest Odysseus in the *Odyssey* and of Virgil's storytelling Aeneas in the analogous scene of banqueting in Dido's Carthage in the *Aeneid*: the reference in book 5 to the fruit that Eve brings to the table, which could be found on "the Punic coast [i.e., the Carthage of the *Aeneid*], or where / Alcinous reigned" (5.340–41), are tip-offs to the epic models of this convivial scene.

Raphael's words have been such, Adam says, that

> while I sit with thee, I seem in heaven,
> And sweeter thy discourse is to my ear
> Than fruits of palm-tree pleasantest to thirst
> And hunger both, from labour, at the hour
> Of sweet repast; they satiate, and soon fill,
> Though pleasant, but thy words with grace divine
> Imbued, bring to their sweetness no satiety.
> *(8.210–16)*

The angel has narrated the War in Heaven and the Creation, the epic and cosmogonic subject matters, respectively, of Alcinous's bard Demodocus (*Odys.*

8.62–82) and Dido's bard Iopas (*Aen*. 1.740–44): here, as in Milton's epic models, the convivial repast is the occasion for the production of poems-within-the-poem.[35] Adam praises the angel's words, which have transported him to the very heaven they describe, a tribute to Raphael's powers as a poet and to his "likening spiritual to corporeal forms" (5.573), a tribute that Milton, like Homer in the *Odyssey*, pays here to his own verse.[36] The words of the angel singer have been even sweeter than the repast that has brought them together. Eating together becomes the figure for the higher experience that accompanies it, the experience of learning produced through what Milton claims in *Of Education* is the best form of teaching: poetry.[37] Adam gives to Raphael, in turn, an account of his own creation and of the creation of Eve. Shared food, shared stories: a form of communion between man and angel. Milton thus uses the epic frame of the *Odyssey*, with its juxtaposition of the "homophrosyne" of wedded love and the "euphrosyne" of the communal feast to spell out the Pauline analogy between marriage and the charitable community of the church. The epic banquet becomes a Christian feast of love.

"Sweeter ... sweet ... sweetness": the harmony of his marriage, Adam says, outdoes the harmony of Raphael's words; the angel singer's words rival and outdo the sweet Edenic meal that has just been served to him: the "dulcet creams" that Eve has pressed from "sweet kernels" (5.346–47), gathered from a garden of fragrances—myrrh, cassia, nard—that Raphael has found to be "a wilderness of sweets" (5.294). Marriage is itself sweet: the narrator has hailed wedded love as the "Perpetual fountain of domestic sweets" (4.760) and Adam will later recall to Raphael the moment when he first saw Eve in his dream: "which from that time infused / Sweetness into my heart" (8.474–75). Adam's first speech in the poem in book 4 ends with the word "sweet": their work as gardeners in Eden is delightful, he tells Eve: "Which were it toilsome, yet with thee were sweet" (4.439). Eve picks up this cue in her love song to Adam later in the book (4.641–56), which perfectly reciprocates by declaring that for all the beauties and sweetness of the day and night in Eden, none of them "without thee is sweet" (4.656). Together the two passages in book 8 name the three components of Milton's Paradise: marital love, storytelling, conviviality—sex, poetry, and food: who could ask for anything more? The three are analogized and compared with one another in books 4–8 of *Paradise Lost* as forms of union and harmony, and they share the common quality and denominator of being *sweet*: "communion sweet" (5.637) as Raphael describes the festive joy of the angels in heaven in book 5.

Milton changed the 1667 reading "refection sweet" in book 5 to "communion sweet" and added verse 638, which describes how the angels "Quaff immortality and joy," in the revised version of *Paradise Lost* in 1674. He did so to spell out the parallel in book 5 between the feast and "sweet repast" (5.630) of the angels, replete with "song and dance" (5.619) and "harmony divine" (5.625), that Raphael recounts having taken place in heaven after God's announcement of the anointment of the Son and the luncheon of sweets that Raphael has consumed with his human hosts to whom he addresses his narration. Both are original versions of communion, versions *before*, and without the necessity of, the Son's sacrifice that institutes the later Lord's Supper. The biblical model of hospitality that Milton superimposes on the model of the epic banquet is the visit of the three angels to Abraham and Sarah at Mamre in Genesis 18: patristic interpretation saw eucharistic overtones in the meal shared by divinity and humans, and early Christian art portrayed the bread that Sarah bakes at the hearth for the occasion as a type for that later communion: the bread of the angels (*panis angelicus*).[38] Adam appreciates Raphael's condescending to eat "Food not of angels, yet accepted so" (5.465). In his speeches about the unity of God's creation as a universal food chain in which the "grosser feeds the purer" (5.404–33, 5.416) and as "one first matter all" (5.469–505, 5.472), Raphael suggests a larger communion, drawing creature toward Creator, built into the cosmos and into the physical act of eating itself.[39] Raphael's own dining with Adam and Eve could token, in turn, a future when human beings would rise to eat the angels' food and find it "no inconvenient diet" (5.495). Through a digestive alchemy that would, in the narrator's loaded word, "transubstantiate" (5.438) nutritional matter into a more "sublimed" form (5.483), "perhaps"—Raphael is careful to qualify to his human hosts—"Your bodies may at last turn all to spirit / Improved by tract of time" (496–98). The monism of the passage differentiates it from Milton's earlier fantasy of the virginal body turned "by degrees to the soul's essence / Till all be made immortal" in *Comus* (461–62), but it is much the same fantasy—the time "when men / With angels may participate" (5.493–94). The mellifluous dews and pearly grains that, Raphael informs us earlier, cover the floor of heaven each morning (5.429–30), and that constitute the angels' diet, are based on the manna that God sent the Israelites during their wanderings in the wilderness; manna, too, as Milton notes in *De Doctrina Christiana*, was "Under the law the type of the Lord's Supper" (*CPW* 6:554), the bread of communion: some earlier form of communion was already shared between man and angel in Milton's Eden.

Milton offers a further etiology of this "angels' food" (5.633) that draws these analogies still tighter to the communion of Christ's postlapsarian Church. He depicts the "communion sweet" that the angels enjoy at their heavenly feast as a new gift to them mediated by the Son of God and future Christ. When God honors and anoints the Son, he declares to the angelic host:

> your head I him appoint;
> And by my self have sworn to him shall bow
> All knees in heaven, and shall confess him Lord:
> Under his great viceregent reign abide
> United as one individual soul
> Forever happy: him who disobeys

> Me disobeys, breaks union ...
>   (5.606–12)

God makes the Son the head of the angels, just as the Son will later head his earthly church. In doing so, Abdiel will argue against Satan at the end of book 5, God has sought "to exalt / Our happy state under one head more near / United" (5.829–31). The quibble in Abdiel's words unites the angels nearer, both to God, a kind of promotion of angelic nature, and to one another. By means of the Son who condescends to be one of their ranks—"One of our number thus reduced" (5.843)—as he will later lower himself to take on human nature, Abdiel argues, God has initiated them into a more perfect union, the union that disobedience breaks. The corporate "individual soul" takes the place in God's words for the Pauline figure of the unified body, a nod to angelic nature that is more soul than body. The "immortality and *joy*" that the angels subsequently quaff (5.637–38) in communion is still more perfect than those earlier occasions Raphael remembers in book 6 when the angels "were wont to meet / So oft in festivals of *joy* and love / *Unanimous*" (6.93–95). Such angelic union is also characterized in book 11 as "fellowships of *joy*" (11.80) and God, in Raphael's recounting of the Creation, promises a similar "*joy* and union, without end" (7.161) to human beings raised by merit and long obedience to heaven. "Joy" is the repeated term here, and it corresponds to the "Euphrosyne"/ "laetitia" of *L'Allegro* that the speaker of *Il Penseroso* begins by disparaging ("Hence vain deluding Joys"). But Milton combines the convivial "euphrosyne" of the angels with "homophrosyne," the state of being one soul—"one individual soul," "Unanimous"—the condition that Paul defines as the essence of charity. This condition is coextensive with, or deeply analogous to, the "Union of mind, or in us both one soul" that Adam ascribes to his marriage with Eve; the "individual solace" he pronounced at their first meeting and wedlock finds its echo in the angels' "individual soul." Marital union is the counterpart, not only to a church on earth but to the community of the angels newly improved by the Son: husband and wife, angel and angel share an analogous happiness.

Abdiel's figure of the angels "under one head more near / United" is subsequently literalized during the War in Heaven in book 6 when Michael rallies the troops of the good angels behind the oncoming Son: "Under their head embodied all in one" (6.779). Book 6 is framed by two moments on either end, first when Abdiel, having separated himself by dissent from Satan and his followers on Satan's falsely named Mountain of the Congregation,[40] is incorporated into God's host—"gladly then he *mixed* / Among those friendly powers" (6.21–22)—and by the Son's excommunication and driving out of the rebel angels: "Then shall thy saints *unmixed*, and from the impure / Far separate, circling thy holy mount / Unfeigned hallelujahs to thee sing, / Hymns of high praise, and I among them chief" (742–45). In loving God through and with his Son, the angels come together as one pure body, and later, Raphael's description of angelic lovemaking picks up the same language: "Total they mix, union of pure with pure / Desiring" (8.627–28). Such angelic intimacy and union make it difficult to say which is a figure for which—the marital body for the communal one or the larger social communion for the unity of marriage.

"Not vastly disproportionall"

Paradise Lost elaborately develops in books 4–8 the analogy between human marriage and a larger charitable community among creatures. Nonetheless, the likeness does not close into an identity between the two.[41] Nor will the plot of the poem have it so: Raphael inserts "perhaps" into his prospect of human beings trading in their human bodies "to turn all to spirit" (5.496–97) because he already knows that the Fall will take place. This is the nature, Milton observes, of analogy, which he terms "proportion" (*proportio*) in *The Art of Logic* (1.21)—"Similarity is called proportion, in Greek usually *analogia*; and similarly things are called proportional, in Greek, *analoga*"—and then cites the scholastic formula that Montaigne had also famously invoked: "nothing similar is identical, the similar thing does not run on four feet, every similarity limps" (*CPW* 8.284–85; *Works* 11.192).

God sanctioned marriage in the first place, after listening and approving the arguments of Adam, as a specifically human relationship that substitutes for the "union or communion deified" to which God can raise his creatures, however homologous the two loving unions may be. By the same analogy, the unions created by love *within* marriage and in other forms of human charity remain incomplete. "Total they mix," Raphael remarks of the angels' lovemaking, but their union of angelic bodies, "As flesh to mix with flesh" (8.629), is physically impossible for human beings, as Milton remarks in *Tetrachordon* where he insists that the "one flesh" of marriage must be interpreted as the "likenes [and] … fitness of mind and disposition, which may breed the Spirit of concord, and union between them" (*CPW* 2:605). Milton's imagination also and equally balks at total spiritual union, "soul with soul" (8.629) with others, even if such union is the goal toward which human charity strives, whether in marital or communal form. When he defines the unanimity created by charity in *De Doctrina Christiana*, Milton twice uses the qualifying phrase, "quantum fieri potest"—"as far as possible"—to leave open a space of individual difference and, hence, freedom. In place of total mixture, this space or gap in marriage, and in the larger Christian community, is both bridged and preserved by "proportion."

When Adam tells Raphael of the "Union of mind" he shares with Eve, which is a "Harmony of mind to behold in wedded pair / More grateful than harmonious sound to the ear," he picks up the extended conceit of a stringed instrument with which he laid down the conditions of marital love earlier in book 8 in his dialogue with God.[42]

> Among unequals what society
> Can sort, what harmony or true delight?
> Which must be mutual, in proportion due
> Given and received; but in disparity
> The one intense, the other still remiss
> Cannot well suit with either ...
>   *(8.383–88)*

Adam primarily argues that the proper "human consort" (8.392)—he continues the musical punning—is another human being, not a brute beast that lacks "rational delight" (8.391) and is too low on the ladder of being as a loosely strung ("remiss") string is too low to be brought into musical "proportion" with a highly strung ("intense") one. But Adam also sets out the terms—"in proportion due"—for the give and take of marriage between partners who are both like and other: "Thy likeness, thy fit help, thy other self" (8.450), God proclaims of the mate he makes for the first man. Ronald Levao detects an echo of Aristotle's definition in the *Nicomachean Ethics* (8.13; 1162b) of the "proportion" (*analogon*) that obtains in the friendship between social superiors and inferiors: "the better should be loved more than he loves" (8.7; 1158b), but mutual love evens out their inequality.[43] Milton, we have seen, describes a "proportiond equalitie" prevailing in the free republican Commonwealth of *The Readie and Easie Way* (*CPW* 7:424), the political equivalent of such friendship. Adam may suggest a similar fitness between the two human sexes of *Paradise Lost*, unequal but in proportion with each other as they are not with lower animal species. Levao, however, argues that, beyond "an equivocation, present throughout the poem and Milton's culture at large, between egalitarian and hierarchical gender relations," Adam's sense of proportion valorizes the autonomy and difference, as well as the likeness and suitability of mind, between husband and wife.[44] One must have differently tuned strings to produce harmony: it is not a question of staying on the same wavelength. The opposite is the grounds for divorce described in *The Doctrine and Discipline of Divorce*, "when the minde hangs off in an unclosing disproportion" (*CPW* 2:246). The marriage of true minds in *Paradise Lost* seeks to close together their differences without closing them up, an individual solace.

The proportionality that applies to human marriage applies as well to Milton's vision of the Christian community of charity—the Church—of which it is a figure. In *Areopagitica*, written and published between *The Doctrine and Discipline of Divorce* and *Tetrachordon*, and in a large part a defense of his publishing these heterodox works, Milton reimagines—in the figures of the ingathering of the broken body of Truth and the building of Solomon's temple—the Pauline metaphors of the Church as the members of the body of Christ (Rom. 12:4–5; 1 Cor. 12:12–30; Eph. 4:3–16) and as the new temple: "Know ye not that ye are the temple of God, and that the Spirit of God dwelleth in you?" (1 Cor.

3:16; 2 Cor. 6:16; Eph. 2:21). Paul joins these two metaphors in his injunction that the spiritual gifts of its individual members, what he calls "prophecies," should "edify" (*oikodomeo*) the Church, both body (Eph. 4:12) and building, "God's building," whose foundation, Paul declares in 1 Corinthians 3:9–10, he has himself laid down, "as skillful master builder." Milton had already mixed Pauline metaphors in *The Reason of Church Government* (1.2), where the carefully measured "materiall Temple" and its future rebuilding foretold by Ezekiel are types for the spiritual "line and level" that God will apply to the soul of man, "the sooner to edifie and accomplish that immortall stature of Christs body which is his Church, in all her glorious lineaments and proportions" (*CPW* 1:757–58).[45] Here, too, "proportion" is the key term: Paul had enjoined the faithful in Romans 12:6, "let us prophecie according to the proportion of faith," where "proportion" translates the Greek *analogian*. So the gloss to 1 Corinthians 12 in the Geneva Bible describes Paul urging that those who offer their prophecies should make the "end proportionable to the beginning." Even as he calls upon the different members of the Church to love one another in unity, Paul seeks, through this appeal to likeness, to rein in prophecy under church discipline, as he would curb the act of speaking in tongues and women speaking at all in 1 Corinthians 14:26–40, and to ensure doctrinal uniformity (i.e., uniformity to Paul's doctrine).

Milton writes *against* the spirit of Paul's admonitions. The figures of the corporate Church in *Areopagitica* insist on difference-in-likeness and on the freedom it postulates. The body hewn into a thousand pieces of Truth, personified as feminine, "*homogeneal,* and proportionall" (*CPW* 2:551), is Milton's revised version of Paul's true Church—a mystical body larger than and not to be identified with any specific confessional or state church—which is to be brought into final form only at "her Masters second comming; he shall bring together every joynt and member, and shall mould them into an immortall feature of lovelines and perfection" (*CPW* 2:549; see Eph. 4:16; we might note the quibble in "loveliness"). Jesus has never seemed so much the son of Joseph the Joiner and carpenter by profession, and here he also—through the gender-inverting comparison of this joining the members of Truth to Isis gathering up the limbs of her spouse Osiris—becomes a marriage partner to his church, answering to "the voice of thy Bride," which called out to him three years earlier at the end of Milton's prose hymn in the 1641 *Animadversions* (*CPW* 1:707).

Milton continues to describe the piecing together of this invisible Church as carpentry in the figure of the building of Solomon's temple with its cutting and hewing, a defense of so-called schisms and an objection against the idea of complete ecclesial unity.

> And when every stone is laid artfully together, it cannot be united into a continuity, it can but be contiguous in this world; neither can every peece of the building be of one form; nay rather the perfection consists in this,

that out of many moderat varieties and brotherly dissimilitudes that are not vastly disproportionall arises the goodly and gracefull symmetry that commends the whole pile and structure. (*CPW* 2:555)

The members of God's building join together without erasing the differences—of religious opinion—among them. These are "not vastly disproportionall" just as the body of Truth is "proportionall."[46] Milton describes the process of fitting together the body and the temple through Paul's "proportion of faith"—by likeness and analogy—as "To be still searching what we know not, by what we know, still closing up truth to truth as we find it" (*CPW* 2:551). The double negative in the formulation "not vastly disproportionall," however, allows for the leeway and freedom necessary to build a church capacious enough for a time when "all the Lord's people are become Prophets" (*CPW* 2:556).[47] The individuality of prophecy, belonging to "those whom God hath fitted for the speciall use of these times with eminent and ample gifts, and those perhaps neither among the Priests" (*CPW* 2:567)—namely, the layman John Milton, prophet of divorce—requires its integration, through the dissemination of print, into a larger body, a super, invisible Church that can contain difference and nonconformity: the pieces of the house of God are not all of one form. Otherwise, this Church could not be *reformed*. The ongoing nature of its building —"the reforming of Reformation it self" (*CPW* 2:553)—in turn demands new forms of doctrine and personal revelation. Truths will never be closed up entirely, and contiguity rather than continuity is the condition of the unity of the Church in this world, the condition that warrants the religious toleration and freedom of expression for which *Areopagitica* argues. Milton invokes Pauline charity—"*the unity of Spirit*" and "*the bond of peace*" (*CPW* 2:565; Eph. 4:3)—over Pauline conformity. The proportion or similitude of charity is not to be collapsed into identity; instead, dissimilitude can be brotherly. Like the verse of *Paradise Lost*, it need not rhyme.

Changing Places

These ideas of analogical proportion, similitude that is not identity, surround Adam's fall. He falls in the name of a loving human relationship that is proportional, based on an incomplete likeness, between husband and wife—and that thus is free. So marriage, "one flesh," is proportional to—both a special instance of and a privileged figure for—an expanded charity, itself proportional and free, among the different members of a corporate human community. It is through marriage that other relations and charities first were known. In the case of Adam and Eve, the only human beings on earth at the time, these are one and the same thing. These human relationships are, in turn, proportional to, distinct from, and (imperfectly) continuous with communion with the angels (the meal with Raphael), and, most important, with "union or communion" with

God. Adam's decision to die with Eve appears to be the choice of one loving union over another, of a part instead of the analogous whole—and an assertion of human freedom. To say so is to repeat the observation that Adam's fall is a version of charity that anticipates the Son's sacrificial willingness to die for his future fellow humans (who are *his* typological bride), already announced in the poem in book 3: "Dwells in all heaven charity so dear?" the Father has asked (3.216)—it is only one of two places where the word "charity" in the singular appears in *Paradise Lost*. The parallel renders Adam's charity heroic, "more heroic" (9.14) than his epic predecessors listed at the opening of book 9 to offer grounds for comparison.[48] But the Son's "immortal love / To mortal men" is itself secondary to and dependent on the "Filial obedience" that shines above it in the Son's heavenly aspect (3.267–69): charity and obedience are aligned in his sacrifice of himself while they are opposed in Adam's fall.

The immediate effects of Adam's disobedient charity—an oxymoron—are ironic. By falling with Eve, Adam, like Satan and the other fallen angels, "breaks union" (5.612) with God. By eating the forbidden fruit together, they leave the communion of God's creatures: "No more of talk where God or angel guest / With man, as with his friend, familiar used / To sit indulgent, and with him partake / Rural repast … ," the narrator remarks at the opening of book 9, announcing not only the change to tragic subject matter in the book, but also the end, "no more," of the Edenic closeness shared among human beings, angels, God, and creation. As God declares in book 11, human beings are ejected from that cosmic unity that knows "no unharmonious mixture foul" (11.51)—as was the case at the end of the War in Heaven, the impure separate from the pure with whom harmonious union is now impossible. Henceforth they will eat "mortal food" (11.54), an "inconvenient diet" that will not let them convene with angels. The marital union of Adam and Eve itself dissolves, after the initial intoxication of sin, into mutual accusation and potentially endless discord by the last lines of the book: "And of their vain contest appeared no end" (9.1189). Their marriage of minds had been founded, more perhaps than Adam realized, on their shared love and obedience to God, "unanimous" in their common prayer. The Son's charity reopens the channel between humans and divinity that Adam's charity had broken off, and, in doing so, also reopens the possibility of human love.

Adam's charity is heroic *and* tragic, the opening of book 9 announces: he is an Achilles, knowingly hastening his own death ("Certain my resolution is to die" [9.907]); Odysseus giving up the substitution of Calypso and immortality ("Should God create another Eve" [9.911]), in order to return to Penelope; an anti-Aeneas ("Astonied stood and blank, while horror chill / Ran through his veins and all his joints relaxed" [9.890–91]) who will not leave a Creusa or Dido behind.[49] But this proem, less dismissive than its tone suggests, notes that such epic heroism later in human history is itself tragic, the inheritance of the world of death and divine wrath—"Neptun's ire or Juno's" (9.18)—into which Adam and Eve plunged humanity, a classical heroic world without the Son's saving charity, where heroism itself takes the form of Achilles's wrath rather than Adam's love. Again, the effect is ironic: book 9 closes and comes around to where it started with Adam's discovering anger—"first incensed" (9.1162)—in his heated rebuke to Eve. Something similar had happened in John Milton's own first marriage.

Charity nonetheless begins at home in *Paradise Lost*, and by its final lines, the reconstituted marriage of Adam and Eve seems very much like the epic's goal. Like Eve's wish for individual spiritual trial and divine approval, Adam's wish for human love and companionship both causes the Fall and seems to be the right choice for men and women after it: the characters may disastrously fail, but Milton's two wishes remain intact and vindicated. For, as Adam's case suggests, charity must begin somewhere. We know where charity will end: the eschatological goal of Christian history when, the Son tells the Father in book 6, "in the end / Thou shalt be all in all, and I in thee / For ever, and in me all whom thou lovest" (6.731–33; cf. 3.341). This all-encompassing and difficult-to-picture oneness on the far side of death is the outer reach and limit to which Milton's mysticism and ideas of corporate love are ultimately directed, *perhaps* what might have been, as Raphael's musings ventured, had the Fall not taken place. But it suggests all too much togetherness for the human here and now, both before and after the Fall, where for Milton, as we have just seen, a proportional charity strives to overcome and acknowledges the finally unclosable differences between loving individuals.[50] The ideal of human marriage in *Paradise Lost* posits a middle ground between Milton's two wishes that seem unassimilable in the career of Abdiel in the poem: the angel's being singled out for his service to God, his being "mixed" into the larger, promiscuous community of servants. The suiting to each other of two separate human beings and minds preserves the individual distinction and resists the potential narcissism of the first of these wishes; it preserves the altruistic love and resists the potential absorption of identity of the second. History may end—and the human individual's own history may end—in an all (or nothing), but *Paradise Lost* ends with Adam and Eve starting out, hand in hand again as they had first entered the poem (12.648; 4.321). Their marriage is what survives of Eden. For it to do so, however, the first man and woman must take up each other's—and Milton's—wishes.

A thought experiment suggests how closely these wishes have been attached to the characters and genders of Adam and Eve. Suppose that their positions had been reversed. Had Adam been the one tempted, he might, so aware of his human deficiency and so in love with Eve, have been less susceptible to Satan's flattery and promise of fame in a larger world; he would not have been without Eve by his side as his best witness, and would have gained strength from the shame of doing wrong in her sight; the more intellectual of the two, he might have reasoned against the devil's arguments. Had Eve been the one to confront a fallen Adam, she, persuaded of her spiritual sufficiency, might have turned away from him, as she did when they first met by the reflecting pool, and preferred to be acknowledged by the witness of God. Neither would have fallen, had they played each other's part. After the Fall, this is what they will do.

Adam feels that he has it all worked out after listening to Michael's narrative of human history and the promise of its end.

Henceforth I learn, that to obey is best,
And love with fear the only God, to walk
As in his presence, ever to observe
His providence, and on him sole depend,
Merciful over all his works, with good
Still overcoming evil, and by small
Accomplishing great things, by things deemed weak
Subverting world strong, and worldly wise
By simply meek;
   (12.561–69)

Adam has readjusted the balance between obedience and love along the model of the Son in heaven. He now places obedience first: it is best and followed by love. The love in question, however, is directed to the same God Adam obeys and on whom Adam will uniquely depend—no more codependency with his wife. Adam expresses the ambitions to spiritual heroism that had belonged to Eve before their fall, ambitions now corrected (and disguised) along the lines of Christ and Abdiel as patience and heroic martyrdom. Eve had argued that God would be "our witness from the event." Now Adam chooses to think of God looking on and present beside him, while he, in turn will "observe"—both to discern and to serve—what God has already foreseen for him. This vertical relationship between individual and deity—Milton's first wish—seems, in fact, to leave little room for the collateral love between humans that is his second.

Accordingly, Michael, after extravagantly praising Adam for his doctrine—"thou hast attained the sum / Of wisdom" (12.575–76)—tacks on an addendum.

only add
Deeds to thy knowledge answerable, add faith,
Add virtue, patience, temperance, add love,
By name to come called Charity, the soul
Of all the rest: then wilt thou not be loath
To leave this Paradise, but shalt possess
A paradise within thee, happier far.
   (12.581–87)

Adam might be taken aback and wonder what it takes to win in God's system: love for his fellow human being is what got him into trouble in the first place. And, in fact, Michael appears to invert the order and the priorities of that other heavenly mediator Raphael, who left the unfallen Adam in book 8, urging him to "Be strong, live happy, and love, but first of all / Him whom to love is to obey"

(8.633–34). Adam thinks he has gotten it straight: obedience, named last, none-theless comes first and appears to be the highest form of love. But now Michael, invoking the word "Charity" in the singular for its only reappearance in the poem since God asked it of the Son in book 3, tells him that this love is "the soul" of an ambiguous "all the rest": whether of all the things added to Adam's newfound knowledge or of these *and* of that knowledge itself. In this rewriting of 2 Peter 1:5–7, where brotherly kindness and love similarly come at the end of a series of theological virtues, Milton insists on their rising order of impor-tance. It is not a traditional Protestant scheme in which works ("deeds") are an addition to the faith that alone justifies salvation (see 12.408–10), since *both* faith and works are add-ons to Adam's pledge of obedience. Rather, Michael guarantees Adam that he can—and must—have it all: charity, experienced most fully in the restored marriage of Adam and Eve, is the sine qua non condition of that happier paradise within which Adam and his descendants will find avail-able in fallen history.[51] Michael's speech concludes with the promise that Adam and Eve will live "in one faith *unanimous* though sad" (12.603), bringing back this word, too, and its promise of marital harmony, from before the Fall.

Michael's injunction and the structure of the end of book 12, which now turns from Adam and Michael to Eve for the final speech of the epic, fit the paradoxical concept of the *supplement* described by Jacques Derrida: what is presented as an addition to a completed structure both questions the latter's completeness and becomes indispensable to it, a necessary addition.[52] So the charity that supplements Adam's knowledge of the primacy of obedience be-comes its fulfillment. In fact, *this is what will happen to the Son's own charity*, which in heaven shone less in him than did his obedience. A reversal will take place, Michael has narrated earlier in book 12, when the Son comes to the earth to save humanity.

> The law of God exact he shall fulfil
> Both by obedience and by love, though love
> Alone fulfil the law;
>   *(12.402–4)*

Milton's application of Romans 13:10 moralizes Christ's sacrifice as the super-session of the Law, which, as Michael goes on to say, is itself nailed to the cross and annulled (12.415–19), and it suggests the limitations, both spiritual and historical, of obedience. It lends to Michael's addition of charity the quality of a new dispensation. With its "one easy prohibition" (4.433), the Eden that Adam and Eve outgrow may now be looked back upon as a period under the Law: Christ will fulfill "that which thou didst want, / Obedience to the law of God" (12.395–96), Michael tells Adam. It is succeeded by a new Christian liberty: love and do what you will.[53]

Eve's final speech may feel tacked on, a little scene granted to a character who is created second and comes second to her husband.[54] Its fourteen lines, it has been pointed out, suggest a sonnet, a lyric coda voiced by the female hero-ine to the epic of the male hero.[55] These are calculated effects of the speech, but Milton has carefully designed it not only to be an addition at the poem's end but to correspond to an earlier passage near the beginning of book 11. Together they frame books 11 and 12, which, we want to remember, were originally one final book 10 in the original 1667 *Paradise Lost*. Back in book 11, Adam, as-sured that their prayers have found favor with God, hails Eve as the "Mother of all Mankind, / Mother of all things living, since by thee / Man is to live and all things live for man" (11.159–61). Eve replies that she is "Ill worthy" (11.164) of the title, and acknowledges the infinite grace of God and the favor of Adam, "next favourable thou, / Who highly thus to entitle me vouchsafest" (11.169–70). Chastened by experience, she also pledges "never from thy side henceforth to stray" (11.176)—a stark revision of her complaint during their quarrel after the Fall in book 9, "Was I to have never parted from thy side? / As good have grown there still a lifeless rib" (9.1153–54)—and a token of the reconciliation that the couple has meanwhile effected in book 10. Collateral love indeed. Now, toward the close of book 12, in the last words spoken in the poem, she reechoes their earlier exchange.

> but now lead on;
> In me is no delay; with thee to go,
> Is to stay here; without thee here to stay,
> Is to go hence unwilling; thou to me
> Art all things under heaven, all places thou,
> Who for my willful crime art banished hence.
> This further consolation yet secure
> I carry hence; though all by me is lost,
> Such favour I unworthy am vouchsafed,
> By me the promised seed shall all restore.
>   *(12.614–23)*

With its recollection of the pledge to Naomi—"whither thou goest, I will go" (Ruth 1:16)—by Ruth, "of whome the Lord Iesus did vouchsafe to come," as the Geneva Bible puts it, Eve now accepts her own role as the first and, in her case, knowing ancestress of Christ, mother of mankind and of one greater man in particular.[56] She declares her readiness to go with Adam into the new Promised Land. The sentiments also recall Eve's love song in book 4 where none of the delights of Eden were sweet to her without the company of Adam. Now Adam is "all places" to her, and their marriage itself her Eden or paradise within. The exchange of the two characters' roles is nowhere more telling than in Eve's reaffirmation of her place by Adam's side: now *she* is the codependent partner in their relationship. But *Paradise Lost* suggests that from here on love in marriage and community may be the best thing human beings can seek for themselves.

This reassignment of roles and of Miltonic wishes to the two characters and to their respective sexes—individual heroism to Adam, loving partnership to Eve—brings the ending of *Paradise Lost* closer to norms of patriarchy and to a gendered division of public, active (masculine) and private, affective (feminine) spheres. In retrospect, the epic even allows us to think that the Fall was caused by their original misalignment, that Milton has redeemed his wish for individual trial and approval by transferring it from his female heroine Eve—and behind Eve from the Lady of *Comus*—to the male hero Adam; *Paradise Regained* awaits, and however Lady-like or like the Lady of Christ's College its Christ may be, he is still a he. Feminist criticism has rightly taught us to be suspicious.

But the ending of the poem does more than set gender roles and hierarchy straight: it rearranges its own priorities. If Milton, in his first wish, identified with Eve before the Fall, he continues, in his second, to identify with Eve in an emancipated Christian future. And this second wish now seems to count for more. Eve's sonnetlike supplement to the poem, like Michael's answer to Adam with which it corresponds, suggests that marriage and the community of charity for which Eve has now become the spokeswoman effectively supersede standing approved in the sight of God.[57] Milton still wants it both ways: the blind poet's composing *Paradise Lost* might be included among the "things deemed weak" posited by Adam, whose accomplishment constitutes a new heroism and personal witness. But the poem itself, which Kerrigan has argued became possible biographically through Milton's own marriage and acceptance of adult sexuality, places its emotional and narrative goal in marital love. Like Adam and Eve in its final lines, *Paradise Lost* comes down to earth, and the weight of feeling of the poem shifts from the reconciliation and renewed obedience of humans to a now distanced, alienated deity to their reconciliation with one another. They leave the Eden that was made for them to the one that they must make for themselves, and the new realm of human autonomy that is specially instanced in their marriage feels like Christian freedom. Eve may come second, but, in so doing, she has the last words of a poem that declares that the last shall be first.

Appendix: A Note on the Separation Scene

Adam's momentous "Go" speech (9.343–75), where he appears to give the persuasive final argument against Eve's going off by herself, only then to turn around and grant her permission to do so, imitates a speech of Goffredo in Tasso's *Gerusalemme liberata* (5.3–5), particularly as Milton would have known it in the Edward Fairfax translation, as well as in the Italian original. The commander of the crusade outlines good reasons why the knights in the group of "adventurers" (*aventurieri*), loosely under his authority, should not go off with the pagan enchantress Armida, who has presented a phony damsel-in-distress story, and meanwhile seduces them with her beauty and flirtation. He then accedes to their request to send out ten champions from the crusader host. Here are the two passages, first Adam:

>   *trial will come unsought.*
> Wouldst thou approve thy constancy, approve
> First thy obedience: the other who can know,
> Not seeing thee attempted, who attest?
> *But if* thou think, *trial unsought* may find
> Us both securer than thus warned thou seem'st,
> *Go*; for thy stay, *not free, absents thee more*;
> *Go* in thy native innocence.
>   *(PL 9.366–73)*

then Goffredo in the Fairfax translation:

> "In following her it may betide you ill;
> Refrain therefore, and change this forward thought
> *For death unsent for, danger comes unsought.*
>
> "*But if* to shun these perils, *sought* so far,
> May seem disgraceful to the place you hold;
> If grave advice and prudent counsel are
> Esteemed detractors from your courage bold;
> Then know, *I none against his will debar*,
> Nor what I granted erst I now withhold;
> But be mine empire, as it ought of right,
> Sweet, easy, pleasant, meek and light.
>
> "*Go* then or tarry, each as likes him best,
> *Free power I grant you* on this enterprise."
>   *(Jerusalem Delivered 5.3.6–8 to 5.5.1–2)*

Goffredo's indulgence is the first cause of all the ensuing problems that block the taking of Jerusalem until the end of Tasso's epic: hero after hero goes AWOL.

The rest of the *Gerusalemme liberata*, as its very first stanza spells out, involves Goffredo's reduction of his errant fellow knights back under his command and beneath the holy auspices of the crusade.

The parallel colors Milton's Eve as a reckless knight-errant, desirous as she is to make trial of her strength, and one easily susceptible to seductive wiles—of which Satan has no shortage. It complicates the recollection in her words (9.335–36) of *Areopagitica* and its chivalric figure of the "warfaring Christian," like Spenser's Sir Guyon (*CPW* 2:515–16). It may lend an added pointedness to Adam's addressing his wife as "adventurous Eve" (9.921), when she returns to him after eating the forbidden fruit. The parallel also could suggest that Adam, as Eve will later claim, was too weak a husband and commander-in-chief: "why didst not thou the head / Command me absolutely not to go, / Going into such danger as thou saidst?" (9.1155–57). Adam replies, however, that "I warned thee, I admonished thee, foretold / The danger ... beyond this had been force / And force upon free will hath here no place" (9.1171–74).

Both Tasso and Milton explore the irresolvable dilemmas of authority and freedom. The comparison brings out Tasso's relative authoritarianism and Milton's commitment to liberty, however great the cost.

Reversing the Fall in Book 10

Has Milton nodded? Though little noticed, there is a logical problem in the order of events in book 10. We are told (10.332–45) that Satan witnessed the Fall but fled terrified from the Son who came to judge Adam and Eve, then returned to eavesdrop on the couple and learned of God's decree upon him, "which understood / Not instant but of future doom" (10.344–45); this conversation is the one between Adam and Eve that begins at 10.867 and concludes the book. Satan now meets with Sin and Death on the outside of the universe and discovers the bridge they have built to hell; they started to build the bridge before the Fall and Judgment (10.220), which by now have taken place. Satan sends them to ravage God's new world (10.346–409); he meanwhile proceeds along the bridge to stage a triumph in Pandaemonium, which will backfire on him as he and his fellow devils are transformed into serpents (10.410–584). Sin and Death set to work (10.585–613), and it is at the sight of Satan's children entering his creation that God himself reacts, and alters the universe and the earth's weather (10.613–714). Adam himself reacts to these changes in a long soliloquy of despair (10.715–866). At this point Eve enters the scene and the dialogue and reconciliation of the couple ensues, the conversation that Satan has supposedly already overheard, *but which he cannot have done*, since he has, in fact, triggered it—through Sin and Death, God's ensuing action, and Adam's consequent despair. The narrative circles back on itself in a moebius strip or loop.[1] Milton may have made a mistake in the epic's chronology, but it is not like him to have done so. He would have been able to correct it, had he so chosen, in the second edition in 1674.

One effect of the confused order of events is to entangle the narratives of Satan and Adam and Eve—the falls of the angels and of mankind, whose parallels have heretofore structured *Paradise Lost*—at the very moment when the poem decisively separates and distinguishes them. From the point at which the despairing Adam declares himself in soliloquy "To Satan only like both crime and doom" (10.841) and cast into an abyss "out of which / I find no way" (10.843–44), fortunes for humanity in fact begin to change. The logic and unity of book 10 depend on the contrast it draws between, on the one hand, Satan and the devils, who in the first half of the book (10.235–584) seem to have achieved their high point of victory over humanity and God only to find themselves back where they started and further degraded in hell, and, on the other, Adam and Eve, who, in the book's second half (10.715–1104), climb up from their low point of despair to reconcile with each other and to reestablish a line of communication with their forgiving Creator. The impossible narrative feedback loop of book 10 suggests no way out of the book itself. It corresponds to the recursive nature of sin that Adam recognizes in his anguish and that indeed characterizes the permanent plight of Satan and his fellow fallen angels, condemned forever to go around in circles. But the regenerate Adam and Eve *do* escape from book 10 and from this vortex of fallenness: the couple will continue into the last books of the poem, while the devil is left behind.

The dialogue between Adam and Eve that Satan is supposed to—but logically cannot—have overheard constitutes the "Crisis of *Paradise Lost*," as E. M. Tillyard terms it in a profound and classic essay, the moment when the human pair become the true heroes of the poem in Satan's place. Tillyard saw the restoration of love between the first couple and of the recovery of hope for a human future not only as the dramatic hinge of the poem but also as Milton's artistic wager: "The main point therefore now is whether in actual fact, as we read, the reconciliation of Adam and Eve and their repentance before God have sufficient weight in the poem to balance the grandeur of Satan and his doings in the first books."[2] The humbleness of a conversation between husband and wife, rebuilding bridges after a terrible quarrel, becomes a graver subject in Milton's epic than the conventional epic of war and empire that finds its Virgilian emblem in the colossal, lifeless bridge that Sin and Death, the book's other couple, build across Chaos. The grandeur of the devils at the opening of the poem has in any case fallen in book 10 into the grotesqueness of Sin and Death and the final metamorphosis into ash-chewing snakes of Satan and his crew. The colloquy of Adam and Eve ends in their humbling themselves before the deity they have offended, the Christian moral counterpart to the aesthetic humility of the scene itself.

The reconciliation of Adam and Eve, the new heroic arena of *Paradise Lost*, thus takes place in book 10 against a design that involves Satan, and, as we shall see, the Son as well. An understanding of this design, which precisely concerns beginnings and endings, is a necessary prelude to a discussion of what Milton is doing with his human heroes. Its terms are drawn, as I have just suggested, from Virgil's *Aeneid*, whose glorification of imperial power and greatness makes it the epic model that the Christian humility of *Paradise Lost* most insistently measures itself against and self-consciously inverts. As a Protestant poet, Milton was bound to oppose the *Aeneid*'s story of Roman power without end, a story that had been eagerly enough embraced by a Roman Catholic papacy that claimed to be the empire's inheritor.[3] It is also the epic that consistently asserts, in Aeneas's loss of Creusa and abandonment of Dido, the incompatibility of marriage and love with the historical mission of its hero: Odyssean domesticity and eros are assigned to the first half of the *Aeneid* and give way to the conquest and battles of its Iliadic second half. In *Paradise Lost*, marital love becomes its human heroes' goal *after* the Son and Satan and their respective forces have fought their epic battles in heaven at the poem's midpoint. The *Odyssey* half of Milton's epic—the story of a private couple—supersedes *its Iliad* half, the grand, all-inclusive history of God and devil, in a pointed reversal both of Virgil's sequence (itself an inversion of Homeric sequence) and of the Roman poet's apparent ethical priorities. The first section of this chapter shows how Milton's studied Virgilian allusions organize and unify the action of book 10 up to the dramatic dialogue of Adam and Eve. The ultimately aimless circularity of the exploits of Satan and his children, Sin and Death, contrasts with the closed, apocalyptic plot accomplished by the victory of the Son, an epic closure that is itself supplemented—and superseded—by his ensuing act of creating a new universe. The open-ended future that begins for Adam and Eve is measured against both of these narrative models and their ethical possibilities: the potential for relapse as well as for creative perseverance. For if the human pair replace Satan as heroes of *Paradise Lost*, Satan, before he disappears from the scene of the poem, has already announced his own successors in Sin and Death. He sends them into the universe as his "Plenipotent" (10.404) substitutes. In the hall of mirrors set up by book 10, Satan's children are shadowy doubles, not only for the Son but for Adam and Eve themselves: they will dog the steps of mankind until the end of time.[4]

Death is, in fact, an option in the dialogue of Adam and Eve, discussed in the chapter's second section: Eve's proposal that they commit a Stoic suicide would end their story, just as Satan's story ends, inside the confines of book 10. But just having an option already distinguishes Adam and Eve from Satan. Unlike the fallen angels, who in book 2 discover no end for their hopeless condition because they cannot die, Adam and Eve find that they have the freedom to die, and therefore can choose to live. They choose to humble themselves before God, while God humiliates the punningly "Reluctant" (10.515) Satan, writhing and unwilling, as a snake. The recovery of choice—of free will—allows the first humans and the poem to go forward.

Adam and Eve choose, above all, to love each other again. There appeared to be "no end" (9.1189) of their mutual accusation at the close of book 9, just as the War in Heaven could have gone on forever—"in perpetual fight they needs must last / Endless" (6.693–94), God had declared—until the Son steps in to stop both conflicts. Book 10 breaks this impasse, but not before Adam drops one rung further down into despair and launches into a misogynistic tirade at Eve's approach (10.867–908). "Out of my sight, thou serpent," cries the angry husband, and we have to wonder how much of his own first marriage to Mary Powell the sightless poet revisits at this moment.[5]

Adam's is a literally textbook misogyny, culled, as we shall see in the chapter's third section, from the best classical sources—Euripides's woman-hating Hippolytus and Hesiod's Pandora. These are of a piece with two other misogynistic stories to which Milton alludes to and revises in book 10: the tragedy of Virgil's abandoned Dido, the most prestigious of epic heroines, and the biblical account of the concubine exposed by her husband at Gibeah in Judges 19. Milton's rewriting of these stories—and he will also glance at Virgil's Creusa at the end of *Paradise Lost*—in order to correct their misogynistic tenor constitute another pattern that unifies the larger book and that reflects Adam's own change of heart. Adam and the Genesis story itself seem to invent a subsequent tradition of Western literary misogyny, but he and Milton's book 10 take it back as part of the book's larger reversal of the effects of the Fall: we learn *not* to identify that tradition with Milton's Eve, nor with her daughters. The temptation to blame women is the last of the "evasions vain" (10.829) by which Adam in his preceding soliloquy admits to trying to avoid his own responsibility for his misery (he has already tried to shift the blame to Eve in the Judgment Scene at the book's beginning). It is the final obstacle that needs to be overcome before Adam can love Eve, and before the reunited couple can chart their way out of the recursive fold of the narrative of book 10. In his portrait of Adam's mixed emotions and not always noble actions, Milton is perhaps facing up, more than two decades later, to his own role in the rocky beginning of his first marriage. But that marriage, too, went forward.

Virgilian Coordinates and the End of Satan

Milton shapes the fiction of book 10 through multiple allusions to beginnings and endings in Virgil's *Aeneid*, and these fit, in turn, into a larger pattern in *Paradise Lost*. We have seen in chapter 1 how the opening of the epic depicts Satan struggling to tend off the Dead Sea–like burning lake and its Sodom-like rain of fire, to find a "harbour" in hell (1.184–85) as Aeneas seeks a haven for his fleet along the shores of Carthage after the storm that opens book 1 of the *Aeneid*. Chapter 5 noted how the duel that fails to take place between Gabriel and Satan at the end of book 4 pointedly avoids a repeat of the narrative ending of the *Aeneid* and the killing by Aeneas of Turnus. Milton, instead, looks for an idea of an ending in the *chronological* endpoint projected by Virgil's epic, the future victory of Augustus Caesar over Antony at Actium and the subsequent triumph of Augustus in Rome, events of Virgil's own lifetime prophesied as the end, goal and conclusion, of history and sculpted by Vulcan on the shield Venus bestows on Aeneas at the conclusion of *Aeneid* 8. These Virgilian coordinates of book 10 are charted in the table below:

Aeneid 1 (opening in storm; Carthage; orator simile; Neptune's trident)	*Aeneid* 8 (triumph of Augustus; bridge over Araxes)
SIN AND DEATH build bridge out of stormy Chaos with Death's trident	Indignation of Chaos (Araxes)
(SON calms Chaos by Word, Bk 7)	(SON's triumph after War in Heaven, Bk 6) (SON's triumph after Creation, Bk 7)
SATAN back in hell; Libyan desert (snakes)	SATAN's "triumph" in hell, bridge as triumphal arch
ADAM and the storm winds; troubled sea of passion	

Milton divides the opening scene of the *Aeneid*, where the speech of Neptune calms the violent storm winds sent by Aeolus at the prompting of Juno—what precedes Aeneas's making for a harbor at Carthage—into two separate episodes in order first to depict the Son's creative word calming Chaos, thus starting up the second half of *Paradise Lost*. He returns to this Virgilian scene in book 10 to describe, by way of contrast and parody, how Sin and Death create through lethal force the bridge that connects earth to hell. That bridge also recalls the final image on the shield of Aeneas, the bridge Augustus rebuilt over the Araxes River, and in effect connects in book 10 both of these Virgilian coordinates: the beginning storm of the *Aeneid* and that poem's prophetic vision of Augustan imperialism and closure upon history. Milton similarly divides up this latter Virgilian scene of imperial triumph into contrasting episodes of *Paradise Lost*. He uses it to portray, on the one hand, the victory of the Son in the War in Heaven and his subsequent entry in triumph into heaven in book 6, an ending that climaxes the first half of the twelve-book 1674 version of the epic and that anticipates the Son's apocalyptic victory over Satan at the true end of history. On the other, Milton depicts the would-be triumph of Satan, celebrating his seduction of humanity in book 10, as a false ending that only returns Satan back to where he began, to the hell that re-evokes the Carthage and Libya of the opening of the *Aeneid*. Milton returns yet again in book 10 to the same opening episode of the *Aeneid*, to the still earlier moment when the storm winds of Aeolus are first unleashed. As an effect of the Fall, the winds of the earth are released from their prison, matched by the storm of Adam's human passion. Adam has fallen into a Chaos or hell of despair: Will he be able to make his way out?

CREATION AND ANTI-CREATION

Through his rewritings of it, Milton engages in a critical reading of the famous first simile of the *Aeneid*. Virgil compares Neptune's calling upon the winds to desist and to return to their imprisonment under their king Aeolus to the words of an unarmed citizen, renowned for his piety and service, calming a great people that rages (*saeuit*) in civil strife (*Aen.* 1.148–53). As we indicated in chapter 5, Milton reproduces this scenario in book 11 in the vision that Michael offers to Adam of Enoch who similarly tries to calm a city fallen into "factious opposition" (11.664)—only to have the crowd hoot him down: Enoch is only saved from their violence by his timely translation into heaven. Milton's version belies the ostensible content of Virgil's simile that most commentators from the Renaissance onward have read straightforwardly as an equation of Neptune's speech with the pacifying words of the statesman.[6] Both god and statesman appear to be figures for Augustus, the restorer of rationality and order to a Rome wracked by civil wars: an announcement in this first simile of the ideological stakes in the poem that is to follow. But Milton has detected the potential irony that Virgil already built into the simile, for Neptune, unlike the orator, is armed, and he not only calms but threatens the winds with his fierce trident ("saeuum tridentem"; *Aen.* 1.138). The adjective indicates a violence in kind that corresponds and responds to the violence of the raging crowd in the simile, as well as to the violence of fierce Juno, who has fomented the storm in the first place, "saeuae ... Iunonis" as she is evoked in the fourth verse of the *Aeneid* —and it suggests the element of force that not only backs up Neptune's words but the reason of state of Augustus. Virgil is having it two ways.

So does Milton as he breaks the simile apart in the action of *Paradise Lost*; he imitates the calming of the storm *twice*.[7] In book 7, the Son begins the act of creating the universe by bringing peace to the storms of Chaos, which is assimilated with the "Deep" of Genesis 1:

> Outrageous as a sea, dark, wasteful, wild,
> Up from the bottom turned by furious winds
> And surging waves, as mountains to assault
> Heaven's highth, and with the centre mix the pole.
>   Silence, ye troubled waves, and thou deep, peace,
> Said then the omnific Word, your discord end:
>   *(7.212–17)*

Chaos, we are told by Raphael, hears the Son's voice (221) and turns into a "watery calm" (234), ready to be infused with the vital virtue of creation.[8] Here, as in book 2, Chaos is like a "dark / Illimitable ocean" (2.891–92), and the Son's command recalls Neptune's speech that sends the winds of Aeolus back to their king. There is an explicit echo here of Virgil's storm in *Aeneid* 1 that churns up the sea from its lowest depths: "a sedibus imis" (*Aen.* 1.84). The quieting of the discord of Chaos through the omnific Word of God alone aligns the Son with the weaponless orator-statesman of Virgil's simile. The scene also conflates the Virgilian model with a future calming of a storm on the Sea of Galilee by the same Son: "And he arose and rebuked the wind, and said unto the sea, Peace, be still. And the wind ceased, and there was a great calm" (Mark 4:39).

In book 10, this sublime scene of creation is parodied when Sin and Death build their bridge across Chaos from hell to God's new universe: Rte. 666. Here, too, a stillness is imposed on the waves of Chaos, but it is the stillness of death.[9]

> what they met
> Solid or slimy, as in raging sea
> Tossed up and down, together crowded drove
> From each side shoaling towards the mouth of hell.
> As when two polar winds blowing adverse
> Upon the Cronian sea, together drive
> Mountains of ice, that stop the imagined way
> Beyond Petsora eastward to the rich
> Cathaian coast. The aggregated soil
> Death with his mace petrific, cold and dry,
> As with a trident smote …
> *(10.285–95)*

Sin and Death first act like the winds of Aeolus themselves, making the sea of Chaos rage; Death finishes the job with his petrifying mace that, with its comparison to a trident, carries associations with Neptune and returns us to the opening scene of the *Aeneid*. Milton's fiction activates the force with which Virgil's Neptune threatens any recalcitrant storm winds and here the force proves both lethal, the icy grip of death, and, in its source, indistinguishable from the disorder to which it puts an end. Built out of imitations of the same *Aeneid* episode, out of the vehicle (the statesman) and the tenor (Neptune and his trident) of its first simile, Milton's contrast between the two episodes of creation could not be clearer. The spiritual goodness of the "omnific Word" of the Son creates new life, the wonderful architecture of the universe, out of the discord of Chaos; the children of Satan use carnal force to make a lifeless edifice. Virgil's Romans were superb builders of roads—roads for military purposes above all—but this is what their and other attempts at human empire building could amount to: so Tacitus has the British chieftain Galgacus, a character in Milton's own *History of Britain*, remark of the Roman conquerors of his island, "they make a wasteland and call it peace" (*Agricola* 1.30).[10]

ANTI-TRIUMPHS

In fact, the building by Sin and Death of their causeway across Chaos alludes not only to the opening of the *Aeneid* but to a symbol of imperial conquest that brings Virgil's epic to a kind of historical end point and high point at the close of its book 8. Aeneas beholds the new shield that the God Vulcan has made for him, sculpted with scenes of future Roman history and its triumphs. The god's prophetic vision and the poet's historical hindsight culminate in the triumph of Augustus in 29 BCE, and the ekphrastic description of the shield concludes with an image-within-the-image, the representation carried in the triumphal procession of the Armenian river Araxes, where Roman power bordered on the Parthian Empire, and of the bridge that Augustus rebuilt over it—"pontem indignatus Araxes" (*Aen.* 8.728). This image of imperial permanence over the flux of time miniaturizes the shield that, in turn, miniaturizes Virgil's epic, and it underscores the sense of an ending that the shield projects: that Roman history from the time of Aeneas has been leading up to and concludes in the power of Augustus.

The "high arched" (10.301) bridge that Sin and Death build over Chaos, which now appears to be a kind of triumphal arch to greet Satan as he returns from earth to hell—"Triumphal with triumphal act have met / Mine with this glorious work" (10.390–91),[11] the devil declares—is a version of Augustus's bridge on a colossal scale.

> The other way Satan went down
> The causey to hell gate; on either side
> Disparted chaos over built exclaimed,
> And with rebounding surge the bars assailed,
> *That scorned his indignation;*
>   (*10.414–18*)

"Pontem indignatus Araxes": Milton insists on the echo; we hear the same indignation earlier in the simile that compares the bridge of Sin and Death to another imperial undertaking.

> So, if great things to small may be compared,
> Xerxes, the liberty of Greece to yoke,
> From Susa his Memnonian palace high
> Came to the sea, and over Hellespont
> Bridging his way, Europe with Asia joined,
> And scourged with many a stroke *the indignant waves.*
>   (*10.306–11*)

Milton borrows the simile from Lucan's *De bello civile* 2.672–77, where it describes, in turn, another Caesarian project, the building by Julius Caesar of a causeway across the harbor of Brindisi, where he sought, unsuccessfully, to block the escape of the fleet of Pompey and the defenders of the republic.[12] But the figure of Xerxes is also linked to Virgil's Araxes. Servius glossed the *Aeneid* 8 passage: "this is a river in Armenia which Xerxes was unable to mount with bridges, and upon which Alexander the Great built a bridge, but the flooding of the river broke it; later Augustus bound it with a stronger bridge, whence it is called, to the glory of Augustus, 'the Araxes indignant at its bridge.'"[13]

The glory of Augustus may not last, however, if the experience of his conqueror predecessors with the river is any evidence. This concluding tag of the description of the shield of Aeneas, like the opening simile of the *Aeneid*, is potentially ironic, and here, too, we can watch Milton exploiting a doubleness already present in his Virgilian model as he rewrites its scene of imperial triumph. Both of Xerxes's bridge projects fail: he has troops scourge the indignant waves of the Hellespont because a storm there washed his pontoon bridge away, just as the Araxes broke his bridge. Alexander has no better luck with the Araxes, and these precedents, in turn, cast doubt in the *Aeneid* on the permanence of Augustus's imperial achievement. By giving the last word of the description of the shield to the indignant Araxes, Virgil hints at another future washing away of the bridge and of new dangers massing at Rome's frontier, a flood of Parthians ready to overflow their boundaries, the same Parthians, "outpoured" from their capital Ctesiphon (*PR* 3.311), that Satan would put at the disposition of Milton's Jesus in *Paradise Regained* to free Israel from the Roman yoke. We should similarly conclude that, despite their use of "pins of adamant" (10.318) that recall the "adamantinos … clavos" of Horace's Necessity (*Odes* 3.24.4–7) and that make this punning hell's pont all "too fast … / And durable" (*PL* 10.319–20), the bridge of Sin and Death is not built to last. No earthly power, human or demonic, is lasting, for the earth itself will pass way. In fact, in the same narrative sequence God will foretell the apocalyptic victory of the Son over both Sin and Death (*PL* 10.631–39) and, in a moment that might give pause to Milton's reader, the angels sing hallelujah (10.642) at the instant that the two are set loose into the world. The good news is that the triumph of Satan, Sin, and Death is fleeting in the eyes of eternity; the bad news is that their bridge will last until the end of human history: long enough.

The building of the bridge over Chaos thus combines the beginning of the *Aeneid*, the calming of the storm winds that strike Aeneas off the coast of Carthage, with the ending Virgil's epic projects beyond the story of Aeneas himself, the triumph of Augustus epitomized in his bridge over the indignant Araxes. Like the raising of Pandaemonium in book 1, the episode builds a Rome in one day, a Rome that is both the empire of Virgil's poem and, with its "wondrous art / Pontifical" (10.312–13) a modern-day papal Rome that through Spanish and Portuguese conquest would extend its power over the "new world" (2.403) and, through the masked Catholicism of the treacherous Stuarts, to the "happy isle" (2.410) of England as well. But these are the small things, mere human empires, to which the great satanic Rome is compared. Milton's fiction dwarfs the Rome celebrated by the *Aeneid*, and in the construction of the bridge that collapses the opening and historical closure of Virgil's poem, he effectively dwarfs the *Aeneid* itself, reducing it to some forty verses (10.282–324): the biggest *Aeneid* ever told in the shortest number of lines. At the same time, he suggests the short-circuited nature of this miniature epic of Satan's children, whose end is already built into its beginning: their bridge is fated, like Roman triumphal arches still visible in Milton's and our own day, to be a ruin of a fallen empire.

THE TRIUMPHS OF THE SON

As he has done with the scene of Neptune calming the storm at the beginning of the *Aeneid*, Milton has similarly distributed his rewriting of this scene on the shield of Aeneas in *Aeneid* 8 into two separate and contrasting episodes, the triumph of the Son after the War in Heaven at the end of book 6 and its parody in Satan's triumphant return to hell along the bridge that his offspring have built in book 10. Where Virgil depicts an end to history two-thirds of the way through his epic, Milton gestures to a similar finality halfway through the twelve-book 1674 *Paradise Lost*: the Son's defeat of Satan in book 6 and the subsequent creation of the universe in book 7 anticipate the apocalyptic battle of Revelation and the creation of a new heaven and new earth at the end of Christian history. The War in Heaven from which the Son returns victorious is itself modeled on Virgil's depiction of Actium on the shield, a battle that is in part a heavenly conflict between the Olympian gods and the monster gods of Cleopatra's East (*Aen.* 8.698–700).[14] The Son receives the acclamation of the angel citizens of heaven.

> Sole victor from the expulsion of his foes
> Messiah his triumphal chariot turned:
> To meet him all his saints, who silent stood
> Eye witnesses of his almighty acts,
> With jubilee advanced; and as they went,
> Shaded with branching palm, each order bright,
> Sung triumph, and him sung victorious king,
> Son, heir, and Lord, to him dominion given,
> Worthiest to reign: he celebrated rode
> Triumphant through mid heaven, into the courts
> And temple of his mighty Father throned
> On high: who in glory him received,
> Where now he sits at the right hand of bliss.
>   (6.880–92)

The Son rides into the forecourts of the temple of his mighty Father and sits at the right hand of bliss, where Virgil's Augustus sits on the threshold of the temple of *his* divine patron, possibly his divine father, Apollo (*Aen.* 8.720–22).[15] The triumph of Augustus projects the fictional world of the *Aeneid* into Virgil's own time and constitutes a culmination and endpoint of the Roman history that is founded in the poem. The Son's triumph, which takes place before human history properly begins, is prophetic both of his triumph over Satan and sin at the Crucifixion—so the Son, in an adaptation of Colossians 2:15, has prophesied: "I through the ample air in triumph high / Shall lead hell captive maugre hell, and show / The powers of darkness bound" (3.254–56; cf. also 12.451–58)—and equally of his triumph over Satan at the end of history at the Last Judgment: Michael ends his narration of history to Adam with the same terminal word "bliss": "To bring forth fruits joy and eternal bliss" (12.551).[16] (In its thirty-seven appearances in *Paradise Lost*, "bliss" comes at the end of the verse twenty-five times, in a kind of verbal tic.) The Son's acclamation by the palm-bearing angels thus anticipates his entrance as Jesus into Jerusalem to a chorus of hosannas on Palm Sunday—itself a version in humility that mocks the pride of the Roman triumph—and his entrance into the temple that initiates the Passion (John 12:12–16, Matt. 21:1–17, Mark 11:1–11, Luke 19). It also anticipates the gathering of the saints before the throne of the Lamb at the end of time (Rev. 7:9–10).

The Son of God takes the place of Virgil's "diui genus" (*Aen.* 6.792), Augustus Caesar, and will, Michael foretells to Adam, "bound his reign / With earth's wide bounds, his glory with the heavens" (12.370–71) as Virgil's Jupiter prophesies of Augustus: "imperium Oceano, famam qui terminet astris" (*Aen.* 1.287). Milton's claiming this triumphal Virgilian typology for his God does not, however, turn the heaven of *Paradise Lost* into Dante's Rome in which Christ is a Roman (*Purg.* 32.102), which would confer a special divine historical dispensation on the Roman Empire and on Virgil, its poetic celebrant and Dante's guide. To the contrary, we should understand Virgil's Augustus to be imitating the triumph of the Son—the *Aeneid* in effect imitating the fiction of *Paradise Lost* rather than the other way around—and, in doing so, to be idolatrously attempting to play God, the only legitimate king.[17] Human tyrants, of whom Nimrod, foretold by Michael in book 12 of *Paradise Lost*, is the prototype, falsely claim "second sovereignty" (*PL* 12.35) from heaven, a supposed divine right of kings. Adam answers Michael by asserting that God gave human beings dominion only over the other animals.

> that right we hold
> By his donation; but man over men
> He made not lord; such title to himself
> Reserving, human left from human free.
> *(12.68–71)*

The distinguishing of true from false donations seems particularly pointed, an attack not merely on temporal monarchy but on the temporal power and monarchical pretensions of the papacy, which, through the so-called Donation of Constantine, claimed to be the heir of the Roman Empire.[18] But that empire, the Rome of Virgil and Augustus, was itself a carnal and profane copy, or diabolic parody, of divine monarchy.[19]

Milton, moreover, stages, at the end of book 7, a *second* entrance of the Son into heaven-Jerusalem and into "God's eternal house" (7.576) and "imperial throne" (7.585) that outdoes his triumph after the War in Heaven at the end of book 6: "greater now in thy return / Than from the giant angels; thee that day / Thy thunders magnified; but to create / Is greater than created to destroy" (7.604–7)—the angels sing to the *Father*, Jehovah (7.602), whose power, manifested in the Son, has topped its earlier achievement. The thirteen verses that described the Son's triumph have now expanded to eighty-two (7.551–632), as the Son returns from creating the universe

> Up to the heaven of heavens his high abode
> Thence to behold this new created world,
> The addition of his empire, how it showed
> In prospect from his throne, how good, how fair
> Answering his great idea. Up he rode
> Followed with acclamation and the sound
> Symphonious of ten thousand harps that tuned
> Angelic harmonies: the earth, the air
> Resounded ...
> (7.553–61)

The music of the angels is amplified by a rare Miltonic use of rhyme—"abode/showed/rode," "fair/air"—and his more customary internal rhyming: "sound/thousand/Resounded," "harps/harmonies," which enacts the resounding it describes. Milton is pulling out all the stops in order to make us feel the greater magnitude of the event. As a supplement to the War in Heaven, God has added to his "empire," but he has done so pointedly by creation, not by the war and conquest celebrated in the Roman triumph and depicted in the Virgilian model that stands behind the Son's earlier victorious entry into heaven. That model now seems to be left behind altogether, and *Paradise Lost* suggests that it has been doubly superseded.

SATAN'S TRIUMPH

By the time, then, that the satanic forces of *Paradise Lost* themselves produce in book 10 their own would-be Virgilian triumph, it can only be an empty parody of the Son's triumph—and, as we have seen, Satan's children also parody the Son's life-giving act of creation by their use of deadly force. They thus disclose the true demonic nature of such human—especially Roman—imperial projects. Satan, indeed, has just made himself the prince of this world, and subjected God's creation and humanity to Sin and Death, as well as to his fellow devils who now have free access to the earth on the bridge that his children have built, "To range in, and to dwell, and over man / To rule" (10.492–93), he tells them in Pandaemonium. They *have* something to celebrate, and Milton's belittling Satan's accomplishment and putting a damper on their festivity can smack of denial and whistling in the dark. Here, too, Milton makes his point by manipulating the Virgilian coordinates of his poem, collapsing together in this episode the sense of an ending contained in the triumph of Augustus on the shield of Aeneas with the shipwreck and disarray on the coastline of Libya that opens the *Aeneid*. Satan and his devils will turn out to have achieved no conclusive victory over mankind and God, and they finish up not only back where they began in hell, but in even greater degradation.

Milton precedes the episode in book 10 by reminding us, once again, of what Satan and his companions are parodying: the narrator refers, in an even more direct citation of Colossians 2:15, to the future triumph of the Son at the Crucifixion, when he "rising from his grave / Spoiled principalities and powers, *triumphed* / In open show" (10.185–87). The episode then divides into two parts. First, Sin and Death, the very principalities and powers whom the Son will despoil, build their triumphal arch (like Augustus's bridge over the Araxes, waiting its destruction), and meet their father; then Satan returns to Pandaemonium expecting acclaim from his fellow devils of the kind the Son received from the angels in heaven: he promises "to lead ye forth / *Triumphant* out of this infernal pit" across the newly created bridge to God's new creation and to earth (10.463–64), an exodus that would parody the Son's harrowing of hell. Instead, he and they are transformed into serpents.

Satan ends his speech to the assembled chiefs of the fallen angels on the same terminal word, "bliss," which had ended Raphael's description of the Son's triumph to the acclaim of the singing angels in book 6; he invites the devils to enter into full "bliss," as he had shortly before told Sin and Death to descend to Paradise: "There dwell and reign in bliss" (10.399).

> what remains, ye gods,
> But up and enter now into full bliss.
>   So having said, a while he stood, expecting
> Their universal shout and high applause
> To fill his ear, when contrary he hears
> On all sides, from innumerable tongues
> A dismal universal hiss, the sound
> Of public scorn;
>   *(10.502–9)*

"Bliss" turns into a divine joke on Satan, for, far from indicating an achieved ending, it already indicates that he is being transformed, along with all the other devils around him, into a hissing serpent.[20] "Thus was the applause they meant, / Turned to exploding hiss, triumph to shame / Cast on themselves from their own mouths" (10.545–47). Deprived of their triumph, this metamorphosis further compels the devils comically to fall down, "supplanted" (10.513), and to reenact a parodic version of original sin, attracted to a grove "laden with fair fruit, like that / Which grew in Paradise, the bait of Eve / Used by the tempter" (10.550–52), only to find it to taste of bitter ashes, "like that which grew / Near that bituminous lake where Sodom flamed" (10.561–62). The Dead Sea fruits of

Sodom were supposed to turn to ashes in one's hands; these go one better and refuse to melt in the mouths of the serpent-devils, who have to chew them and spit them out over and over again, falling repeatedly "Into the same illusion, not as man / Whom they triumphed once lapsed" (10.571–72).

The whole scene not only depicts Satan's literal return to hell but also brings him back to the beginning of the poem, and suggests that his heroic career has gone in a circle and made no real progress at all. As we noted in chapter 1, he finds himself again in the same symbolic landscape of hell, but a landscape raised to a new level of quasi-burlesque grotesqueness in which he is forced to participate. Through the ashy fruit, it is another version of Sodom and the Dead Sea[21]—and through the snake metamorphosis, it is another version of the Libyan desert beside Carthage as well.

> dreadful was the din
> Of hissing through the hall, thick swarming now
> With complicated monsters head and tail,
> Scorpion and asp, and amphisbaena dire,
> Cerastes horned, hydrus, and ellops drear,
> And dipsas (not so thick swarmed once the soil
> Bedropped with blood of Gorgon, or the isle
> Of Ophiusa)
>   *(10.521–28)*

The soil sprinkled with the blood of the Gorgon Medusa is Libya in the account that Lucan gives in the *De bello civile* (*BC* 9.619–937) of why the region teems in venomous serpents: among its snakes are the amphisbaena, cerastes, and dipsas—and Lucan also describes a particularly deadly scorpion (*BC* 9.833–36). Milton's poem returns with Satan to the Carthaginian-Libyan landscape of its opening book and of the opening of the *Aeneid*, now demonized even further as a realm of serpents and poison. The biggest of these snakes is Satan himself, likened to "whom the sun / Ingendered in the Pythian vale on slime, / Huge *Python*" (10.529–31); this last simile describing Satan returns us again to the beginning of the poem and to the *first* simile that governs our first sight of him: "in bulk as huge / As whom the fables name of monstrous size, / Titanian, or Earth-born, that warred on Jove, / Briareos or *Typhon*" (1.196–99). Huge Typhon, huge Python: the two snaky monsters were identified with each other through mythographical conflation and typographical inversion, and Milton's pattern suggests reversion and circularity.[22] Satan exits the poem in simile as he had entered it. If the Son's triumph corresponds to the politico-historical climax or "ending" of the *Aeneid* at the end of its book 8, Satan's failed parody of that triumph brings him back to where he started in *Paradise Lost*, and back to the corresponding beginning of the *Aeneid* as well: in a doomed Carthage rather than all-victorious Rome. Even the hiss of the mutually entangled ("complicated") devils-turned-serpents—"hissing through the hall, thick swarming now"—merely repeats the noise and situation of their initial entrance into Pandaemonium in book 1, as they bumped into each other in its too narrow confines: "*Thick swarmed*, both on the ground and in the air / Brushed with the *hiss* of rustling wings" (1.767–68).[23] The sense that the devils and their evil have gone around in a circle and will only keep doing so is strengthened by the report—"some say"—that they must repeat their metamorphosis: "Yearly enjoined, some say, to undergo / This annual humbling certain numbered days" (10.575–76), a compulsory feast of atonement. Condemned with the serpent at the opening of book 10 "Upon thy belly grovelling thou shalt go" (10.177), Satan is last glimpsed in *Paradise Lost* as "A monstrous serpent on his belly prone" (10.514); he is in the same "abject posture" (1.322) in which he was first found, "prone on the flood" (1.195) with his "Grovelling and prostrate" (1.280) companions: there a storm-tossed Aeneas seeking a harbor near Carthage, now a snake on its Libyan sands.

ADAM AND THE WINDS

This is the posture and also the Virgilian situation of the despairing, fallen Adam whom we meet shortly later in book 10. Milton describes him, after his long soliloquy, "on the ground / *Outstretched he lay*, on the cold ground" (10.850–51); so Satan is first seen in the poem: "So *stretched out* huge in length the arch-fiend *lay* / Chained on the burning lake" (1.209–10). Adam's soliloquy is preceded by the work of God's angels changing the weather on earth. The winds are released in a full catalog, classical and modern, that is a Miltonic tour de force.

> now from the north
> Of Norumbega, and the Samoed shore
> Bursting their brazen dungeon, armed with ice
> And snow and hail and stormy gust and flaw,
> Boreas, and Caecias and Argestes loud
> And Thrascias rend the woods and seas upturn;
> With adverse blast upturns them from the south
> Notus and Afer black with thunderous clouds
> From Serraliona; thwart of these as fierce
> Forth rush the Levant and the ponent winds
> Eurus and Zephir, with their lateral noise,
> Sirocco, and Libecchio, thus began
> Outrage from lifeless things;
> (10.695–707)

The action recalls once again the beginning of the *Aeneid* when, at Juno's bidding, Aeolus looses the imprisoned winds that attack Aeneas and his fleet; four that attack the Trojan ships in Virgil's epic—Eurus, Notus, Afer-Africus, and Zephyr (*Aen.* 1.85–86, 131)—are present and accounted for here. And Adam himself recalls the gale-tossed Aeneas of *Aeneid* 1, as the storm raging outside becomes a storm within.

> these were from without
> The growing miseries, which Adam saw
> Already in part, though hid in gloomiest shade,
> To sorrow abandoned, but worse felt within,
> And in a troubled sea of passion tossed,
> Thus to disburden sought with sad complaint.
> *(10.714–19)*

In a way that is typical of Milton's method, the epic landscape becomes internalized: Satan discovered that he carried hell within him when he thinks to have escaped it by arriving on earth in book 4 (18–23, 75); Adam will receive a "paradise within thee, happier far" at the end of the epic (12.587). Here the fallen Adam is tossed on a sea of inner turmoil that, together with the winds that rage without, puts him in the position of Virgil's Aeneas off the coast of Carthage, the same position in which Satan is first introduced in book 1, trying to find a way "From off the tossing of these fiery waves" (1.184).[24] The scene returns us to the openings both of the *Aeneid* and of *Paradise Lost* itself. The latter, in hell, is the literal low point of Milton's epic, and Adam similarly has hit rock bottom.

Milton, however, develops these parallels between the fallen Satan and the fallen Adam—and aligns them with the same Virgilian coordinates—in order finally to contrast the careers of devil and man in book 10. In a book whose narrative appears to loop back upon itself, Satan himself returns to where he started. He is an Aeneas who never really gets out of the storm or the Carthage-hell that he has himself built. In Adam's case, the allusion to the opening of the *Aeneid* signals a genuine new beginning. Adam will start over, thanks to the intervention of Eve and, so the narrator, Son, and Father will each declare in book 11, thanks to prevenient grace (11.3; 11.23; 11.91). He is an Aeneas with the world all before him after the fall of Troy, and, as we shall see, he keeps his Dido-Creusa. Like Satan in the larger poem, Adam will apparently end up as we first see him in book 10 and in a similar prone posture: "prostrate" (10.1087; 10.1099) on the ground. But appearances are deceiving and the similarity that carefully unifies the fiction of the book points out the saving difference between the regenerated Adam and Eve and the forever fallen angels.

The Recovery of Human Choice

We are now, finally, in a position to read the colloquy between Adam and Eve against the preceding first seven hundred lines of book 10, with their insistent pattern of Virgilian ending collapsed with beginning, with their literal Sturm und Drang. Neither triumph, nor mock-triumph in a cycle of defeat, the respective properties of the divine and diabolic protagonists of *Paradise Lost* and of the martial winners and losers of earlier epic, the victory of Adam and Eve over despair is human and everyday—it is no final victory but must be won every day—and it is no less, but more heroic for that. The couple's reconciliation with each other in marital love is the model for their reconciliation with God—the poem leaves open which causes which. Both allow them to escape the recursive pull of their own fallenness, and to find their way out of a book that seems to have no exit.

At first, in his grand, tragic "complaint" of one hundred and twenty-five verses that now follows (10.720–844), Adam cannot argue his way out of despair and concludes himself, "To Satan only like both crime and doom" (10.841). His soliloquy in fact echoes Satan's earlier spoken soliloquies, paired by their respective addresses to the sun and to the earth, at the openings of book 4 (4.32–113) and book 9 (9.99–178). Adam crucially submits—"I submit" (10.769)—to the justice of God's punishment where Satan had disdained the very word "submission" (4.81–86), and he thus leaves himself open to Eve's subsequent intervention and example, "submissive in distress" (942). But Adam is no less despairing than the Satan who explicitly bid farewell to hope (4.108), and where Satan, in his resolution to embrace evil, also bid farewell to fear, Adam ends his speech driven into an "abyss of fears / And horrors" (10.842–43). Adam finds that rock bottom is itself notional, and feels himself falling ever spiritually downward, "from deep to deeper plunged" (10.844), as Satan had earlier testified in book 4—"in the lowest deep a lower deep / Still threatening to devour me opens wide" (4.76–77)—and the poem has just depicted Satan experiencing the indeed greater mortification of falling down and crawling on his belly as a serpent. As Belial had suggested to the devils in book 2, things can get worse for them. Adam, too, repeatedly discovers the circularity of sin and of his fallen existence. The curse of his posterity whom he has made like him in original sin "Shall with a fierce reflux on me redound" (10.739; compare Satan, who deliberately seeks "others to make such / As I, though thereby worse to me redound" [9.127–28]). Adam's "sense of endless woes" (10.754), which becomes specified as the fear that death is "endless misery" (10.810), "Comes thundering back, with dreadful revolution / On my defenseless head" (10.814–15). His "reasonings, though through mazes" return him to his own conviction: "first and last / On me, me only, as the source and spring / Of all corruption, all the blame lights due" (10.831–33). The plotting out in book 10 of returns to epic beginnings, both its three evocations of the opening of the *Aeneid* (Sin and Death impose stillness on Chaos; hell as Libya; the release of the winds) and the literal return of Satan to the hell of book 1, are thus internalized in the hopeless circles of Adam's remorse. He cannot get out of his own mind by himself, and needs the partnership of Eve and/or of grace.

We have also seen this circularity in the plight of the fallen angels in Pandaemonium in book 2, whirled about in their chariot races or by whirlwinds, lost in the wandering mazes of thought, brought by revolution from hot to cold in order to suffer seasonal change. The no-exit nature of the devils' situation depended there—as the initial exchange between Belial and Moloch spelled out—on their inability to die and the "Ages of hopeless end" (2.186) of their punishment. All other choices they make turn out to be versions of each other, and no choice at all, in light of this bad eternity. The fallen Adam, too, begins to intuit and dread an endless suffering. He overcomes his fear, "lest all I cannot die" (10.783) by reasoning out Milton's mortalist, materialist position that the soul dies (or sleeps) with the body that it has vivified (10.783–808)—only to raise the specter that death, as it is for fallen angels, is the experience of his own remorse for an unforgiven sin: "endless misery / From this day onward, which I feel begun / Both in me, and without me, and so last / To perpetuity" (10.810–13). As he contemplates the prospect of this "second death," the hell of the damned, Adam asks again for physical death: "Why comes not death, / Said he, with one thrice acceptable stroke / To end me?" (10.854–56). Instead, Eve approaches Adam to restore him to life: she does so not least by offering him the choice of death.

The reconciliation of the couple is exquisitely balanced so that they each in succession save the other from despair.[25] After Adam lashes out at her in a general misogynistic outburst—whose literary and possibly biographical associations will be discussed in our next section—Eve begins the couple's mutual process of spiritual recovery by four actions. The first is a physical example: she "Fell humble" (10.912) in tears and embraced Adam's feet as a suppliant and is subsequently "upraised" (10.946) by her appeased husband. Adam is himself upraised, this time mentally and internally, from despair; after her second speech, "To better hopes his more attentive mind / Labouring had raised" (10.1011–12): he begins to work for a solution, and the curse of labor that comes with the Fall becomes a blessing. Second, Eve calls to mind the "oracle" (10.182) about the enmity between her seed and the serpent (10.925–27) expressed in the Son's judgment on them at the beginning of the book. Third, she volunteers to return to the "place of judgment" (10.932–36). Fourth, she offers to ask God to remove his punishment from the head of Adam and to let it fall "On me, sole cause to thee of all this woe, / Me me only just object of his ire" (10.935–36).

Adam appears distracted from the first three of these actions by the fourth and last. Eve's offer to take God's sentence upon herself is Christological and with its repetition of "me" echoes, as commentators have pointed out, the Son's offer to die for humanity in book 3: "Behold me then, me for him, life for life / I offer, on me let thine anger fall; / Account me man" (3.236–38).[26] Adam takes this option off the table, telling Eve that she is not capable of bearing the full wrath of God, and suggesting that if it would work, he would do it himself. It is not Adam's finest moment. He refuses to Eve an ethical heroism that he himself rejected in his soliloquy where, though he recognized himself as culprit—"me, me only" he had said, now echoed by Eve—he had felt unable to bear the burden of wrath "Than all the world much heavier, though divided / With that bad woman?" (10.836–37): no question here of his taking the punishment all by himself. Moreover, he had fully considered and rejected, at the moment of God's judgment earlier in the book, the option of shielding Eve, whose guilt "I should conceal and not expose to blame" (10.130), a moment he or the poem subsequently recalls: "To me committed and by me exposed" (10.957). The unfallen Adam passes the test of love by falling and dying with Eve; once fallen, he twice fails to die for her.[27] Adam may be doctrinally correct, and the Christian plot of the poem appears to reserve the salvation of humanity for the Son, who at the beginning of book 10 has stated that "the worst on me must light, / When time shall be" (10.73–74). Eve may be trying once again, as in her setting out "to make trial of her strength" before her fall in book 9, to play a heroic role that she is not quite up to. And Adam may fear losing Eve. Again. But he is ungallant, to say the least, in attributing his own deficiency in heroism to Eve and denying her the chance to die for him.

Thwarted, Eve resolves to die, period. Rather than give birth to a posterity cursed with their original sin, she first proposes sexual abstinence and then the quickest way out.

> Then both ourselves and seed at once to free
> From what we fear for both, let us make short,
> Let us seek death, or he not found, supply
> With our own hands his office on our selves;
> Why stand we longer shivering under fears,
> That show no end but death, and have the power,
> Of many ways to die the shortest choosing,
> Destruction with destruction to destroy.
>   She ended here, or vehement despair
> Broke off the rest; so much of death her thoughts
> Had entertained, as dyed her cheeks with pale.
>   (10.999-1009)

Eve invents Stoicism: Seneca writes of the many exits to life that lie open to men and women in his letters and in his tragedy, the *Phoenissae*.[28] Her attempt to short-circuit human history through suicide is a pagan alternative to the Christological model she first proposed, but Eve still seems to usurp or parody the role of the Son. Her destroying of destruction is a counterpart to his passion, itself a kind of suicide mission, through which "Death his death's wound shall then receive" (3.252). The difference is that the Son would overcome Death as the "second death," a spiritual rather than a merely physical condition. Adam spells out the difference in his response to Eve when he fears that God would "make death in us live" (10.1028), as it lives in the fallen angels, who are unable to find death, that is, annihilation, in hell.

The poetic logic of this moment of *Paradise Lost* depends, nonetheless, on our bearing in mind the similarity between the endless, futile misery of the fallen angels and the existence of fallen human beings on earth—in order that Eve's discovery of suicide can decisively distinguish the two. Human beings can find many ways to death; the fallen angels cannot die. (Milton does not seem interested in representing eternal punishment of human beings after death.) One may speculate to what extent John Milton, after the affliction of his blindness and the defeat of his political cause, faced suicide as a daily existential choice. The chorus of *Samson Agonistes* carefully addresses its hero, "Among thy slain self-killed / Not willingly" (*SA* 1664–65), but the play testifies to thinking about how to end it all.

For the Stoic, the possibility of suicide is the ultimate expression of human liberty. It is paradoxically no less of one in Milton's fiction, even if suicide is to be rejected. Eve offers the wrong choice, but it now appears that human beings, unlike the devils, *have* a choice. In book 9, Eve unknowingly and Adam, against his better knowledge, had chosen death. Now, together, they will choose to live.[29] In preserving, rather than destroying "our selves and seed," the human race itself, they anticipate the choice proffered to the Israelites in Deuteronomy 30:19: "I have set before you life and death, blessing and cursing: therefore choose life, that both thou and thy seed may live." In this section of the epic, Milton doubly justifies death to man, the most difficult of the ways of God to understand. At the opening of book 11, God will declare that death is the "final remedy" (11.62) to human life that would have otherwise "served but to eternize woe" (11.60) after the Fall. Human life becomes livable because we know that it will end.[30] But already here in book 10, death restores the choice that seemed to be lost by the Fall: because death is available as a way out, living on becomes something we will ourselves to do, a "better fortitude." Death becomes the ground of human freedom.

Given the choice, Adam rescues Eve from her despair as she had shaken him out of his own. He envisions a human future of "labour" (10.1054), both his and men's work and the labor of Eve's and women's childbirth, both forms of creation, and by the end of the book, Adam's laboring mind will have discovered fire like a new Prometheus.[31] "To create / Is greater than created to destroy," and the reconciliation of the couple is itself a creative act aligned with the creativity of God and contrasted to the creation-through-destruction of that other couple of book 10, Sin and Death, as they build their bridge across Chaos. Adam now takes up the cues of Eve's first speech. He remembers the oracle of the serpent and women's seed (10.1030–36). He repeats her plan to return to the "the place of judgment." He imitates her tearful prostration:

> What better can we do, than to the place
> Repairing where he judged us, prostrate fall
> Before him reverent, and there confess

Humbly our faults, and pardon beg, with tears
Watering the ground, and with our sighs the air
Frequenting, sent from hearts contrite, in sign
Of sorrow unfeigned, and humiliation meek.
    (10.1086–92)

Adam disconcertingly presents these actions as if they were his own ideas—but in some ways they are. He appears to realize for the first time that the serpent was, in fact, Satan (10.1033–35); he urges that they pray not to take all the punishment onto one or the other of themselves but to seek forgiveness together. Milton delicately insists on the mutuality of the first couple's finding their course to spiritual renewal: it belongs to both of them, the product of the give-and-take that characterizes his ideal of marriage in *The Doctrine and Discipline of Divorce*: "a meet and happy conversation is the chiefest and noblest end of marriage" (*CPW* 2:246). Whatever they accomplish, they accomplish together. The spectacular triple pun of "Repairing"—the primary sense is "returning," but it also connotes "putting a pair or couple together again" and "making reparation"—suggests that the reconciliation of Adam and Eve, particularly Adam's relenting forgiveness to the penitent Eve, who fell humble at his feet ("at his feet submissive in distress, / Creature so fair his reconcilement seeking" [10.942–43]), is the condition, as well as the model, for their reconciliation with God: "let him live / Before thee reconciled" (11.38–39), says the Son, carrying their prayers to the Father as their advocate and interpreter. The resolution that the couple "prostrate fall" before the offended deity transforms Adam's earlier lying in despair, outstretched upon the cold ground, into a posture now of penitence and prayer.[32] The contrast with the fall of Satan and his cohorts prone on the ground, as serpents in enforced "penance," indicates that one will either prostrate oneself to God willingly or God will make one bow down to him willing or no. Adam and Eve prostrate themselves in order to rise, while the fallen angels fall down only to fall further, over and over. One is surprised, on turning the page to the first verse of book 11, to find the human couple in a different stance: "Thus they in lowliest plight repentant *stood*"; they may have gotten up, but the verb certainly refers to their spiritual state.

Milton remarkably repeats Adam's injunction to prostration and prayer, altered into narrative form, to end book 10 (10.1098–1104); the Homeric-style repetition contributes to the sense of both formal and symbolic closure, the sense that *Paradise Lost* has reached its heroic climax, which is nothing more, but also nothing less, than the restoration of the marriage of Adam and Eve.[33] Quieter, as Tillyard pointed out, than the mock-triumph of Satan to which it is contrasted inside the book or than the heroic triumphs of the Son at the ends of books 6 and 7, it does not correspond to the Virgilian coordinates of beginning and ending discussed in the preceding section. Adam and Eve escape the circular return to spiritual storm and shipwreck that claims Satan;[34] they do not achieve the apocalyptic finality of the triumphant Son. By contrast, the peace Adam and Eve have achieved is provisional and open-ended: "My motions in him, longer than they move, / His heart I know, how variable and vain / Self-left" (11.91–93) comments God in the following book 11, as he unpleasantly takes credit for the human drama we have just watched unfold. The subsequent history of mankind narrated by Michael in books 11 and 12 will recount a depressing series of relapses. But the reconciliation of Adam and Eve ensures that there will be a human history at all, a history into which they enter at the close of *Paradise Lost* with wandering steps and slow, their thoughts, Michael tells them, to be cheered by a "happy end" (12.605) not soon or anywhere in sight. They leave Eden to go in medias res, so to speak, into history's middle and its human muddle, which may have to be enough for them, as well as for Milton's readers. It will be up to them "to choose / Their place of rest" (12.646–47): the idea returns, in these final lines summing up the poem, that death haunts human choice as both its limit and condition of freedom.[35] Like the deity they worship anew, Adam and Eve have chosen creation over destruction; following the instructions Raphael gave them when they were immortal (8.633), they resolve, now in the face of death, to live happy and love.

Cherishing Eve

The careful balancing of the back-and-forth efforts of Adam and Eve to achieve a new start for their marriage and for human life—one lifting the other, in turn, from despondency and despair—corresponds to the larger balancing of our sympathies toward the two characters that are made to shift between book 9 and book 10. To put it schematically, Eve acts badly toward Adam, Adam acts nobly toward her in book 9; Adam acts badly toward Eve, Eve acts nobly toward him in book 10. The bad actions in question are not their respective falls, but how Eve and Adam behave *after* they have fallen. Even the most sympathetic reader of Eve must be taken aback when in book 9, as she contemplates her own death and "Adam wedded to another Eve" (9.828), she decides to take her husband with her: "Adam shall share with me in bliss or woe" (9.831). Marriage for better or for worse: Eve's plan, little short of murderous, is a measure of her fallenness. Nevertheless, through the cunning of Milton's plotting and art, Eve hardly needs to put her plan into effect and play the role of a Circean or Duessa-like seductress, for Adam resolves to fall beside her "soon as he heard / The fatal trespass done by Eve" (9.888–89).[36] He cannot live without her, and his love is enough to ensure that they will fall and stay together. He eats the forbidden fruit, the narrator informs us, "Against his better knowledge, not deceived / But fondly overcome with female charm" (9.998–99). However one understands the second of these verses, Eve has not seduced Adam as she was seduced by Satan, and Adam scarcely seems to be listening to her arguments as he asserts to himself in inward, silent soliloquy: "Certain my resolution is to die" (9.907).

But it is not for want of Eve's trying, and this gap between her criminal intent and action and Adam's quite independent response and responsibility for his fall allows us to see her as both more and less guilty. Eve, in fact, feels guilty, and in the shift between the behavior of the two characters between books 9 and 10, she is the member of the couple who confesses soon to the Son who has come in judgment over them (10.160) at the beginning of book 10, and who subsequently inaugurates the reconciliation with Adam, acknowledging that she has sinned "against God and thee" (10.931). In book 10, it is Adam's turn, and he is a cad. In a measure of *his* fallenness, he first attempts to lay the blame on Eve to the judging Son (10.125–43). Later, he rejects Eve when she approaches him, and he launches an invective against both her and womankind: "Out of my sight, thou serpent" (10.867). Eve perseveres and the couple "repair" in book 10—this time in true unity and repentance—as they had partnered in sin in book 9.

Paradise Lost makes available a reading of Eve as an epic femme fatale, if only, through an ironic twist of plot, to complicate such a conventional understanding of its action and of Eve herself. It is part of the work of book 10 to undo the aspersions that both Adam and the poem cast upon his wife. William Kerrigan comments, "As the theodicy gradually succeeds in establishing God's innocence of responsibility for the fall, Eve in particular stands accused, and the last three books of the poem seek to make peace with the ambivalent gift of life and death she bequeaths to her children. Ultimately Eve is to be cherished and celebrated."[37] Kerrigan relates the poem's ambivalence to Milton's own experience of his three marriages.

Book 10 contributes to this revaluation of Eve through a series of literary allusions—to Virgil's Dido and Tasso's Armida, to the myth of Pandora, and to the concubine exposed at Gibeah in Judges 19—that both link up to other passages in *Paradise Lost* and suggest a shared pattern within the book itself. As I identify and examine the latter two cases, I will, like Kerrigan, attempt to show how they may be intertwined with Milton's biography. Such biographical links are necessarily tentative and speculative: that they are inferred through buried literary allusions may indicate something of their personal, private nature. All three allusions are revisionary: they overturn misogynistic precedents and teach the reader, as well as Adam, to celebrate Eve.

DIDO AND ARMIDA; CREUSA

The reconciliation of Adam and Eve evokes, if only to invert, one further Virgilian coordinate, and turn the moment into a specifically epic choice. In Eve's counsel of suicide, thoughts of death have "dyed her cheeks with pale" (10.1009). The line is a direct allusion to Tasso's heroine Armida in the last canto of the *Gerusalemme liberata*: "già tinta in viso di pallor di morte" (*GL* 20.127.6; her face already *dyed* with the pallor of death). Torn by the passions of Love and Disdain for Rinaldo, the hero and former lover who has earlier abandoned her after their erotic idyll together on her Eden-like island paradise in the Fortunate Isles, the pagan Armida prepares, in the aftermath of the final battle and Crusader victory outside of Jerusalem, to take her life with an arrow, a literal weapon symbolically charged as an arrow of love. She cites Seneca's *Phoenissae* (*GL* 20.132) on suicide. Rinaldo saves her at the last minute and the couple reach an ambiguous reconciliation.[38]

And behind Tasso's Armida lies Virgil's Dido, abandoned by Aeneas, whom Rome's destiny has called away from his love for her. At the moment Dido rushes to kill herself in book 4 of the *Aeneid*, she wears the pallor of her approaching death—"pallida morte futura" (*Aen.* 4:644). So Virgil portrays the historical figure for whom Dido is in part a fictional stand-in, the Egyptian queen Cleopatra—"pallentem morte futura" (8.709)—as she flees from defeat at Actium toward her own suicide by the Nile, on the reliefs sculpted on the shield of Aeneas in book 8. The telltale pallor of Milton's Eve is overdetermined. Tasso makes Armida a combination of Virgil's Dido and Cleopatra, but he is primarily interested in casting her as a Dido whom his poem will not allow to destroy herself. *That* suicidal Dido is pointedly reserved for the demonic parodists of the enchanted woods of canto 18 who produce before Rinaldo a specter of Armida among myrtle trees (*GL* 18.25–37) that evoke the *Lugentes campi*, the Mournful Fields of Virgil's underworld where Aeneas sees the ghost of Dido flee away from him (*Aen.* 6.440–76). Earlier in the poem in canto 13, the same woods had taken on the appearance of another underworld explicitly linked to suicide, Dante's forest of suicides in *Inferno* 13.

Milton pursues similar ends when he portrays the pale-cheeked Eve taking up the role of Armida and, through Armida, of Dido. Her first words in the colloquy, "Forsake me not thus, Adam" (10.914) not only align her with Jesus suffering on the cross (Matt. 27:46), but with Dido and other abandoned epic heroines. Ovid's version of Dido in the *Heroides*, whose imagining of Aeneas in a new homeland with another Dido—"altera Dido" (*Heroides* 7.17)—may lie behind both Eve's and Adam's speculations on "another Eve" (9.828; 9.911) in book 9, also suggests that Aeneas may be forsaking a pregnant Dido (*Heroides* 7.133); her ensuing self-immolation will take his posterity with her, much as Eve's proposed suicide aims to do.[39] Tasso has Rinaldo abandon Armida in a full-scale reenactment of Aeneas leaving Dido (*GL* 16.29–74), and he waits until the final stanzas of the *Gerusalemme liberata* to bring them back together. Adam's speechless astonishment—"Astonied stood and blank" (9.890)—on seeing the fallen Eve return to him with the forbidden fruit (9.890–94) recalled the reaction of Aeneas in *Aeneid* 4 when Mercury orders him to depart from Dido and Carthage (*Aen.* 4.278–80). But Adam chose not to pick up the Virgilian cue and he fell with Eve rather than abandon her.[40] In fact, Milton has served notice from the very beginning of the relationship of the first husband and wife that *Paradise Lost* would be an epic that will save its Dido-like heroine and the sexual love that Virgil's hero Aeneas had to give up. When Adam now dissuades Eve from the fate of Dido in book 10, he evokes his very first inter-action with her, the *first* words that Eve, recalling the scene of her creation in book 4, remembers Adam crying to her as she turned back to her watery image in the pool: "Whom fly'st thou? Whom thou fly'st, of him thou art" (4.482), he called out before he took her hand in wedlock. "Quem fugis?" are the *last* words Aeneas addresses to the ghost of the self-slain Dido (*Aen.* 6.466), who tears herself away from him into the shadowy grove of the *Lugentes campi* and out of the *Aeneid*.[41] Milton had carefully inverted his Virgilian model in book 4 to indicate that Eve's narcissism was a kind of suicide, and there, too, it might have spelled the end of the human race. Now he suggests that Adam's talking Eve out of a Dido-like suicide returns to the couple's first meeting and starts their marriage over again.

Milton, following Tasso, rejects the tragic scenario of the *Aeneid* that depicts the incompatibility of private, erotic experience, identified through Dido with womankind, with the public, masculine, heroic mission of epic. The domestic sphere of married love becomes the central heroic arena of *Paradise Lost*, and the stakes in Adam and Eve's relationship are higher than in the Christian/pagan (Muslim) reconciliation of Tasso's Rinaldo and Armida: the reunion of the first couple ensures the future of humanity, and, more emphatically than Tasso's fiction, it asserts the value of the sexual life. Eve offers sexual abstinence as an alternative option to suicide, but the two are the same if humans are to increase and multiply—"Our maker bids increase, who bids abstain / But our destroyer?" (4.748–49), the narrator has earlier asked, defending the depiction of sexual intercourse in Eden against theologians he dismisses as hypocrites. Adam rejects both of Eve's options in his reclaiming their marriage. He is also reclaiming in Eve the dignity of woman as the vessel of human reproduction—"Hail mother of mankind" (5.388), Raphael had addressed her before the Fall—against a tradition of misogyny to which the *Aeneid* had offered the most prestigious literary contribution. The blocking divine antagonist of the hero in Virgil's epic is *pronuba* Juno (*Aen.* 4.166), the very goddess who furthers marriage and family: Dido's suicide by the sword Aeneas has left behind is a grotesque sexual act, the prolonged agonies by which her soul seeks to leave her body a ghastly version of childbirth.[42] Adam's rescue of Eve overturns this Virgilian model and its portrait of the feminine.[43] This Aeneas comes around and cherishes his Dido.

Outside of book 10, Milton will again counter Virgil's relegation of the fem-inine and of sexual love when he returns to the model of the *Aeneid* at the close of *Paradise Lost*. God's sending Michael to inform Adam that he and Eve must leave Eden and its comforts repeats the descent of Mercury in *Aeneid* 4 to bid Aeneas to leave Dido's Carthage. Milton signals the analogy, as well as the difference, in the two fictions by dressing up Michael in Aeneas's clothes.[44] The archangel wears "A military vest of purple ... / Livelier than Meliboean, or the grain / Of Sarra" (11.241–43), while his sword hangs by his side "As in a glistering zodiac" (11.247): an unmistakable recollection of the starry sword and of the mantle shining with the purple of Tyre (Sarra)—"atque illi stellatus iaspide fulua / ensis erat Tyrioque ardebat murice laena" (*Aen.* 4.261–62)—the gifts of Dido that Aeneas is wearing when Mercury appears to him.[45] The reversal of who is wearing what signals yet once more that in *Paradise Lost* the military heroism of the classical epic hero has been transferred away from the human to the combatants of the War in Heaven: it is not a proper heroic option for Adam or for his descendants. But it also suggests that this version of leaving Carthage will be different. In the final lines of the poem, as Adam and Eve look back together in book 12 on Eden, over which the "flaming brand" of the sword of God is blazing, and see its gate thronged with "fiery arms" (12.643–44), they recall not only Lot and his wife leaving burning Sodom, but also the Aeneas of *Aeneid* 5 looking back—"respiciens"—from the sea on the walls of Carthage lit by the flames of Dido's funeral pyre (*Aen.* 5.1–7).[46] (The comparison of the heat and vapor of the sword of God to "the Libyan air adust" [12.635] reinforces the parallel.) But Adam does not abandon his Dido: Eve leaves Eden beside him.

Dido is not the first beloved woman, nor Carthage the first city in flames, that Aeneas's historical mission causes him to leave behind in Virgil's epic. Carthage was itself the last of a whole series of substitutes in books 1–4 of the *Aeneid* for the Troy he has lost, Dido a possible second spouse. As Troy is set ablaze in book 2, Aeneas famously lifts up and carries his father Anchises on his shoulders while he takes his little son Iulus by the hand—an image of patriarchal piety and continuity, particularly of the Julian lineage of Augustus—while his beloved wife Creusa follows behind him. But in a moment of panic created by Anchises, Aeneas loses Creusa as he is leaving his smoldering city, and when he returns to find her inside Troy, he encounters her ghost, who tells him he must go to Italy without her (*Aen.* 2.701–95): here, too, Aeneas is rendered speechless (*Aen.* 2.774). Milton pointedly makes a different choice for his hero. In the final words spoken in the poem, Eve tells Adam in book 12 that she is ready to leave Eden, over which she and Adam will see the flaming brand of God's sword.

> but now lead on;
> In me is no delay; with thee to go,
> Is to stay here; ...
>   (12.614–16)

She echoes the words of Virgil's *Anchises*: "iam iam nulla mora est; sequor et qua ducitis adsum" (*Aen.* 2.701; Now, now there is no delay; I follow and where you lead, there I am). The omen of the Julian destiny that will produce Augustus moves Anchises to leave Troy, and Eve, too, has the consolation that "By me the promised seed shall all restore" (12.623), the expected Christ. But the larger import of the allusion puts Eve, wife and partner, in the future of humanity in place of the Virgilian father and son: she is no Creusa to be left behind.[47] Nor, in the evocation of the destruction of Sodom a few lines later (12.636–44), will Eve suffer the analogous fate of Lot's wife: she and Adam *both* look back on the Eden they have lost, now seemingly ablaze with angelic arms; they shed a few tears and move on. Like all future husbands in the marriage that he institutes, Adam leaves his father and cleaves unto his wife—"so that marriage requireth a greater duetie of us toward our wives, then otherwise we are bounde to shewe to our parents," the Geneva Bible comments on Genesis 2:23; in *Paradise Lost* the moral seems to apply even to one's divine parent. No father on his back, Adam leaves Eden with Eve hand in hand.

PANDORA

It is difficult to read the scene of Eve's falling at the feet of Adam and seeking his forgiveness and *not* connect it to the account that Milton's nephew Edward Phillips gives of the drama of the poet's first marriage to Mary Powell.[48] After only one month of wedded life with the poet, this daughter of a royalist family had returned to her father's house in Oxfordshire in 1642. Milton sent for her by letter and then messenger, who, Phillips writes, "reported that he was dismissed with some sort of contempt."[49] Milton had been abandoned. Incensed, he wrote his divorce tracts, frequented as "a single man again" the company of the married Margaret Lee, and began a "design" to marry one of the daughters of a Dr. Davis, who was "a very handsome and witty gentlewoman, but averse, as it is said, to this motion."[50] In 1645, the Powells saw the king's cause and their own circumstances in decline, and sought to renew the alliance; friends of each party brought Milton and Mary Powell together in the house of one of his relatives.

> One time above the rest, he making his usual visit, the wife was ready in the next room, and on a sudden he was surprised to see one whom he thought to have never seen more, making submission and begging pardon on her knees before him. He might probably at first make some show of aversion and rejection; but partly his own generous nature, more inclinable to reconciliation than to perseverance in anger and revenge, and partly the strong intercession of friends on both sides, soon brought him to an act of oblivion and firm league of peace for the future.[51]

Eve's submission to Adam and his relenting in *Paradise Lost* appear to rewrite this scene of Milton's biography, although we cannot know to what extent Phillips's narrative, penned in 1694, has been influenced, even inspired, by the poem. Milton's initial "show of aversion and rejection" on that occasion becomes something more heated and complicated in Adam's outburst against his wife, one of the main bases, Edward Le Comte points out, for "Milton's reputation as a misogynist poet."[52]

O why did God,
Creator wise, that peopled highest heaven
With spirits masculine, create at last
This novelty on earth, this fair defect
Of nature, and not fill the world at once
With man as angels without feminine,
Or find some other way to generate
Mankind? This mischief had not then befallen,
And more that shall befall, innumerable
Disturbances on earth through female snares,
And straight conjunction with this sex: for either
He never shall find out fit mate, but such
As some misfortune brings him, or mistake,
Or whom he wishes most shall seldom gain
Through her perverseness, but shall see her gained
By a far worse, or if she love, withheld
By parents, or his happiest choice too late
Shall meet, already linked and wedlock-bound
To a fell adversary, his hate or shame:
Which infinite calamity shall cause
To human life, and household peace confound.
    (10.888–908)

In this blanket rejection of the female sex, Adam echoes the personal griefs of his poet-creator as he lists the possible alternatives of the mating game: the mistake in Mary Powell, perverseness in the averse Ms. Davis, the already-married Margaret Lee. Milton evokes here his own "lot unfortunate in nuptial choice" (SA 1743), as Manoa, the father of the hero in the unmistakably autobiographical Samson Agonistes, remarks on his son.[53] But Milton could both give voice to felt wrongs and discontents *and* look back at them with a sense of distance and, perhaps, even of self-criticism. Consider the source of this speech: he puts these complaints in the mouth of an Adam in despair and at his lowest moral point in the poem, ready to blame Eve, women, and anyone else for the misery that he has less than fifty verses earlier admitted falls due "first and last / On me, me only" (10.831–32). He both recognizes and cannot bear his own guilt: male self-hatred, Milton suggests, lies at the basis of the hatred of women. Adam's excessive and almost comically sputtering tone contributes to the distancing effect: it is misogyny placed within quotation marks.[54]

One should also consider the literary source(s). As with his recall of Tasso's Armida and Virgil's Dido, Milton makes a double allusion. It has been recognized that Adam's rant is a citation of a speech by the hero of Euripides's *Hippolytus* (616–37), delivered at the moment when Hippolytus has been shocked by the sexual proposition made to him by the Nurse on behalf of her mistress, his stepmother Phaedra. Adam takes up the question that Hippolytus addresses to Zeus about why there could not have been some means other than women to propagate the human race, and he additionally cites the case of the angels in heaven as an all-male fellowship, something like the Cambridge in the sky, the "sweet societies," that the speaker of *Lycidas* envisions for the dead swain; he does not appear to know, and the poem itself seems to have forgotten, what it has told us back in book 1, that angelic spirits—or is it only the fallen spirits?—are versatile and "when they please / Can either sex assume, or both" (1.423–24). But Hippolytus, even before he is propositioned to commit incest, was already a woman hater, an exemplar of what Cicero defines as a pathological condition (*Tusculan Disputations* 4.11.27). Caspar Stiblin, an influential Renaissance commentator on Euripides, cautions the reader not to confuse the misogynistic attitudes of an enraged character with that of his author, and notes the over-the-top quality of Hippolytus's speech: "The calumny against women is vehement; but it is very well suited to Hippolytus, who naturally pursued women with hatred because of his perpetual vow of virginity."[55] As Aphrodite complains at the beginning of Euripides's play (14), Hippolytus had dedicated himself to virginal chastity. So had the young Milton, the poet of *Lycidas*, as well as of *Comus* and other poems of the 1645 volume, a man, we might presume, still a virgin at thirty-four on his wedding three years earlier to Mary Powell—the marriage that initially did not turn out well. Adam has regressed to attitudes that he never shared—he knew from the moment of his creation that it was not good for man to be alone—but that did belong to an earlier period of his poet-creator's biography. By casting Adam and his former self as another Hippolytus, Milton lends a measure of self-awareness—an acknowledgment that he, too, may have been part of the problem—to this restaging of his marital crisis with its invective against womankind.

The speech of Euripides's Hippolytus offers a model for the "either" and the succession of "or's" of Adam's listing of the alternatives, one as bad as the next, that women will offer to the men who court them in the future: either one gets good in-laws and a bad wife, Hippolytus says, or a good wife and in-laws who make one miserable (634–37). The Euripidean passage, in turn, alludes to an earlier Greek classic, the description of the original creation of women in the form of the maleficent Pandora in Hesiod's *Theogony* (570–616): women are an evil to men, "anthropois kakòn" for Hippolytus (616); "andressi kakòn" (606) in Hesiod's poem.[56] Hesiod also spells out a set of undesirable alternatives or mixed blessings that await future men that are perhaps closer than the Euripides passage to Adam's prophetic tone and to Milton's experience: either you reach old age without support (something for a blind man to think about) or you suffer a mixture of good and evil in marriage (*Theogony* 603–12). Women: you can't live with them or without them. One might not emphasize the double allusion that Milton is making here, to the Hesiodic text inside the Euripidean one, were it not for the poem's earlier identification of Eve with Pandora in book 4 and, more pointedly, for the way in which the action of book 10 is framed first by Adam's complaining to the Son about the "gift" of his wife and last by his invention of fire in the manner of Prometheus, a sequence that seems to reverse and revise that identification.

The likening of Eve to the mythical Pandora, the first woman whom Zeus caused to be molded out of earth by the metalworking God Hephaestus, was traditional. In Hesiod's second telling of the story, which names Pandora, in the *Works and the Days* (42–104), her jar or box brought misfortunes to mankind, just as Eve brought the forbidden fruit to Adam.[57] Woman, according to both Hesiodic versions, was a punishment or evening of the score that Zeus wrought on humanity for the crime of Prometheus, son of the Titan Iapetus, who had stolen the fire of Zeus and given it to mankind. Milton's comparison of Eve to Pandora in book 4 follows the usual conflation, and misogynistic bent, of the biblical and classical stories.

> more adorned,
> More lovely than Pandora, whom the gods
> Endowed with all their gifts, and O too like
> In sad event, when to the unwiser son
> Of Japhet brought by Hermes, she ensnared
> Mankind with her fair looks, to be avenged
> On him who had stole Jove's authentic fire.
> *(4.713–19)*

In the *Works and the Days*, the gods contribute gifts to Pandora—hence her name, "All-Gift"—and then Zeus bestows her on Epimetheus, the brother of Prometheus, as a countergift for Prometheus's gift of fire. Prometheus had warned his unwiser brother not to accept presents from Zeus, but to no avail. Adam describes Eve as just such a fatal gift in the Judgment Scene at the beginning of book 10 when he tries to shift the blame to "This woman whom thou madest to be my help, / And gavest me as thy perfect gift, so good / … Her doing seemed to justify the deed" (10.137–38, 142). The sarcasm transforms Adam's earlier praise of his wife, "Heaven's last best gift" (5.19), "fairest this / Of all thy gifts" (8.493–94). Now he complains, in an evident rewriting of the events, that he was taken in by appearances and that God's gift has turned out to be a Pandora. The Son's reply denies this charge, but at the same time picks up the same language as the book 4 simile: "*adorned* / She was indeed, and *lovely* to attract / Thy love, not thy subjection, and her *gifts* / Were such as under government well seemed" (10.151–54). Pandora's looks, the simile had declared, "ensnared" mankind: in his tirade against Eve and women more generally, Adam would warn all creatures away, "lest that too heavenly form, pretended / To hellish falsehood, snare them" (10.872–73), and he insists on the term, condemning the "female snares" (10.897) that will confound men in the future. Eve herself penitently acknowledges to Adam that she, "for thee ordained / A help, became thy snare" (11.164–65), and the word, with its associations, like Pandora's box, with the female pudenda, comes back in full force and exuding sexual disgust in Samson's recriminations of his marriage to Dalila in *Samson Agonistes*: "into the snare I fell / Of fair fallacious looks" (*SA* 532–33; cf. 230, 365, 409, 845, 860, 931).[58] Women and sexuality prove to be man's downfall and Adam can still speak in this vein in book 11, where he invents the hoarily conventional pun—"the tenor of man's woe / Holds on the same, from woman to begin" (11.632–33)—before he is corrected, if not completely contradicted, by Michael, who tells him and future men to look for the woman within: "From man's effeminate slackness it begins" (11.634).

Yet already in book 4, Milton distances himself from the likeness he draws between Eve and Pandora—"O too like." By following Renaissance mythographers who identified the Greek Japet with Japhet, Noah's son,[59] he underscores the lack of correspondence between the classical myth and his own true scriptural story of Adam and Eve on the other side of the Flood.[60] Moreover, the likeness confuses causality. The Pandora-Eve of the simile seems to occasion the crime for which she is the instrument of divine punishment, if we are to understand the stealing of fire by Prometheus as a figure for original sin. Milton had earlier read the Prometheus story in just such terms in his second Latin prolusion at Cambridge, "On the Harmony of the Spheres": "The fact that we are unable to hear this harmony seems to be due to the presumption of that thief Prometheus, which brought so many evils upon men, and robbed us of that happiness which we may never again enjoy so long as we remain buried in sin [*sceleribus cooperti*] and degraded by brutish desires" (*CPW* 1.238–39, *Works* 12:156–57). The Pandora simile, that is, seems to share much of the misogyny of the Adam who lashes out at Eve after the Fall in book 10 and whose outburst against women alludes again to Pandora, the Adam who blames his wife and who sees nothing but trouble—"innumerable / Disturbances"—from women thenceforth.

Adam's resolution in the final verses of book 10, just before he takes up Eve's earlier advice and urges them both to return to the place of their judgment and offer up prayer to God, answers to and corrects these earlier evocations of Pandora. Remembering how the pitying Son had clothed them after his judgment upon them, and facing the changes in weather that God is bringing on after their Fall, Adam begins, in a pointedly drawn-out meditation, to find a way to keep themselves warm. Before the sun goes down they should seek

> how we his gathered beams
> Reflected, may with matter sere foment,
> Or by collision of two bodies grind
> The air attrite to fire, as late the clouds
> Justling or pushed with winds rude in their shock
> Tine the slant lightning, whose thwart flame driven down

Kindles the gummy bark of fir or pine,
And sends a comfortable heat from far,
Which might supply the sun; such fire to use,
And what may else be remedy or cure
To evils which our own misdeeds have wrought,
He will instruct us praying, and of grace
Beseeching him ...
    (10.1070–82)

Adam himself becomes a Prometheus, discovering fire. The passage balances, on the one hand, human invention and action, the grinding of bodies, with, on the other, dependence on the fires of heaven, on lightning, and on the very sun that the possession of fire will "supply" or replace, dependence ultimately on divine instruction that will supply in turn what human beings have lost.[61] Milton creates an area of autonomous human action—and those generative grinding bodies are also sexualized[62]—that will build a technological future at the same time that he insists on divine cooperation: these are "My motions in him" (11.91), God announces at the opening of book 11.

The purely secular, and therefore sinful version of such technological advances through fire are the metalworking children of Cain subsequently revealed in a vision by Michael to Adam in the following book (11.558–92), "inventors rare" who, in pointed contrast to Adam, refuse to acknowledge the gifts of the Spirit who taught them their "arts that polish life" (11.610). "Yet they a beauteous offspring shall beget" (11.613), Michael says of these first artisans, and a momentary quibble makes us think that he is referring to their handiworks before the next verse reveals their attractive daughters, themselves works of art, so many Pandoras "that seemed / Of goddesses, so blithe, so smooth, so gay, / Yet empty of all good wherein consists / Woman's domestic honour and chief praise" (11.614–16), who snare the righteous "sons of God" (11.622) of Genesis 6:1 in "the amorous net" (11.586). They are the ones whom Adam terms man's woe. "Ill-mated marriages" (11.684) will, indeed, lead to human misery and sin, Michael says (and thereby justifies Milton's writings on divorce). Milton seems to be redistributing the motifs of the Prometheus-Pandora story in this later episode of fallen human history, playing on a Renaissance mythographical identification of Pandora's maker Vulcan/Hephaestus with Tubalcain, the blacksmith descendant of Cain (Genesis 4:22).[63] But here in book 10 Adam is an innocent Prometheus, and the Prometheus story itself no longer stands in for the original sin of the Fall: the discovery of fire is instead part of a "remedy or cure" for the effects of the Fall.

This Prometheus, moreover, reverses the order of events in the Pandora myth and, in effect, undoes its meaning. Adam invents fire at the end of book 10, *after* he has received the "perfect gift" of the first woman about whom he complains at the Judgment Scene at the book's beginning, *after* his invective against Eve and womankind has evoked Hesiod's Pandora. Milton runs the tale of Pandora backward so that the first woman is already on the scene when the invention of fire takes place, and cannot be its subsequent punishment. This reversal dissociates the Pandora myth from Milton's own biblical story that it had seemed all "too like": it corrects both the simile in book 4 and Adam's framing of his story in the misogynistic terms of the myth. The fallen Adam of book 10 gives voice to the idea that Eve, women, women's beauty, and human sexual experience itself are some kind of divine mistake that has caused the Fall or a divine retribution that punishes it in the future—but he has moved beyond this idea by the book's end. Eve is put under accusation, but acquitted as well as forgiven: she is not Pandora.[64]

THE EXPOSED MATRON

In the 1674 second version of *Paradise Lost*, Milton changed the wording of the two verses in book 1 that complete the description of Belial, the lewd demon, a passage given prominence by its coming at the very end of the catalog of the chief devils who will come to inhabit the Holy Land of the Bible in future times. Belial had been present in spirit in the Sodom of Genesis 19, when the townsmen of the city that was soon to be destroyed demanded that Lot send out his two angelic guests so that they might sexually abuse them, present as well in the biblical rewriting of the Sodom episode in Judges 19, the account of the Levite and his concubine in Gibeah. Milton's mention of this latter story reads as follows in the 1667 *Paradise Lost*:

> and that night
> In Gibeah, when hospitable Dores
> Yielded thir Matrons to prevent worse rape
> *(1.503–5)*

The version of 1674 makes these changes:

> and that night
> In Gibeah, when *the* hospitable *door*
> *Exposed a matron* to *avoid* worse rape.
> *(1.503–5)*

The revision follows the scriptural story more exactly.[65] When the Benjamite inhabitants of Gibeah, "certain sons of Belial," demand that the Levite be sent out so that they "may know him," his Ephraimite host, also a stranger in the city, offers to send out his maiden daughter and the Levite's concubine: plural victims. In the event, however, it is the Levite husband and not the hospitable Ephraimite who takes his concubine and brings her out to them. The woman is gang-raped and turns up fallen on the threshold of the house the next morning (Judges 19:22–27). The Geneva Bible commentary pronounces her dead, though the text is unclear.[66] One can only hope so, for in the still more horrifying continuation of the story, the Levite puts her body over his donkey, carries it to his house, cuts it up, dead or alive, into twelve pieces, sends them throughout Israel as an emblem of the crime committed against the community of tribes, and thereby instigates a war of near extermination against the Benjamites.

What also catches the eye in this revision is the change of the verbs, "Exposed" in place of "Yielded," which now suggests less a helpless surrender to the crowd outside than the Levite's active exercise of his power over the concubine. Similarly, the substitution of "avoid" for "prevent" seems to lessen the urgency of the husband's choice, to make it more of a deliberate choice. There is a secret wit in the coupling of "Exposed" and "avoid," which can be near synonyms meaning "to expel" or "to banish." But Milton's change of the wording to "Exposed" is calculated, above all, to link this passage to the drama of book 10 and to Adam, the first human husband who chooses "to expose" his wife (10.130) and later admits to having done so: "To me committed and by me exposed" (10.957).

The link suggests another autobiographical layer in Milton's depiction of Adam and Eve's marriage in Eden. The Gibeah story, as Louise Simons and Michael Lieb have shown, haunted Milton's imagination and dots his prose works throughout his career; it was one of the scenarios—the destruction of Sodom was another—in the list that Milton compiled of possible subjects on which to write a tragedy (*CPW* 8:556).[67] His most significant discussion of the Judges episode, however, lies in *The Doctrine and Discipline of Divorce*, where Milton's personal experience frequently seeps into the argument. There was a parallel, in fact, between Mary Powell and the Levite's concubine in the story. Both had left their husbands and returned to their father's house, and it is on his return from retrieving the concubine that the Levite stops for the night in Gibeah: "when Milton read Judges," Simons writes, "he may have pictured Mary Powell as the headstrong wife and himself as the long-suffering husband."[68]

Milton brings up the Judges passage in *The Doctrine and Discipline of Divorce* in order to practice a bit of philological legerdemain. He does not argue that the phrase in the English version, "And his concubine played the whore against him [the Levite]" (Judges 19:2), is a mistranslation, as he would have known it was, but that it should be understood *to mean* only that she was stubborn and rebellious: "Fornication then in this place of Judges is understood for stubborn disobedience against the husband, and not for adultery" (*CPW* 2:336).[69] The point not only serves Milton's purpose to prove that the fornication for which scripture allows the husband to seek divorce can extend to temperamental differences that can make a marriage untenable. It also absolves Mary Powell of anything worse than leaving John Milton and refusing to come back to him: humiliating enough, perhaps, for the author of the divorce tracts. Additionally, it challenges commentators who complacently concluded that the whoring concubine had gotten what was coming to her during the night in Gibeah.[70] It refocuses attention on the husband who sacrifices her to save himself from violation, and by the time of the epic, Milton appears to feel some discomfort with his identification with the Levite. Was he, as Lieb suggests, expressing an unacknowledged, avoided bisexuality that complicated his marriage?[71] Had Milton done nothing else, he had exposed Mary Powell multiple times in print as the wife of the man seeking divorce. The link between the Gibeah story and the epic's main story of the Fall had been implicit in 1667; the 1674 substitution of "exposed" for "yielded" now created an explicit verbal link and suggested that both Adam and Milton—like the Levite—may have done their first wives wrong.

The appearances of the verb "expose" in book 10 have been mentioned above. To examine its resonance further, let us return to Adam's answer to the judging Son, who asks him if he has eaten of the tree of the forbidden fruit. Adam elaborates the plainer answer of the Adam of Genesis 3:12, "The woman whom thou gavest to be with me, she gave me of the tree, and I did eat," with its hint that God may have been to blame in creating woman, into a complaint about God's "perfect gift" that turns Eve, as we have seen, into a kind of Pandora.[72] But before Adam does so, Milton provides for him a long speech of apparent soul-searching that expands the scriptural passage.

> To whom thus Adam sore beset replied.
> O heaven! In evil strait this day I stand
> Before my judge, either to undergo
> My self the total crime, or to accuse
> My other self, the partner of my life;
> Whose failing, while her faith to me remains,
> I should conceal, *and not expose to blame*
> By my complaint: but strict necessity
> Subdues me, and calamitous constraint
> Lest on my head both sin and punishment,
> However insupportable, be all
> Devolved; though should I hold my peace, yet thou
> Wouldst easily detect what I conceal.
> *(10.124–36)*

Adam's words have the sound of a soliloquy, but they are in fact spoken out loud as a performance of self-division, perhaps sincere but certainly for the benefit of his judge. In this forensic setting, Adam has recourse to the law court's oratorical trick of *praeteritio*, declaring what he will or should conceal, and in doing so, not concealing it at all. In any event, he concludes at the end, God would see through his ploy, so he might as well be honest. He invokes "necessity, / The tyrant's plea" (4.393–94), as Milton's narrator had called it in book 4 with reference to Satan's supposed reluctance to make victims of mankind in order to pursue his imperial ambitions and revenge on God: the claim that one has no choice but to pursue self-serving actions that do harm to others. And so, acting against his better knowledge once again, Adam accuses Eve and exposes her to blame, lest he have to take all the punishment—and perhaps with the hope that all the punishment will fall on her. He exposes this matron, as it were, to avoid a worse rap.

In the scene of their reconciliation later in the book, Adam looks back on his behavior, and seems to acknowledge, perhaps grudgingly, that he has been at some fault. If he thought it would work, he says, in response to Eve's suggestion that she pray to God so that all of the punishment for the Fall might indeed fall upon her rather than on him, he would do the same for her:

> That on my head all might be visited,
> Thy frailty and infirmer sex forgiven,
> To me committed and by me exposed.
> *(10.955–57)*

Adam now confesses to having exposed his wife, and the verb is given emphasis by the full stop at the end of the line and of the verse sentence, by its juxtaposition within the balanced line to what seems to be its antonym, "committed." He may refer in retrospect not only to his evasion before the Son's judgment but to his fatally having allowed Eve to go off by herself in book 9, leaving her open to Satan's temptation: she returned to him, in Adam's own words, "deflowered" (9.901). He exposed Eve in spite of his sententious assertion of the duties of husband to wife, "Who guards her, or with her the worst endures" (9.269). In their apparently endless mutual recrimination at the end of the book, Eve upbraids Adam for not having commanded her "absolutely not to go" (9.1156), for not being "firm and fixed in thy dissent" (9.1160): he had failed, she implies, to play the role of the man, and she raises the question of which is the "infirmer sex."

The admission of shared responsibility by the first man goes together with a reassertion of gender hierarchy that is not liable to find much sympathy among today's readers. So the Son had answered Adam's complaint against Eve at the Judgment Scene with the rebuke that Adam's "perfection far excelled / Hers in all real dignity" (10.150–51), and so Michael in book 11 similarly reminds Adam when he puts the onus first ("it begins") on the "effeminate slackness," infirm indeed, of man who was endowed from the start with "superior gifts" (11.636) than was woman. The repeated logic asserts that if the man is woman's superior, he must be held to a stricter account and assume the greater culpability for their mutual transgression. The idea accords with Milton's early pronouncements on male chastity: as the behavior of the "perfecter sex," the unchastity of a man, "though commonly not so thought, be much more deflouering and dishonourable" than a woman's, he wrote in *An Apology Against a Pamphlet* in 1642 (*CPW* 1:892)—a worse disgrace that is a worse rape.[73] Pat and patriarchal as it may be, this logic nonetheless runs counter to the biblical myth that *Paradise Lost* takes as its subject matter, a myth that expresses the misogyny and double standard that *is* commonly so thought, and that exposes a matron in place of her husband. Beyond the myths of Dido and Pandora, this is the myth that book 10 attempts to reverse and redress.

8

Leaving Eden

The first 1667 version of *Paradise Lost* arranges its ten books in a concentric and symmetrical scheme, outlined in the following table.

1 The building of Pandaemonium; the devils' future enshrinement; idolatry. Catalog of devils and shrines.	10 (1674 *11–12*) The leaving of Eden; the cessation of oracles; living temples. Catalog of seats of empire.
2 The devils's lack of choice. Satan acclaimed.	9 (1674 *10*) Adam and Eve recover human choice. Satan hissed.
3 The Son's charity and offer to redeem humanity.	8 (1674 9) The Fall. Adam's choice to fall with Eve.
4 Eden. Eve's story of her creation, meeting with Adam.	7 (1674 *7–8*) The Creation. Adam's story of his meeting with Eve.
5 War in Heaven. Abdiel.	6 (1674 *6*) War in Heaven. Son.

Milton's 1674 revision of the poem into the twelve-book version we now read changes the center of the poem so that books 6 and 7 depict the double heroism of the Son as victor over Satan and as cosmic creator, the actions he will repeat at the end of time in apocalyptic battle and as maker of a new heaven and earth. In doing so, it obscures the earlier pattern, whose center, we observed in chapter 1, pivoted around the character of Abdiel, the lone individual who dissents from his satanic company at the end of the 1667 book 5 and wounds Satan at the beginning of book 6 before yielding place to the greater, if not necessarily more heroic, exploits of the Son. It also obscures other correspondences between books of the 1667 *Paradise Lost*.[1] When the poem is read from its inside out, books 4 and 7, respectively, contain Eve's and Adam's contrasting accounts of the first moments of their creation and of their first meeting and marriage; 3 and 8 juxtapose the Son's promised redemption of humanity and the Fall of humanity to which it already answers, a Fall in which Adam's choice to die with the Eve he loves reflects the Son's greater charity; 2 and 9, as I have argued in chapter 7, differentiate the fallen angels' inability to die and lack of real alternatives (Scylla and Charybdis) from the real choice between living and dying that Adam and Eve can make—through God's grace; in book 2, Satan leaves the council hall of Pandaemonium to the "loud acclaim" (2.520) of his fellow devils, in book 9 to their universal hiss. Relatives of classical ring composition, such concentric patterns are a feature of some of the greatest works of Renaissance literature, as Edwin Duval's studies of the Rabelaisian books and James Nohrnberg's analysis of the *Faerie Queene* have demonstrated.[2]

The correspondence between the outermost of these books of *Paradise Lost*, between books 1 and 10 or, in the 1674 version of the poem, books 1 and 11–12, concerns the devil's building of Pandaemonium and Adam's and Eve's departure from Eden before it becomes a false temple, that is, a correspondence between the inauguration of Milton's poem itself and the reader's leaving its spell. In the catalog of devils in book 1, we are told how the demons created idols and cults by falsities and lies—"gay religions full of pomp and gold" (1.372)—and "durst fix / Their seats long after next the seat of God" (1.382–83), the Jerusalem temple. The parallel catalog of book 11 lists one after another future "seat / Of mightiest empire" (11.386–87) and of *gold*, the worldly forces that will profane and substitute themselves for the worship of the true God. The empires include "Sofala thought Ophir" (11.400), the realm from which Solomon imported the gold that placed the potential for corruption in the temple from its beginning.[3] In books 11 and 12 God closes down Eden lest the devil possess it as well, but as I shall argue below, Eden seems preordained for Satan's takeover from the moment he jumps over the garden's wall in book 4, the first pollution by "lucre and ambition" (12.511) of a shrine or church that is too rich for its own good. In book 1 Milton suggests his own complicity as poet in raising the devil; in the last two books he disenchants his epic's poetic world.

This coda on the final two books of *Paradise Lost* accordingly itself looks back on the discussion of book 1 in this study's own first chapter. It suggests that the first and last books framing the epic both share a continuity with Milton's first great poem, *On the Morning of Christ's Nativity* (the *Nativity Ode*), and its final section where the newborn true God expels their resident demons from the pagan oracles. The motif of the cessation of oracles, to which Milton also returns at the end of book 1 of *Paradise Regained*, shapes the double structure of the 1667 book 10, which naturally divided into the 1674 books 11 and 12: Eden as a possible temple and oracular shrine is destroyed in prophecy at the end of book 11 so that the utterance of the true oracle, the Son, his curse against the serpent at the Judgment Scene in book 10, can reecho through Michael's narrative in book 12. Eden, I shall finally argue, is by the end of *Paradise Lost* an image of the poem itself, and in the loss of the garden, Milton's epic depicts the relinquishing of its own imaginative plenitude and riches, the end of epic poetry itself.

Deconsecrated Earth

In his instruction to Michael before he sends the archangel to earth, God spells out this double plan for the last two books of the poem. Michael is first to "drive out the sinful pair, / From hallowed ground the unholy" (11.105–6), then to initiate them into a holiness that lies in the promised Christian future. Adam and Eve, God has earlier stated, can no longer dwell in Paradise because they are now themselves a polluting, fallen human presence:

> Those pure immortal elements that know
> No gross, no unharmonious mixture foul,
> Eject him, tainted now, and purge him off
> As a distemper, gross to air as gross,
> And mortal food, as may dispose him best
> For dissolution wrought by sin, that first
> Distempered all things, and of incorrupt
> Corrupted.
>   *(11.50–57)*

God similarly instructs the Son to eject Satan and the fallen angels at the end of the War in Heaven—"drive them out / From all heaven's bounds" (6.715–16)—in order that the good angels, in the answering words of the Son, might be *"unmixed*, and from the impure / Far separate, circling thy holy mount" (6.742–43); so the Son, in his next appearance as Jesus, will drive out the profane money changers and cleanse the temple.[4]

Distempered by sin, man is himself a distemper to the purity of Eden. The passage announces the motif that makes of the last two books a kind of Spenserian Legend of Temperance: the moderation of the appetites, "The rule of not too much" (11.531) that Michael teaches Adam to observe but which original sin has made difficult to follow, whether with regard to the diseases of the body in book 11, "Inductive mainly to the sin of Eve" (11.519; cf. 11.476: "the inabstinence of Eve") or the maladies of the body politic, kingship and tyranny, in book 12, due to the "original lapse" (12.83) of Adam. This immoderation is characterized by further "unharmonious *mixture*," the marriages of the daughters of men with the "grave" sons of God (11.585)—"Where good with bad were matched, who of themselves / Abhor to join; and by imprudence *mixed*" (11.685–86; cf. 3.456: "unkindly mixed")—and a further confusion within the civilization of conqueror "giants" to which they gave birth, "Gray headed men and grave, with warriors *mixed*" (11.662). Michael's task is thus, on the one hand, to separate the sinful Adam and Eve from the purity of Eden, and near the end of book 11, he foretells Eden's eventual fate to be uprooted by the Flood; at the end of book 12, the sword of God has already begun to parch the garden's "*temperate* clime" (12.636). On the other, God instructs the archangel to "*inter-mix* / My Covenant in the woman's seed renewed" (11.115–16) as he reveals to Adam the Christian history that is to come. This story culminates when "God with man unites" (12.382) in the Son, and it will be the result of the Son's offer seventy verses earlier in book 11 to "ingraft" (11.35) the sinful works of men and to make the redeemed "one with me" (11.44); Adam and Eve, that is, are to be detached physically from a former holiness in order to be joined in spirit to a future one.

The last two books of the 1674 poem divide accordingly. Once the visions that Michael offers Adam close in book 11 with the washing away of Eden and a new start and covenant for humanity, he turns in book 12 to his second assignment, and in his plainer narration mentions some seven times the judgment-prophecy of the woman's seed, which will bruise the head of the serpent (12.148–51; 233–35; 311–14; 327; 430–33; 542–44, 600–601). In book 11 humans have mixed their fallen motives and carnal imaginings with the holy, and by its end they have polluted the entire globe. The view from the Mountain of Speculation to which Michael leads Adam is compared to the vision of "all earth's kingdoms and their glory" with which Satan will later tempt Jesus (Matt. 3:8; Luke 4:5–7). It leads into the resonant list of future empires (11.385–411), associated with golden riches, and of the names and titles of their monarchs (khan, Temir, king, mogul, czar, sultan, negus, Almansor, Motezume, Atalipa). These are balanced at the end of the book by the submersion and wiping out of their antediluvian prototypes, the giant-conquerors who enjoyed "triumph and luxurious wealth" (11.788), the fame and renown that they achieved (11.698–99) perishing with them, along with their names.[5] In book 12, God will himself mix with human beings—"God who oft descends to visit men" (12.48)—until, after Nimrod and his ilk again try at Babel to "get themselves a name" (12.45), he decides to limit his presence and "one peculiar nation to select" (12.111) from amid the idolatrous rest. The description of the borders of the land granted to Abraham (12.135–46) with its succession of place-names— "Things by their names I call, though yet unnamed" (12.140), says Michael—is a reduced version and substitute for the earlier catalog of global empires. It is at the end of this humbler description of Canaan, but of names that will really count, that Michael first mentions to Adam God's covenant and promise of "thy great deliverer, who shall bruise / The serpent's head" (12.149–50). The lost Eden of book 11 is replaced by the territorially demarcated Promised Land of book 12, before this elect nation and the House of God it builds are themselves corrupted by kingship, wealth, and idolatry—virtual synonyms—and are replaced by the "living temples" (12.527) that are individual believers.

Milton has all along coordinated Adam and Eve with Abraham and Sarah: the first couple hosts Raphael as the later one entertains the visiting God and his two angels at Mamre in Genesis 18. He renews the comparison through allusion. The questions that structure the lament of Eve at the news that they will have to leave Eden,

> Must I thus leave thee Paradise? Thus leave
> Thee native soil, these happy walks and shades,
> Fit haunt of gods?
> (11.269–71)

recall the situation and long complaint of Abraham in the *Divine Weeks* of Du Bartas in Josuah Sylvester's translation, at the moment when the patriarch answers God's call and leaves Chaldea for Canaan:

> Alas (sayd *Abrahm*) must I needs forgoe
> These happie fields wheare *Euphrates* doth flowe?
> . . . .
> O can I thus my Native soile forsake?
> O with what words shall I my farewell take?
> Farewell Chaldea, deere delights adieu.
> (*The Vocation* 147–48; 187–89)

Eve's overhearing Michael pronounce God's sentence of banishment in "the place of her retire" is itself based on another Abrahamic moment, the same Genesis 18 episode at Mamre, now reutilized as a model for the embassy of a second angel of God. God announces the future birth of Isaac, the child of the promise and God's seed (Gal. 4:28; Rom. 9:7), and the aged Sarah, concealed behind the tent flap, laughs in incredulity (Gen. 18:9–15). Milton's double allusion suggests that Eve, for all the grief her lament expresses at leaving her nursery of flowers to whom she has given names (11.273–79), is now destined to leave this dollhouse for real motherhood, in Adam's words, "Mother of all Mankind" (11.159) and, down the line, as she will realize, of the "promised seed" (12.623). It further indicates that on leaving Eden, Adam and Eve are already entering into a Promised Land. Their later counterparts, Abraham and Sarah, are called away from "his father's house" (12.121) and from an upbringing in "idol-worship" (12.115). For, hard as it is to believe, Michael says, men had grown so stupid, even while Noah was still alive, "As to forsake the living God, and fall / To worship their own work in wood and stone / For gods" (12.118–20; cf. 1.367–75). Eden was the house of Adam and Eve's divine Father; now they leave the garden before it can be turned into a sanctuary of idols and demons.

"Fit haunt of gods," Eve says of their lost home. The prospect that Eden might indeed be haunted prompts God to block access to the garden, "Lest Paradise a receptacle prove / To spirits foul, and all my trees their prey, / With whose stolen fruit man once more to delude" (11.123–25), like the wood enchanted with diabolic spirits in the *Gerusalemme liberata* that proves an obstacle to Tasso's crusaders. Both Tasso and Milton are imagining a cross between the mythological dryads who were supposed to have inhabited trees (see *GL* 18.27) and the darker demons who were the reality beneath those classical nature spirits, the demons whom the Canaanites of the Bible worshipped in the groves on high places. Hosea inveighs against such rites, whether forms of Canaanite religion or contaminated by them: "They sacrifice upon the tops of the mountains, and burn incense upon the hills, under oaks and poplars and elms, because the shadow thereof is good" (Hosea 4:13). Abraham himself imitated his idol-making neighbors and "planted a grove in Beersheba, and called there on the name of the LORD, the everlasting God" (Gen. 21:33), and such cult centers to the Israelite God were still active when Hezekiah set out to destroy them and give a monopoly of worship to the Jerusalem temple (2 Kings 18:4; 18:22). But nearby the temple itself, book 1 of *Paradise Lost* records, Solomon had built to Moloch a "grove / The pleasant valley of Hinnom" (1.403–4), that Josiah, later than both Solomon and Hezekiah, would hew down.[6] (The "grove" that stood hard by the false temple of Pandaemonium in book 10 [547–72], its fair but ashen fruit a punishment for Satan and his companions, is likely its hellish relative.) Eve herself initiated such idolatrous worship when, after the Fall, she bowed down to the tree of the knowledge of good and evil "as to the power / That dwelt within" (9.835–36). In retrospect, there is something ominous in the earlier comparison in book 9 of Eve to "a wood-nymph light / Oread or dryad" at the momentous occasion when she leaves Adam and "Betook her to the groves" (9.386–88), as if her Fall summons such tree gods into being. In attributing such power to the tree, Eve invents idolatry and—according to the influential account of the origins of pagan cult by Augustine in the *City of God* discussed in chapter 1—would be extending an invitation to Satan's devils to take the tree over as their "receptacle." Eden, which Raphael refers to as "this delicious grove, / This garden" (7.537–38), could become itself a demonic grove; George Sandys writes in his traveler's description of Jerusalem that the grove of Moloch that Josiah would cut down had been "before a Paradise."[7] God forestalls the possibility of turning Eden into a false, haunted Paradise.

But it is the fallen Adam, who, in his very piety, may pose the greater danger of desecration to Eden. His own lament at leaving Eden, voiced to Michael, describes his plans, which would have turned the garden into a memorial park.[8]

> here I could frequent
> With worship, place by place where he vouchsafed
> Presence divine, and to my sons relate;
> On this mount he appeared; under this tree
> Stood visible, among these pines his voice
> I heard, here with him at this fountain talked:
> So many grateful altars I would rear

Of grassy turf, and pile up every stone
Of lustre from the brook, in memory,
Or monument to ages, and thereon
Offer sweet smelling gums and fruits and flowers:
    (11.317–27)

Adam's project also anticipates Abraham, who would build altars at Moreh—
"there builded he an altar unto the LORD, who appeared unto him" (Gen.12:7)—
and at Bethel and Mamre (Gen. 12:8; 13:18) before he planted the grove to God
in Beersheba. Adam wants to convert Eden into a cult site; he has yet to learn
the lesson contained at the end of the book in Michael's prophecy that Eden
will be washed away in the Flood, "To teach thee that God attributes to place /
No sanctity" (11.836–37). Michael speculates that if Adam had remained unfallen Eden "had been / Perhaps thy capital seat," to which his future posterity
would have come "From all the ends of the earth, to celebrate / And reverence
thee their great progenitor" (11.342–46): the angel indicates just why, after
the Fall, Eden cannot be left in human hands. The garden would become a
religious center and goal of pilgrimage—Michael pointedly refers to Eden as
"this rock" (11.336), but no Petrine church will be built on it. The other "high
capital" (1.756) of the poem is Pandaemonium, a combination of the Jerusalem temple and Saint Peter's in Rome, the latter viewed by Protestants
as a profane replacement and continuation of the cult of the Roman *capi-
tol*—the cult of temporal state power itself in perhaps the supreme "seat /
Of mightiest empire" (11.386–87) listed in the ensuing catalog, forty verses
later, of the earth's future kingdoms and their glory that Satan will offer
to Jesus (see 11.405–6). Adam's impulse to decorate his altars with shiny
stones, gums, and flowers is the first step to church ornaments that can be
confused with the pagan religions, full of pomp and gold—and there are
indeed "sands of gold" (4.238) in the streams of Eden. Such ornate houses
of worship, in the case of Pandaemonium, turn pilgrimage into tourism
directed at the rich artwork rather than the deity—"the work some praise
/ And some the architect" (1.731–32). Adam is not Mulciber, nor a Michel-
angelo or Bernini, but his attempt to consecrate Eden through his human
means is liable to have the opposite effect, the worship of his own work in
wood and stone. Milton comments in *De Doctrina Christiana*, with a particular eye to Catholics who "call idols the layman's books" (*CPW* 6:693,
Works 17:142), that "the worship of the true God in the form of an idol
is accounted no less grave a sin than the worship of devils" (*CPW* 6:692;
Works 17:140). It is nonetheless the case that Adam's stones of luster and
flowers could be read as a figure for Milton's poetry itself in relation to its
sacred subject.

    Adam misses and wants to recapture God's absent voice. Milton connects
the shrine that Eden might become with a particular pagan form of pilgrimage

and worship, the cult of oracles. At the beginning of his career, Milton had exploited the tradition that the pagan oracles had ceased to prophecy at the birth of Christ in *On the Morning of Christ's Nativity*, the great ode that opened the *Poems* of 1645. The last third of the poem's Hymn, stanzas 19–27, assimilates the cessation of oracles with the expulsion of the pagan gods, so many demons, from their temples.

> The oracles are dumb
> No voice or hideous hum
>> Runs through the arched roof in words deceiving.
> Apollo from his shrine
> Can no more divine,
>> With hollow shriek the steep of Delphos leaving.
> No nightly trance, or breathed spell,
> Inspires the pale-eyed priest from the prophetic cell.
>
> . . . .
> From haunted spring, and dale
> Edged with poplar pale,
>> The parting genius is with sighing sent,
> With flower-inwoven tresses torn
> The nymphs in twilight shade of tangled thickets mourn.
>> *(173–80, 184–88)*

The first two stanzas of the roll call of defunct and superseded gods pairs Delphic Apollo, excluded from his famous oracle, with everyday nature spirits, elegiacally invoked, but demons nonetheless, leaving the groves they have "haunted"—and Milton probably alludes here to Hosea's poplar and its good shade, a kind of pagan darkness.[9] Virtually all of the dethroned deities of the *Ode*—Apollo, Peor, Baal, Ashtaroth, Hammon, Thammuz, Moloch, Isis, and Osiris—reappear in book 1 of *Paradise Lost* in the catalog of demons who will in later times be enshrined under their names. Apollo comes near the end, in the inventory, almost as an afterthought, of the Greek gods, among those "on the Delphian cliff / Or in Dodona" (1.517–18). Reversing the *Nativity Ode*, the epic's catalog mentions oracles last: the oracle at Dodona was in an oak or oak grove. It will take the coming of Christ to drive out these demons—although the *Nativity Ode* simultaneously suggests that they may have crept back into Catholic idolatry. The Jesus of *Paradise Regained* breaks the Good News to Satan: "henceforth the oracles are ceased, / And thou no more with pomp and sacrifice / Shalt be inquired at Delphos or elsewhere" (*PR* 1.456–58). *Paradise Lost* already foreshadows the oracles' end with the closing down of Eden.

Milton associates Eden with the two most famous oracles of Apollo, Delphi and Delos; Adam and Eve have returned to pray at the place where the Son had judged them, and are compared in simile to Deucalion and Pyrrha, survivors of a universal flood in pagan myth:

>   the ancient pair
> In fables old, less ancient yet than these,
> Deucalion and chaste Pyrrha to restore
> The race of mankind drowned, before the shrine
> Of Themis stood devout.
>   (11.10–14)

The simile elegantly frames the book, which will end with the biblical Flood and the survival and new start for Noah and his family—perhaps a more ancient fable itself if one accepts a quibble on "these." But it also suggests a second frame that links Eden to Delphi at the beginning of the book, to Delos at its end. The place of judgment in Eden is a potential site of cult, and indeed the prayers of Adam and Eve are treated as sacrificial offerings, "first fruits" (11.22) by the priestly Son, who proffers them, in turn, to the Father. The fuming "golden altar" at which the Son adds incense to the prayers (11.18) is, however, *in heaven*. It is not to be confused with an earthly shrine and oracle like that of Themis, consulted by Deucalion and Pyrrha in order to learn how to repopulate the world. This oracle, in most versions of the myth, including its Ovidian retelling in *Metamorphoses* 1 (316–415), was the oracle at Delphi, which in those days—"tunc," Ovid says—belonged to Themis before Apollo dispossessed her in order to gain its cult and wealth.[10] It is, in fact, Euripides's account, in a choral ode in the *Iphigenia in Tauris*, of how Apollo took over the oracle at Delphi and expelled the older nocturnal visions sent by Themis that provided the classical model for Milton's depiction in the *Nativity Ode* of Apollo himself and the other oracles and pagan deities being sent packing, in their turn, to be replaced by Christ.[11] In *Paradise Lost*, the Son prophesied as a true oracle at the place of judgment where Adam and Eve now stand—"So spake this oracle" (10.182)—that the woman's seed shall bruise and be bruised in turn by the serpent. But this oracle spoke once and for all time—it foretells all the future, as the narrator's ensuing gloss reveals: the course of Christian history up to its apocalyptic end, when the Son will tread Satan "at last under our feet" (10.190). After this divine utterance, Eden falls silent, as will the pagan oracles when the Son next returns to speak truth on earth.

At the end of book 11, Michael foretells how the garden itself, its human inhabitants and potential cult worshippers long since expelled, will be upended in the Flood and carried down the Euphrates to the Persian Gulf, "And there take root an island salt and bare, / The haunt of seals and orcs, and sea-mews' clang" (11.834–35). James Nohrnberg has pointed out, in unpublished work to which I am indebted, that Milton alludes here to the *Homeric Hymn to Apollo*, which recounts that when Leto sought to give birth to Apollo on Delos, the island feared that the god would disdain its hard, rocky terrain and overturn it: "So, many-footed creatures of the sea will make their lairs in me and black seals their dwellings undisturbed because I lack people" (77–78). Delos obtains from the goddess her oath that Apollo will establish an oracle and temple on its barren earth, before he sets up temples and groves elsewhere—at Delphi, as the hymn goes on to relate in its second part.[12] Milton has already identified Eden with Delos in book 5 when Raphael first sees earth and the garden of God from the air as a sea pilot "amidst the Cyclades / Delos or Samos first appearing kens / A cloudy spot" (5.264–65). Here he reverses the order of Apollo's career in his allusions in book 11, and suggests that Eden suffers the fate that Delos feared for itself, disdained by its deity: fit haunt of seals, *not* of gods.

Both allusions—to Delphi as shrine of Themis and to Delos as an already rocky and barren isle—evoke these sites *before* they were to become the oracles of Apollo, before their treasuries would be filled with visitors' offerings and their temples adorned with sculptures that made them both good places to find ancient statuary, according to the odd *Of Statues and Antiquities* included in the Columbia Manuscript, along with works of Milton (*Works* 18: 258–61). The oracles' treasuries were de facto banks, money changers in their temples, and they were the targets of sacrilegious robbery: the Athenians' appropriation of the treasury of the Delian league, the plunderings of Delphi by the Phocians, Sulla, and Nero. God moves preemptively so that Eden cannot become an Apollonian oracular site, ordaining the cessation of oracles before oracles will have come into being.

Shrine, oracle, pilgrimage site: Eden is a temple or church that has been desecrated by sin and now risks being further infiltrated by pagan, worldly motives of power and wealth. The garden is closed off and then destroyed at the end of *Paradise Lost* so that a new Pandaemonium like the one raised at its beginning cannot be built there, a receptacle to foul spirits and a profane replica of itself. *Paradise Lost* announced this prospect of desecration when it depicted Satan first entering the garden, "at one slight bound," in book 4; the ensuing simile already anticipates Eden's demise at the epic's end.

> As when a prowling wolf,
> Whom hunger drives to seek new haunt for prey,
> Watching where shepherds pen their flocks at eve
> In hurdled cotes amid the field secure,
> Leaps o'er the fence with ease into the fold:
> Or as a thief bent to unhoard the cash
> Of some rich burgher, whose substantial doors,
> Cross-barred and bolted fast, fear no assault,
> In at the window climbs, or o'er the tiles;
> So clomb this first grand thief into God's fold:
> So since into his church lewd hirelings climb.
>   (4.183–93)

The remarkable double simile combines and juxtaposes epic and biblical motifs and allusions. The hungry wolf had described Tasso's crusader Rinaldo during the eleventh-century conquest of Jerusalem in the *Gerusalemme liberata* (19.35.1–4). The hero is standing outside the Al-Aqsa mosque, which housed the pagan (Muslim) defenders of the city and which rested on the site of the Jewish temple, "nel tempio che, più volte arso e disfatto, / si noma ancor, dal fondator primiero, / di Salamone" (*GL* 19.33.2–5; Which burned and builded oft, still keeps the name / Of the first founder, wise King Solomon [Fairfax]). He eventually bursts its doors open with blows of a giant beam against its locks and hinges; a massacre of the Muslims ensues. Satan is a false crusader invading Eden's sanctuary, and the scenario may suggest the demonic nature of the crusade celebrated by the Catholic Tasso.[13] Disdaining the gate of Eden—we only later begin to suspect why when we learn that Gabriel is posted there with the angelic guards (4.542–54) who will catch up to Satan at the book's end—Satan is further compared to the thief who climbs into the sheepfold in Jesus's parable in John 10:1–18: Jesus goes on to explain that he himself is the door that leads to salvation (10:9), but "He that entereth not by the door into the sheepfold, but climbeth up some other way, the same is a thief and a robber" (10:1). Jesus's parabolic discourse is itself double, and the figure of the thief is succeeded by that of the hireling who, in contrast to Jesus the messianic good shepherd (10:14), neglects the sheep, and "the wolf catcheth them" (10:12). The epic wolf—behind Rinaldo lies Virgil's Turnus prowling outside the Trojan camp (*Aen.* 9.57–66)—becomes the wolf of the Christian pastoral metaphor, threatening the sheepfold that is the Church; so, in book 12, the wolf and hireling minister moved by "lucre and ambition" have become one: after the ministry of the apostles, "Wolves shall succeed for teachers, grievous wolves" (12.508).

The succession of similes and allusive contexts comes—by now we have expected this—at Satan's expense. They transform him from a superhuman epic hero Rinaldo wielding, in frontal martial assault, a timber that, Tasso says, was taller and thicker than the masts of a Genoese ship (*GL* 19.36.3–4)—a model for Milton's earlier comparison of Satan's spear to "the tallest pine / Hewn on Norwegian hills, to be the mast / On some great ammiral" (1.292–94)—to a common thief breaking furtively into a moneyed, citizen household. The drop in poetic diction signaled by "cash" at the end of verse 188 signals something lower than the *sermo humilis* of biblical language and enacts the devil's heroic comedown, from force to fraud, a descent, too, in class. Satan's, we might say, is no longer a class act (or all too typically an aristocratic one, revealed for the low-down looting it is). By the same token, the sequence suggests how the substitution in *Paradise Lost* of biblical epic and spiritual heroism for military valor, even, or especially, for the Christian crusader warfare of Tasso's epic, "Wars, hitherto the only argument / Heroic deemed" (9.28–29), implies both a new bourgeois—as opposed to aristocratic—subject matter and audience. In contrast to the cavalier devil, Adam and Eve and their garden are a model of middle-class domesticity. The simile suggests why, fourteen verses later, Satan's view of Eden in which is "exposed / In narrow room nature's whole wealth" (4.206–7) should echo the counting house of Marlowe's Barabas, the Jew of Malta, which would "inclose / Infinite riches in a little room" (1.1.36–37). Paradise looks a bit like the childhood home of the poet, son of John Milton Sr., scrivener and moneylender. It had been lost in the Great Fire of London one year before the epic appeared in print.[14]

The substitution of the rich burgher's house for the humble sheepfold is Milton's innovation with respect to John's Gospel. The real treasure of Eden is its human worshippers, like the good shepherd's flock. But both parts of the double simile suggest that Eden is a church that is already proleptically violated before Satan leaps inside it. Tasso's Rinaldo breaks down the doors of a "temple" in eleventh-century Jerusalem profaned by pagan rites; in the slaughter that follows "Lavò co 'l sangue suo l'empio pagano / quel tempio che già fatto avea profano" (*GL* 19.38.7–8; with their heart's blood the Pagans vile / This temple washed which they did late defile [Fairfax]). Similarly, the figuring of Eden as a cash-rich burgher's house describes a church that is a sure target for thievish hirelings, whose ejection Milton had proposed in his *Considerations Touching the Likeliest Means to Remove Hirelings Out of the Church* (1659) through the elimination of tithes. There Milton had repeatedly argued that the Jewish practice of tithing had depended on the existence of a "national church" centered in its capital seat, the Jerusalem temple, and had ceased once the temple was destroyed (*CPW* 7:282, 289, and 292). That temple was "a den of thieves" in the prophecy of its destruction uttered by Jeremiah (7:11) and cited by Jesus (Matt. 21:13; Mark 11:17, Luke 19:46) as he casts out all who bought and sold there, and predicts that nothing will remain of it: "there shall not be left one stone upon another, that shall not be thrown down" (Matt. 24:2, Mark 13:2; Luke 21:6). The closure of Eden and its eventual washing away by the Flood removes its latent, linked dangers of pagan idolatry and simoniac wealth, a future state church: God destroys the garden before it can become a temple that will be destroyed again.[15] And again.

Good-bye

This reduction of Eden to an island salt and bare also implies a willed foregoing of the imaginative riches of the poem that has gone before.[16] Satan's entrance into a wealthy Eden precedes Milton's luxuriant verse description and creation of the garden, akin to Mammon's and Mulciber's (and Milton's) raising of Pandaemonium through musical exhalations in book 1. Now the lost Paradise that could only be summoned up by poetry has been emptied out as the epic reaches its end. The desolation of Eden coincides with the shift in Michael's mode of exposition (12.8–11) from the visions that he has presented to Adam to sparer narration, a shift that aesthetically divides the once composite books 11 and 12 (six visions in 11, six speeches by Michael in 12: these suggest a little twelve-book epic at the end of the poem). The visions are begun when Michael instills drops from the well of life into Adam's eyes. The drops have the effect of curing the spiritual blindness Adam has incurred with the Fall, but when they are applied, he is literally blinded—"enforced to close his eyes" (11.419). We are reminded of Adam's earlier dream of the creation of Eve in book 8 that: "closed mine eyes. / Mine eyes he closed, but open left the cell / Of fancy my internal sight" (8.459–61). Both moments, in turn, recall and enact the divine illumination that the blind poet of *Paradise Lost* has invoked for himself at the opening of book 3. The visions of book 11 are tagged by such metaliterary markers as the depiction of the invention of the "arts that polish life" themselves in Jubalcain the musician and Tubalcain the metalworker; the modeling of the episode of the warrior giants on the episode of the two cities on the shield of Achilles in the *Iliad*, forged there by the metalworker Hephaestus-Vulcan, with whom Tubalcain was identified and itself a work of art that occasions a passage of ekphrasis within the larger poem of which it seems to be a miniaturized version; and the sequence of the visions, beginning with the story of Cain and Abel and leading to the "triumphs or festivals" (11.723) of the giant conquerors, which recalls the similar shield forged by Vulcan for Aeneas in *Aeneid* 8, whose sculpted scenes begin with Romulus and Remus and end with the triple triumph of Augustus. Hephaestus, Tubalcain, and Vulcan are other names for Mulciber, the architect of Pandaemonium, whose specter has briefly reappeared and now will be banished, as Michael shifts from the visual to the auditory.[17]

The cessation with Noah's Flood of these visions of humanity's first stage of history consigns them to a poetically fabulous, if also spiritually emblematic or allegorical, status, "fables old"—for who knows what transpired before the Flood?—and it may consign Milton's fable of Eden and the Fall with them.[18] From hereon, as Michael moves quickly from the story of Nimrod and Babel, where the confusion of tongues similarly ensured the loss of memory that the tower was built to prevent (12.45–47), to the history, on what feels like firmer ground, of Abraham and his descendants up to the Second Coming, the archangel and the poem shift to a simpler chronicle. For a while the words of Michael—"seer blest"(12.553), Adam calls him at the end of the angel's narration—are still studded with invocations to sight: "I see him, but thou canst not" (12.128); "I see his tents" (12.135); "each place behold / In prospect, as I point them" (12.142–43); "the river Nile; / See where it flows" (12.158). Adam initially responds in similar terms: "now first I find / Mine eyes true opening" (12.273–74); "but now I see / His day in whom all nations shall be blest" (12.276–77). But these figures of seeing soon disappear, as the severer Protestant practice of hearing the word of God replaces visualization, the mode attached to the idols that Catholics call the layman's books. Michael's dry narrative has occasioned critical censure, but the impoverishment of its style is Milton's self-conscious choice, a choice imaged in a salt and bare Eden. It is probably significant that

Michael does not show Adam the fate of Eden in a vision but *tells* him about it: the shift to narration has already begun, and this new mode enacts the aridity it portrays. Noah has built his ark to survive the Flood, but the circus animals have deserted.

Milton thus places the grand epic edifice of *Paradise Lost* between its idolatrous double, the temple of Pandaemonium, and a desert isle whose bareness is a related, bleaker version of the "universal blank" (3.48) of his poet-narrator's blindness. From its opening invocation, *Paradise Lost* has been about the cessation of external oracles and supersession of state temples in favor of an internal shrine: the "oracle of God" (1.12) of the Jerusalem Temple Mount is replaced six verses later by "the upright heart and pure" (1.18) of the individual believer that the Spirit prefers before all temples. So, in the last section of Michael's narrative, the few endangered true believers have become the Spirit's "living temples, built by faith to stand, / Their own faith not another's" (12.527–28). So Michael's final advice to Adam will return to the catalog of golden, earthly empires in book 11 (all once part, we want to remember, of the same 1667 book 10) and will urge him, in place of "all the riches of this world ... / And all the rule, one empire" (12.580–81), and in place of Eden itself, to embrace "A paradise within thee, happier far" (12.587) of spirituality and love. So readers at the end of *Paradise Lost* walk away from the poem itself, leaving its riches behind for—or making those riches part of—their own inner resources.[19]

Tied to this final, unequivocal rejection of empire is Milton's ambivalence toward the power of his own imagination and the wealth of the classical literary tradition that *Paradise Lost* has housed as treasure in its memory palace.[20] *Paradise Regained* will end with a similar supersession of the temple on which Jesus stands; Samson destroys the profane temple and theater of Dagon at the climax of *Samson Agonistes*. But these iconoclastic, farewell gestures, like the washing away of Eden, only come at the conclusion of these works, when their poetic achievements are assured: Milton has become the oracle he promised for the man of letters in his early Latin *Prolusion* 7 at Cambridge—"to be the oracle of many nations, to find one's home regarded as a kind of temple" (*CPW* 1:297, *Works* 12:266; Multarum Gentium oraculum esse, domum quasi templum habere)—but this oracle, too, ceases and its living temple shuts down.[21] *Paradise Lost* is not a self-consuming artifact, but it appears to have consumed its tradition and genre: once utilized as the building block of Milton's inspired poem, epic cannot be salvaged to carry out its former business as usual. As an image of the larger *Paradise Lost*, Eden is the realization of the opportunity for a true, sacred epic that was already potentially compromised by its own bounty and that will not come again, its riches too dangerous to be left in others' profane hands.[22] That is, the critical chestnut that the epic tradition finishes with *Paradise Lost* is scripted by the poem itself.

Michael's prophecy of Eden's destruction forecloses the epic field to others, as does its primary epic model, the prophecy in *Iliad* 12 (10–33) that the wide wall surrounding the Greek ships would stand so long as Hector was alive and Achilles was angry—that is, for the duration of the *Iliad* itself—but that after the fall of Troy the gods would turn the rivers of Ida upon it and wash it out to sea, leaving a sand beach: no later bard would or should be able to revisit this poetic terrain.[23] The angelic guard posted by the gate of Eden serves a similar purpose: no one will tread on the sacred ground of Milton's epic, whether demons or poetic successors—the difference scarcely seems to matter. The original garden will eventually be swept away, beyond recovery. At the beginning of Milton's epic tradition, the *Iliad* had warned its readers to beware of imitations. Now *Paradise Lost*, which tells the beginning and *ending* of history, contests the priority of the *Iliad* and takes over its claim to nonrepeatability: Milton would begin and end a literary history as well. Adam and Eve in the poem's final lines descend from the wealth of Eden to the "subjected plain" (12.640) of plainer style and subject. They have a world all before them, but one of lower generic expectations; the gates of epic close behind them.

Notes

Note on italics and emphasis: All appearances of italics in verse citations in this book, whether of Milton's poetry or the works of other poets, represent my emphases designed to bring out key terms and correspondences among passages. The texts of Milton's poetry that I follow in the edition of John Carey and Alastair Fowler do not use italic script except in the case of *Paradise Lost* 5.513–14.

Notes to the Introduction

1. Barthes, *S/Z: An Essay*, 3–4.
2. Does Milton expect the reader of *Paradise Lost* to know his *Poems* of 1645 in the same way that Virgil expects the reader of the *Aeneid* to know and catch echoes of his earlier *Eclogues* and *Georgics*? Did he intend, that is, to invent the Miltonist? This book begs the question.
3. *Paradise Lost* follows traditional epic form and divides into books that can be read for their own internal structure, logic, and coherence. These divisions counter the poem's narrative exuberance: its *action* spills over from book to book and only comes to a full stop at the end of book 8 (book 7 in the 1667 version) where, like the Creator-God it describes, the poem takes a Sabbatarian rest; Satan himself takes a seven-day sabbatical before resuming his assault on humanity in book 9. Satan seems similarly to have dropped out of the narrative at the end of book 4, when he flees from Gabriel before the judgment of God; but the dream he has induced continues to operate in Eve's memory at the beginning of book 5, and Satan soon reappears as the protagonist of Raphael's narrative of the rebellion and War in Heaven. He is only absent from the poem during its books or book of creation, 7–8, before he definitively exits from its action in book 10, his place taken by his children Sin and Death. The overflowing of its container books by the narrative in *Paradise Lost* is typically Miltonic and resembles its long verse sentences and their frequent enjambment. Both resemble his writing in the modern Italian sonnet form of Della Casa and Tasso, in which sentences run across the formal divide between octave and sestet, and the couplets in *Lycidas* that frequently bridge the ending of one verse paragraph and the beginning of the next. On these latter cases, see Prince, *The Italian Element in Milton's Verse*, 14–33, 85–88.
4. Frye, "Literature as Context: Milton's Lycidas," in Frye, *Fables of Identity: Studies in Poetic Mythology*, 125.
5. Hinds, *Allusion and Intertext: Dynamics of Appropriation in Roman Poetry*.
6. All citations of Milton's verse, both English and Latin, are taken from *The Poems of John Milton*, ed. John Carey and Alastair Fowler, Longmans Annotated English Poets (Harlow, UK: Longmans, 1968). When I refer to Fowler's notes to *Paradise Lost*, I am citing from his 2nd ed. (New York: Longman, 1998), hereafter referred to as *PL*. Citations from Milton's prose are taken from *The Complete Prose Works of John Milton*, ed. Don M. Wolfe, 8 vols. (New Haven, CT: Yale University Press, 1953–82), hereafter referred to as *CPW*. Where the original of the prose is in Latin, the text is taken from *The Works of John Milton*, ed. Frank Patterson (New York: Columbia University Press, 1931–38); hereafter referred to as *Works*.
7. Ariosto's passage (especially 17.73.7–8; *Orlando furioso* [*OF*]) echoes, in turn, a similar

invective in Petrarch's *Triumph of Fame* 2.143–45: "gite superbi, o miseri Cristiani / consumando l'un l'altro, e non vi caglia / che'l sepolcro di Cristo è in man de' cani!" (go your proud ways, wretched Christians, consuming each other, while it matters not to you that the sepulcher of Christ lies in the hands of dogs!). Milton is tapping into a long poetic history.

8. See Davies, *Images of Kingship in "Paradise Lost": Milton's Politics and Christian Liberty*, 51–88; Davies, 71–72, correctly senses that unity of the devils at 2.495–505 glances at the unity of the Turks under their sultan, but she does not cite the specific allusions to the Camões and Ariosto passages.

9. Milton, in fact, equates Turkish Islam, maintained by force, with Catholicism and, finally, with any state-enforced or pecuniary religion in *Considerations Touching the Likeliest Means to Remove Hirelings out of the Church* (*CPW*, 7:318).

10. Bloom, *The Map of Misreading*, 125–43. See also Teskey, *Delirious Milton*, 123–27, for the idea that Milton practices a kind of Christian spoliation of classical literary tradition, leaving that tradition defaced and incomplete.

11. Hampton, "'Turkish Dogs': Rabelais, Erasmus and the Rhetoric of Alterity," 58–82, and, a subsequent version in *Literature and Nation in the Sixteenth Century: Inventing Renaissance France*, 35–65.

12. This view of *Paradise Lost* runs counter to Frank Kermode's insistence on its tragic effect and its origins *as* a tragedy. See his essay, "Adam Unparadised," in *Shakespeare, Spenser, Donne*, 260–97; see also Wilson, *Mocked with Death: Tragic Overliving from Sophocles to Milton*, 164–206.

Notes to Chapter 1

1. Colin Burrow notes how the martial energies and action of book 1 take a "nosedive" in *Epic Romance: Homer to Milton*, 263–68.

2. On Satan's most spectacular use of force—his invention of artillery—already as a form of fraud, see Murrin, *History and Warfare in Renaissance Epic*, 131–32.

3. Two notable critical discussions of the catalog are found in Rosenblatt, "'Audacious Neighborhood': Idolatry in *Paradise Lost*, Book I," 553–68, which relates the contagion of idolatry and the need to divorce and separate the impure from the pure to later developments in the Fall of Adam and Eve, and Lyle, "Architecture and Idolatry in Paradise Lost," 129–55, which traces a narrative progression, a falling into ever worse forms of idolatry in the catalog; Lyle sees the poem taking a more neutral attitude toward the Jerusalem temple itself than the critical one I shall ascribe to it below. See also Broadbent, who emphasizes the anti-Catholic elements of the catalog, in *Some Graver Subject: An Essay on "Paradise Lost,"* 88–95; Leonard, *Naming in Paradise: Milton and the Language of Adam and Eve*, 67–85; Archer, *Old Worlds: Egypt, Southwest Asia, India, and Russia in Early Modern English Writing*, 83–87.

4. On Belial, on Milton's conflation of Sodom and Gibeah, and on Milton's intention to write a drama on the Sodom story, see Lieb, *Milton and the Culture of Violence*, 114–55; Leonard, *Naming in Paradise*, 72–73.

5. Vossius, *De Theologia Gentili et Physiologia Christiana*, 345–46; Vossius, 346, notes the discrimination that the Greeks made between Comus and Priapus; Fowler indicates Jerome's commentary in his note to 1.415–17. John Selden discusses Chemos-Priapus in his *De Diis Syris*, 161; Selden's work was Milton's most important source of information about the gods of the ancient Near East.

6. Diodorus Siculus 20.14.4–7 and the passages in Quintus Curtius, Lactantius, and Augustine cited below. On the whole subject, see Warmington, *Carthage*, 155–62.

7. Biblical references are to the King James Version of the Bible unless indicated otherwise.

8. Curtius, *History of Alexander*, 1:195.

9. Lactantius, *Divine Institutes, Books I–VII*, 82. The Lactantius passage is cited by Selden, *De Diis Syris*, 181–82.

10. Augustine, *City of God*, 233–34.

11. Blessington, *"Paradise Lost" and the Classical Epic*, 6; Lewalski, *"Paradise Lost" and the Rhetoric of Literary Forms*, 58–59.

12. *The Geneva Bible: A Facsimile of the 1560 Edition*, 120.

13. Rebecca W. Smith, "The Source of Milton's Pandemonium," 187–98.

14. In book 2, Mammon proposes that the devils build a "nether empire, which might rise / By policy, and long process of time, / In emulation *opposite to heaven*" (2.296–98), a Carthage against God's true and only Rome. For some of the parallels to Virgil's Carthage that follow, see Blessington, *Paradise Lost and the Classical Epic*, 7–8. Charles Martindale criticizes Blessington's exclusive identification of Pandaemonium with Carthage and Dido in his *John Milton and the Transformation of Ancient Epic*, 4–5.

15. On Michael's action, see Lieb, *Milton and the Culture of Violence*, 123–24; Fowler on 12.637–38.

16. Cicero, *De Natura Deorum, Academica*, 331–33.

17. Selden, *De Diis Syris*, 151.

18. Lewalski, *"Paradise Lost" and the Rhetoric of Literary Forms*, 76–77.

19. Riggs, *The Christian Poet in "Paradise Lost,"* 32–33.

20. Lieb, *Poetics of the Holy*, 127–28, within his larger discussion, 119–70, of Milton's use of the Bible's sacred geography—Mount Zion versus Mount Sinai—in *Paradise Lost*.

21. See the discussion in Manley, *Literature and Culture in Early Modern London*, 568–74. I am also indebted to an unpublished paper by James Nohrnberg, "Jerusalem Transposed: On the Axes of Western Epic."

22. Murrin, *The Allegorical Epic*, 153–71; Lieb, *Poetics of the Holy*, 140–52.

23. *Geneva Bible* (New Testament), 58 recto.

24. Calvin, *Commentary on the Acts of the Apostles*, 302.

25. Bloom, *Map of Misreading*, 125–43.

26. The Miltonic polemic against numbers continues in *Paradise Regained*; see Quint, *Epic and Empire*, 325–40. See also Forsyth, *The Satanic Epic*, 87–90.

27. The model here, as I have argued in an earlier study, is the *Iliad* where the absence of the sulking Achilles creates a kind of heroic vacuum that is eventually filled with the massed Greek and Trojan forces and the predominance of missile weapons, a threat to the individual heroism that the return of Achilles will restore. See Quint, *Epic and Empire*, 47–48.

28. Hartman, "Milton's Counterplot," in *Beyond Formalism*, 120–23; Parker, *Inescapable Romance*, 153–57.

29. Milton gathers the scriptural testimony about devils as well as angels in book 1, chapter 9 of his *De Doctrina Christiana*; *CPW* 6:343–50. On the fallen angels' loss of their names, see Leonard, *Naming in Paradise*, 67–85.

30. Broadbent, *Some Graver Subject*, 95–97.

31. Corbet, *Poems of Richard Corbet*, 50–51.

32. Augustine, *City of God*, 235.

33. Nock, ed., *Corpus Hermeticum 2: Traités XIII–XVIII; Asclepius*, 347; Copenhaver, trans., *Hermetica: The Greek Corpus Hermeticum and the Latin Asclepius*, 90; cited by Augustine in *City of God* (8.24), 272.

34. Augustine, *City of God*, 274.

35. What follows takes up the observation of Hartman, "Milton's Counterplot," 122: "Thus the whole cycle of to and fro, big and small ... is continued when we learn, in the final lines of Book 1, that far within Pandemonium, perhaps as far from consciousness as hell is from the thoughts of the Peasant or demonic power from the jocund if intent music of the fairy revelers, Satan and the greatest Lords sit in their own, unreduced dimensions."

36. Murrin, *Allegorical Epic*, 17, invokes the empty inner sanctum of the temple in his analysis of Milton's depiction of heaven.

37. On Babelic noise in *Paradise Lost*, see Sauer, *Barbarous Dissonance and Images of Voice in Milton's Epics*, 14–34.

38. Polybius, *Rise of the Roman Empire*, 476. See Cowan, "The Clashing of Weapons and Silent Advances in Roman Battles," 114–17.

39. Ammianus Marcellinus, *Historia* 16.12.13, in *Ammianus Marcellinus*, 1:270–71.

40. Fuller, *History of the Worthies of England*, 199.

Notes to Chapter 2

1. This chapter, as later notes will also indicate, is indebted to the teaching of and conversations with James Nohrnberg, to his unpublished essay, "Jerusalem Transposed on the Axes of Western Epic," and to his article, "*Paradise Regained* by One Greater Man," 83–114. For some other treatments of the figure of Ulysses in *Paradise Lost*, see Lewalski, "*Paradise Lost*" and the Rhetoric of Literary Forms, 65–68; Blessington, "*Paradise Lost*" and the Classical Epic, 1–18, 50–67; Webber, *Milton and His Epic Tradition*, 131–36; Steadman, *Milton's Epic Characters*, 194–208.

2. The fiction of book 2 is further populated—and further unified—by its allusions to later epic voyagers who recall and are modeled on Homer's Ulysses: Jason in the *Argonautica* of Apollonius Rhodius (2.1016–18); and Virgil's Aeneas, who also sailed past Scylla and Charybdis, following in the literal and literary historical wake of Homer's Ulysses. Satan's fall through Chaos alludes, as we shall see in chapter 3, to Dante's Ulysses in *Inferno* 26, his ship swallowed by the sea on his final journey outside the Mediterranean. Satan's trip to what Beelzebub terms "The happy isle" (2.410) of God's "new world" (2.403) recalls, too, the Atlantic voyage of Tasso's knights, Carlo and Ubaldo, to the Fortunate Isles in canto 15 of Tasso's *Gerusalemme liberata* (*GL*): these crusaders are explicitly told that they are sailing, as will the future Columbus, on the westward course that earlier claimed Dante's unfortunate Ulysses (*GL* 15.25–32). Critics have further seen in Satan's trip across Chaos a complex of allusions to Vasco da Gama's eastern voyage of discovery to India in Camões's *Os Lusíadas* around the Cape of Good Hope (4.159–65) in search of a route to India and the Spice Islands Ternate and Tidore (2.636–42); Camões touts his hero as a superior Ulysses from his epic's third stanza. See Sims, "Camoens' *Lusiads* and Milton's *Paradise Lost*: Satan's Voyage to Eden," in *Papers on Milton*, 36–46; Quint, *Epic and Empire*, 253–66. To these versions of Ulysses one may add one more, surprising figure. Satan promises his fellow fallen angels to "seek / Deliverance for us all" (2.464–65). He tells Sin and Death that he comes "to set free / From out this dark and dismal house of pain, / Both him and thee" (2.822–24); he will "search with wandering quest a place foretold / Should be" (2.830–31). The associations with Moses are unmistakable, and they reappear when Satan lets Chaos know that he has been "Wandering this darksome desert" (2.973). As noted in the preceding chapter, hell is a kind of Egypt—or rather the Egypt of the Exodus was a biblical type of hell—and Satan becomes a Moses freeing the devils/Israelites and wandering in the desert, or, in his guise as "spy" (2.970) a Joshua or Caleb sent to spy out (Num. 13:16) the land of Canaan: the latter are recalled again when Satan first looks down in book 3 on God's creation through an opening compared to the passageway that would in later times open over that Promised Land (3.531). Satan is himself compared in simile to "a scout / Through dark and desert ways with peril gone" (3.543–44), who now eyes "The goodly prospect of some foreign land / First seen" (3.548–49). The alignment of the wanderings of Moses in search of an ancestral homeland with the wanderings of Ulysses was not a commonplace, but it turns up within a few years of *Paradise Lost*, in the 1656 preface to Abraham Cowley's *Poems*. In defending the biblical subject matter of his epic poem, the *Davideis*, Cowley asks, "Does not the passage of *Moses* and the *Israelites* into the *Holy Land* yield incomparably more Poetical variety then [sic] the voyages of *Ulysses* or *Æneas*?" *Critical Essays of the Seventeenth Century*, 2:89. Milton's fiction, I think, picks up on this suggestion. By effecting a worldly deliverance of his devils and leading them into a takeover of God's Holy Land, Satan has rewritten the Exodus all too much into a pagan *Odyssey*. Satan as Moses is one more version of Ulysses in book 2.

3. Unflattering portraits of Ulysses in Greek tragedy (Sophocles's *Philoctetes* and Euripides's *Hecuba* and *Rhesus*) precede the censorious Roman view of his Greek guile in Virgil's *Aeneid*. Plutarch feels called upon to defend the hero's actions from his critics in *De audiendis poetis* [*How a Young Man Ought to Hear Poems*], 8.

4. On *contaminatio*, a nonclassical term, and its Renaissance practice, see Greene, *The Light in Troy: Imitation and Discovery in Renaissance Poetry*, 156–69; but, against my argument, see 40, where Greene distinguishes Milton's imitation *from* the *contaminatio* of a Poliziano.
5. Blumenberg discusses the Ulysses of Dante's *Inferno* 26 as the avatar of modernity and its spirit of curiosity and free inquiry in *The Legitimacy of the Modern Age*, 338–40.
6. On wandering and wandering thoughts in *Paradise Lost*, see Parker, *Inescapable Romance*, 140–41, 156–58.
7. Stanford, *The Ulysses Theme: A Study in the Adaptability of a Traditional Hero*. Milton's criticism of the humanistic Ulysses is close to Dante's condemnation of the hero in *Inferno* 26. See Mazzotta, *Dante's Poet of the Desert: History and Allegory in the Divine Comedy*, 65–106: of particular interest for Milton are Mazzotta's remarks on the circularity that surrounds the existence of Ulysses; see also Freccero, *Dante: The Poetics of Conversion*, 15–28, 138–51. I will argue in chapter 3 for a textual connection to Dante's Ulysses in Satan's fall through Chaos at *Paradise Lost* 2.927–38.
8. On the demonic council of book 2, see the fundamental discussion by Broadbent in *Some Graver Subject*, 110–20.
9. The debate between Ovid's Ulysses and Ajax in *Metamorphoses* 13 is a master structuring model for the episodes and characters of Tasso's *Gerusalemme liberata*, the most prestigious among the modern epics preceding *Paradise Lost*; see Quint, "The Debate between Arms and Letters in the *Gerusalemme Liberata*," in *Sparks and Seeds: Medieval Literature and its Aftermath; Essays in Honor of John Freccero*, ed. Stewart and Cornish, 241–66.
10. See Hardie, "Fame and Defamation in the *Aeneid*, in *Vergil's "Aeneid": Augustan Epic and Political Context*, ed. Stahl, 243–70, 262–63.
11. Cicero, *De Officiis*, 115.
12. "Peroratio plàne tragicus es, immo Ajax Lorarius ..." *Works* 7:40.
13. "An Poeta non meministi, cùm de Achillis mortui armis, Ajax & Ulysses contenderent, non Graecos populares sed Troianos hostes ex sententia Nestoris Judices datos?" *Works* 8:82.
14. "quamquam enim Ulyssem, id est, quàm optimè de patria meritum me esse sane perquàm vellem, tamen Achilleïa arma non ambio; coelum in clypeo pictum, quod alii, non ego, in certamine aspiciant, praeferre, onus non pictum sed verum, humeris portare, quod ego, non alii sentiant, non quaero." *Works* 8:84.
15. The posture recalls the paralysis of the seated Lady in *Comus* and the invitations of Satan to Jesus in *Paradise Regained* to "Sit down and eat" (2.375) or to sit on "David's throne" (3.153) and/or "Moses' chair" (4.219), all Miltonic figures of immobility.
16. See Broadbent, *Some Graver Subject*, 116.
17. Hamlet's soliloquy is one Shakespearean model. Fowler's note to 2.146–51 connects Belial's fear of death and to be "devoid of sense and motion" to the speech of Shakespeare's Claudio in *Measure for Measure* 3.1.117–18: "This sensible warm motion to become / A kneaded clod." I am grateful to Lawrence Manley and Harold Bloom for pointing out to me how Claudio's entire speech is distributed in the fiction of book 2:

> Ay, but to die and go we know not where;
> To lie in cold obstruction, and to rot;
> This *sensible warm motion* to become
> A kneaded clod; and the delighted spirit
> *To bathe in fiery floods*, or to reside
> *In thrilling region of thick-ribbed ice*;
> To be *imprison'd in the viewless winds*
> *And blown with restless violence round about*
> *The pendant world*; or to *be worse than worst*
> Of those that lawless and incertain thought
> Imagine howling—'tis too horrible!

> The weariest and most loathed worldly life
> That age, ache, [penury], and imprisonment
> Can lay on nature is a paradise
> To what we fear of death.
>   (*Measure for Measure* 3.1.117–31)

Compare Claudio's dread "to be worse than worst / Of those that lawless and uncertain thought / Imagine howling" (125–27) to Belial's comments on what would be "worse," Claudio's fear of being imprisoned in the winds to Belial's vision of being the sport of winds, Claudio's prospect of fiery floods and thicked-ribbed ice, to the landscape of hell described later in the book where the devils at certain revolutions are brought "From beds of raging fire to starve in ice" (2.600). "The pendant world" is the original for Milton's "This pendent world" at the end of the book (2.1052).

18. The opening of spaces for human choice in Milton's poetry, including the reader's choosing among its possible meanings, is the subject of Brisman, *Milton's Poetry of Choice and Its Romantic Heirs*.

19. See Lewalski, *"Paradise Lost" and the Rhetoric of Literary Forms*, 86–87, for the general parallel to the council in *Iliad* 2.

20. Hoxby, *Mammon's Music: Literature and Economics in the Age of Milton*, 154–55, 174–77. See Forsyth, *Satanic Epic*, 110–13.

21. On Thersites, see the studies collected in La Penna, *Tersite censurato e altri studi letteratura fra antico e moderno*. La Penna points out the connection between Thersites and Virgil's Drances (113–20), and Milton may here, too, have already intuited this connection in his pairing of the Drances figure Belial with the Thersites figure Mammon.

22. Tasso's Goffredo wields a golden scepter when he puts down the rebellion of the Thersites-like Argillano in canto 8 of the *Gerusalemme liberata* (8.78).

23. Rumrich, *Matter of Glory*.

24. Broadbent, *Some Graver Subject*, 110–15. For Milton's general polemic against human kingship, see Davies, *Images of Kingship*, and the fundamental remarks of Frye, *The Return of Eden*, 106–14.

25. Many critics disagree, but they seem to me to be the heirs of a romantic tradition that identified Milton's revolutionary politics with Satan's; both regimes and parliaments may, of course, be implicated in the satire. For some more recent views, see Norbrook, *Writing the English Republic: Poetry, Rhetoric and Politics, 1627–1660*, 442, 452–55; Corns, *Regaining "Paradise Lost,"* 134–38; Achinstein, *Milton and the Revolutionary Reader*, 199–210; Armitage, "John Milton: Poet against Empire," in *Milton and Republicanism*, ed. Armitage, Himy, and Skinner, 206–25; Dzelzainis, "Milton and the Protectorate in 1658," in *Milton and Republicanism*, 181–205; Fallon, *Divided Empire: Milton's Political Imagery*, especially 55–81. For a discussion of Satan as a modern politician, whether royalist or republican, and the tradition of the parliament of devils in pamphlet literature contemporary to Milton, see Benet, "Hell, Satan, and the New Politician," in *Literary Milton: Text, Pretext, Context*, ed. Benet and Lieb, 98–113.

26. Colin Burrow identifies this model in *Epic Romance*, 265–66; it was first pointed out to me by James Nohrnberg. The episode is retold in the *Rhesus* of Euripides. It also stands, as Burrow's study shows, at the beginning of a whole series of subsequent epic imitations, starting with Virgil's Nisus and Euryalus episode in the *Aeneid*. Burrow notes, 67, that Ariosto's version of the night exploit, modeled on the Nisus and Euryalus episode and *its* imitation in Statius's *Thebaid* (10.346–48), is the episode of Medoro and Cloridano that leads to the love story of Medoro and Angelica, the cause, in turn of Orlando's madness, and the turning point of the *Orlando furioso*: "Ariosto makes Virgil's dead episode thrill with continuing life, and causes the main action of his poem." Tasso's version, the celebrated duel between Tancredi and Clorinda in canto 12 of the *Gerusalemme liberata*, is modeled on Virgil's episode and a *different* imitation of that episode in later Roman epic, a vignette of confused identity and patricide in the darkness of night in the *Punica*

of Silius Italicus (9.66–177), and it similarly is the pivotal event of its epic. The wounded Medoro is rewarded by being brought to life and receiving the love of the universally desired Angelica; Clorinda dies, but receives baptism and eternal life before she expires. Milton's Italian predecessors had thus already made the *Doloneia*-type episode central to their poem; and Milton's explicit return to the model of *Iliad* 10 followed a modern practice that inverted the epic tradition and turned apparent defeat, in this case the Son's future death, into victory.

27. Burrow, *Epic Romance*, 266, notes that ancient Homeric scholia that doubted the authenticity of the *Doloneia* were available in print from 1521 onward.

28. Fowler, note to 4.894.

29. For the version that Enceladus is buried beneath Aetna, see *Aeneid* 3.578–82; for the version that it is Typhoeus, see *Metamorphoses* 5.346–58. The Hercules who dies in flames in the *Hercules Oetaeus* of Seneca is compared to *both* Typhoeus (Typhon) and Enceladus; see vv. 1732–34. For the conventional pairing of the two giants, see Claudian, *De tertio consulatu Honorii* 159–61; *De sexto consulatu Honorii, praef.* 17; *Gigantomachia* 32–33.

30. Quintus Smyrnaeus, *The Fall of Troy*, 253.

31. A bill to enforce transportation failed to pass Parliament in 1663; its place was supplied by royal warrant. See Beattie, *Crime and the Courts in England, 1660–1800*, 470–83. For the argument that hell is a penal colony and part of God's "empire," see Evans, *Milton's Imperial Epic: Paradise Lost and the Discourse of Colonialism*.

32. Fowler, note to 2.628. "How false and vain is this opinion they know well from their own bitter experience who have ever felt the pangs of guilty consciences: they are beset by Sphinxes and Harpies, Gorgons and Chimeras, who hunt their victims down with flaming torches in their hands" (*CPW* 1:230–31; namque hanc vanam esse & nugatoriam opinionem infoelici nôrunt experientia, quicunque sceleris cujuspiam conscii sibi fuere; quos tunc Sphinges & Haryiae, quos tunc Gorgones & Chimaerae intentatis facibus insequuntur), *Works*, 12:144.

33. In his *Adagia*, Erasmus explains the proverbial state of being between Scylla and Charybdis as the acceptance of a lesser evil in place of a greater one or of steering a middle course between two equal dangers; see *The Collected Works of Erasmus*, 387–89 (adage 4.4).

34. For commentary on the Sin and Death episode, see Kahn, *Machiavellian Rhetoric*, 215–25; Martin, *The Ruins of Allegory*, 165–67, 182–94; Summers, *The Muse's Method*, 32–70.

35. The model of the *Telegony* for Milton's Sin and Death is pointed out and discussed by James Nohrnberg, "*Paradise Regained* by One Greater Man," 22, and by Don Cameron Allen in *Mysteriously Meant: The Rediscovery of Pagan Symbolism and Allegorical Interpretation in the Renaissance*, 298–99. For the myth, see the ancient summary in *Hesiod, the Homeric Hymns, and Homerica*, trans. Evelyn-White, 530–31. The detail that the spear of Telegonus was tipped with the sting of a stingray is found in Oppian, *Halieutica* 2.496–505. See Nohrnberg, "*Paradise Regained* by One Greater Man," 11n22.

36. *Geneva Bible: A Facsimile of the 1560 edition*.

37. *Apocryphal New Testament*, 134. Compare Vida's rewriting of the *Gospel of Nicodemus* in book 6.198–215 of the *Christiad*, where the devils, human to the waist, serpents below (209), are so many versions of Milton's Sin. Milton is also influenced by Spenser's rewritings of the harrowing of hell in book 1 of the *Faerie Queene*, especially Arthur's rescue of the Redcrosse knight from Orgoglio's castle—the prison of Redcrosse's own pride—in canto 8, which opens to the horn of Arthur's squire Timias: "And every dore of freewill *open flew*" (1.8.5.3); Arthur himself rends the iron door to the seemingly bottomless pit, "as darke as hell" where Redcrosse is imprisoned (1.8.39.5–9) when none of Ignaro's keys fit the lock. Ignaro, the refusal to recognize one's own sin, suggests, too, Milton's key-holding Sin, whom Satan does not recognize. The parody makes Satan the savior of the devils, who, through Sin and the subsequent Fall, will be released from hell to wander over the earth. It is in line with Satan's parody in book 1 of the awakening of the sleeping dead at the Resurrection: "Awake, arise or be forever fallen" (1.330; Eph. 5:14), when he gets his fallen companions going again. It is also in line

with the role of the Moses-like deliverer that Satan also assumes in the poem: see note 2 above.

38. See Lapide, *Commentaria in Scripturam Sacram*, 21:360. "S. Augustinus, Primasius, Ticonius, Viegas, et Ribera, per infernum et mortem metonymice accipiunt diabolum, qui est princeps mortis et inferni."

39. Ibid., 21:361. "Hucusque Alcazar, Arabicus pro *mors*, vertit *abyssus*, quia mors vastissimum habet os et ventrem, quo omnes morientes complectitur, instar abyssi horribilis: 'Et abyssus,' inquit, et infernus projecti sunt in stagnum ignis plenum sulphure."

40. The "loudest vehemence" of Chaos parodies the "sonus tamquam advenientis spiritus vehementis" in the Vulgate Bible's description of the descent of the Holy Spirit on the apostles in Acts 2:2; we are meant to think of the Spirit brooding over the abyss at the Creation described in the opening invocation to the poem in book 1 (1.19–22) and again in the depiction of the Creation in book 7 (7.233–36).

41. This is not the only myth invoked by Satan's fall through Chaos; see chapter 3 for the model of the fall of Icarus. Teskey notes that Milton's Chaos is "a greedy gulf like Charybdis," in *Delirious Milton*, 73.

42. The *Odyssey* parallel is discussed in Gallagher, *Milton, the Bible, and Misogyny*, 144–48, and by van der Laan, "Milton's Odyssean Ethics: Homeric Allusions and Arminian Thought in *Paradise Lost*," 48–76. See also Frye, *Return of Eden*, 99; Lewalski, "*Paradise Lost*" *and the Rhetoric of Literary Forms*, 115–16.

43. *Odyssey of Homer*, 28.

Notes to Chapter 3

1. *Metamorphoses* 1.750–2.400, 8.183–235; *Tristia* 1.1.79–91, 3.4.21–30. For some Renaissance examples, see Ronsard, *Le Second Livre des Sonnets pour Helene* 1.11, "Discours à Monsieur de Cheverny, garde des Seaux de France," in the second part of the *Bocage Royal*, 95–108; Camões, *Os Lusíadas* 4.104.1–4; Shakespeare, *3 Henry VI* 1.4.33–34, 2.6.11–13, 5.6.18–25. On Icarus as an image of excess and aspiration in seventeenth-century English writing, see Scodel, *Excess and the Mean in Early Modern English Literature*, 148–53. Late medieval allegorizers of Ovid identified Phaethon's fall with the fall of Satan; see Davis Harding, *Milton and the Renaissance Ovid*, 15–16; Mulryan, *Through a Glass Darkly: Milton's Reinvention of the Mythological Tradition*, 50.

2. Borris, "Allegory in *Paradise Lost*: Satan's Cosmic Journey," 101–33, has compared Satan's flight through Chaos to other instances of flight, real, metaphorical, and poetic, in *Paradise Lost*. He does not note the mythic parallels of Icarus and Phaethon that I explore here; there is nonetheless some overlap in our discussions. Patrick Cheney examines the figure of poetic flight in the case of Spenser in *Spenser's Famous Flight: A Renaissance Idea of a Literary Career*.

3. Segal, "*Aeternum per saecula nomen*, the Golden Bough and the Tragedy of History: Part II," 50–52; Putnam, *Virgil's Epic Designs: Ekphrasis in the Aeneid*, 95.

4. Virgil, *Aeneid VI*, 33; see also P. *Vergili Maronis Opera*, 2:38, with reference to Virgil's other use of "remigio alarum," at *Aeneid* 1.301, describing the winged flight of Mercury.

5. For the doctrine of the void from antiquity into Milton's seventeenth century, see Grant, *Much Ado about Nothing: Theories of Space and Vacuum from the Middle Ages to the Scientific Revolution*.

6. A distinguished exposition of this reading of the relationship of the two poets is found in Hardie, *Virgil's Aeneid: Cosmos and Imperium*, 157–240. See also Dyson, "Dido the Epicurean," 203–21, and the critical response to Dyson by Gordon, "Dido the Phaeacian: Lost Pleasures of an Epicurean Intertext," 188–211.

7. A similar Lucretian reading of the gates of ivory, reached by different arguments, is found in Michels, "Lucretius and the Sixth Book of the *Aeneid*," 147.

8. Freccero, *Dante*, 15–24. Freccero acknowledges his debt to Courcelle, "Quelques symboles funéraires du néoplaonisme latin: Le vol de Dédale—Ulysses et les Sirènes," 65–93. See also Thompson, *Dante's Epic Journeys*. Borris, "Allegory," evokes similar Platonic

flights of the unaided contemplative intellect to gloss bad, satanic flight in *Paradise Lost*.

9. One can compare the formulation in Ovid's other retelling of the Icarus story at the opening of the second book of the *Ars Amatoria*: "Remigium volucrum disponit in ordine pinnas" (2.45); here, too, Icarus is characterized by the audacity of his flight: "Icarus *audaci fortius arte volat*" (2.76).

10. I have contrasted the voyage of Ulysses, the voyage of Tasso's boat of Fortune, and the voyage of Columbus in Quint, *Epic and Empire*, 248–67. The same discussion compares Tasso's sea voyagers to the Satan who flies through Chaos in book 2 of *Paradise Lost*. The present discussion offers new interpretations that I think complement rather than contradict the findings in that earlier study.

11. The allegorization of Columbus's name is elaborated upon in the first chapter of the biography of the explorer written by his son Fernando Colombo (1488–1539), a work that circulated in manuscript form and that was first published in an Italian translation in 1571—the original Spanish version is lost.

> If we consider the common surname of his ancestors, we will say that he was truly a dove, because he carried the grace of the Holy Ghost to that New World which he discovered: he showed who was God's beloved Son to the peoples there who did not know Him, just as the Holy Spirit did in the figure of a dove at the baptism of Jesus by St. John the Baptist; and because he similarly carried over the waters of the ocean, like the dove of Noah's ark, the olive branch and oil of baptism for the unity and peace that those peoples were to achieve with the Church, because they had until then been shut up in the ark of shadowy darkness and confusion.

See Colombo, *Storie del Nuovo Mondo*, 23. Tasso reinforces the analogy between the voyage of Columbus and the sea journey of his personified Fortuna through the extended octave-long simile that compares the iridescent dress of the latter to the plumage of a dove—*colomba*—at canto 15, stanza 5 of the *Liberata*. The little ship of Fortune travels so fast that it appears to fly—"così la nave sua sembra che vole" (15.14.5): one of Tasso's models are the semimagical ships of the Phaeacians in the *Odyssey*, which "move swift as thought, or as winged creature" (7.36); one of these, running faster than "a falcon / That hawk that flies lightest of creatures" (13.86–87), carries Ulysses home after his romance wanderings.

12. Tasso's fiction contains a further, parodic version of Elijah's chariot, the enchanted chariot on which Armida flies to and back from her island.

> Ella su 'l carro suo, che presto aveva
> s'assise, e come ha in uso al ciel si leva.
>   (16.70.7–8)

> Calca le nubi e tratta l'aure a volo,
> cinta di nimbi e turbini sonori,
> passa i lidi soggetti a l'altro polo
> e le terre d'ignoti abitatori;
> passa d'Alcide i termini …
>   (71.1–5)

> [She seated herself in her chariot, which she had ready to hand, and, as is its custom, it rises to the heavens. It treads the clouds and cleaves the winds in flight, girded with rain-clouds and loud whirlwinds, it passes the shores subject to the other pole, and the lands of unknown inhabitants, it passes the boundaries of Hercules …]

This magic chariot evokes the flying chariot of Medea, but it just as surely recalls the chariot of Elijah described by Dante in *Inferno* 26. Surrounded by clouds and whirlwinds in her chariot, which rises to heaven, Armida seems to be another version of the Dantesque Elijah at the moment when his horses reared and rose toward heaven—"quando i cavalli al cielo erti levorsi"; the prophet, we should recall, ascended by a whirlwind into heaven: "ascendit Elias per *turbinem* in caelum" (2 Kings 1:11).

Milton had himself evoked the chariot of Elijah in one of his earliest Latin poems, *In Proditionem Bombardicam* (On the Gunpowder Plot), probably written in 1626. The speaker of the epigram sarcastically addresses Guy Fawkes and asks him whether he intended an evil sort of piety in his attempt to blow up the King and Parliament and to send them to heaven like deathless Elijah.

> Scilicet hos alti missurus ad atria caeli,
> Sulphureo curru flammivolisque rotis.
> Qualiter ille feris caput inviolabile Parcis
> Liquit Iordanios turbine raptus agros.   (5-8)

> [It was I take it, to the halls of high heaven that you meant to blow them up in their sulphurous chariot with its wheels of whirling flame: you meant to blow them up just as that man whose life the fierce Parcae could not harm was swept up from Jordan's banks in a whirlwind.]

The terms of this early poem return in our episode in book 2 of *Paradise Lost* when Satan appears to rise through Chaos "as in a cloudy chair [i.e. chariot] ascending" (930) only to start to fall through its depths. The devil is then hurried back aloft by an explosion "of some tumultuous cloud / Instinct with fire and nitre (936-37), natural gunpowder of the type that Satan has earlier, we subsequently learn, dug up out of the substrate of heaven for his canons in the celestial war (6.469-520). Satan is no Elijah, but he is a kind of Fawkes. Milton recalls his own juvenilia as well as the models of Tasso and Dante.

13. See Leonard, "Milton, Lucretius and the 'Void Profound of Unessential Night,'" in *Living Texts*, ed. Pruitt and Durham, 198-210.

14. I enter into a much-contested area of Milton criticism: the nature of Chaos in *Paradise Lost*. It will be clear that my description is close to that presented by Rumrich, "Of Chaos and Nightingales," in *Living Texts*, ed. Pruitt and Durham, 218-27. Rumrich is responding to the powerful criticism of Leonard, "Milton, Lucretius," in the same volume: Leonard emphasizes the horror of Chaos, a literal *horror vacui*; Rumrich both defends and moves slightly away from his earlier formulation about the goodness of Chaos in Rumrich, *Milton Unbound: Controversy and Reinterpretation*; there, 118-33, he understood Chaos to constitute a passive, feminine aspect of God. Rumrich also offers a thoughtful rejoinder to the position of Rogers, *The Matter of Revolution: Science, Poetry, and Politics in the Age of Milton*, 130-43, who sees the goodness of Chaos fatally compromised by its "tartareous cold infernal dregs / Adverse to life" (7.238-39). These correspond to Lucretius's "faex" in *De rerum natura* 5.497, and may be more morally and politically neutral than Rogers suggests. These dregs seem to me to be the stuff out of which God makes hell, his Tartarus (2.858) and Inferno, a frozen "universe of death" (2.622), and thus serve his purpose: nothing is wasted, not even the waste products. I thus disagree with Sugimura's contention that these dregs are assimilated into Night; Sugimura, *"Matter of Glorious Trial": Spiritual and Material Substance in "Paradise Lost,"* 275-76. I agree with Rumrich and others in rejecting the quasi-Manichaean position of Schwartz, "Milton's Hostile Chaos: ... and the Sea Was No More," 337-74, which assimilates Chaos with evil. Adams, "A Little Look into Chaos," in *Illustrious Evidence: Approaches to English Literature in the Early Seventeenth Century*, ed. Miner, 71-89, places Chaos in opposition both to divine and satanic creativity. For a further discussion, see Hunter, "The Confounded Confusion of Chaos," in *Living Texts*, ed. Pruitt and Durham, 228-36; Lieb, *The Dialectics of Creation: Patterns of Birth and Regeneration in "Paradise Lost,"* 16-24; Martin, *Ruins of Allegory: "Paradise Lost" and the Metamorphoses of Epic Convention*, 186-200; Teskey, *Delirious Milton*, 65-85. The classic account of the cosmological learning behind Milton's Chaos is Chambers, "Chaos in *Paradise Lost*," 55-84.

15. Lewalski, *"Paradise Lost" and the Rhetoric of Literary Forms*, 117-18. Lewalski points out

the difference between Phaethon's near destruction of the earth by fire and the final apocalyptic fiery destruction of the earth that will lead to a new creation—this opposition, as we shall see below, is already found in Milton's *Natura non pati senium*.

16. Harding, *Milton and the Renaissance Ovid*, 89–93; DuRocher, *Milton and Ovid*, 55–56.
17. See the note by Fowler to 6.100–102.
18. For related remarks on the War in Heaven and a return to Chaos, see Lieb, *Dialectics of Creation*, 118–24.
19. The assonance repeats the pattern already set at greater length in the first shock of the angelic forces encountering one another in battle:

> Nor less hideous joined
> The *h*orrid shock; now *st*orming *fu*ry *r*ose,
> And *cl*amour, such as *heard* in heaven till now
> Was ne*ver*, a*rms* on *armour* clashing brayed
> *H*orrible dis*cord* ...
> (6.206–10)

20. In the war of the Olympian gods against the Titans, Pan blew on a conch shell trumpet, sending the Titans into panicked flight; on panic terror, see Dempsey, *Inventing the Renaissance Putto*, 115–46. The similarity to the Gadarene swine is spelled out at the end of *Paradise Regained*, 4.626–32. Note that there Jesus "all *unarmed* / Shall chase thee with the *terror* of his voice." For the parallel to the sight of Apollo causing the panic of the foes of Augustus at Actium as it is depicted on the shield of Aeneas in *Aeneid* 8.704–6, see Quint, *Epic and Empire*, 41.
21. Hillier makes a similar argument in "'By force or fraud / Weening to prosper': Miton's Satanic and Messianic Modes of Heroism," 17–38, 31. Von Maltzahn describes the irony of literary history that would see the imitation of the War in Heaven, particularly of its mock-heroic depiction of the devils' artillery, in poems celebrating the victories of William III and Marlborough; see von Maltzahn, "The War in Heaven and the Miltonic Sublime," in *A Nation Transformed: England after the Restoration*, ed. Houston and Pincus, 154–79.
22. The echo is pointed out in Leonard, "Milton, Lucretius," 200–204.
23. Bush, in his edition of *The Complete Poems of John Milton*, 52 and 334, notes Milton's later echo in the War in Heaven at *Paradise Lost* 6.673 of these lines in *Natura non pati senium*, and he cites their Ovidian provenance.
24. See DuRocher, *Milton among the Romans: The Pedagogy and Influence of Milton's Latin Curriculum*, 145–47, for a critical discussion of another Miltonic "denial of Lucretius's denials," in this case focused on the wounds that earth feels at *PL* 9.782 and 9.1000–1004 in the wake of original sin.
25. See *De Doctrina Christiana*, chapter 13 in *CPW* 6:399–424; *Works* 15:214–50. DuRocher, *Milton among the Romans*, 174, notes the similarity between Lucretian teaching and Milton's mortalism.
26. Lieb, *Dialectics of Creation*, 30.
27. For a discussion of Milton's early interest in the bodily assumption of saints and its relation to his later embrace of mortalist doctrine, see Kerrigan, "The Heretical Milton: From Assumption to Mortalism," 125–66.
28. Fowler, note to 6.520–22.
29. Lewalski, *The Life of John Milton*, 402–7, 670n38.
30. Du Bartas, *La Sepmaine texte de 1581*, 7.
31. Sylvester, trans., *The Divine Weeks and Works of Guillaume de Saluste Sieur du Bartas*, 1:115.
32. I owe this observation to conversations with Jennifer Clarvoe.
33. For another reading of the figure of Bellerophon that emphasizes the hero's chastity, see Fallon, "Intention and Its Limits in *Paradise Lost*: The Case of Bellerophon," in *Literary Milton*, ed. Benet and Lieb, 161–79.
34. Horace, *Odes and Epodes*, 286.

35. Ellen Oliensis, "Return to Sender: The Rhetoric of *Nomina* in Ovid's *Tristia*," 192n18, notes how Ovid presents himself in the *Tristia* (1.1.89–90; 3.4.21–24) as a poetic Icarus, whose highflying may have resulted in a fall but who has nonetheless gained a famous name for himself. Hardie, *Ovid's Poetics of Illusion*, 294–96, takes up Oliensis's suggestions; Hardie points out the Horatian intertext of *Odes* 4.2.

36. There may be an obscene double entendre in this passage, as Milton tells Diodati he is not doing much of anything.

37. Appropriately enough, the *Oxford English Dictionary* notes the first use of "depressed" with this sense in *The Anatomy of Melancholy* (1621), II.ii.6.2, where Robert Burton is translating Cicero on the power of oratory to cure melancholy: "Assuredly a wise and well-spoken man may do what he will in such a case; a good orator alone, as Tully holds, can alter affections by the power of his eloquence, 'comfort such as are afflicted, erect such as are *depressed*, expel and mitigate fear lust, anger,' etc." Burton, *The Anatomy of Melancholy*, 2:113. Burton goes on in the next section of his book to praise the remedy of music, including the music of poets like Orpheus, Amphion, and Arion.

38. Compare, too, the music that alleviates the state of the fallen angels in hell in book 1.556–59: "Nor wanting power to mitigate and swage, / With solemn touches, troubled thoughts, and chase / Anguish and doubt and fear and sorrow and pain / From mortal or immortal minds."

Notes to Chapter 4

1. Greene discusses these patterns in *The Descent from Heaven: A Study in Epic Continuity*, 388, as markers of two insistent dimensions of *Paradise Lost* that play on verticality and on light and darkness.

2. MacCaffrey, "The Theme of *Paradise Lost*, Book 3," in *New Essays on Paradise Lost*, ed. Kranidas, 58–85. My discussion covers some of the same ground as MacCaffrey's essay, particularly her discussion on different kinds of vision, though largely to different ends. MacCaffrey emphasizes the difference between vision and the hearing of God's word, and notes the space that divine dialogue takes up in the episode of Milton's heaven.

3. Milton appears wistfully to echo *On Education* when Adam responds to Raphael's "one first matter all" speech by declaring that the angel has shown him the scale of nature "whereon / In contemplation of created things / By steps we may ascend to God" (5.510–12). In one sense, he is right: Raphael has shown Adam and Eve how, by analogy with the odors given off by the flowers of a plant, the human body can rise to reason and contemplation itself. But this is not the same thing as forming an idea of an invisible heaven and deity from the created universe. Moreover, Raphael has proposed a possible—"perhaps" (5.496)—human future of participation in angelic food (not exactly contemplation, in any case) and winged travel to heaven that he already knows will not take place because of the Fall. Adam, in fact, immediately follows his words by asking Raphael what he could have meant by "*If ye be found / Obedient*," as if to cancel out this idea of contemplative ascent.

4. Bacon, *The Advancement of Learning and New Atlantis*, 104.

5. Ibid.

6. Ibid.

7. The argument that follows shares much with the discussion of accommodation in Madsen's *From Shadowy Types to Truth*, particularly where Madsen discusses Milton's uneasiness about reading the world and Book of Nature in terms of Neoplatonic correspondences (85–144); Madsen may overly emphasize the gap between prelapsarian and postlapsarian experience to explain the discontinuity between created world and Creator. Victoria Silver insists on this discontinuity, perhaps to the point of rending the unity of creation in *Paradise Lost* in *Imperfect Sense: The Predicament of Milton's Irony*; she questions the monism attributed to Milton on 359–63n12. On the material unity of Milton's universe, see, among others, Kerrigan, *The Sacred Complex: On the Psychogenesis of "Paradise Lost*," 192–262; Rumrich, *Matter of Glory*, 53–82; Stephen Fallon, *Milton among the Philosophers: Poetry and Materialism in Seventeenth-Century England*; Rogers, *Matter of Revolution*, 103–43.

8. Jackson I. Cope maps out some of the patterns of light in book 3 in a discussion of light

and darkness in the larger epic; see Cope, *The Metaphoric Structure of "Paradise Lost,"* 106–10.

9. Broadbent notes the framing pattern in *Some Graver Subject*, 157.

10. For the tradition, see Dölger, *Sol Salutis*.

11. *Hesiod, the Homeric Hymns, and Homerica*, 325.

12. Ibid., 337.

13. *Callimachus, Hymns and Epigrams, Lycophron, Aratus*, trans. A. W. Mair and G. R. Mair, 51. The translators are evidently influenced by Milton's language in book 3.

14. On the Son as feminized moon, see Kerrigan, *Sacred Complex*, 185–86.

15. Many of the solar terms of *Elegy V*, of *On the Morning of Christ's Nativity*, and of the discussion of light, sunlight, and darkness in book 3 of *Paradise Lost* were already set out in one of the very first works from Milton's pen, the first Latin prolusion presented at Cambridge on *Whether Day is more excellent than Night* (*Works* 12:118–49; *CPW* 1:218–33). For the earth decking herself out for the Sun, and the ubiquity of solar worship, including among the Indians of the New World, see *Works* 12:139; *CPW* 1:228. Tillyard further relates *Prolusion 1* to the daytime and nocturnal worlds of the *L'Allegro* and *Il Penseroso* in *The Miltonic Setting*, 1–27. There is a special pathos, perhaps recognized by the blind elderly Milton, when he first published this piece of juvenilia in 1674, in its prospect of a realm of darkness, where the eye of the world has been put out, descending back into ancient Chaos. *Works* 12:142; *CPW* 1:229–230.

16. One can compare the similar ambition that Milton expressed in the verses of *At a Vacation Exercise in the College*, originally attached to the sixth of his Latin prolusions, and probably composed just before *Elegy V*:

> the deep transported mind may soar
> Above the wheeling poles, and at heaven's door
> Look in, and see each blissful deity
> How he before the thunderous throne doth lie,
> Listening to what unshorn Apollo sings
> To the touch of golden wires, while Hebe brings
> Immortal nectar to her kingly sire;
> (33–39)

17. See Pecheux, "The Image of the Sun in Milton's *Nativity Ode*," 315–33; Quint, "Expectation and Prematurity in Milton's *Nativity Ode*," 195–219.

18. See Kerrigan, *Sacred Complex*, 181–92, on this inspiration as a form of divine impregnation of the poet, made empty and thus feminized by his blindness.

19. Phillips, *The Life of Milton*, in John Milton, *Complete Poems and Major Verse*, ed. Hughes, 1035.

20. *Works*, 15:28: "INVISIBILIUM saltem nobis, sunt coelum supremum, qui thronus est et habitaculum Dei et coelites sive Angeli."

21. Baxter, *The Life of Faith*, 150. For a salutary caution against the uncritical use of Baxter to gloss Milton's writings, see Rumrich, *Milton Unbound*, 29–33.

22. For the hidden nature of Milton's God, and for the closed system of signification that governs Milton's depiction of heaven, see chapter 6, "The Language of Milton's Heaven," in Murrin, *Allegorical Epic*, 153–71.

23. See especially 1.571–73; 6.791.

24. Samuel, "The Dialogue in Heaven: A Reconsideration of *Paradise Lost*, III, 173–202," 601–11.

25. See Wilson, *Mocked with Death*, 152–53, 176–78.

26. MacCaffrey, "The Theme," 61.

27. "I come no spy" (2.970) Satan lies to the personified Chaos in book 2, and goes on to say that he is "Wandering this darksome desert" (2.973) of Chaos itself. See chapter 2, note 2.

28. *The Orphic Hymns*, trans. Athanassakis, 12–15. See also Ovid, *Metamorphoses* 4:228, where Apollo declares himself "mundi oculus." Waddington looks at the tradition and the typology of Christ as the Sun of righteousness in "Here Comes the Son: Providential

Theme and Symbolic Pattern in *Paradise Lost*, Book 3," 256–66. Waddington's allegorical reading of the created world seems to collapse what he calls the "pious and conventional distinction between the created and the Creator" (257).

29. Pseudo-Dionysius, *The Complete Works*, 162.

30. Milton probably has a particular royal hypocrite in mind in his portrait of the false piety of Satan that fools Uriel: Charles I, the same figure he has in mind in his book 4 portrait of a Satan who, if offered an "act of grace," would "recant / Vows made in pain, as violent and void" (4.93–97), and start his nefarious ways again. He is rewriting his earlier attack on the portrait of the executed king in the hagiographic *Eikon Basilike*. In Milton's own response to this piece of royalist propaganda in *Eikonoklastes* (1649), he had ridiculed Charles's supposed prayer for the eventual conversion to Protestantism of his Catholic wife Maria-Henrietta, and concludes the chapter:

> But what is it that the blindness of hypocrisy dares not doe? It dares pray, and thinks to hide that from the eyes of God, which it cannot hide from the op'n view of man? (*CPW* 3:422)

In the earlier controversial work, Milton had insisted on the perfect legibility of Charles's hypocrisy: it would be hard to fool God, if you cannot fool human sight. By the time of *Paradise Lost*, however, the Restoration had ensued and *Eikonoklastes* had been burned by the public executioner. Milton had to admit that yes, you could fool all of the people all of the time, and in his poem, he reversed the terms of his earlier tract. Blindness belonged not to the kingly hypocrite but to his subjects, who had welcomed back Charles's no less hypocritical son and namesake.

31. *Third Letter on Sunspots*, in the *Discoveries and Opinions of Galileo*, 143. In the *First Letter*, Galileo wrote, "I do not assert on this account that the spots are clouds of the same material as ours, or aqueous vapors raised from the earth and attracted by the sun. I merely say that we have no knowledge of anything that more closely resembles them. Let them be vapors or exhalations then, or clouds, or fumes sent out from the sun's globe or attracted there from other places; I do not decide on this—and they may be any of a thousand other things not perceived by us" (100).

32. For some rich discussion, along other lines, of the sun in *Paradise Lost*, see Hartman, "Adam on the Grass with Balsamum," in Hartman, *Beyond Formalism*, 124–50.

33. *Discoveries and Opinions of Galileo*, 38. See *PL* 5.261–63.

34. Murrin, *Allegorical Epic*, 160–61, for similar doubts.

35. Compare book 5, vv. 439–44.

36. MacCaffrey, "The Theme," 80.

37. On the bad winds of Chaos and of the Paradise of Fools, see Lieb, *Dialectics of Creation*, 30–34. See also Martin, "'What If the Sun Be Centre to the World?': Milton's Epistemology, Cosmology and Paradise of Fools Reconsidered," 231–65, for an analysis of Milton's confrontation with Dante in the episode.

38. Joseph Addison objected to the episode in *The Spectator* 297: "I must in the next Place observe that *Milton* has interwoven in the Texture of his Fable some Particulars which do not seem to have Probability enough for an Epic Poem, particularly in the actions he ascribes to *Sin* and *Death*, and the Picture he draws of the *Limbo of Vanity*, with other Passages in the second Book. Such allegories rather savour of the spirit of *Spencer* and *Ariosto*, than of Homer and Virgil." *The Spectator* (London, 1712), 4:174; italics in original. See also Broadbent, *Some Graver Subject*, 162–63. The comedy of the passage is defended in Summers, *The Muse's Method: An Introduction to "Paradise Lost,"* 55–58; Summers responds to Addison whom he cites earlier, 35–36. MacCaffrey, "The Theme," 76–77, describes the role of the episode in the larger thematic structure of book 3.

39. Ficino, "Concerning the Sun," chapter 3 in *Renaissance Philosophy*, 121.

40. Ibid., chapter 6, 128. In chapter 11, 135, Ficino distinguishes divine Light from the "weak mass of the light of the sun," and attributes to God what was merely a *symbolic* Platonic principle: "the *Soul of the World* generates, moves and warms everything by its vital heat."

See also the commentary by Ficino's follower, Giovanni Nesi, to the Pythagorean saying, "Do not speak against the sun," in his *Symbolum Nesianum*; Celenza, *Piety and Pythagoras in Renaissance Florence: The Symbolum Nesianum*, 94–97.

41. Martin, " 'What If the Sun,' " 261–62.

42. The passage appears in chapter 10 of part 1 of *De revolutionibus*, cited in Kuhn, *The Copernican Revolution*, 179–80. Garin shows the provenance of Copernicus's language from Ficino's *De Sole* in "Per la storia della cultura filosofica del rinascimento: Letteratura 'solare,' " 3–16.

43. Galileo, *Dialogue Concerning the Two Chief World Systems*, 268–69.

44. More, *The Argument of Psychathanasia or The Immortality of the Soul* 3.3.11.2–3, in *The Complete Poems of Dr. Henry More*, 77. The passage is cited in Nicolson, *The Breaking of the Circle*, 160. On Kepler, see Nicolson, *The Breaking of the Circle*, 150–54, and Lawson, " 'The Golden Sun in Splendor Likest Heaven': Johannes Kepler's *Epitome* and *Paradise Lost*, Book 3," 46–51.

45. It might also lead to a non-Christian deism, perhaps an intermediate stop on the way to sheer materialism. Selden's *De Diis Syris*, published in 1617 and much reprinted throughout the century, was Milton's source for knowledge of ancient Near Eastern sun cults; Milton could also have followed the arguments of Gerhard Vossius in the second book of his *De Theologia Gentili*, which deals with the pagan worship of heavenly bodies. D. P. Walker notes that Vossius, more than Selden, insists that ancient solar cults were not to be read symbolically—in Neoplatonic fashion—but as idolatrous worship of created nature; this seems to be Milton's position. See Walker, *The Ancient Theology: Studies in Christian Platonism from the Fifteenth to the Eighteenth Centuries*, 186–87. Walker's remarks appear in a discussion on the deist Edward Lord Herbert of Cherbury's *De Religione Gentilium*, published posthumously in 1663. Herbert used Vossius as a source, but in fact defended the symbolic astral religion of the ancients; for Herbert's remarks on solar worship, see Walker, 177–78.

46. *The history of Diodorus Siculus Containing all that is Most Memorable and of greatest Antiquity in the first Ages of the World until the War of Troy*, trans. Henry Cogan (London, 1653), 105, cited in Broadbent, *Some Graver Subject*, 167. There is, however, no suggestion in this passage on natural history of the solar cult that Broadbent describes. My discussion is indebted to, even as it revises Broadbent's bringing together of, the passages of *Paradise Lost* that refer to the sun. Broadbent argues that the verse of book 3 that describes the visible sun, precisely because it deals with the visible manifestation of a creative potency that Milton could not otherwise depict in his God, is too magnificent and tips the balance of the book, against the poet's intentions, in favor of a carnal, pagan worldview: "instead of attributing to God, at reverent secondhand, the power and the glory which could not be manifest in Heaven itself, it tends towards a rationalisation of sun-worship."

47. Julian, Letter 47, to the Alexandrians, *The Works of the Emperor Julian*, 3:149. Garin, "Letteratura 'solare,' " 5–6, discusses how Julian's worship of the sun was revived in the fifteenth-century neopaganism of Gemisthus Pletho and in the natural hymn to the Sun of the Neo-Latin poet Michael Marullus; see the commentary by Donatella Coppini in Marullus [Michele Marullo Tarcaniota], *Inni naturali*, 227–45.

48. See also Julian, *Oration 4: Hymn to King Helios*, 150a, in *The Works of the Emperor Julian*, 1:411. Julian may be indebted to Iamblichus, to whom Proclus, in his *Commentary on the Timaeus*, attributed the doctrine that the moon was the mother of creation in collaboration with the father sun. Proclus, *Commentaire sur le Timée*, 4:90. In his 1642 *Apology against a Pamphlet* [*Apology for Smectymnus*], Milton defends his prayer in section 4 of the 1641 *Animadversions* (see *CPW* 1:704–7) as "a hymn in prose, frequent both in the Prophets, and in humane authors" (*CPW* 1:930). He probably has Julian's hymns in mind among the latter, especially the *Hymn to King Helios*; the *Animadversions* prayer depended heavily on light and sun imagery to describe the Reformation coming to rescue England from spiritual blindness (Julian in the *Hymn*, 131a, had referred to his own past *as a Christian* as a time of darkness), and Milton prayed against his country's backsliding:

"O if we freeze at noone after their earely thaw, let us feare lest the Sunne for ever hide himselfe, and turne his orient steps from our ingratefull Horizon justly condemn'd to be eternally benighted. Which dreadfull judgement O thou the ever-begotten light, and perfect Image of the Father, intercede may never come upon us, as we trust thou hast" (*CPW* 1:705).

49. Satan echoes and epitomizes his longer description of a seemingly—"as seems" (9.105)—geocentric universe in his earlier soliloquy addressed to the earth in book 9:

> O earth, how like to heaven, if not preferred
> More justly, seat worthier of gods, as built
> With second thoughts, reforming what was old!
> For what god after better worse would build?
> Terrestrial heaven, danced round by other heavens
> That shine, yet bear their bright officious lamps,
> Light above light, for thee alone, as seems,
> In thee concentring all their precious beams
> Of sacred influence: as God in heaven
> Is centre, yet extends to all, so thou
> Centring receives from all those orbs; in thee,
> Not in themselves, all their known virtue appears
> Productive in herb, plant, and nobler birth
> Of creatures animate with gradual life
> Of growth, sense, reason, all summed up in man.
> (9.99–113)

No sooner does Satan recognize the earth as built by a god, if not God, than he sets it up as a rival to God. His geocentrism is pointedly more materialist and actually less anthropocentric than Raphael's heliocentric model, which has already conceded that the "bright luminaries" of the solar system are not to the earth "Officious, but to thee, earth's habitant" (8.98–99). It is Satan who here makes literal the likeness of earth to heaven that Raphael had made iffy: "what if earth / Be but the shadow of heaven, and things therein / Each to the other like, more than earth is thought" (5.574–76). We should be suspicious of the devil's science.

50. Broadbent, *Some Graver Subject*, 166.
51. Harrison, *The Bible, Protestantism, and the Rise of Natural Science*, on iconoclasm, 116–17. See also Westfall, *Science and Religion in Seventeenth-Century England*, and Hooykaas, *Religion and the Rise of Modern Science*. The relationship of Reformation thought and the New Science has been debated since the salvos of Tawney, *Religion and the Rise of Capitalism* and Weber, *The Protestant Ethic and the Spirit of Capitalism*. Theodore K. Rabb has objected that before the mid-seventeenth century, that is, in the period of the New Science's emergence, scientific discoveries and developments took place and were shared in Catholic and Protestant countries alike; see Rabb, "Religion and the Rise of Modern Science," 111–26. The relationship of science to Puritan millenarianism is the subject of Charles Webster's important *The Great Instauration*.
52. Bacon, *New Organon and Related Writings*, 1.62; 59; *Bacon's Novum Organum*, 235.
53. *New Organon*, 1.65, 62; *Bacon's Novum Organum*, 243.
54. *New Organon*, preface, 36; *Bacon's Novum Organum*, 183. Bacon repeats the idea with identical language in aphorism 1.128, 116; 327.
55. Garin, "La nuova scienza e il simbolo del 'libro'" (1954), in *La cultura filosofica del rinascimento italiano*, 450–67, 457; Foucault, *The Order of Things*.

Notes to Chapter 5

1. At the beginning of Abraham Cowley's unfinished epic *Davideis*, Cowley's Satan, determined to rouse King Saul's hatred against David, God's anointed (1.115–16), calls for help from his infernal crew: "dares none / Attempt what becomes Furies?" he asks (1.137–38).

The scene imitates the *Doloneia* in *Iliad* 10, the same episode that we have seen Milton use both to depict Satan's volunteering to journey to earth in the council scene in hell in book 2 and for the Son's volunteering in book 3 to save mankind. There ensues the same silence that is found in both the Greek and Trojan camps in *Iliad* 10 and in both Milton's hell and heaven, where devils and angels, respectively, sit and stand mute. Cowley draws this silence out and builds the suspense with further elaboration. At last, a volunteer is found.

> The quaking Pow'ers of Night stood in amaze,
> And at each other first could onely gaze.
> A dreadful *Silence* fill'd the hollow place,
> Doubling the native terror of *Hells* face;
> Rivers of flaming Brimstone, which before
> So loudly rag'd, crept softly by the shore;
> No hiss of *Snakes*, no clanck of *Chains* was knowne,
> The *Souls* amidst their *Tortures* durst not groan.
> *Envy* at last crawls forth from that dire throng,
> Of all, the direfulst; her black locks hung long,
> Attir'd with curling *Serpents*; ...
>   thus from the accursed crew
> *Envy*, the worst of *Fiends*, herself presents
> *Envy, good* onely when she her self *torments*.
>   (1.145–55, 166–68)

Envy crawls to the fore. Taking credit for Cain's murder of Abel, for having driven Pharaoh into the Red Sea, and for the rebellion of Korah, Cowley's Envy now proceeds to the task at hand and enters into the mind of Saul, making him envious of David (cf. 1 Sam. 18:9–10). This infernal council that gets the action going in the *Davideis* is one more suggestive precedent for *Paradise Lost*, where Satan will himself volunteer for the dirty warfare of the *Doloneia* in place of Cowley's Envy. The difference is slight, however, because Milton's Satan is the virtual personification of envy. Cowley, *Davideis*, 7. In Du Bartas, *The Divine Weeks* 2.1.2, *The Imposture*, the Satan who sets out to tempt Eve, the "old *Python* which through hundred throtes / Doth proudly hisse" (58–59; see *Paradise Lost* 10.529–31) is spurred and characterized by his envy: "His envious hart, self-swoln with sullen spight / Brooks neither greater, like, nor lesser wight: / Dreads th'one, as Lord; as equall, hates another; / And (jealous) doubts the rising of the other" (61–64). *Divine Weeks*, 1:340.

2. On Satan's envy, see Revard, "Satan's Envy of the Kingship of the Son of God: A Reconsideration of *Paradise Lost*, Book 5, and its Theological Background," 190–98, and *The War in Heaven: "Paradise Lost" and the Tradition of Satan's Rebellion*, 67–85; and the recent study of Kilgour, *Milton and the Metamorphosis of Ovid*, 233–64; Kilgour, 232, cites Wisdom 2:23, and more generally opposes satanic envy as a mirror, perverted or revealing, to Milton's own poetic creativity and emulation.

3. Verbart puts the three passages together in "Milton on Vergil: Dido and Aeneas in *Paradise Lost*," 111–26. Both DuRocher and Strier have discussed echoes of *Aeneid* 1.11 in *Paradise Lost* 6.788, 9.929–30, and in a third passage (4.118–19) that I do not discuss here. DuRocher, "Passion and Allusion in *Paradise Lost*," 124–45; Strier, "Milton's fetters, or, why Eden is better than Heaven," 169–97. Neither critic discusses the Father's echo of the line *in bono* in 3.216; it is noted by Martindale, *John Milton and the Transformation*, 3. See also Kilgour, "Satan and the Wrath of Juno," 653–71.

4. In the invocation to book 9, Milton aligns God's anger at the Fall—"Anger and just rebuke" (9.10) with the wrath of Achilles in the *Iliad* (14–15) and rage of Turnus, the second Achilles of the *Aeneid* (16–17), and then with the divine ire of Neptune in the *Odyssey* and, finally, of Juno in the *Aeneid* (18–19).

5. DuRocher, "Passion and Allusion," 142, "Envy *can* dwell in heavenly breasts, Satan and his followers show. But such spirits do not remain heavenly for long."

6. Rosenblatt, "Structural Unity and Temporal Concordance: The War in Heaven in *Paradise Lost*," 33–34. DuRocher, "Passion and Allusion," points out the verbal echo of *Aeneid* 7.583–84, the clamoring of the Italians for war, "perverso numine," in spite of divine omens and oracles.

7. Cicero, *Tusculan Disputations*, 3.9.20–21. See also Fresch, "'Aside the Devil Turned / For Envy': The Evil Eye in *Paradise Lost*, Book 4," in *Living Texts*, ed. Pruitt and Durham, 118–30.

8. Bacon, *Essays*, 83.

9. Alciati, *Emblemata, Lyons, 1550*, 79.

10. The begetting and exaltation of the Son, and its repercussions, are an obligatory topic in criticism of *Paradise Lost*. For some important discussions, see Revard, "Satan's Envy" and *The War in Heaven*; James Nohrnberg, "On Literature and the Bible," 36–38; Davies, *Images of Kingship*, 133–63; Nyquist, "The Father's Word/Satan's Wrath," 187–202; Ide, "On the Begetting of the Son in *Paradise Lost*," 141–55; Williams, "The Motivation of Satan's Rebellion in *Paradise* Lost," 253–68; Gilbert, "The Theological Basis of Satan's Rebellion and the Function of Abdiel in *Paradise* Lost," 19–42; W. B. Hunter, "Milton on the Exaltation of the Son: The War in Heaven in *Paradise Lost*," 215–31, and, against Hunter, Rumrich, *Matter of Glory*, 155–65; MacCallum, *Milton and the Sons of God: The Divine Image in Milton's Epic Poetry*, 79–87; Rogers, *Matter of Revolution*, 122–29; Labriola, "'Thy Humiliation Shall Exalt': The Christology of *Paradise Lost*," 29–42.

11. See Pitt Harding, "'Strange point and new!': Satan's Challenge to Nascent Christianity," in *Uncircumscribed Minds*, ed. Durham and Pruitt, 113–28.

12. "Loud o'er the rest Cremona's trump doth sound" (26), says Milton in "The Passion," paying tribute to Vida and the *Christiad*.

13. Cyril of Alexandria, *On the Gospel of John*, Book 5, 73:482.

14. "Opponitur huic, religionis quam sequimur dissimulatio. Qualis erat Nicodemi." *Works* 17:164–65.

15. *The Apocryphal New Testament*, 101.

16. Citations are taken from Vida, *Christiad*; translations are my own.

17. Samuel Fallon examines the problem that Milton confronts in depicting an unchanging God operating—through the Son—in time and narrative, principally in connection with the dialogue between God and the Son in book 3, in "Milton's Strange God: Theology and Narrative Form in Paradise Lost," 48; the problem, he suggests, becomes an interpretative crux for Satan at the moment of the Son's exaltation in book 5.

18. On Milton's form of Arianism, see Rumrich, "Milton's Arianism: Why It Matters," in *Milton and Heresy*, ed. Dobranski and Rumrich, 75–92; Gregory Chaplin, "Beyond Sacrifice: Milton and the Atonement," 354–69.

19. Chrysostom, *Homilies on the Gospel of Saint Matthew*, in *A Select Library of the Nicene and Post-Nicene Fathers of the Christian Church*, ed. Schaff, 10:43.

20. On linear versus cyclical ideas of time in Christian thought and in relationship to Milton's poems, see Tayler, *Milton's Poetry: Its Development in Time*, 8–17.

21. For the critical argument that the Son has been begotten *as* an angel, see Labriola, "'Thy Humiliation Shall Exalt'" and "The Son as an Angel in *Paradise Lost*," in *Milton in the Age of Fish*, ed. Lieb and Labriola, 105–13.

22. In *The Legitimacy of the Modern Age*, 594, Hans Blumenberg remarks on this problem in Christian thought from the beginnings of the religion: "the Hellenistic world had also developed the philosophical critique of the myth of the gods and their 'stories,' and for this critique the metamorphoses of myth were in essence a lie, deceitful deception, misuse of the power of a god. He who was supposed to have brought the final truth could not get involved in a dimension of such ambiguity." Milton's anti-Trinitarianism is one way out of the dilemma, but it opens up new problems for Satan.

23. See Pelikan, *The Emergence of the Catholic Tradition (100–600)*, 197–98; Labriola, "The Son as Angel." I am indebted to discussions with John Rogers on Milton's Christology.

24. Nohrnberg, "On Literature and the Bible," 36–38. See the description of the Greek gods in book 1 who are born out of heaven itself: "Titan Heaven's first born / With his enormous brood, and birthright seized / By younger Saturn, he from mightier Jove / His own and Rhea's son like measure found" (1.510–13). In this pagan genealogy, usurpation is at the basis of rulership, and Satan hopes himself to usurp God's throne.

25. In *Milton's God*, William Empson provocatively asserts that Satan "is talking standard republican theory" when he protests the regency of the Son: "How can one of us justly become King over the rest, and give us laws though we arrange our affairs better without such an institution? And if he could, how could this be an adequate reason … for him to seek to be worshipped as a God, by misusing our customary terms of honour?" (75–76). This will be the question that Adam, as we shall see below, addresses to the earthly conquerors and kings of books 11 and 12 (see 12.64–71). But Empson's view fails on two counts: like Satan, he treats God *as* one of those earthly kings, and despite some immediate qualifications, he downplays Satan's own monarchical ambitions that arise precisely from this category error. The prince of this world does not, pace Empson, repent "for having let himself be adored on the throne of Hell" (76), and he is hardly a "conscientious republican" (77).

26. Although he does not mention envy, Roland Mushat Frye gives a trenchant and memorable account of the nihilism of Milton's Satan in *God, Man, and Satan: Patterns of Christian Thought and Life in "Paradise Lost," "Pilgrim's Progress," and the Great Theologians*, 21–41.

27. Kerrigan remarks on this passage in *The Sacred Complex*, 172–73.

28. Bandello, *Tutte le opere di Matteo Bandello*, 1:41.

29. Tasso, *Tasso's Dialogues: A Selection with the Discourse of the Art of the Dialogue*, 162–63.

30. Samuel Taylor Coleridge heard an echo in the Father's begetting and anointing of the Son (5.600–615) of Duncan's promotion of Malcolm in *Macbeth* (1.4.35–42). "Messiah-Satan," he commented, on the Shakespearean scene that, in a break with the previous tanistry prevailing in Scotland, lifts a son over Macbeth and his fellow thanes. See *Coleridge's Writings on Shakespeare*, 192. Like God in *Paradise Lost*, Duncan promises that this exaltation of his son will be good for everyone: the "honour must / Not unaccompanied invest him only, / But signs of nobleness, like stars, shall shine / On all deservers."

31. Simmel, *The Sociology of Georg Simmel*, 197–98. For a socially conservative consideration of the problem of envy and equality, see Schoeck, *Envy: A Theory of Social Behaviour*, 231–56.

32. Simmel, *Sociology of Georg Simmel*, 197.

33. Bacon, *Essays*, 84–85.

34. The best and most thorough analysis of the analogy between Milton's God and earthly king is Davies, *Images of Kingship*. See also Frye, *Return of Eden*, 64–71, 108–15; Bennett, *Reviving Liberty: Radical Christian Humanism in Milton's Great Poems*, 33–58; Lewalski, "*Paradise Lost* and Milton's Politics," 141–68; and Nigel Smith, *Is Milton Better than Shakespeare?*, 86–131. For a discussion of the analogy between courtier and prince/human being and God, see Langer, *Divine and Poetic Freedom in the Renaissance: Nominalist Theology and Literature in France and Italy*, 51–83.

35. For Milton's equation of monarchy and idolatry, and for the relationship to rabbinic commentary of his "exclusive" view that republics are the only legitimate form of government, see Nelson, " 'Talmudical Commonwealthsmen' and the Rise of Republican Exclusivism," 809–35.

36. Revard, "Satan's Envy," 197: "Ironically enough, Satan's kingship is not patterned on the *real* kingship of either Messiah or God, but upon the *misconstrued definition* of kingship by which Satan has denounced Messiah." Revard emphasizes the tradition that the envy that caused Satan's fall was envy of the Son's kingship more than envy of his Incarnation or envy of the creation of human beings. For a defense of the satanic position that sees God indeed as the type of monarch whom Milton attacked in his republican writings, see Bryson, *The Tyranny of Heaven: Milton's Rejection of God as King*.

37. Broadbent describes Mammon as "a plutocrat co-opted to government, wondering what

all the political fuss is about." Broadbent, *Some Graver Subject*, 117. For Mammon as a type of hardworking New England colonist or Dutch republican, see Hoxby, *Mammon's Music*, 154–55, 174–77. For the political failure of Mammon's class, see Dzelzainis, "Milton's Classic Republicanism," in *Milton and Republicanism*, ed. Armitage, Himy, and Skinner, 3–24.

38. Stone, *The Crisis of the Aristocracy, 1558–1641*; Elias, *The Civilizing Process*, vol. 1, *The History of Manners* and vol. 2, *Power and Civility*.

39. The fight of the underdog David against Goliath in 1 Samuel 17:4–54 directly follows David's being taking up by Saul as his court harpist, 1 Samuel 16:14–23.

40. See Empson, *Milton's God*, 77, on Satan: "We also need to realize that he is a rippingly grand aristocrat." For a correction of Empson, see Davies, *Images of Kingship*, 127–63.

41. In *Images of Kingship*, Davies states that "God is shown as presiding over a court rich in chivalric motifs as an absolute ruler over a rigidly formulated and militaristic hierarchy dressed with medieval splendor according to degree" (129). I think one should remove "chivalric" and "militaristic" from this description. It is not a small quibble: only after Satan's rebellion, it appears, do the angels become soldiers.

42. This discussion draws on materials in Quint, "Duelling and Civility in Sixteenth-Century Italy," 231–78, especially 272–74. On the duel, see Kiernan, *The Duel in European History*; Billacois, *The Duel: Its Rise and Fall in Early Modern France*; Erspamer, *La biblioteca di don Ferrante: Duello e onore nella cutura del Cinquecento*; Muir, *Mad Blood Stirring: Vendetta and Faction in Friuli during the Renaissance*; Peltonen, "Francis Bacon, the Earl of Northampton, and the Jacobean Anti-Duelling Campaign," 1–28.

43. Carlyle, *The Life of Oliver Cromwell, With a Selection from His Letters and Speeches*, 126. Bacon specifically addresses the giving of the lie in his *The Charge touching duels*; see *Francis Bacon: The Major Works*, 310. For Touchstone, see *As You Like It* 5.4.50–104.

44. On this distinction and for a fine discussion of courtliness in *Paradise Lost*, see Schoenfeldt, "'Among Unequals What Society': Strategic Courtesy and Christian Humility in *Paradise Lost*," 69–90, especially 77. For critical reflections on the difficulty of representing worship and the humiliation of creatureliness, see Barnaby, "Cringing Before the Lord: Milton's Satan, Samuel Johnson, and the Anxiety of Worship," in *The Sacred and the Profane in English Renaissance Literature*, ed. Papazian, 321–44.

45. Romei, *Courtiers Academie*, 147–48. Bacon makes the related argument: "But much more it is to be deplored when so much noble and gentle blood shall be spilt upon such follies, as, if it were adventured in the field in service of the King and realm, were able to make the fortune of a day, and to change the fortune of a kingdom." *Francis Bacon*, 305.

46. Fish discusses how this episode already suggests the logic of the War in Heaven in *Surprised by Sin: The Reader in Paradise Lost*, 173–76.

47. Lieb, *Poetics of the Holy*, 297–304; on the humiliation of the good angels during the War in Heaven, see 277–82. For a discussion of how Milton's depiction of the War in Heaven takes a generally ironic attitude toward the battles of the English Civil War, see Bedford, "Milton's Military Heaven Revisited," 123–48. Of particular interest is Bedford's discussion on 136–37 of the "Lobsters," a parliamentary regiment impeded by their full-body armor, at the Battle of Roundway Down; both Milton's good and bad angels find their armor to be an encumbrance.

48. It may be indicative of Milton's discomfort with Jesus's example of the server at table, omitted from his citation of Luke 22 in *The Readie and Easie Way*, that there are no waiters at the heavenly banquet in book 5 that follows the proclamation of the exaltation of the Son. Everything happens in the passive voice: "all in circles as they stood, / Tables are set, and on a sudden piled / With angels' food ..." (631–33). No one clears or does the dishes.

49. Burrow, *Epic Romance*, 273; Michael Putnam, "The *Aeneid* and *Paradise Lost*: Ends and Conclusions," 387–410.

50. Compare the parallel evocation of Luke 22:25 to describe earthly conquerors in *Paradise Regained* 3.81–82: "and must be titled gods / Great benefactors of mankind." Alexander is alluded to in the following verses 84–87. "Plagues of men" echoes Milton's *First Defense*

of the English People, chapter 5, which terms Homer's Agamemnon a plague of his people, "pestem populi." See *CPW* 4.441; *Works* 7.312–13.

51. Milton's dialogue with *The City of God* in books 11–12 is understudied; Fowler's notes make little mention of it. For brief discussions, see Loewenstein, *Milton and the Drama of History: Historical Vision, Iconoclasm, and the Literary Imagination*, 95–96; Tayler, *Milton's Poetry: Its Development in Time*, 71–72. For Milton's interest in the bodily assumption of Enoch in relationship to his mortalist beliefs, see Kerrigan, "The Heretical Milton: From Assumption to Mortalism," 125–66.

52. *Sallust*, 20–23.

53. Augustine, *City of God*, 57.

54. On the polemic against the linking of patriarchy and kingship in these verses, specifically in response to Filmer, see Patterson, "His Singing Robes," 191.

55. "This paternal power continued monarchical to the Floud, and after the Floud to the confusion of *Babel* when Kingdomes were first erected, planted, or scattered over the face of the world; we find, Gen. 10.11. It was done by Colonies of whole families, over which, the prime Fathers had supream power, and were Kings, who were all the sons or grand-children of *Noah*, from whom they derived a fatherly and regall power over their families. Now if this supream power was settled and founded by God himself in the fatherhood, how is it possible for the people to have any right or title to alter and dispose of it otherwise?" Filmer, *The Anarchy of a Limited or Mixed Monarchy*, 7. In his *Concerning the Originall of Governments*, Filmer takes up Milton's contention in chapter 1 of the *First Defense* (*CPW* 4:327, *Works* 7:46) that kings and fathers are in fact very different, and that, even if we were to grant the analogy and think of a king as a kind of father, he should be held accountable if he kills his subject—sons. Filmer responds by first insisting that "every King that now is hath a paternall Empire, either by inheritance, or by translation or usurpation, so a Father and King may be all one." He continues, "A Father may die for the murther of his Son, where there is a superior Father to them both, or the right of such a supreme Father; but where there are only Father and Sons, no Sons can question the Father for the death of their brother: the reason why a King cannot be punished is not because he is excepted from punishment, or doth not deserve it, but because there is no superior to judge him, but God onely, to whom hee is reserved" (19).

56. Another possible reading: in the case of these biblical kings puissant deeds may be admirable when they are accompanied by piety; wealth may be well used when coupled with wisdom. The context of books 11 and 12 makes the ironic, antimonarchical construction of these verses more likely. David and Solomon, the "uxorious king" (1.444), are both subject to unflattering treatment in Milton's poetry and prose. On the criticism of David in *Paradise Regained* and its relationship to Stuart propaganda, see Quint, *Epic and Empire*, 325–34. Hoxby, *Mammon's Music*, 99–100, 164–65, describes how the comparison of Charles II to Solomon could praise him for his furthering of wealth and trade. For James I and Solomon, see Tate, "King James I and the Queen of Sheba," 561–85.

57. Summers, *The Muse's Method*, 208–10.

58. Leonard, *Naming in Paradise*, 56.

59. *City of God*, 482–83.

60. In *The Legitimacy of the Modern Age*, 207–26, Blumenberg suggests how the modern recognition of the purely material nature of the universe—not divinely disposed for human use and subject to human exploitation—leads to the scarcity predicted by Malthus. The intermediary development in Blumenberg's scheme is the rise of the modern state, identified with absolutism and given theoretical foundation in Hobbes's "state of nature." Here Blumenberg is anticipated by Burckhardt, who described the individualistic culture of Renaissance Italy as the reflection of its new state system. On the zero-sum game structure of this competitive individualism, see Kerrigan and Braden, *The Idea of the Renaissance*, 3–35. The history that is inaugurated in Milton's heaven at the beginning of time is a mirror, this chapter has suggested, of this envious modern age. Milton pushes back

against its implications by having Raphael assert to Adam, as we saw in chapter 4, that the universe, at least the part of it that Adam occupies, *is* made for human beings (8.98–99).

61. See chapter 6, note 40.

62. Milton describes the personified Wisdom of the book as the sister and playmate of the Muse Urania he invokes in book 7 (9–12).

Notes to Chapter 6

1. The wordplay is already present in Shakespeare; see Sonnet 93. See the commentary of John Leonard to 1.35 in his edition of *Paradise Lost*, 293, where "dis-Eve-d" would denote Satan's deprivation of Eve of her immortality, and again, 431, on 10.917. In *Paradise Regained*, Milton places "Eve" and "deceive" in successive verses three times (1.51–52; 2.141–42, 3.36–37); at least it is a verbal tic. On the classical "Dis," the underworld and its king, involved in Milton's usage, see the excellent chapter in Forsyth, *Satanic Epic*, 217–38.

2. Gallagher, *Milton, the Bible*, 49–130, connects the two passage in a chapter devoted to Milton's response to the tradition surrounding 1 Timothy 2:11–15; Burden, *The Logical Epic: A Study of the Argument of "Paradise Lost,"* 77–89, endorses Paul, who "rightly saw that Adam could not have been deceived at the moment he ate the Fruit" (89). Genesis 3, however, offers little evidence.

3. Ronald Levao describes Milton's exploration in *Paradise Lost* of "two of his own most cherished formal and ethical assumptions: that the self can be a 'true poem,' a composition, and patterne of the best and honorablest things' (*Apology for Smectymnus* in *CPW* 1:890), and that such perfection ought to ensure its natural congruence with a virtuous other." See Levao, "'Among Unequals': *Paradise Lost* and the Forms of Intimacy," 98. Rosenblatt, commenting on the first words of Milton's *Of Education* (1644), connects the first sentence of the pamphlet —"no purpose or respect should sooner move us than simply the love of God and of mankind"—to *Paradise Lost*: "'Faith and virtue' and 'love of God and of mankind' appear in Milton's *De Doctrina Christiana* (*CPW* 6:353) as the two commands in paradise beyond natural law: those concerning the tree of knowledge and marriage. These are precise Edenic counterparts to postlapsarian dispensations." See *Milton's Selected Poetry and Prose*, ed. Rosenblatt, 320.

4. Howard, "'The Invention' of Milton's 'Great Argument': A Study in of the Logic of 'God's Ways to Men,'" 149–73.

5. Kerrigan, *Sacred Complex* and "The Irrational Coherence of *Samson Agonistes*," 217–32.

6. Kerrigan, "The Irrational Coherence," 228, suggests that Milton's poems in the 1671 volume "halve his life, *Paradise Regained* being, as psychic autobiography, primarily about his youth and *Samson Agonistes* primarily about his maturity and old age." My thinking is indebted to the different tracing of Milton's (psycho)biography in *Paradise Regained* by James Nohrnberg, "*Paradise Regained* by One Greater Man."

7. On the dynamic nature of the state of innocence that allows Adam and Eve to develop in virtue, see Lewalski, "Innocence and Experience in Milton's Eden," in *New Essays on "Paradise Lost,"* ed. Kranidas, 86–117.

8. The dramatic action of the Separation Scene is analyzed by Nyquist, "Reading the Fall: Discourse in Drama in *Paradise Lost*," 209–14, and Bennett, *Reviving Liberty: Radical Christian Humanism in Milton's Great Poems*, 94–118.

9. McColley, "Free Will and Obedience in the Separation Scene of *Paradise Lost*," 103–20, subsequently developed in McColley, *Milton's Eve*, 172–81; Blackburn, "'Uncloistered Virtue': Adam and Eve in Milton's Paradise," 119–37; Revard, "Eve and the Doctrine of Responsibility in *Paradise Lost*," 69–78; Ulreich, "'Argument Not Less But More Heroic': Eve as the Hero of *Paradise Lost*," in *"All in All": Unity, Diversity and the Miltonic Perspective*, ed. Durham and Pruitt, 67–82.

10. In his satirical vignette in *Areopagitica*, Milton compares the Christian who lets outside authorities determine his belief to a rich man who employs "some factor to whose care and credit he may commit the whole managing of his religious affairs." *CPW* 2:544.

11. On Eve and Abdiel, see Benet, "Abdiel and the Son in the Separation Scene," 129–43.

12. Campbell and Corns, *John Milton: Life, Work, Thought*, 60.

13. On the coordination of these episodes in the *Faerie Queene*, see O'Connell, *Mirror and Veil: The Historical Dimension of Spenser's Faerie Queene*, 101–7; see also Watkins, *The Spectre of Dido: Spenser and Virgilian Epic*, 114–19.

14. Klemp, "Milton's Pastourelle Vision in *Paradise Lost*," 257–71; Paden, *The Medieval Pastourelle*; Jones, *The Pastourelle*.

15. Manley, *Literature and Culture*, 487.

16. On Milton's continuing concern with the parable of the talents, see Haskin, *Milton's Burden of Interpretation*, 29–117.

17. For the tradition of pastoral elegy, see Lambert, *Placing Sorrow: A Study of the Pastoral Elegy Convention from Theocritus to Milton*.

18. Kahn offers a reading of these lines and of the antinomies in *Comus* of "the force of grace and the force of individual virtue" (202) in her chapter "Virtue and Virtù in *Comus*," in *Machiavellian Rhetoric: From the Counter-Reformation to Milton*, 185–208.

19. This self-approval can be linked to the virtuous self-esteem that Raphael counsels Adam to seek for himself at 8.571–72: "oft times nothing profits more / Than self-esteem." Scodel, *Excess and the Mean*, 269–84, discusses this passage and others in connection with Milton's description in *The Reason of Church Government* of the "honest shame, or call it if you will an esteem, whereby men bear an inward reverence toward their own person" (*CPW* 1:841). Scodel traces the classical and Christian traditions of the idea and its role in *Paradise Lost*, in dialogue and at times in disagreement with Quint, *Epic and Empire*, 283–99; see also, Guillory, "Milton, Narcissism, Gender: On the Genealogy of Male Self-Esteem," in *Critical Essays on John Milton*, ed. Kendrick, 194–234; and Strier, "Milton against Humility," in *Religion and Culture in Renaissance England*, ed. McEachern and Shuger, 258–86. Kerrigan and Braden, *The Idea of the Renaissance* (212), argue that Milton fulfills his ambition to fame by denying it to Eve. The action and meaning of *Paradise Lost* hinge to a large degree on finding a balance between satanic pride on the one hand and, on the other, that "just honoring of ourselves," which *The Reason of Church Government* passage declares to be a "principle of all godly and virtuous actions," second only to the love of God itself.

20. As has been well noted, the cave and its waters recall the cave of the nymphs described in the landscape of Ithaca in the *Odyssey* (13.102–12) and allegorized by the third-century Neoplatonist Porphyry as the entrance by which the human soul enters into material existence, a gateway of birth.

21. See Rumrich, *Matter of Glory*, 79–81; on God's seeking glory for himself, 131–46.

22. For the Jesus of *Paradise Regained* as the new Adam, see Lewalski, *Milton's Brief Epic: The Genre, Meaning, and Art of Paradise Regained*, 165–82, 222–27; Frye, *Return of Eden*, 118–43.

23. On these scenes of lovemaking in *Paradise Lost* and *Iliad* 14, see Nyquist, "Textual Overlapping and Delilah's Harlot-Lap," in *Literary Theory/Renaissance Texts*, ed. Parker and Quint, 355–69.

24. *Samson Agonistes*, 562–72.

25. Annabel Patterson pointed out to me the correspondence, which I discuss above in chapter 2, p.45, between the description of Belial and the passage in *The Reason of Church Government*. The accusatory words of the early treatise seem to have haunted Milton.

26. The parallel is noted by Nyquist, "Reading the Fall," 212.

27. Milton's potentially contradictory ideas about fame and his desire to affirm in *Paradise Regained* "the lasting recognition of true merit" were lucidly noted nearly a century ago by Hanford in "The Temptation Motive in Milton," in *John Milton, Poet and Humanist: Essays by James Holly Hanford*, ed. Diekhoff, 253–55. They are forcefully restated by Miller in "Milton's *Paradise Regained*," *Explicator* 56.1 (1997): 14–17; see also Strier, "Milton against Humility," 277–78. Other commentators take a softer line: Kermode, "Milton's Hero," 325–26; Stein, "The Kingdoms of the World: *Paradise Regained*," 114–16; Lewalski, *Milton's Brief Epic*, 227–56; Bennett, *Reviving Liberty*, 173–79.

28. These Johannine passages are variously crucial to Milton's Arian argument for the creation

and subordination of the Son in *On Christian Doctrine* 1.5. See *CPW* 6:214–15, 220, 230; on the Son's glorification, see 6:272–78.

29. Virgil's hymn to Hercules smacks of euhemerism, placed as it is in book 8 in juxtaposition with the later depiction of Augustus at Actium, accompanied by the star of his deified father, Julius Caesar. Earlier in the *Aeneid* in book 6 (130–31, the Cumaean Sibyl's description of those sons of gods whose burning virtue has lifted them to heaven ["ardens euexit ad aethera uirtus, / dis geniti"])—a passage that we have seen Milton echo and imitate above in the *Mansus*, 95–96: "in aethera divum / Quo labor et mens pura vehunt, atque ignea virtus"—and who have been able to descend to and return from the underworld is similarly juxtaposed with Anchises's later description of "Augustus Caesar, Diui genus" (6.791), whose extension of Rome's empire outdoes the deeds of the divine sons Hercules and Bacchus (6.801–5). The strong suggestion is that the deification of Hercules and of Augustus is a metaphor for the *fame* that great conquerors achieve for themselves and that allows them to survive death. That they become the objects of hero and emperor cults would only confirm Euhemerus's recursive argument that all the gods began as human heroes or kings. Virgil seems indeed to conflate power and fame in his first description of Augustus in *Aeneid* 1:287, "whose rule will be bound by the Ocean, his fame by the stars" (imperium Oceano, famam qui terminet astris). Milton will apply these terms to the Son in *Paradise Lost*: he will "bound his reign / With earth's wide bounds, his glory with the heavens" (12.370–71). This *glory* is otherworldly and worldly, too.

30. For the first sense of indivisibility, applied to the Genesis marriage formula, "And they shall be one flesh," see *Tetrachordon*, in *CPW* 2:605: "These words also inferre that there ought to be an individualty in Mariage." For the second sense of an individual person, see *Animadversions* 13, in *CPW* 1:712. See Stein, *Answerable Style: Essays on "Paradise Lost,"* 110–13; Levao, "'Among Unequals,'" 94.

31. A defense of Adam against the narrator's judgment is mounted by James Grantham Turner, *One Flesh: Paradisal Marriage and Sexual Relations in the Age of Milton*, 288–89.

32. Fowler, note to 9.913–16, cites, inter alia, Rosenblatt, *Torah and Law in Paradise Lost*, 196. On the sexual intimacy that seems to add a dimension to human marriage for which God or the poet cannot fully account, see Rogers, "Transported Touch: The Fruit of Marriage in *Paradise Lost*." On the repetition of the Genesis marriage formula, "bone of my bones, flesh of my flesh," as part of a story of Eve's (and woman's) willing subjection to Adam, see Nyquist, "The Genesis of Gendered Subjectivity in the Divorce Tracts and in *Paradise Lost*," 99–127.

33. *Homophrosyne* appears only one other place in the *Odyssey* 15.198, when Telemachus speaks of his concord of mind with Peisistratus, the son of Nestor.

34. Homer, *Homeri quae extant omnia Ilias, Odyssea, Batrachomyomachia, Hymni, Poemata aliquot*. See Fletcher, "Milton's Homer," 229–32.

35. We have observed that the luncheon that Eve serves up to Raphael in book 5 locates this scene of hospitality in the epic tradition.

> Whatever Earth all-bearing mother yields
> In India east or west, or middle shore
> In Pontus or the Punic coast, or where
> Alcinous reigned, fruit of all kinds ...
> (5.338–41)

Alcinous, king of the Phaeacians on the island of Scheria, entertained Odysseus as a guest at a banquet in books 8–12 of the *Odyssey*; Dido banqueted Aeneas in Carthage on the Punic coast in books 1–3 of the *Aeneid*; Aeëtes banqueted Jason—although grudgingly— in his Black Sea (Pontic) Kingdom of Colchis in book 5 of the *Argonautica* of Valerius Flaccus. Milton indicates these models in reverse order of their dates and succession in the literary tradition that goes back to Homer. The Phaeacian episode of the *Odyssey* is the most important epic model for books 5–8 of *Paradise Lost*. Before he narrates the story of his own wanderings to Alcinous and the assembled nobles of Scheria, Odysseus is entertained by the bard Demodocus with three songs—inset poems within the larger epic. The first (*Odys.* 8.72–82) and last (8.499–366) retell the Fall of Troy and make Odysseus weep at the memory of war. The second (8.266–366) recounts, in a humorous key, the adultery of Aphrodite and Ares and their being caught out and ensnared by the cuckolded Hephaestus. This latter story of immoral behavior among the gods, which inside the poem might make Odysseus think about the possible infidelity of Penelope, created scandal among ancient readers. As was usual in such cases, the episode was allegorized: Heraclitus, the first-century allegorist, declares that it is a cosmogonic fable and that Aphrodite and Ares represent the Empedoclean principles of love and strife through and by which the world was created. Virgil appears to have been aware of this reading. In the fourth *Georgic*, he depicts the nymph Clymene singing about Mars and Venus—the Roman versions of Ares and Aphrodite—and of the loves of the gods going back to ancient Chaos (*Georgics* 4.345–47): the history of the world from its creation. More pointedly, Virgil presents a version of Demodocus's songs in the first book of the *Aeneid*, in the analogous situation of the reception of Aeneas in Dido's Carthage. First, Aeneas famously weeps, like Odysseus, when he sees scenes of the Trojan War depicted on the walls of the temple that Dido has built to Juno (*Aen.* 1.453–93). Second, at the banquet itself and at the end of book 1, just before he retells in books 2 and 3 the travails and journeys that have brought him to Carthage, Aeneas hears the bard Iopas sing of the moon and the sun and the origin of human beings and beasts, of the stars and constellations, a song of didactic cosmogony (1.740–46). Valerius Flaccus condenses his models by describing *reliefs* on the walls of the Colchian temple that first portray the sun and the moon and then depict, prophetically, the deeds of Jason and the Argonauts both before and after their coming to the realm of Aeëtes (*Arg.* 5.410–54). What Milton takes from this pattern, established at Alcinous's banquet and subsequently varied by the ensuing epic tradition, is that the epic banquet scene should contain three elements: on the host's part two kinds of songs, one of them retelling events of epic warfare, the other a cosmogony; on the part of the guest and epic hero a retrospective narrative of his previous experiences. Milton works his own variation on this pattern and tradition, for his hero Adam is the host, who recounts to Raphael his life story from the moment of his creation to his marriage with Eve (8.249–559), while Raphael the guest tells him first of the epic War in Heaven (5.561–6.912) and then, in a second narrative, recounts the story of the six days of the Creation of the universe (7.110–640). Milton has not only changed who, host or guest, is to tell which kind of story, but he has greatly altered the proportions of the stories themselves. Adam's previous life has admittedly been a limited one, a matter of weeks, and he takes up only three hundred lines to tell what it takes Odysseus four and Aeneas two whole books to recount. The bard's songs in Homer, which run from a dozen to a hundred verses, now have expanded: the War in Heaven runs across books 5 and 6 while the Creation takes up book 7. Milton has managed to incorporate both a martial, if at times mock-heroic, epic and a hexameral cosmogonic epic into his larger poem. One reason for this disproportion is ready to hand: the protagonist of both Raphael's epics is the Son, vanquisher of Satan and demiurge of the universe. At the center of *Paradise Lost*—especially in the revised twelve-book version of 1674 that we normally read—Raphael's twin narratives break into the story of the poem's human hero to celebrate its divine hero, the second Adam. Books 6 and 7 each feature an angelic hymn near their conclusions; book 6 honors the Son (6.886–92), while book 7 moves from hymning the Son (7.566–73) to climax with praise of the Father himself (7.601–32).

36. Milton had aspired to the role of Demodocus since his verses in *At a Vacation Exercise in the College*, written when he was nineteen:

> And last of kings and queens and heroes old,
> Such as the wise Demodocus once told
> In solemn songs at king Alcinous' feast,
> While sad Ulysses's soul and all the rest

> Are held with his melodious harmony
> In willing chains and sweet captivity.
> *(47–52)*

In this instance, too, in the immediately preceding verses, Milton pairs epic heroism with cosmogony as possible poetic subjects: "Then sing of secret things that came to pass / When beldam Nature in her cradle was" (45–46). The third subject Milton announces is theophany or divinity itself.

37. Kerrigan, *Sacred Complex*, 207–62, argues for the literal transmutation of food into thought and poetry in *Paradise Lost*.

38. The reciprocity between Abraham's hospitality and divine nourishment is spelled out in the preface, 39–68 to the *Psychomachia* of Prudentius, which combines the visit of the angels at Mamre with the episode that precedes it, the bringing of bread and wine by the high priest Melchizedek (Gen. 14:18–19), a traditional prefiguring of the Eucharist: "mox ipse Christus, qui sacerdos verus est, / parente inenarribili atque uno satus, / cibum beatis offerens victoribus / parvam pudici cordis intrabit casam, / monstrans honorem Trinitatis hospitae" (59–63; Then Christ himself, who is the true priest, born of a Father unutterable and one, bringing food for the blessed victors, will enter the humble abode of the pure heart and give it the privilege of entertaining the Trinity). Prudentius, *Prudentius*, ed. Thomson, 1:278–79. In his *De Abraham* 1.40, Ambrose compares the calf that Abraham serves up to the angels (Gen. 18:7) to the Paschal lamb (12:5–6); see Saint Ambrose of Milan, *On Abraham*, 22–23; and *De Abraham*, 2.2:78–81. For similar arguments, including the idea that the three cakes that Sarah bakes prefigure the human race descended from the sons of Noah, which will be "brought together into the one bread of the body of Christ," see Rabanus Maurus, *Commentariorum in Genesim Libri Quatuor* 2.21, in *Patrologiae cursus completus, Series Latina*, 107:551. In a thirteenth-century Psalter, MS. K.26, Saint John's College, Cambridge, Abraham is depicted offering three bread wafers and wine to the three angels depicted as the Trinity: the caption reads, "De Abraham offerente panem et vinū t[ri]bus angelis." See Brieger, *English Art, 1216–1307*, plate 67b. See also Brenk, *Die Frühchristlichen Mosaiken in S. Maria Maggiore zu Rom*, 61; Brenk acknowledges the Eucharistic overtones of the scene, but argues that they are peripheral to its interpretation.

39. Schwartz, "Real Hunger: Milton's Version of the Eucharist," 1–17, argues that Eden offers a version of a lost natural fullness, "materiality without violence and hierarchy" (13), to whose apocalyptic restoration the sacrament of the Lord's Supper (her use of "eucharist" is non-Miltonic), instituted by the sacrifice of Christ, can only point but not fulfill in history; Schwartz corrects the satirical reading by King, "Miltonic Transubstantiation," 41–58.

40. Satan's language picks up too, but in a parodic mode, the language of communion. The dream that Satan infuses into the sleeping Eve parodies in advance Raphael's prediction of a gradual and gradated ascent—as Adam responds to the angel, "By steps we may ascend to God" (5.512)—and substitutes for this long process of physical and mental digestion the quick fix of the forbidden fruit: "Taste this, and be henceforth among the gods / Thy self a goddess" (5.77–78). Satan falsely argues that the fruit forbidden to humans must therefore be a kind of angelic food, "as only fit / For gods" (5.69–70), but that there is no reason it should not be shared: "since good, the more / *Communicated*, more abundant grows" (5.71–72). The loaded language not only substitutes the forbidden fruit for the communion meal, but it also anticipates Adam's description of the plenty of Eden that he and Eve are to share with Raphael: "where nature multiplies / Her fertile growth, and by disburdening grows / More fruitful ..." (5.318–20). In the story of the War in Heaven that Raphael recounts, communion is parodied in Satan's naming his royal seat, "The Mountain of the Congregation called" (5.766), but this structure, "as a mount / Raised on mount with pyramids and towers" (5.757–58), suggests the typology of Egypt and Babel, the latter traditionally associated as it is here with the classical giants who piled Mount Pelion on Mount Ossa. The Tower of Babel is the emblem not of unity but of dispersal

and, as book 12 will put it in an echo of this book 5 passage, "the work Confusion named" (12.62). Satan is first introduced by Raphael as "Contemptuous" (5.671), and the pun suggests that the union Satan creates among his crew is their common temptation; Abdiel later speaks of a "contagion" (5.880).

41. For analogous and admirably concise arguments, see Rumrich, *Matter of Glory*, 105–6.

42. See Fowler's note to 8.384–89.

43. Levao, "'Among Unequals,'" 96.

44. Ibid. On gender hierarchy in *Paradise Lost*, and more general discussion of the marital relationship and household of Adam and Eve, see Scodel, *Excess and the Mean*, 255–84.

45. The chapter summary on 1 Corinthians 12 in the 1560 Geneva Bible, "The diversitie of the giftes of the holie God oght to be used to the edifying of Christs Church 12 As the members of mans bodie serve to the use of one another," along with that Bible's summary of the whole Pauline letter that describes how Paul "behaved him self skilfully, according to the foundation (which is Christ) and exhorteth others to make the end proportionable to the beginning … seeing they are the Temple of God," provide the metaphors for the last sections of Milton's *Areopagitica*, which proclaim "some new and great period" in the Church. *CPW* 2:553–70.

46. On Milton's use of the negative and double negative, see Patterson, *Milton's Words*, 165–95.

47. *Areopagitica* intimates at times that this church is being realized in London itself—"this vast city, a city of refuge," which, as a kind of New Jerusalem replaces the temple—"I saw no temple therein" (Rev. 21:22), and which is "prepared as a bride adorned for her husband" (Rev. 21:2). *CPW* 2:553–54.

48. In an essay that succinctly spells out the case against Adam, John C. Ulreich observes that, in a perfect imitation of the Son, Adam "might offer to die *for* Eve rather than *with* her"; "'Sufficient to Have Stood': Adam's Responsibility in Book IX," 41. Choosing to die with her is impressive nonetheless. The superiority of charity—modeled on Christ's sacrifice for a fallen humanity—over classical heroism is the subject of a brief treatise of Tasso, *Della virtù eroica e della carità: Opere di Torquato Tasso colle controversie della Gerusalemme*, 11:168–84. For a brief discussion, see Kermode, "The Cave of Mammon," 80–83.

49. Cf. *Aen.* 2.744; 4.279–82, where Aeneas respectively confronts the ghost of Creusa who bids him farewell and the god Mercury who tells him he must leave Dido. Aeneas also stands voiceless and with his limbs chilled at *Aen.* 1.92 (when the storm winds attack his fleet), and 3.29–30, 48 (before the speaking tree Polydorus), but the context of Adam's beholding the fallen Eve suggests that we think of him as an Aeneas faced with the loss of the women he has loved. On further allusions, which reverse the Virgilian scenarios so that Adam and Eve may remain together, see chapter 7, pp. 219–23.

50. See Benet, "'All in All': The Threat of Bliss,"; 48–66; McColley, "'All in All': The Individuality of Creatures in *Paradise Lost*," 21–38.

51. In contradistinction to the argument of Schwartz, "Real Hunger," 14, perhaps applicable to Adam and Eve *before* the Fall, that gives priority to obedience.

52. Derrida, *De la grammatologie*, 208, where Derrida discusses writing itself as a "supplement" to the meaning it is supposed to reproduce. I am indebted to Patricia Parker's development of this Derridean idea into the feminist argument of "Coming Second: Woman's Place," in *Literary Fat Ladies: Rhetoric, Gender, Property*, 178–233; for *Paradise Lost*, see 191–201. A similar argument is made by Nyquist in "Gynesis, Genesis, Exegesis and Milton's Eve," in *Cannibals, Witches, and Divorce: Estranging the Renaissance*, 159–60.

53. Rogers has described, apropos of the human history narrated in the last two books of *Paradise Lost*, a double vision of divine constraint and human freedom that nonetheless moves from "the theocentric to the anthropocentric basis of causation" (176) in his chapter "Milton and the Mysterious Terms of History," in *The Matter of Revolution*, 144–76. On a Miltonic strain of antinomianism that both leads to the Fall and to postlapsarian freedom, see Bennett, *Reviving Liberty*, 94–118; Bennett notes, 118, that it is Eve, in the reconciliation of the first couple in book 10, "who 'takes the lead'" into praxis, opening the road to postlapsarian liberty.

54. Parker, "Coming Second." Nyquist, "Gynesis, Genesis," contends that Milton's placement of Adam's account of the creation of Eve in book 8 of *Paradise Lost*, four books later than Eve's own account in book 4, is determined by his desire not "to risk allowing her to appear as the necessary and hence, in a certain sense, superior creature suggested by the logic of the supplement, undeniably set in motion by Adam's self-confessed 'single imperfection'" (192). I acknowledge the force of this critical observation and I do not question—how could one?—that *Paradise Lost* articulates a hierarchy of genders; yet, at the same time, I argue that, in a countercurrent of ideas and feeling, Milton gives the last word of the poem to Eve and to the marital love and charity that now seem attached to her rather than to Adam—and sets in motion "the logic of the supplement." Nyquist notes that in Milton's Christian culture, "the manifold dynamics of this logic are most clearly at work in hermeneutical reflections on the relations of the New to the Old Testament" (159–60).

55. Johnson, "Milton's Blank Verse Sonnets," 129–53, 143–45; Nardo, *Milton's Sonnets and the Ideal of Community*.

56. The Ruth echo is noted by Bush, ed., *Complete Poetic Works of John Milton*, 458; Leonard, ed., *Paradise Lost*, 452.

57. Eve and Michael's speeches may be related *formally*; Johnson, "Milton's Blank Verse Sonnets," 134, suggests that Michael's reply to Adam (12.574–87) is also sonnet-length; he subsequently, 143–44, connects Michael's speech to Eve's final words in the epic.

Notes to Chapter 7

1. In his notes to his edition of *Paradise Lost*, 428, John Leonard would save appearances by arguing that when "Adam saw / Already in part" of the "growing miseries" consequent on the Fall (10.715–16), he was anticipating them, and that the wording implies that "Sin and Death have not yet entered our universe, and Satan has not yet left it. Satan is still in Paradise, eavesdropping, at the end of book x." But these growing miseries depend on the actions of Sin and Death and the reaction of God: there would be nothing for Adam to see.

2. Tillyard, "The Crisis of *Paradise Lost*," 8–52, 49.

3. The claim of continuity between imperial and papal Rome was long-standing. Stinger, *The Renaissance in Rome*, 235–91, offers a valuable account of the modern permutations it underwent in the papal ideology of the fifteenth and sixteenth centuries.

4. While Satan's conferral of "matchless might / Issuing from me" (10.404–5) on Sin and Death recall God's similar bestowing of power on the Son (3.317–43), his parting injunction, "go and be strong" (10.409), echoes the parting words of Raphael to Adam at the end of book 8: "Be strong, live happy, and love" (8.633).

5. Mary Powell had literally disappeared from sight when she returned to her father's house. She died in 1652 around the same time that Milton became totally blind.

6. Quintilian singles out the simile to describe the power of his ideal orator in the *Institutio Oratoria* 12.1.27. For a reading that argues for the ironic cross-purposes of the simile, see Quint, "Virgil's Doublecross: Chiasmus and the *Aeneid*," 273–300.

7. Fowler, notes to 7.210–15 and 10.289–93, comments on the similarity of Virgil's Neptune to both the pacifying Son in book 7 and trident-bearing Death in book 10.

8. For the parallel to the Son's restoration, by his command and voice, of the terrain of heaven that the War in Heaven has begun to turn into Chaos, 6.781–84, see chapter 3, pp. 79–80.

9. Tillyard pointed out the relationship between the two scenes of creation in "The Causeway from Hell to the World of *Paradise Lost*," 266–70. Lieb offers a rich discussion in *The Dialectics of Creation*, 172–83.

10. The speech of Calgacus/Galgacus is briefly recalled by Milton in book 2 of *The History of Britain*; see CPW 5:1.89.

11. Lewalski, *Paradise Lost and the Rhetoric of Literary Forms*, 107, reads the bridge as a triumphal arch, and later, 162–63, notes the contrast of the triumph of the Son to Satan's

aborted triumph. See Davies, *Images of Kingship*, 9, and, more generally, 89–126; for an earlier version of her argument, see Davies, "Triumph and Anti-Triumph: Milton's Satan and the Roman Emperors in *Paradise Lost*," 385–98.

12. There is still another Caesarian project involved in this complex of images. The Araxes indignant at its bridge in the *Aeneid* echoes Virgil's own poetry, his description in the *Georgics* of the breakwater that Augustus's general Agrippa built at the mouth of the Lucrine Lake against the sea: "an memorem portus Lucrinoque addita claustra / atque *indignatum* magnis stridoribus *aequor*, / Iulia qua ponto longe sonat unda refuso / Tyrrhenusque fretis immittitur aestus Auernis?" (2.161–64; or shall I tell of our harbors and the dam joined to the Lucrine, and of the indignant sea that roars greatly, where the Julian waves resound with the noise of the sea being beaten back, and the Tyrrhenian billows are channelled into the straits of Avernus). Milton seems to be recalling these lines in his description of Chaos as a "rebounding surge"—"ponto ... refuso"—assailing the bridge that Sin and Death build over it at 10.417. Note the proximity to Avernus (hell).

13. P. *Vergilii Maronis Opera, quae quidem extant, omnia*, 1359.

14. On the War in Heaven and Virgil's depiction of Actium, see Quint, *Epic and Empire*, 41–45; on the dimension of theomachy and gigantomachy in Virgil's Actium, see Hardie, *Vergil's Aeneid*, 97–110.

15. Milton would have known through Suetonius (*Augustus* 94) of the dynastic myth that Augustus was the son of Apollo. It is not clear that the myth was already current when Virgil wrote the *Aeneid*. See Galinsky, *Augustan Culture*, 215–20.

16. In Vida's *Christiad*, 6.701–7, the return of Christ to heaven at his ascension is directly compared in simile to a triumph by a victorious Roman consul.

17. See Sims, "A Greater than Rome: The Inversion of a Virgilian Symbol from Camoens to Milton," 333–44.

18. Compare *Paradise Regained* 4.184, where Jesus contests Satan's claim that he has been given the kingdoms of the world, and asserts that the devil has instead usurped them: "Other *donation* none thou canst produce." It is the only other appearance of the word in Milton's poetry. Milton discusses the Donation of Constantine in *Of Reformation, CPW* 1:552–60, where he includes his own translations of passages from Dante, Petrarch, and Ariosto that condemn the Donation. See Stinger, *The Renaissance in Rome*, 248–54, on the survival of the Donation in papal ideology in spite of its exposure as an eighth-century forgery by Lorenzo Valla in 1440.

19. Northrop Frye remarks: "The heaven of *Paradise Lost*, with God the supreme sovereign and the angels in a state of unquestioning obedience to his will, can only be set up on earth inside the individual's mind. The free man's mind is a dictatorship of reason obeyed by the will without argument: we go wrong only when we take these conceptions of kingship and service of freedom as *social* models. Absolute monarchs and their flunkeys on earth always follow the model of hell, not of heaven." *Return of Eden*, 111. For the contrast to Dante, see 109.

20. Quilligan observes Satan's hissing in *Milton's Spenser: The Politics of Reading*, 114.

21. Lieb, *Dialectics of Creation*, 123.

22. On this lore, see Fontenrose, *Python*, 70–93. For the relation of the tradition of Python to Spenser's Error, see Nohrnberg, *The Analogy of "The Faerie Queene*," 135–51; Nohrnberg, 145, discusses Milton's use of the figure of Python in *The Reason of Church Government*.

23. The correspondence is noted by Kerrigan, Rumrich, and Fallon in their note to 1.767–75 in their edition of *Paradise Lost*.

24. When Satan reaches earth in book 4 of *Paradise Lost*, horror and doubt "from the bottom stir / The hell within him" (4.19–20). There may be another echo here of Virgil's storm raising the sea "a sedibus imis" that we have seen in the description of the Son calming Chaos at 7.213. Satan would thus contain his own Virgilian sea of stormy passion within him, equivalent to hell, in the same way Adam does, reinforcing the similarity between the two characters in their fallenness. Milton's description of Adam at 10.718 may itself look back at Virgil's own internalization of the the storm that opens the *Aeneid* within its

hero, the description of Aeneas in book 8 tossing on a great sea of cares—"magno curarum fluctuat aestu" (*Aen.* 8.19).

25. Tillyard, "The Crisis of *Paradise Lost.*" Wilson presents an important rereading of the scene in *Mocked with Death*, 164–206.

26. Shoulson, *Milton and the Rabbis*, 117–31; Summers, *The Muse's Method*, 178–84; Shuellenberger, "Wrestling with the Angel: *Paradise Lost* and Feminist Criticism," 76. For a discussion of the echo of Virgil's Nisus—"me, me adsum, qui feci, in me convertite ferrum" (*Aen.* 9.427)—see Lewalski, *"Paradise Lost" and the Rhetoric of Literary Forms*, 116–17; Chaplin, "Beyond Sacrifice," 362–67; Whittington, "Vergil's Nisus and the Language of Self-Sacrifice in *Paradise Lost*," 586–606. See also Green, "Softening the Stony: Deucalion, Pyrrha and the Process of Regeneration in *Paradise Lost*," 9–21.

27. Ronald Levao comments that Adam's choice to fall with Eve "tests a difficult honesty: our admission that Adam's choice is one we might *not* have made. We might well have shrunk under the threat of incalculable Paternal wrath and slunk (to use that Miltonic word) behind the shelter of piety, hoping that if heartfelt motives could not excuse Adam's disobedience, ignoble ones would not be held against us." Levao, "'Among Unequals,'" 102. For the measured counterargument, see Ulreich, "'Sufficient to Have Stood.'"

28. Seneca, *Phoenissae* 153; *Epistulae morales* 70.14.

29. I am indebted to conversations with Stephen Fallon and James Nohrnberg, who pointed out this symmetry and its implications to me. Wilson, *Mocked with Death*, 202, notes how Michael's promise of a "paradise within thee, happier far" (12.587) echoes not only the "far happier place" (12.464) of the new heaven and new earth of the Last Judgment, but also the annihilation, "happier far / Than miserable to have eternal being" (2.97–98), which Moloch sought in book 2. Perhaps, Sam Bendinelli has pointed out to me, the choice Adam and Eve make to live is not so free. Adam reasons that suicide would lead to further punishment: God would "make death live in us" (10.1028). This possible second death would be the equivalent of what, before the Fall, has been that mysterious thing called death whose "after-bands," Eve had reasoned earlier as she chose to eat the forbidden fruit, would limit her "inward freedom" (9.761–62). Some degree of coercion, a fear of unknown consequences, remains in place.

30. Annabel Patterson has analyzed how the meaning of death changes over the course of *Paradise Lost* in *Milton's Words*, 94–113.

31. On work in *Paradise Lost*, see Goodman, "'Wasted Labor'? Milton's Eve, the Poet's Work, and the Challenge of Sympathy," 415–46.

32. For a related discussion of the posture of prostration, see Schoenfeldt, "'Among Unequals What Society?'" 69–90.

33. See Tillyard, "The Crisis," 49–50.

34. The regenerate Adam and Eve are compared at the opening of book 11 to Deucalion and Pyrrha rescued from the universal flood (*PL* 11.8–15); the book ends with still another rescue from drowning, the survival of humanity, the race of Adam and Eve, in the family of Noah.

35. One can contrast Satan's first survey and recognition of his new condition in the second death of hell, "where peace / And rest can never dwell" (1.65–66), and his subsequent attempt to get "off the tossing of these fiery waves, / There rest, if any rest can harbor there" (1.184–85).

36. For Eve as Duessa *and* Una, see Bond, *Spenser, Milton, and the Redemption of the Epic Hero*, 81–84. The still innocent Eve is implicitly compared to Circe at 9.521–22.

37. Kerrigan, *Sacred Complex*, 205.

38. This comparison of Rinaldo and Armida to Adam and Eve was suggested to me by the late Phillip Damon.

39. "I am with childe, and yive my child his lyf," pleads Dido to Aeneas in Chaucer's *Legend of Good Women* (1323). She has already abased herself: "She falleth him to fote, and swoneth there / Dischevele" (1314–15); compare Milton's Eve: "And tresses all disordered, at his feet / Fell humble" (10.911–12); Chaucer, *The Workes of Our Ancient and Learned Poet*

Geoffrey Chaucer, fol. 191v. The last words of Tasso's Armida, "Ecco l'ancilla tua" (*GL* 20.136.7) echo the Virgin Mary at the Annunciation; Tasso, as my former student John Hill pointed out to me, may glance at the idea that this rescued Dido figure, too, is in a family way.

40. See chapter 6, note 49.

41. Goodman, " 'Wasted Labor'?," 432, notes the echo. A full discussion, beginning with the question of why Milton should "translate Aeneas's last words to Dido in Adam's first words to Eve?" (112) is presented in Verbart, "Milton on Vergil." Commentators have seen an allusion to Apollo's pursuit of Daphne in *Metamorphoses* 1.514–15; see Green, "The Virgin in the Garden: Milton's Ovidian Eve," 911–912. But the form of the question, "Whom fly'st thou?" links Adam's words more closely to those of Aeneas to the departing Dido.

42. Phillips, "Juno in *Aeneid* 4.693–705," 30–33; Quint, *Epic and Empire*, 111–13.

43. When Adam in book 8 recounts his marriage and the moment when he led Eve to their nuptial bower and first lovemaking, he tells Raphael that "the earth / Gave sign of gratulation" (8.513–14); this happy scene replaces and pointedly contrasts with the first lovemaking of Aeneas and Dido in their cave in book 4 of the *Aeneid*, where earth and Juno give ominous signs—"dant signum" (4.166)—as witness and wedding matron, the first day of death and beginning of Dido's tragedy. It is rather when Eve and then Adam disobey and eat the forbidden fruit of book 9 that the earth and nature "gave signs of woe" (9.783) and "a second groan" (9.1001), and with these pangs seem to break their sympathetic relationship with humanity: it is sin, not sexual love, which proves tragic in *Paradise Lost*, as the poem measures itself against Virgil's model. Along somewhat different lines, see Verbart, "Milton on Vergil," 113–14.

44. I owe the observation of this allusion to Madeline Wong, who also points out the earlier passage describing the cohort of cherubim accompanying Michael, "Spangled with eyes more numerous than those / Of Argus, and more wakeful than to drowse, / Charmed with Arcadian pipe, the pastoral reed / Of Hermes, or his opiate rod" (11.130–33). Their immunity to the power of Hermes-Mercury, Wong argues, suggests the superiority of Milton's biblical fiction and of his own Mercury-figure Michael over his Virgilian-Homeric model.

45. The "vest" (11.241) of Milton's Michael follows the gloss of Servius, "Genus vestis," on Virgil's unusual word, "laena," a mantle worn by augurers that may lend the apparition of Mercury something of a prophetic vision. Michael will go on to prophesy the history of history itself. See Virgil, *P. Virgili Maronis Opera, quae quidem extant, omnia*, 833.

46. Verbart, "Milton on Vergil," 120. I am grateful to the observations of Alexandra van Nievelt on this passage.

47. Verbart describes the parallel and contrast to Virgil's episode in *Fellowship in "Paradise Lost": Vergil, Milton, Wordsworth*, 240–42. Song, *Dominion Undeserved*, 109, has noted the allusion.

48. For clearheaded and humane accounts of the mishaps of Milton's first marriage, read through the evasive prose of the Divorce Tracts, see Patterson, *Reading between the Lines*, 276–97, and *Milton's Words*, 32–53.

49. Hughes, ed., *John Milton: Complete Poems and Major Prose*, 1031.

50. Ibid., 1032.

51. Ibid.

52. Le Comte, *Milton and Sex*, 113.

53. Ibid., 37, offers a slightly different series of biographical correspondences to this passage; critics who would like to see none at all are Tillyard, "The Crisis," 39; and Hanford, "The Dramatic Element in *Paradise Lost*," 234.

54. Fowler's note to 10.898–908 suggests that "even if M. might once have sympathized with Adam's execrations, here he is more rational—and the exaggerated multiplication of griefs ludicrous."

55. Euripides, *Euripides Poeta Tragicorum princeps in Latinum sermonem conversus*, 211.

Stiblin continues: "It seems that the poet has indulged his affect (which he often does) and in this place most freely, when he so invidiously drags down poor women. Against this calumny of Hippolytus which thus is not considered, but excessive and inflammatory, one should read Heinrich Cornelius Agrippa's book *On the Nobility and Excellences of Women*. It therefore appears that Euripides should not, on the basis of this passage, be named a misogynist, nor rashly insulted by Aristophanes as an intractable hater of women." Modern commentators might take note.

56. See Zeitlin, *Playing the Other: Gender and Society in Classical Greek Literature*, 259 and 59–72. The Hesiod passage is noted as an analogue or model for the speech of Hippolytus by David Kovacs in his edition and translation of *Euripides: Children of Heracles, Hippolytus, Andromache, Hecuba*, 185.

57. Panofsky and Panofsky, *Pandora's Box: The Changing Aspects of a Mythical Symbol*, 12–13; 64–65. On the Pandora myth and *Paradise Lost*, see Revard, "Milton and Myth," 23–48, 37–44; Butler, "Milton's Pandora: Eve, Sin, and the Mythographic Tradition," 153–78.

58. Le Comte, *Milton and Sex*, 112–13.

59. On Prometheus and Noah, see Allen, *Mysteriously Meant*, 68, 73, 162; for Prometheus and Adam, see 243, 293; and on Milton's use of the classical myths, 290–301. For some allegorists, the Prometheus *in bono* of Ovid's *Metamorphoses* 1.82–84 is the creator of man from an earth that may still retain bits of divine fire in it; others interpret the fire that the Titan steals from heaven as intellectual power and knowledge of astronomy and divine mysteries; the traces of this fire are to be found in poetry, Milton writes to his father in *Ad Patrem*, 17–23.

60. Vossius, *De Theologia Gentili*, 142, notes the error of the myth that portrays Prometheus as the son of Japhet, since, Vossius maintains, Prometheus was really a version of Noah himself.

61. Wilson, *Mocked with Death*, 188.

62. On "grinding," Milton's unpleasing euphemism for sexual intercourse, see Patterson, *Milton's Words*, 51–53.

63. The association between Tubalcain and Vulcan is made by Du Bartas/Sylvester in the section of the second of the *Divine Weeks*, "The Handy-Crafts," devoted to Cain and his metalworking descendants. Tubal(cain)'s fellow workmen at his smithy are Brontes and Steropes ("The Handy crafts," 525–28) , the same cyclopes who labor at the forge of Virgil's Vulcan in book 8 of the *Aeneid* (8.423–25). See also Vossius, *De Theologia Gentili*, 224. For the connection of Vulcan's artifice and paternity, see 658: "For Vulcan, as we have shown, is the creative fire of the smithy. But it is the instrument of this art: instruments do not pertain to the material, which is called such from *mater*, but from the efficient cause, as a father (*pater*)." Vossius does not mention Pandora.

64. Milton may remind us of the identification at second hand, in his comparison of Adam and Eve to Deucalion and Pyrrha at the opening of book 11.9–14. In Ovid's version of the pagan myth of the Flood in *Metamorphoses* 1, the Roman poet refers to the couple as Promethides and Epimethida (390), as the son of Prometheus and the daughter of Epimetheus (and hence daughter of Pandora). See Revard, "Milton and Myth," 42–44.

65. I follow closely the analysis of Lieb, *Milton and the Culture of Violence*, 147–55.

66. So the Levite later says in his own version of the events in Judges 20:5; see the version of Josephus, *Jewish Antiquities* 5.2.8.

67. Simons "'An Immortality Rather than a Life': Milton and the Concubine of Judges 19–21;" Lieb, *Milton and the Culture of Violence*, 125–55.

68. Simons, "'An Immortality Rather than a Life,'" 155.

69. The evidence that would have been available to Milton was gathered by Lapide in his *Commentarius in Iosue, Iudicum, Ruth, IV; Libros Regum et II Paralipomenon*. See Lapide, *Commentarii in Sacram Scripturam*, 2.1:195. "Our translator elongates *tiznach*, that is *she left*, for they read *tizna*, that is, *she fornicated*. Hence the Rabbis say that she was sent away from the Levite for adultery. But in truth neither the Septuagint, nor the Chaldean, nor Josephus make mention of this crime. The Septuagint translates, *she was angry at him*, the

Chaldean *she had contempt for him.* Josephus says that she separated from her husband because of his jealousy. It is likely that they had different manners and customs, whence arose strifes, quarrels, and altercations among them, which are frequent among spouses, and for that reason the wife left her husband to go to her parents. This is to be linked to verse 3: *her man followed her wishing for a reconciliation.*"

70. Lieb, *Milton and the Culture of Violence*, 133–34.

71. Ibid., 154–55.

72. Commentators perceived that the Adam of Genesis 3:12 was blaming God in blaming the woman whom God had given him. In his *Commentarii in Pentateuchum Mosis*, Lapide writes, "The just man is his own accuser from the beginning: Adam, after his sin full of concupiscence, pride, and self-love, preferred to seek excuses for his sins. Whence he transferred the fault from himself to his wife, and indeed traced it to God himself, who had given him such a wife." Augustine comments on Adam shifting the blame to Eve out of pride in *City of God* 14.14.

73. Le Comte, *Milton and Sex*, 18.

Notes to Chapter 8

1. G. K. Hunter reads a concentric structure in the 1674, twelve-book *Paradise Lost*; he had the right idea, but, I would argue, the wrong version of the epic: the concentric scheme can be discerned more clearly in Milton's original plan of the poem in ten books. See Hunter, *Paradise Lost*, 37–41. On the two centers of the poem, see Summers, *The Muse's Method*, 112–46.

2. Nohrnberg, *The Analogy of "The Faerie Queene"*; and Duval, *The Design of Rabelais's Pantagruel*, *The Design of Rabelais's Tiers Livre de Pantagruel*, and *The Design of Rabelais's Quart Livre de Pantagruel*.

3. For a discussion of the view of world empires from the mount of speculation, see Hoxby, *Mammon's Music*, 160–77; on Charles II as a new Solomon in the propaganda of his entry into London in 1661, see 99–100. See also Archer, *Old Worlds*, 88–89. Almansor, king of Morocco, listed in the rulers of the empire at 11.403–4, is almost certainly to be identified with Ahmed Al-Mansur (1549–1603), known as the "Golden" (al-Dhahabi) after he conquered the Songhai Empire in present-day Mali and gained access to its sub-Saharan gold, an epithet that corresponds to the "El Dorado" of Guiana a few verses later (11.411); see Smith, *Ahmad al-Mansur: Islamic Visionary*, 80, 124. Milton would probably not have known that Al-Mansur compared himself to Solomon; see Mouline, *Le califat imaginaire d'Ahmad al-Mansur*, 346. Because of his diplomatic negotiations with England, Al-Mansur acquired a place in the Elizabethan imagination; he is the character Muly Mahamet Seth in Peele's *The Battle of Alcazar*, and he may be recalled in the Prince of Morocco, who wrongly chooses the golden casket in Portia's test in *The Merchant of Venice*; see Ungerer, "Portia and the Prince of Morocco," 89–126.

4. For the parallel between Eden and the Jerusalem temple, both destroyed, see Rosenblatt, "'Audacious Neighborhood,'" 553–68, 563–64; Frye, *Return of Eden*, 141. I am also indebted to the unpublished paper of James Nohrnberg, "Jerusalem Transposed," cited again below (notes 12 and 23). The comparison of the thunderstruck fallen angels driven by the Son over the verge of heaven to "a herd / Of goats or timorous flock together thronged" at 6.856–57 suggests the parable of Matthew 25:32–34, as well as the episode of the Gadarene swine, possessed by a legion of demons, who charge down a steep place into the Sea of Galilee (Matt. 8:28–33; Mark 5:1–20; Luke 8:26–39); they may also recall the sheep and oxen that Jesus drives out of the temple (John 2:14–15).

5. Leonard, *Naming in Eden*, 51–56.

6. In his discussion of idolatry in book 2, chapter 5 of *On Christian Doctrine*, Milton cites Deuteronomy 16:21–22, "you shalt not plant a grove [lucum] for yourself near the altar of Jehovah," and goes on to remark, "Idolatry is described in Isa. lvii.9, etc: *getting heated in the groves* [lucis]." *CPW* 6:691; *Works* 17:134–36.

7. Sandys, *A Relation of a Iourney Begun An: Dom: 1610*, 186. Cited by Fowler in his note to 1.403–5.

8. On this passage and on the role of place, with its implications for urban settlement—Eden versus Pandaemonium—in the last books of *Paradise Lost*, see Manley, *Literature and Culture*, 566–82.
9. The tree is mentioned only one other time in the Bible. Carey, *The Poems*, 109, suggests a reminiscence of the *albaque populus* of Horace *Odes* 2.3.9; this silver poplar, too, is associated with its welcoming shade (*umbram hospitalem*).
10. Fontenrose, *Python*, 395–97, 417.
11. Quint, "Expectation and Prematurity." For the cessation of oracles at the Nativity, Christian poets looked back to Prudentius, *Apotheosis* 435–43. See Patrides, "The Cessation of the Oracles: The History of a Legend," 500–507.
12. Nohrnberg, "Jerusalem Transposed." As Nohrnberg points out, Milton glances at the variant myth that Delos once floated unmoored on the sea before the birth of Apollo, when, according to Callimachus (*Hymn* 4.53–54), the island grew roots, or, in Virgil's retelling, the grateful Apollo bound it to the neighboring islands of Mykonos and Gyaros (*Aen.* 3.75–76).
13. Milton's only mention of crusading, in his early *Apology against a Pamphlet*, ties it and his opponent, the remonstrant Joseph Hall, to Catholic violence (*CPW* 1:896) against fellow Christians, notably to the Saint Bartholomew's Day massacre. See the remarks on Tasso, Ariosto, and Camões as epic poets of the crusade against Islam in the introduction.
14. Hoxby, *Mammon's Music*, 157, suggests the echo of Marlowe. On Milton's home, see Nohrnberg, "*Paradise Regained* by One Greater Man," 114n53. Jameson asserts that the pendent world that Satan sees hanging from God's aristocratic heaven "is the market system and capitalism itself." A sentence earlier, he comments, "Alongside the feudal world of God and his court, of Satan, and his host, Adam is clearly of another species—the commoner, the first bourgeois, that extraordinary mutation which is middle-class man, destined as we know today to be fruitful and multiply, and to inherit the earth." See Jameson, "Religion and Ideology," 332. Baldly stated as it is, this observation survives the critique of Jameson's essay by Goldberg, "The Politics of Renaissance Literature: A Review Essay," 514–42.
15. In his extended address to Cromwell toward the end of the *Second Defense of the English People* (1654), Milton urges the separation of church and state: "Next, I would have you leave the church to the church and shrewdly relieve yourself and the government of half your burden (one that is at the same time completely alien to you), and not permit two powers, utterly diverse, the civil and the ecclesiastical, to make harlots of each other, and while appearing to strengthen, by their mingled and spurious riches, actually to undermine and at length destroy each other. I would have you remove all power from the church (but power will never be absent so long as money, the poison of the church, the quinsy of truth, extorted by force even from those who are unwilling, remains the price of preaching the Gospel). *I would have you drive from the temple the money-changers, who buy and sell, not doves, but the Dove, the Holy Spirit Himself*" (*CPW* 4:678).
16. Welch, "Milton's Forsaken Proserpine," 527–56, suggests that the Eden washed away at the end of book 11 is the "landscape of literary romance" (555), a mode that Milton is giving up at the end of *Paradise Lost*.
17. On Vulcan and Tubalcain, see chapter 7, note 63. These remarks, and the general contrast in this chapter between the Pandaemonium raised in book 1 and the Eden destroyed in book 11, are a variation on the observations of Bloom, who sees in the building of Pandaemonium by Mulciber "the anxiety of influence and an anxiety of morality about the secondariness of any poetic creation, even Milton's own." Bloom, *Map of Misreading*, 139.
18. Allen suggests, to the contrary, that Milton wrote *Paradise Lost* "to reaffirm his faith in the Pentateuch story and to oppose in this fashion the manifold doubts of his age," in *The Legend of Noah: Renaissance Rationalism in Art, Science, and Letters*, 39.
19. There is a parallel here, I think, to the argument of Rogers, *The Matter of Revolution*, 144–76, that the last two books of *Paradise Lost* chart a greater human independence from divine constraint; see Rogers, chapter 6, note 53.

20. See Armitage, "John Milton: Poet against Empire," 206–25; Quint, *Epic and Empire*. Michael's blunt disparagement of empire creates some difficulty for contrary views that would see the Milton of *Paradise Lost* as favorable to empire and implicated in the history of British colonialism and imperialism (there may be some difference between the poet and the Secretary for the Foreign Tongues of the Commonwealth and Protectorate governments). See Evans, *Milton's Imperial Epic*; Stevens, "Paradise Lost and the Colonial Imperative," 3–21; Barnaby, "'Another Rome in the West'? Milton and the Imperial Republic, 1654–1670," 67–84; and the essays collected in *Milton and the Imperial Vision*, ed. Rajan and Sauer.
21. Milton's phrase contains a reminiscence of Quintilian, *Institutio Oratoria* 12.11.5.
22. On the condition of Milton's poetry, mediated by a potentially idolatrous literary tradition, necessarily mediated with relationship to its divine subject, see the eloquent comments of Parker, *Inescapable Romance*, 135–37. Leonard, *Naming in Paradise*, 290, notes, "When Paradise is lost, *Paradise Lost* must be fallen." Leonard discusses, following and answering earlier critics, the relationship of Milton's fallen language and tradition to the prelapsarian subject matter of the epic, 233–92.
23. Nohrnberg, "Jerusalem Transposed"; Martindale, *John Milton and the Transformation of Ancient Epic*, 105n51.

Bibliography

Editions of Milton's Works

The Complete Poetic Works of John Milton. Edited by Douglas Bush. Boston, MA: Houghton Mifflin, 1965.

The Complete Prose Works of John Milton. Edited by Don M. Wolfe. 8 vols. New Haven, CT: Yale University Press, 1953–82.

John Milton: Complete Poems and Major Prose. Edited by Merritt Hughes. New York: Odyssey Press, 1957.

Milton's Selected Poetry and Prose. Edited by Jason Rosenblatt. New York: W. W. Norton Press, 2011.

Paradise Lost. Edited by Alastair Fowler. 2nd ed. New York: Longman, 1998.

Paradise Lost. Edited by John Leonard. London: Penguin Press, 2000; repr., 2003.

Paradise Lost. Edited by William Kerrigan, John Rumrich, and Stephen M. Fallon. New York: Modern Library, 2007.

The Poems of John Milton. Edited by John Carey and Alastair Fowler. Longmans Annotated English Poets. Harlow, UK: Longmans, 1968.

The Works of John Milton. Edited Frank Patterson. 18 vols. New York: Columbia University Press, 1931–38.

General Bibliography

Achinstein, Sharon. *Milton and the Revolutionary Reader.* Princeton, NJ: Princeton University Press, 1994.

Adams, Robert Martin. "A Look into Chaos." In *Illustrious Evidence: Approaches to English Literature in the Early Seventeenth Century,* edited by Earl Miner. Berkeley and Los Angeles: University of California Press, 1975.

Alciati, Andrea. *Emblemata, Lyons, 1550.* Translated by Betty I. Knott. Brookfield, VT: Ashgate, 1996.

Allen, Don Cameron. *The Legend of Noah: Renaissance Rationalism in Art, Science, and Letters.* Urbana: University of Illinois Press, 1963.

———. *Mysteriously Meant: The Rediscovery of Pagan Symbolism and Allegorical Interpretation in the Renaissance.* Baltimore, MD: Johns Hopkins University Press, 1970.

Ambrose. *On Abraham.* Translated by Theodosia Tomkinson. Etna, CA: Center for Traditionalist Orthodox Studies, 2000.

———.*De Abraham,* ed. Franco Gori. *Tutte le opere di Sant'Ambrogio.* 25 vols. Milan: Città Nuova, 1977–2004.

Ammianus Marcellinus. *Ammianus Marcellinus.* 3 vols. Translated by John Carew Rolfe. Loeb Classical Library. London: W. Heinemann, 1935.

Apocryphal New Testament. Translated by Montague Rhodes James. Oxford, UK: Clarendon Press, 1953.

Ariosto, Ludovico. *Orlando furioso*. Edited by Emilio Bigi. 2 vols. Milan: Rusconi, 1982.

Archer, John Michael. *Old Worlds: Egypt, Southwest Asia, India, and Russia in Early Modern English Writing*. Stanford, CA: Stanford University Press, 2001.

Armitage, David. "John Milton: Poet against Empire." In *Milton and Republicanism*, edited by Armand Himy, David Armitage, and Quentin Skinner, 206–25. Cambridge, UK: Cambridge University Press, 1995.

Augustine. *The City of God*. Translated by Marcus Dods. New York: Modern Library, 1950.

Bacon, Francis. *The Advancement of Learning and New Atlantis*. Edited by Thomas Case. New York: Oxford University Press, 1956.

———. *Bacon's Novum Organum*. Edited by Thomas Fowler. Oxford, UK: Clarendon Press, 1878.

———. *The Charge touching duels*. In *Francis Bacon: The Major Works*, edited by Brian Vickers. Oxford, UK: Oxford University Press, 1996.

———. *The Essays*. Edited by John Pitcher. Hammondsworth: Penguin Books, 1985.

———. *Francis Bacon: The Major Works*. Edited by Brian Vickers. Oxford, UK: Oxford University Press, 1996.

———. *The New Organon and Related Writing*. Edited by Fulton Anderson. New York: Bobbs-Merrill, 1960.

Bandello, Matteo. *Tutte le Opere di Matteo Bandello*. 2 vols. Edited by Francesco Flora. Verona, Italy: Mondadori, 1966.

Barnaby, Andrew. " 'Another Rome in the West': Milton and the Imperial Republic, 1654–1670." *Milton Studies* 30 (1993): 67–84.

———. "Cringing before the Lord: Milton's Satan, Samuel Johnson, and the Anxiety of Worship." In *The Sacred and Profane in English Renaissance Literature*, edited by Mary A. Papazian, 321–44. Newark: University of Delaware Press, 2008.

Barthes, Roland. *S/Z*. 1st American ed. New York: Hill and Wang, 1974.

Baxter, Richard. *The Life of Faith*. London: Nevil Simmons, 1670.

Beattie, J. M. *Crime and the Courts in England, 1660–1800*. Princeton, NJ: Princeton University Press, 1986.

Bedford, Ronald. "Milton's Military Heaven Revisited." *AUMLA: Journal of the Australian Universities Modern Language Association* 106 (2006): 123–48.

Benet, Diana Treviño. "Abdiel and the Son in the Separation Scene." *Milton Studies* 18 (1983): 129–43.

———. " 'All in All': The Threat of Bliss." In *"All in All": Unity, Diversity and the Miltonic Perspective*, edited by Charles W. Durham and Kristin A. Pruitt, 48–66. Selingsgrove, PA: Susquehanna University Press.

———. "Hell, Satan, and the New Politician." In *Literary Milton: Text, Pretext, Context*, edited by Diana T. Benet and Michael Lieb, 81–113. Pittsburgh, PA: Duquesne University Press, 1994.

———, and Michael Lieb, eds. *Literary Milton: Text, Pretext, Context*. Pittsburgh, PA: Duquesne University Press, 1994.

Bennett, Joan S. *Reviving Liberty: Radical Christian Humanism in Milton's Great Poems*. Cambridge, MA: Harvard University Press, 1989.

Berry, Lloyd E., ed. *The Geneva Bible: A Facsimile of the 1650 Edition*. Madison: University of Wisconsin Press, 1969.

Billacois, François. *The Duel: Its Rise and Fall in Early Modern France*. Translated by Trista Selous. New Haven, CT: Yale University Press, 1990.

Blackburn, Thomas H. " 'Uncloistered Virtue': Adam and Eve in Milton's Paradise." *Milton Studies* 3 (1971): 119–37.

Blessington, Francis C. *"Paradise Lost" and the Classical Epic*. Boston, MA: Routledge & K. Paul, 1979.

Bloom, Harold. *A Map of Misreading*. New York: Oxford University Press, 1975.

Blumenberg, Hans. *The Legitimacy of the Modern Age*. Translated by Robert M. Wallace Cambridge, MA: MIT Press, 1983.

Bond, Christopher. *Spenser, Milton, and the Redemption of the Epic Hero.* Newark: University of Delaware Press, 2011.

Borris, Kenneth. "Allegory in *Paradise Lost*: Satan's Cosmic Journey." *Milton Studies* (1990): 101–33.

Brenk, Beat. *Die Frühchristlichen Mosaiken in S. Maria Maggiore zu Rom.* Wiesbaden, Germany: Franz Steiner, 1975.

Brieger, Peter. *English Art, 1216–1307.* Oxford, UK: Clarendon Press, 1957.

Brisman, Leslie. *Milton's Poetry of Choice and Its Romantic Heirs.* Ithaca, NY: Cornell University Press, 1975.

Broadbent, J. B. *Some Graver Subject: An Essay on "Paradise Lost."* London: Chatto & Windus Press, 1960.

Bryson, Michael. *The Tyranny of Heaven: Milton's Rejection of God as King.* Newark: University of Delaware Press, 2004.

Burden, Dennis H. *The Logical Epic: A Study of the Argument of "Paradise Lost."* Cambridge, MA: Harvard University Press, 1967.

Burrow, Colin. *Epic Romance: Homer to Milton.* New York: Oxford University Press, 1993.

Burton, Robert. *The Anatomy of Melancholy.* Edited by Holbrook Jackson. 3 vols. in 1. New York: Vintage, 1977.

Butler, George F. "Milton's Pandora: Eve, Sin, and the Mythographic Tradition." *Milton Studies* 44 (2005): 153–78.

Callimachus, Lycophron, and Aratus. *Callimachus: Hymns and Epigrams, Lycophron, and Aratus.* Translated by A. W. Mair and G. R. Mair. Loeb Classical Library. 2nd edition. Cambridge, MA: Harvard University Press, 1977.

Calvin, John. *Commentary on the Acts of the Apostles.* Edited by Christopher Fetherstone. Grand Rapids, MI: Eerdmans, 1949.

Camões, Luís de. *Obra Completa.* Edited by Antônio Salgado Júnior. Rio de Janeiro: Editora Nova Aguilar, 1988.

Campbell, Gordon, and Thomas Corns. *John Milton: Life, Work, Thought.* New York: Oxford University Press, 2008.

Carlyle, Thomas. *The Life of Oliver Cromwell, with a Selection from His Letters and Speeches.* Amsterdam: Fredonia, 2002.

Celenza, Christopher S. *Piety and Pythagoras in Renaissance Florence: The Symbolum Nesianum.* Studies in the History of Christian Thought. Leiden: Brill, 2001.

Chambers, A. B. "Chaos in *Paradise Lost*." *Journal of the History of Ideas* 24 (1963): 55–84.

Chaplin, Gregory. "Beyond Sacrifice: Milton and the Atonement." *Publications of the Modern Language Association* 125 (2010): 354–369.

Chaucer, Geoffrey. *The Workes of Our Ancient and Learned Poet Geoffrey Chaucer.* London: Adam Islip, 1602.

———. *The Works of Geoffrey Chaucer.* Edited by F. N. Robinson. 2nd ed. Boston: Houghton Mifflin, 1957.

Cheney, Patrick Gerard. *Spenser's Famous Flight: A Renaissance Idea of a Literary Career.* Toronto: University of Toronto Press, 1993.

Chrysostom, John. *Homilies on the Gospel of Saint Matthew.* In *A Select Library of the Nicene and Post-Nicene Fathers of the Christian Church.* Edited by Philip Schaff. Vol. 10. New York: Christian Literature Company, 1988.

Cicero. *De Natura Deorum; Academica.* Loeb Classical Library. London: William Heinemann, 1951.

———. *De Officiis.* Translated by Walter Miller. Loeb Classical Library. Cambridge, MA: Harvard University Press, 1975.

Coleridge, Samuel Taylor. *Coleridge's Writings on Shakespeare.* Edited by Terence Hawkes. New York: Capricorn Books, 1959.

Colombo [Columbus], Fernando. *Storie Del Nuovo Mondo.* Edited by R. Caddeo. Genoa: Dioscuri, 1989.

Cope, Jackson I. *The Metaphoric Structure of "Paradise Lost."* Baltimore, MD: Johns Hopkins Press, 1962.

Copenhaver, Brian P., trans. *Hermetica: The Greek Corpus Hermeticum and the Latin Asclepius.* Cambridge, UK: Cambridge University Press, 1992.

Corbet, Richard. *The Poems of Richard Corbet.* Edited by J. W. Bennett and H. R. Trevor-Roper. Oxford, UK: Clarendon Press, 1955.

Corns, Thomas N. *Regaining "Paradise Lost."* Longman Medieval and Renaissance Library. New York: Longman, 1994.

Courcelle, Pierre. "Quelques symboles funéraires du néoplatonisme latin: Le vol de Dédale; Ulysses et les Sirènes." *Revue des études anciennes* 46 (1944): 65–93.

Cowan, Ross. "The Clashing of Weapons and Silent Advances in Roman Battles." *Historia* 56.1 (2007): 114–17.

Cowley, Abraham. *Davideis: A Sacred Poem of the Troubles of David.* London: Humphrey Moseley, 1656.

Curtius Rufus, Quintus. *Quintus Curtius* [History of Alexander]. Edited by John Carew Wolfe. Loeb Classical Library. 2 vols. Cambridge, MA: Harvard University Press, 1962.

Cyril of Alexandria. *On the Gospel of John.* In *Patrologia Cursus Completus, Series Graeca,* edited by J. P. Migne. 166 vols. Vol. 73. Paris: L'Imprimerie Catholique, 1857–66.

Dante Alighieri. *La Divina Commedia.* Edited by Giuseppe Vandelli. Milan: Hoepli, 1983.

Davies, Stevie. *Images of Kingship in "Paradise Lost": Milton's Politics and Christian Liberty.* Columbia: University of Missouri Press, 1983.

———. "Triumph and Anti-Triumph: Milton's Satan and the Roman Emperors in *Paradise Lost.*" *Études Anglaises* 34 (1981): 385–98.

Dempsey, Charles. *Inventing the Renaissance Putto.* Bettie Allison Rand Lectures in Art History. Chapel Hill: University of North Carolina Press, 2001.

Derrida, Jacques. *De la Grammatologie.* Paris: Les Éditions de Minuit, 1967.

Diodorus, Siculus. *The History of Diodorus Siculus Containing All That Is Most Memorable and of Greatest Antiquity in the First Ages of the World until the War of Troy.* London: John Macock, 1653.

Dobranski, Stephen B., and John P. Rumrich, eds. *Milton and Heresy.* Cambridge, UK: Cambridge University Press, 1998.

Dölger, Franz. *Sol Salutis.* Münster: Aschendorff, 1925.

Du Bartas, Guillaume. *La Sepmaine, 1581.* Edited by Yvonne Bellenger. Paris: Société des Textes Français Modernes, 1993.

Durham, Charles W., and Kristin A. Pruitt, eds. *"All in All": Unity, Diversity and the Miltonic Perspective.* Selinsgrove, PA: Susquehanna University Press.

———. *Reassembling Truth: Twenty-First Century Milton.* Selinsgrove, PA: Susquehanna University Press, 2003.

———. *Uncircumscribed Minds.* Selinsgrove, PA: Susquehanna University Press, 2008.

DuRocher, Richard J. *Milton among the Romans: The Pedagogy and Influence of Milton's Latin Curriculum.* Medieval & Renaissance Literary Studies. Pittsburgh, PA: Duquesne University Press, 2001.

———. *Milton and Ovid.* Ithaca, NY: Cornell University Press, 1985.

———. "Passion and Allusion in *Paradise Lost.*" *Milton Studies* 49 (2009): 124–45.

Duval, Edwin M. *The Design of Rabelais's Pantagruel.* New Haven, CT: Yale University Press, 1991.

———. *The Design of Rabelais's Tiers Livre De Pantagruel.* Geneva: Droz, 1997.

———. *The Design of Rabelais's Quart Livre De Pantagruel.* Geneva: Droz, 1998.

Dyson, Julia. "Dido the Epicurean." *Classical Antiquity* 15 (1996): 203–21.

Dzelzainis, Martin. "Milton and the Protectorate in 1658." In *Milton and Republicanism,* edited by Armand Himy, David Armitage, and Quentin Skinner. Cambridge, UK: Cambridge University Press, 1995.

———. "Milton's Classic Republicanism." In *Milton and Republicanism*, edited by Armand Himy, David Armitage, and Quentin Skinner, 3–24. Cambridge, UK: Cambridge University Press, 1995.

Elias, Norbert. *The Civilizing Process: I. The History of Manners*. Translated by Edmund Jephcott. New York: Pantheon Books, 1978.

———. *The Civilizing Process: II. Power and Civility*. Translated by Edmund Jephcott. New York: Pantheon Books, 1982.

Empson, William. *Milton's God*. Rev. ed. Cambridge, UK: Cambridge University Press, 1981.

Erasmus, Desiderius. *Adages*. Edited by R.A.B. Mynors, Margaret M. Phillips, Denis L. Drysdall, and John N. Grant. In *Collected Works of Erasmus*. Vol. 31. Toronto: University of Toronto Press, 1982.

Erspamer, Francesco. *La biblioteca di Don Ferrante: Duello e onore nella cultura del Cinquecento*. Rome: Bulzoni, 1982.

Euripides. *Euripides: Children of Heracles, Hippolytus, Andromache, Hecuba*. Edited and translated by David Kovacs. Loeb Classical Library. Cambridge, MA: Harvard University Press, 1995.

———. *Euripides Poeta Tragicorum Princeps in Latinum Sermonem Conversus*. Basel: Oporinus, 1562.

Evans, J. Martin. *Milton's Imperial Epic: "Paradise Lost" and the Colonial Imperative*. Ithaca, NY: Cornell University Press, 1996.

Fallon, Robert Thomas. *Divided Empire: Milton's Political Imagery*. University Park: Pennsylvania State University Press, 1995.

Fallon, Samuel. "Milton's Strange God: Theology and Narrative Form in *Paradise Lost*." *English Literary History* 79 (2012): 32–57.

Fallon, Stephen M. "Intention and Its Limits in *Paradise Lost*: The Case of Bellerophon." In *Literary Milton: Text, Pretext, Context*, edited by Diana T. Benet and Michael Lieb, 161–79. Pittsburgh, PA: Duquesne University Press, 1994.

———. *Milton among the Philosophers: Poetry and Materialism in Seventeenth-Century England*. Ithaca, NY: Cornell University Press, 1991.

Ficino, Marsilio. "Concerning the Sun." Translated by Arturo B. Fallico and Herman Shapiro. In *Renaissance Philosophy*. Vol. 1, *The Italian Philosophers*. New York: Modern Library, 1967.

Filmer, Robert. *The Anarchy of a Limited or Mixed Monarchy*. London: s.n., 1648.

———. *Concerning the Originall of Government*. London: R. Royston, 1652.

Fish, Stanley. *Surprised by Sin: The Reader in "Paradise Lost."* [1967] Berkeley and Los Angeles: University of California Press, 1971.

Fletcher, Harris. "Milton's Homer." *Journal of English and Germanic Philology* (1939): 229–32.

Fontenrose, Joseph. *Python: A Study of Delphic Myth and Its Origins*. Berkeley and Los Angeles: University of California Press, 1959.

Forsyth, Neil. *The Satanic Epic*. Princeton, NJ: Princeton University Press, 2003.

Foucault, Michel. *The Order of Things: An Archaeology of the Human Sciences*. New York: Vintage Books, 1970.

Freccero, John. *Dante: The Poetics of Conversion*. Cambridge, MA: Harvard University Press, 1986.

Fresch, Cheryl H. "'Aside the Devil Turned / for Envy': The Evil Eye in *Paradise Lost*, Book 4." In *Living Texts: Interpreting Milton*, edited by Kristin A. Pruitt and Charles W. Durham, 118–30. Selinsgrove, PA: Susquehanna University Press, 2000.

Frye, Northrop. *Fables of Identity: Studies in Poetic Mythology*. New York: Harcourt, Brace & World, 1963.

———. *The Return of Eden*. Toronto: University of Toronto Press, 1965.

Frye, Roland Mushat. *God, Man, and Satan: Patterns of Christian Thought and Life in "Paradise Lost," "Pilgrim's Progress," and the Great Theologians*. Princeton, NJ: Princeton University Press, 1960.

Fuller, Thomas. *The History of the Worthies of England*. London: J.G.W.L. and W. G. for Thomas Williams, 1662.

Galileo. *Dialogue Concerning the Two Chief World Systems*. Translated by Stillman Drake. Berkeley and Los Angeles: University of California Press, 1967.

———. *Discoveries and Opinions of Galileo*. Translated by Stillman Drake. Garden City, NY: Doubleday Anchor Books, 1957.

Galinsky, Karl. *Augustan Culture*. Princeton, NJ: Princeton University Press, 1996.

Gallagher, Philip J. *Milton, the Bible, and Misogyny*. Edited by Eugene R. Cunnar and Gail L. Mortimer. Columbia: University of Missouri Press, 1990.

Garin, Eugenio. "La nuova scienza e il simbolo del 'libro.'" In *La cultura filosofica del Rinascimento italiano*, 450–67. Florence: Sansoni, 1979.

———. "Per la storia della cultura filosofica del Rinascimento: Letteratura 'solare.'" *Rivista critica della storia della filosofica* 12 (1957): 3–16.

The Geneva Bible: A Facsimile of the 1560 Edition. Madison: University of Wisconsin Press, 1969.

Gilbert, Allan H. "The Theological Basis of Satan's Rebellion and the Function of Abdiel in *Paradise Lost*." *Modern Philology* 40 (1942): 19–42.

Goldberg, Jonathan. "The Politics of Renaissance Literature: A Review Essay." *English Literary History* 49 (1982): 514–42.

Goodman, Kevis. "'Wasted Labor'? Milton's Eve, the Poet's Work, and the Challenge of Sympathy." *English Literary History* (1997): 415–46.

Gordon, Pamela. "Dido the Phaeacian: Lost Pleasures of an Epicurean Intertext." *Classical Antiquity* 17 (1998): 188–211.

Gori, Franco, ed. *Tutte le Opere Di Sant'Ambrogio*. Milan: Bibliotheca Ambrosiana and Città Nuova, 1984.

Grant, Edward. *Much Ado About Nothing: Theories of Space and Vacuum from the Middle Ages to the Scientific Revolution*. Cambridge, UK: Cambridge University Press, 1981.

Green, Mandy. "Softening the Stony: Deucalion, Pyrrha and the Process of Regeneration in *Paradise Lost*." *Milton Quarterly* 35 (2001): 9–21.

———. "The Virgin in the Garden: Milton's Ovidian Eve." *Modern Language Review* 100 (2005): 903–92

Greene, Thomas M. *The Descent from Heaven: A Study in Epic Continuity*. New Haven, CT: Yale University Press, 1963.

———. *The Light in Troy: Imitation and Discovery in Renaissance Poetry*. Elizabethan Club Series. New Haven, CT: Yale University Press, 1982.

Guillory, John. "Milton, Narcissism, Gender: On the Genalogy of Male Self–Esteem." In *Critical Essays on John Milton*, edited by Christopher Kendrick, 194–234. New York: G. K. Hall, 1995.

Hampton, Timothy. *Literature and Nation in the Sixteenth Century: Inventing Renaissance France*. Ithaca, NY: Cornell University Press, 2001.

———. "'Turkish Dogs': Rabelais, Erasmus, and the Rhetoric of Alterity." *Representations* 41 (1993): 58–82.

Hanford, James Holly. "The Dramatic Element in *Paradise Lost*." In *John Milton, Poet and Humanist*, edited by John S. Diekhoff, 224-43. Cleveland, OH: Press of Western Reserve, 1966.

———. "The Temptation Motive in Milton." In *John Milton, Poet and Humanist: Essays by James Holly Hanford*, edited by John S. Diekhoff, 263–55. Cleveland, OH: Press of Western Reserve University, 1966.

Hardie, Philip. "Fame and Defamation in the Aeneid: The Council of the Latins." In *Virgil's "Aeneid": Augustan Epic and Political Context*, edited by Hans-Peter Stahl, 243–70. London: Duckworth Press, 1998.

———. *Ovid's Poetics of Illusion*. New York: Cambridge University Press, 2002.

———. *Virgil's Aeneid: Cosmos and Imperium*. New York: Oxford University Press, 1986.

Harding, Davis P. *Milton and the Renaissance Ovid*. Illinois Studies in Language and Literature. Urbana: University of Illinois Press, 1946.

Harding, Pitt. "'Strange Point and New!': Satan's Challenge to Nascent Christianity." In *Uncircumscribed Minds: Reading Milton Deeply*, edited by Charles W. Durham and Kristin S. Pruitt, 113–28. Selinsgrove, PA: Susquehanna University Press, 2008.

Harrison, Peter. *The Bible, Protestantism, and the Rise of Natural Science*. Cambridge, UK: Cambridge University Press, 1998.

Hartman, Geoffrey H. *Beyond Formalism: Literary Essays, 1958–1970*. New Haven, CT: Yale University Press, 1970.

Haskin, Dayton. *Milton's Burden of Interpretation*. Philadelphia: University of Pennsylvania Press, 1994.

Herbert of Cherbury, Edward Herbert. *De Religione Gentilium*. Faksimile-Neudruck der Ausg. Stuttgart-Bad Cannstatt: Frommann Holzboog, 1967.

Hesiod. *Hesiod, the Homeric Hymns, and Homerica*. Edited and translated by Hugh G. Evelyn-White. Loeb Classical Library. New York: Macmillan, 1977.

Hillier, Russell M. "'By force or fraud / Weening to prosper': Milton's Satanic and Messianic Modes of Heroism," *Milton Quarterly* 43 (2009): 31.

Hinds, Stephen. *Allusion and Intertext: Dynamics of Appropriation in Roman Poetry*. Roman Literature and Its Contexts. New York: Cambridge University Press, 1998.

Homer. *Homeri Quae Extant Omnia Ilias, Odyssea, Batrachomyomachia, Hymni, Poemata Aliquot*. Basil: Eusebius Episcopius, 1583.

———. *The Odyssey of Homer*. Translated by Richard Alexander Lattimore. New York: Harper & Row, 1967.

Hooykaas, R. *Religion and the Rise of Modern Science*. 1st American ed. Grand Rapids, MI: Eerdmans, 1972.

Horace. *Odes and Epodes*. Translated by C. E. Bennett. Loeb Classical Library. Cambridge, MA: Harvard University Press, 1968.

Howard, Leon. "'The Invention' of Milton's 'Great Argument': A Study of the Logic of 'God's Ways to Men.'" *Huntington Library Quarterly* 9 (1945): 149–73.

Hoxby, Blair. *Mammon's Music: Literature and Economics in the Age of Milton*. New Haven, CT: Yale University Press, 2002.

Hunter, G. K. *Paradise Lost*. London: George Allen and Unwin, 1980.

Hunter, William B. "The Confounded Confusion of Chaos." In *Living Texts: Interpreting Milton*, edited by Kristin A. Pruitt and Charles W. Durgam, 228–36. Selinsgrove, PA: Susquehanna University Press, 2000.

———. "Milton on the Exaltation of the Son: The War in Heven in *Paradise Lost*." *English Literary History* 36 (1969): 215–31.

Ide, Richard S. "On the Begetting of the Son in *Paradise Lost*." *Studies in English Literature* 24 (1984): 141–55.

Jameson, Fredric. "Religion and Ideology." In *1642: Literature and Power in the Seventeenth Century: Proceedings of the Essex Conference on the Sociology of Literature, July 1980*, 315–36. Essex, UK: University of Essex, 1981.

Johnson, Lee M. "Milton's Blank Verse Sonnets." *Milton Studies* 5 (1973): 129–53.

Jones, William Powell. *The Pastourelle*. Cambridge, MA: Harvard University Press, 1931.

Julian. *The Works of the Emperor Julian*. Translated by Wilmer C. F. Wright. Loeb Classical Library. 3 vols. Cambridge, MA: Harvard University Press, 2003.

Kahn, Victoria Ann. *Machiavellian Rhetoric: From the Counter-Reformation to Milton*. Princeton, NJ: Princeton University Press, 1994.

Kermode, Frank. "The Cave of Mammon." In *Shakespeare, Spenser, Donne*, 80–83. New York: Viking Press, 1971.

———. "Milton's Hero." *Review of English Studies*, New Series 4, no. 16 (1953): 317–30.

———. *Shakespeare, Spenser, Donne: Renaissance Essays*. New York: Viking Press, 1971.

Kerrigan, William. "The Heretical Milton: From Assumption to Mortalism." *English Literary Renaissance* 5 (1975): 125–66.

———. "The Irrational Coherence of *Samson Agonistes*." *Milton Studies* (1986): 217–32.

———. *The Sacred Complex: On the Psychogenesis of "Paradise Lost."* Cambridge, MA: Harvard University Press, 1983.

Kerrigan, William, and Gordon Braden. *The Idea of the Renaissance*. Baltimore, MD: Johns Hopkins University Press, 1989.

Kiernan, V. G. *The Duel in European History*. Oxford, UK: Oxford University Press, 1988.

Kilgour, Maggie. *Milton and the Metamorphosis of Ovid*. Oxford, UK: Oxford University Press, 2012.

———. "Satan and the Wrath of Juno." *English Literary History* 75 (2008): 653–71.

King, John N. "Miltonic Transubstantiation." *Milton Studies* 36 (1998): 41–58.

Klemp, Paul J. "Milton's Pastourelle Vision in *Paradise Lost*." *Études anglaises* 46 (1993): 257–71.

Kuhn, Thomas S. *The Copernican Revolution: Planetary Astronomy in the Development of Western Thought*. Cambridge, MA: Harvard University Press, 1957.

Labriola, Albert C. "The Son as an Angel in *Paradise Lost*." In *Milton in the Age of Fish*, edited by Michael Lieb and Albert C. Labriola, 105–13. Pittsburgh, PA: Duquesne University Press, 2006.

———. " 'Thy Humiliation Shall Exalt': The Christology of *Paradise Lost*." *Milton Studies* 15 (1981): 29–42.

Lactantius. *The Divine Institutes: Books I–VII*. Translated by Mary Francis McDonald. The Fathers of the Church, a New Translation (Patristic series). Washington, DC: Catholic University of America Press, 1964.

Lambert, Ellen Zetzel. *Placing Sorrow: A Study of the Pastoral Elegy Convention from Theocritus to Milton*. Chapel Hill: University of North Carolina Press, 1976.

Langer, Ullrich. *Divine and Poetic Freedom in the Renaissance: Nominalist Theology and Literature in France and Italy*. Princeton, NJ: Princeton University Press, 1990.

La Penna, Antonio. *Tersite censurato e altri studi di letteratura fra antico e moderno*. Saggi di Varia Umanità. Pisa: Nistri-Lischi, 1991.

Lapide, Cornelius à. *Commentaria in Sacram Scripturam*. 21 vols. Vol. 21. Paris: Louis Vivès, 1876.

———. *Commentarii in Pentateuchum Mosis*. Antwerp: Martinus Nutius, 1630.

———. *Commentarii in Sacram Scripturam*. 10 vols. Vol. 2. Malta: Tonna, Banchii & Soc., 1843–51.

———. *Commentarius in Iosue, Iudicum, Ruth, IV; Libros Regum et II Paralipomenon* (Antwerp: Johannes Meursius, 1642).

Lawson, Anita. " 'The Golden Sun in Splendor Likest Heaven': Johannes Kepler's Epitome and *Paradise Lost*, Book 3." *Milton Quarterly* 21 (1987): 46–51.

Le Comte, Edward. *Milton and Sex*. London: Macmillan, 1978.

Leonard, John. "Milton, Lucretius and the 'Void Profound of Unessential Night.' " In *Interpreting Milton*, edited by Kristin A. Pruitt and Charles W. Durham. Selinsgrove, PA: Susquehanna University Press, 2000.

———. *Naming in Paradise: Milton and the Language of Adam and Eve*. Oxford, UK: Clarendon Press; New York: Oxford University Press, 1990.

Levao, Ronald. " 'Among Unequals What Society': *Paradise Lost* and the Forms of Intimacy." *Modern Language Quarterly* 61 (2000): 79–107.

Lewalski, Barbara Kiefer. "Innocence and Experience in Milton's Eden." In *New Essays on "Paradise Lost,"* edited by Thomas Kranidas, 86–117. Berkeley and Los Angeles: University of California Press, 1969.

———. *The Life of John Milton: A Critical Biography*. Blackwell Critical Biographies. Malden, MA: Blackwell, 2000.

———. *Milton's Brief Epic: The Genre, Meaning and Art of Paradise Regained*. Providence, RI: Methuen, 1966.

———. "*Paradise Lost* and Milton's Politics." *Milton Studies* 38 (2000): 141–68.

———. "*Paradise Lost*" *and the Rhetoric of Literary Forms*. Princeton, NJ: Princeton University Press, 1985.

Lieb, Michael. *The Dialectics of Creation: Patterns of Birth and Regeneration in "Paradise Lost."* Amherst: University of Massachusetts Press, 1970.

———. *Milton and the Culture of Violence*. Ithaca, NY: Cornell University Press, 1994.

———, and Albert C. Labriola, eds. *Milton in the Age of Fish*. Pittsburgh, PA: Duquesne University Press, 2006.

———. *Poetics of the Holy: A Reading of Paradise Lost*. Chapel Hill: University of North Carolina Press, 1981.

Loewenstein, David. *Milton and the Drama of History: Historical Vision, Iconoclasm, and the Literary Imagination*. Cambridge, UK: Cambridge University Press, 1990.

Lucan, *The Civil War*. Translated by J. D. Duff. Loeb Classical Library. Cambridge, MA: Harvard University Press, 1962.

Lucretius. *De Rerum Natura*. Translated by W.H.D. Rouse. Loeb Classical Library. Cambridge, MA: Harvard University Press, 1966.

Lyle, Joseph. "Architecture and Idolatry in '*Paradise Lost*.'" *Studies in English Literature, 1500–1900* 40, no. 1 (2000): 139–55.

MacCaffrey, Isabel G. "The Theme of *Paradise Lost*, Book 3." In *New Essays on Paradise Lost*, edited by Thomas Kranidas, 55–85. Berkeley and Los Angeles: University of California Press, 1969.

MacCallum, Hugh. *Milton and the Sons of God: The Divine Image in Milton's Epic Poetry*. Toronto: University of Toronto Press, 1986.

Madsen, William G. *From Shadowy Types to Truth: Studies in Milton's Symbolism*. New Haven, CT: Yale University Press, 1968.

Manley, Lawrence. *Literature and Culture in Early Modern London*. New York: Cambridge University Press, 1995.

Martin, Catherine Gimelli. *The Ruins of Allegory: Paradise Lost and the Metamorphosis of Epic Convention*. Durham, NC: Duke University Press, 1998.

———. "'What If the Sun Be Centre to the World?' Milton's Epistemology, Cosmology, and Paradise of Fools Reconsidered." *Modern Philology* 99 (2001): 231–65.

Martindale, Charles. *John Milton and the Transformation of Ancient Epic*. London: Croom Helm, 1986.

Marullus [Michele Marullo Tarcaniota]. *Inni naturali*. Edited by Donatella Coppini. Florence: Le Lettere, 1995.

Mazzotta, Giuseppe. *Dante, Poet of the Desert: History and Allegory in the Divine Comedy*. Princeton, NJ: Princeton University Press, 1979.

McColley, Diana Kelsey. "'All in All': The Individuality of Creatures in *Paradise Lost*." In *"All in All": Unity, Diversity and the Miltonic Perspective*, edited by Charles W. Durham and Kristin A. Pruitt. Selingsgrove, PA: Susquehanna University Press.

———. "Free Will and Obedience in the Separation Scene of *Paradise Lost*." *Studies in English Literature* 12 (1972): 103–20.

———. *Milton's Eve*. Urbana: University of Illinois Press, 1983.

Michels, Agnes Kirsopp. "Lucretius and the Sixth Book of the Aeneid." *American Journal of Philology* 65 (1944): 135–48.

Miller, Timothy C. "Milton's Paradise Regained." *Explicator* 56 (1997): 14–17.

More, Henry. *The Complete Poems of Dr. Henry More*, edited by Alexander B. Grosart. Edinburgh: Edinburgh University, 1878.

Mouline, Nabil. *Le Califat Imaginaire d'Ahmad Al-Mansûr*. Paris: Presses Universitaires de France, 2009.

Muir, Edward. *Mad Blood Stirring: Vendetta and Faction in Friuli during the Renaissance*. Baltimore, MD: Johns Hopkins University Press, 1993.

Mulryan, John. *Through a Glass Darkly: Milton's Reinvention of the Mythological Tradition*. Pittsburgh: Duquesne University Press, 1996.

Murrin, Michael. *The Allegorical Epic: Essays in Its Rise and Decline*. Chicago: University of Chicago Press, 1980.

———. *History and Warfare in Renaissance Epic*. Chicago: University of Chicago Press, 1994.

Nardo, Anna K. *Milton's Sonnets and the Ideal of Community*. Lincoln: University of Nebraska Press, 1979.

Nelson, Eric. "'Talmudical Commonwealthsmen' and the Rise of Republican Exclusivism." *Historical Journal* 50 (2007): 809–35.

Nicolson, Majorie Hope. *The Breaking of the Circle*. New York: Columbia University Press, 1960.

Nock, A. D., ed. *Corpus Hermeticum 2: Traités XIII–XVIII; Asclepius*. Translated by A. J. Festugière. Paris: Société d'édition "Les Belles Lettres," 1960.

Nohrnberg, James. *The Analogy of "The Faerie Queene."* Princeton, NJ: Princeton University Press, 1976.

———. "Jerusalem Transposed on the Axes of Western Epic." Unpublished paper

———. "On Literature and the Bible." *Centrum* 2, no. 2 (1974): 5–43.

———. "*Paradise Regained* by One Greater Man: Milton's Wisdom Epic as a 'Fable of Identity.'" In *Centre and Labyrinth: Essays in Honour of Northrop Frye*, edited by Eleanor Cook et. al., 83–114. Toronto: University of Toronto Press, 1983.

Norbrook, David. *Writing the English Republic: Poetry, Rhetoric, and Politics, 1627–1660*. New York: Cambridge University Press, 1999.

Nyquist, Mary. "The Father's Word/Satan's Wrath." *PMLA* 100 (1985): 187–202.

———. "The Genesis of Gendered Subjectivity in the Divorce Tracts and in *Paradise Lost*." In *Re-Membering Milton*, edited by Mary Nyquist and Margaret W. Ferguson, 99–127. New York: Methuen, 1997.

———. "Gynesis, Genesis, Exegesis, and Milton's Eve." In *Cannibals, Witches, and Divorce: Estranging the Renaissance*, edited by Majorie Garber. Selected Papers from the English Institute, New Series. Baltimore, MD: Johns Hopkins University Press, 1987.

———. "Reading the Fall: Discourse in Drama in *Paradise Lost*." *English Literary Renaissance* 14 (1984): 199–229.

———. "Textual Overlapping and Dalilah's Harlot-Lap." In *Literary Theory / Renaissance Texts*, edited by Patricia Parker and David Quint, 341–71. Baltimore, MD: Johns Hopkins University Press, 1986.

O'Connell, Michael. *Mirror and Veil: The Historical Dimension of Spenser's Faerie Queene*. Chapel Hill: University of North Carolina Press, 1977.

Oliensis, Ellen. "Return to Sender: The Rhetoric of Nomina in Ovid's Tristia." *Ramus* 26 (1997): 177–93.

The Orphic Hymns. Translated by Apostolos Athanassakis. Missoula, MT: Scholars Press, 1977.

Ovid. *The Art of Love and Other Poems*. Translated by J. Mozeley. 2nd ed. revised by G. P. Goold. Loeb Classical Library. Cambridge, MA: Harvard University Press, 1985.

———. *Heroides and Amores*. Translated by Grant Showerman. Loeb Classical Library. Cambridge, MA: Harvard University Press, 1977.

———. *Metamorphoses*. Translated Frank Justus Miller. Revised by G. P. Goold. Loeb Classical Library. 2 vols. Cambridge, MA: Harvard University Press, 1999.

———. *Tristia ex Ponto*. Translated by A. L. Wheeler. Revised by G. P. Goold. Loeb Classical Library. Cambridge, MA: Harvard University Press, 1988.

Paden, William D., ed. *The Medieval Pastourelle*. New York: Garland, 1987.

Panofsky, Dora, and Erwin Panofsky. *Pandora's Box: The Changing Aspects of a Mythical Symbol*. 2nd ed. New York: Pantheon Books, 1962.

Parker, Patricia A. *Inescapable Romance: Studies in the Poetics of a Mode*. Princeton, NJ: Princeton University Press, 1979.

———. *Literary Fat Ladies: Rhetoric, Gender, Property*. New York: Methuen, 1987.

Patrides, C. A. "The Cessation of Oracles: The History of a Legend." *Modern Language Review* 60 (1965): 500–507.

Patterson, Annabel. "His Singing Robes." *Milton Studies* 48 (2008): 178–94.

———. *Milton's Words*. Oxford, UK: Oxford University Press, 2009.

———. *Reading between the Lines*. Madison: University of Wisconsin Press, 1993.

Pecheux, Mother M. Christopher. "The Image of the Sun in Milton's Nativity Ode." *Huntington Library Quarterly* 38 (1973–1974): 315–33.

Pelikan, Jaroslav. *The Emergence of the Catholic Tradition (100–600)*. Vol. 1 of *The Christian Tradition: A History of the Development of Doctrine*. Edited by Jaroslav Pelikan. 5 vols. Chicago: University of Chicago Press, 1971.

Peltonen, Markku. "Francis Bacon, the Earl of Northampton, and the Jacobean Anti-Duelling Campaign." *Historical Journal* 44 (2001): 1–28.

Phillips, Jane E. "Juno in *Aeneid* 4.693–705." *Vergilius* 23 (1977): 30–33.

Polybius. *The Rise of the Roman Empire*. Translated by Ian Scott-Kivert. New York: Penguin Classics, 1979.

Prince, F. T. *The Italian Element in Milton's Verse*. Oxford, UK: Clarendon Press, 1954.

Proclus. *Commentaire Sur Le Timée*. Translated by A. J. Festugière. Paris: Vrin, 1968.

Prudentius. *Prudentius*. Translated by H. J. Thomson. Loeb Classical Library. 2 vols. Cambridge, MA: Harvard University Press, 1969.

Pruitt, Kristin A., and Charles W. Durham, eds. *Living Texts: Interpreting Milton*. Selinsgrove, PA: Susquehanna University Press, 2000.

Pseudo-Dionysius. *The Complete Works*. Translated by Colm Luibheid. Mahwah, NJ: Paulist Press, 1987.

Putnam, Michael C. J. "The Aeneid and *Paradise Lost*: Ends and Conclusions." *Literary Imagination* 8 (2006): 387–410.

———. *Virgil's Epic Designs: Ekphrasis in the Aeneid*. New Haven, CT: Yale University Press, 1998.

Quilligan, Maureen. *The Politics of Reading*. Ithaca, NY: Cornell University Press, 1983.

Quint, David. "The Debate between Arms and Letters in the Gerusalemme Liberata." In *Sparks and Seeds: Medieval Literature and Its Aftermath: Essays in Honor of John Freccero*, edited by Dana E. Stewart and Alison Cornish, 241–66. Turnhout, Belgium: Brepols, 2000.

———. "Duelling and Civility in Sixteenth-Century Italy." *I Tatti Studies* 7 (1997): 231–78.

———. *Epic and Empire: Politics and Generic Form from Virgil to Milton*. Literature in History. Princeton, NJ: Princeton University Press, 1993.

———. "Expectation and Prematurity in Milton's Nativity Ode." *Modern Philology* 97 (1999): 195–219.

———. "Virgil's Doublecross: Chiasmus and the *Aeneid*." *American Journal of Philology* 132 (2011): 273–300.

Quintus Smyrnaeus. *The Fall of Troy*. Translated by Arthur S. Way. Loeb Classical Library. Cambridge, MA: Harvard University Press, 1955.

Rabanus Maurus. *Commentariorum in Genesim Libri Quatuor: Patrologiae Cursus Completus; Series Latina*. Edited by J. P. Migne. Paris: J. P. Migne, 1844–64.

Rabb, Theodore K. "Religion and the Rise of Modern Science." *Past and Present* 31 (1965): 111–26.

Rajan, Balachandra, and Elizabeth Sauer, eds. *Milton and the Imperial Vision*. Pittsburgh, PA: Duquesne University Press, 1999.

Revard, Stella Purce. "Eve and the Doctrine of Responsibility in *Paradise Lost*." *PMLA* 88 (1973): 69–78.

———. "Milton and Myth." In *Reassembling Truth: Twenty-First Century Milton*, edited by Charles W. Durham and Kristin A. Pruitt, 23–47. Selinsgrove, PA: Susquehanna University Press.

———. "Satan's Envy of the Kingship of the Son of God: A Reconsideration of *Paradise Lost*, Book 5, and Its Theological Background." *Modern Philology* 70 (1973): 190–98.

———. *The War in Heaven: "Paradise Lost" and the Tradition of Satan's Rebellion*. Ithaca, NY: Cornell University Press, 1980.

Riggs, William G. *The Christian Poet in "Paradise Lost."* Berkeley and Los Angeles: University of California Press, 1972.

Rogers, John. *The Matter of Revolution: Science, Poetry, and Politics in the Age of Milton*. Ithaca, NY: Cornell University Press, 1996.

———. "Transported Touch: The Fruit of Marriage in *Paradise Lost*." In *Milton and Gender*, edited by Catherine Gimelli Martin. Cambridge, UK: Cambridge University Press, 2004.

Romei, Annibale. *Courtiers Academie.* Translated by John Kepter. London: Valentine Sims, 1598.

Rosenblatt, Jason P. "'Audacious Neighborhood': Idolatry in *Paradise Lost,* Book 1." *Philological Quarterly* 54 (1975): 553–68.

———. "Structural Unity and Temporal Concordance: The War in Heaven in *Paradise Lost.*" *PMLA* 87 (1972): 31–41.

———. *Torah and Law in Paradise Lost.* Princeton, NJ: Princeton University Press, 1994.

Rumrich, John Peter. "Of Chaos and Nightingales." In *Living Texts: Interpreting Milton,* edited by Kristin A. Pruitt and Charles W. Durham, 218–27. Selinsgrove, PA: Susquehanna University Press, 2000.

———. *Matter of Glory: A New Preface to "Paradise Lost."* Pittsburgh, PA: University of Pittsburgh Press, 1987.

———. "Milton's Arianism: Why It Matters." In *Milton and Heresy,* edited by Stephen B. Dobranski and John P. Rumrich, 75–92. Cambridge, UK: Cambridge University Press, 1998.

———. *Milton Unbound: Controversy and Reinterpretation.* New York: Cambridge University Press, 1996.

Sallust. *Sallust.* Translated by J. C. Rolfe. Cambridge, MA: Harvard University Press, 1995.

Samuel, Irene. "The Dialogue in Heaven: A Reconsideration of *Paradise Lost,* III.173–202." *PMLA* 72 (1957): 601–11.

Sandys, George. *A Relation of a Iourney Begun An: Dom: 1610 Foure Bookes. Containing a Description of the Turkish Empire, of Aegypt, of the Holy Land, of the Remote Parts of Italy, and Ilands Adioyning.* London: Printed by Richard Field for W. Barrett, 1615.

Sauer, Elizabeth. *Barbarous Dissonance and Images of Voice in Milton's Epics.* Buffalo, NY: McGill-Queen's University Press, 1996.

Schoeck, Helmut. *Envy: A Theory of Social Behavior.* Translated by Michael Gleeny. London: Secker & Warburg, 1966.

Schoenfeldt, Michael. "'Among Unequals What Society': Strategic Courtesy and Christian Humility in *Paradise Lost.*" *Milton Studies* 28 (1992): 69–90.

Schwartz, Regina. "Milton's Hostile Chaos: … and the Sea Was No More." *English Literary History* 52 (1985): 337–74.

———. "Real Hunger: Milton's Version of the Eucharist." *Religion and Literature* 31, no. 3 (1999): 1–17.

Scodel, Joshua. *Excess and the Mean in Early Modern English Literature.* Literature in History. Princeton, NJ: Princeton University Press, 2002.

Segal, Charles. "Aeternum Per Saecula Nomen, the Golden Bough and the Tragedy of History: Part II." *Arion* 5 (1966): 34–72.

Selden, John. *De Diis Syris Syntagmata Ii. Adversaria Nempe De Numinibus Commentitiis in Veteri Instrumento Memoratis. Accedunt Fere Qvae Sunt Reliqua Syrorum, Prisca Porrò Arabum, Aegyptiorum, Persarum, Afrorum, Europaeorum Item Theologia, Subinde Illustratur.* Brendel. 3rd ed. Leipzig: Johann, 1662.

Shakespeare, William. *The Riverside Shakespeare.* Edited by G. Blakemore Evans. Boston, MA: Houghton Mifflin, 1974.

Shoulson, Jeffrey S. *Milton and the Rabbis.* New York: Columbia University Press, 2001.

Shuellenberger, William. "Wrestling with the Angel: *Paradise Lost* and Feminist Criticism." *Milton Quarterly* 20 (1986): 69–85.

Silver, Victoria. *Imperfect Sense: The Predicament of Milton's Irony.* Princeton, NJ: Princeton University Press, 2001.

Simmel, Georg. *The Sociology of Georg Simmel.* Translated and edited by Kurt H. Wolff. London: Free Press, 1950.

Simons, Louise. "'An Immortality Rather than a Life': Milton and the Concubine of Judges 19–21." In *Old Testament Women in Western Literature,* edited by Raymond-Jean Frontain and Jan Wojcik, 145–73. Conway: University of Central Arkansas Press, 1991.

Sims, James H. "Camoens' *Lusiads* and Milton's *Paradise Lost*: Satan's Voyage to Eden." In *Papers on Milton,* edited by Philip Mahone Griffith and Lester F. Zimmerman. Tulsa, OK: University of Tulsa, 1969.

——. "A Greater than Rome: The Inversion of a Virgilian Symbol from Camoens to Milton." In *Rome in the Renaissance: The City and the Myth*, edited by P. A. Ramsay, 333–44. Binghamton, NY: MRTS, 1982.

Smith, Nigel. *Is Milton Better than Shakespeare?* Cambridge, MA: Harvard University Press, 2008.

Smith, Rebecca W. "The Source of Milton's Pandemonium." *Modern Philology* 29, no. 187–198 (1931).

Smith, Richard L. *Ahmad Al-Mansur: Islamic Visionary.* New York: Pearson Longman, 2006.

Song, Eric B. *Dominion Undeserved: Milton and the Perils of Creation.* Ithaca and London: Cornell University Press, 2013.

The Spectator. 8 vols. Vol. 4. London: S. Buckley and J. Jonson, 1712.

Spenser, Edmund. *The Faerie Queene.* Edited by A. C. Hamilton, Hiroshi Yamashita, Toshiyuki Suzuki, and Shohachi Fukuda. 2nd ed. New York: Pearson Longman, 2007.

Spingarn, Joel Elias, ed. *Critical Essays of the Seventeenth Century.* 3 vols. Bloomington: Indiana University Press, 1957.

Stanford, William Bedell. *The Ulysses Theme: A Study in the Adaptability of a Traditional Hero.* 2nd ed. Oxford, UK: Blackwell Press, 1954.

Steadman, John M. *Milton's Epic Characters: Image and Idol.* Chapel Hill: University of North Carolina Press, 1959.

Stein, Arnold. *Answerable Style: Essays on "Paradise Lost."* Minneapolis: University of Minnesota Press, 1953.

——. "The Kingdoms of the World: *Paradise Regained.*" *English Literary History* 23 (1956): 112–26.

Stevens, Paul. "*Paradise Lost* and the Colonial Imperative." *Milton Studies* 34 (1996): 3–21.

Stinger, Charles L. *The Renaissance in Rome.* Bloomington: Indiana University Press, 1985.

Stone, Lawrence. *The Crisis of the Aristocracy, 1558–1641.* Oxford, UK: Oxford University Press, 1965.

Strier, Richard. "Milton against Humility." In *Religion and Culture in Renaissance England*, edited by Claire McEachern and Debora Shuger, 258–86. Cambridge, UK: Cambridge University Press, 1997.

——. "Milton's fetters, or, why Eden is better than Heaven." *Milton Studies* 38 (2000): 169–97.

Sugimura, N. K. *"Matter of Glorious Trial": Spiritual and Material Substance in "Paradise Lost."* New Haven, CT: Yale University Press, 2009.

Summers, Joseph H. *The Muse's Method: An Introduction to "Paradise Lost."* Cambridge, MA: Harvard University Press, 1970.

Sylvester, Josuah, trans. *The Divine Weeks and Works of Guillaume de Saluste Sieur du Bartas.* Edited by Susan Snyder. Oxford: Clarendon Press, 1979.

Tasso, Torquato. *Della virtù eroica e della carità; Opere di Torquato Tasso colle controversie della Gerusalemme.* Edited by Giovanni Rosini. Vol. 11. Pisa, Italy: Niccolò Capurro, 1823.

——. *Gerusalemme liberata.* Edited by Bruno Maier. Milan, Italy: Rizzoli, 1964.

——. *Jerusalem Delivered.* Translated by Edward Fairfax. Edited by Henry Morley. London: George Routledge and Sons, 1890.

——. *Tasso's Dialogues: A Selection with the Discourse of the Art of the Dialogue.* Translated by Carnes Lord and Dain A. Trafton. Edited by Biblioteca Italiana. Berkeley and Los Angeles: University of California Press, 1982.

Tate, William. "King James I and the Queen of Sheba." *English Literary Renaissance* 26 (1996): 561–85.

Tawney, R. H. *Religion and the Rise of Capitalism: A Historical Study.* New York: Harcourt, Brace, 1926.

Tayler, Edward. *Milton's Poetry: Its Development in Time.* Pittsburgh, PA: Dusquesne University Press, 1979.

Teskey, Gordon. *Delirious Milton: The Fate of the Poet in Modernity.* Cambridge, MA: Harvard University Press, 2006.

Thompson, David. *Dante's Epic Journeys*. Baltimore, MD: Johns Hopkins University Press, 1974.

Thomson, H. J., ed. *Prudentius*. 2 vols. Loeb Classical Library. Cambridge, MA: Harvard University Press 1969.

Tillyard, E.M.W. "The Causeway from Hell to the World of *Paradise Lost*." *Studies in Philology* 38 (1941): 266–70.

———. "The Crisis of *Paradise Lost*." In *Studies in Milton*, 8–52. London: Chatto and Windus, 1960.

———. *The Miltonic Setting, Past and Present*. New York: Macmillan, 1929.

Turner, James Grantham. *One Flesh: Paradisal Marriage and Sexual Relations in the Age of Milton*. Oxford, UK: Clarendon Press, 1987.

Ulreich, John C. " 'Argument Not Less but More Heroic': Eve as the Hero of *Paradise Lost*." In *"All in All": Unity, Diversity and the Miltonic Perspective*, edited by Charles W. Durham and Kristin A. Pruitt, 67–82. Selinsgrove, PA: Susquehanna University Press.

———. " 'Sufficient to Have Stood': Adam's Responsability in Book IX." *Milton Quarterly* 5 (1971): 38–42.

Ungerer, Gustave. "Portia and the Prince of Morocco." *Shakespeare Studies* 31 (2003): 89–126.

Van der Laan, Sarah. "Milton's Odyssean Ethics: Homeric Allusions and Arminian Thought in *Paradise Lost*." *Milton Studies* (2009): 48–76.

Verbart, André. *Fellowship in "Paradise Lost": Vergil, Milton, Wordsworth*. Costerus New Series 97. Atlanta, GA: Rodopi, 1995.

———."Milton on Vergil: Dido and Aeneas in *Paradise Lost*." *English Studies* 78 (1997): 111–26.

Vida, Marco Girolamo. *The Christiad*. Translated and edited by Gertrude C. Drake and Clarence A. Forbes. Carbondale: Southern Illinois University Press, 1978.

———. *The Christiad*. Trans. James Gardner. Edited by James Hankins. I Tatti Renaissance Library. Cambridge, MA: Harvard University Press, 2009.

Virgil. *Aeneid VI*. Edited by Sir Frank Fletcher. Oxford, UK: Clarendon Press, 1941.

———. *P. Vergili Maronis Opera*. Edited by John Conington and Henry Nettleship. 3 vols. London: C. Bell and Sons, 1884.

———. *P. Vergili Maronis Opera*. Edited by R.A.B. Mynors. Oxford, UK: Clarrendon Press, 1969.

———. *P. Vergili Maronis Opera, quae quidem extant, omnia*. Edited by Georgius Fabricius. Basel, Switzerland: Henricus Petrus, 1561.

Von Maltzahn, Nicholas. "The War in Heaven and the Miltonic Sublime." In *A Nation Transformed: England after the Restoration*, edited by Alan Houston and Steven Pincus, 154–79. Cambridge, UK: Cambridge University Press, 2001.

Vossius, Gerardus Joannes. *De Theologia Gentili et Physiologia Christiana sive De Origine ac Progressu Idololatriae*. 2 vols. Amsterdam: Johannes and Cornelius Blaeu, 1641.

Waddington, Raymond. "Here Comes the Son: Providential Theme and Symbolic Pattern in *Paradise Lost*, Book 3." *Modern Philology* 79 (1982): 256–66.

Walker, D. P. *The Ancient Theology: Studies in Christian Platonism from the Fifteenth to the Eighteenth Century*. London: Duckworth Press, 1972.

Warmington, B. H. *Carthage*. New York: Penguin Press, 1964.

Watkins, John. *The Spectre of Dido: Spenser and Virgilian Epic*. New Haven, CT: Yale University Press, 1995.

Webber, Joan. *Milton and His Epic Tradition*. Seattle: University of Washington Press, 1979.

Weber, Max. *The Protestant Ethic and the Spirit of Capitalism*. Translated by T. Parsons. New York: Charles Scribner's Sons, 1930.

Webster, Charles. *The Great Instauration*. London: Duckworth Press, 1975.

Welch, Anthony. "Milton's Forsaken Proserpine." *English Literary Renaissance* 39 (2009): 527–56.

Westfall, Richard S. *Science and Religion in Seventeenth-Century England.* Yale Historical Publications Miscellany. New Haven, CT: Yale University Press, 1958.

Whittington, Leah. "Vergil's Nisus and the Language of Self-Sacrifice in *Paradise Lost.*" *Modern Philology* 107 (2002): 586–606.

Williams, Arnold. "The Motivation of Satan's Rebellion in *Paradise Lost.*" *Studies in Philology* 42 (1945): 253–68.

Wilson, Emily R. *Mocked with Death: Tragic Overliving from Sophocles to Milton.* Baltimore, MD: Johns Hopkins University Press, 2004.

Zeitlin, Froma. *Playing the Other: Gender and Society in Classical Greek Literature.* Chicago: University of Chicago Press, 1996.

Index

Roman Catholicism, 21, 205; and demons, 241; and fairies, 31, 32; and Islam, 250n9; and Paradise of Fools, 10, 85; perpetuation of paganism in, 32; and works, 112
romance, 31
romances of chivalry, 30–31, 136
Roman Empire: and barbarian invaders, 17, 21; as diabolic parody of divine monarchy, 207; papacy as heir of, 207
Roman republic, 148
Roman senate, 21
Roman soldiers, 36
Roman triumph, 207
Rome, 172, 176, 200; and Augustine, 148, 151; and bridge over Araxes, 204; and Cain and Abel, 148, 151; and Carthage, 20, 21, 22, 23; and devils, 8, 24; imperial, 5, 276n3; and kingdoms temptation, 174; and Pandaemonium, 20, 21, 205; papal, 5, 21, 205, 276n3; power of, 198–99, 240; roads and empire of, 203; and Saint Peter, 240; and Saturn, 19; and Virgil's *Aeneid*, 12; and war and luxury, 148; as Whore of Babylon, 21
Romei, Annibale, *Discorsi (Courtiers Academie)*, 141
Romulus, 148, 151, 246
Ronsard, Pierre de, *Le Second Livre des Sonnets pour Helene*, 256n1
Rosenblatt, Jason P., 250n3, 266n6, 270n3, 272n32, 281n4
royalists, 103, 140, 150
Rumrich, John Peter, 254n23, 258n14, 260n7, 261n21, 266n18, 271n21, 275n41, 277n23
Ruth, 193

Sabrina (*Comus*), 159
Saint Bartholomew's Day massacre, 282n13
Saint Peter's Basilica, 21, 24, 240
saints, 207, 259n27
Sallust, Conspiracy of Catiline, 148
salvation, 107, 112, 128, 129, 175, 179
Samson (*Samson Agonistes*), 105, 154, 155–56, 172, 177, 216, 224, 227
Samuel, Irene, 261n24
Sandys, George, 239
Sanhedrin, 2, 10
Sarah, 183, 238
Satan: and Abdiel, 11, 29, 127, 128, 142, 151–52, 158, 184; and accommodation of Son, 134; and Achilles, 41; and Adam, 154, 190, 211, 212, 217, 277n24; Adam and Eve as heroes in place of, 198, 199; Adam as echoing soliloquies of, 213; and

Aeneas, 20, 212; as angel of light, 108; and Apollo, 76; and aristocracy, 51, 52, 136, 138, 139, 244; and artillery, 137, 142, 250n2, 259n21; as attracted to substitutes for God, 97, 264n49; and Augustus, 204; as awakening dead at Resurrection, 255n37; and Babel, 78; belittling of, 74, 208; and Braggadocchio, 161; and Cain and Abel, 11, 146; and Caleb and Joshua, 107; capture of, 51–52, 61; and Carthage, 210; and chance, 73–74, 75, 84; and Chaos, 54, 77–79, 84; Chaos crossed by, 3, 9, 24, 38, 39, 40, 54, 55, 58–59, 64, 71–75, 80, 84, 85–86, 107, 252n2, 257n10; Charybdis carried within, 59; as cherub, 96, 108, 112, 117, 139; and Christian equality, 134; circular existence of, 57, 132, 198, 199, 210, 217; and Comus, 159, 160, 161; conferral of power on Sin and Death, 276n4; and confused order of events after Fall, 197; and court service, 133, 134; in Cowley, 264–65n1; Creator denied by, 130; and Death, 40, 54, 55–58, 59, 199, 252n2; as decreative, 75, 80; defeat in War in Heaven, 15, 85; degradation of, 198, 209; deprived of light, 97; desire to be envied, 131; desire to be king, 49, 130, 144, 145; despair of, 213; and destruction, 7, 131, 132; devils as reverencing, 3; as devils' savior, 255n37; as disfigured, 109; and Dolon, 51, 61; and *Doloneia*, 39, 51; in Du Bartas, 264–65n1; Eden entered by, 243–44, 245; and Elijah's ascension, 73, 257–58n12; and Envy in Cowley, 264–65n1; envy of, 1, 7, 10–11, 107, 117, 122–32, 133, 134, 135, 144, 146, 150, 152, 264–65n2, 267n36; and Eve, 8, 10, 11, 170; Eve given dream by, 51, 61, 86–87, 125, 151, 167, 274n40; and Eve's question about stars, 95–96; and Eve's spiritual ambition, 166–67; Eve tempted by, 117, 124–25, 159–60, 162, 163, 167, 168, 170–71, 172, 173, 174, 190; evidence of eyes of, 121, 122, 128–29; evil embraced by, 213; evil eye of, 126; and failed parody of Son's triumph, 210; and falling feeling, 59, 75, 84, 88, 132, 213, 217; fall in vacuity (Lucretian void), 73; as false crusader, 244; false piety of, 262n30; fiction about as fiction, 34; final punishment of, 57; as floating on version of Dead Sea, 18; and fraud, 16, 51, 61; Gabriel's duel with, 11, 123, 124, 138, 139–42, 143, 200; and geocentric universe, 96, 264n49;